ISLAM IN GLOBAL POLITICS

Reaching beyond currently politicized scholarship to provide a unique perspective on the place of religion and culture in global and local politics, this book examines the impact of Islam on 'civilizational' relations between different groups and polities.

Bassam Tibi takes a highly original approach to the topic of religion in world politics, exploring the place of Islam in society and its frequent distortion in world politics to the more radical Islamism. Looking at how this becomes an immediate source of tension and conflict between the secular and the religious, Tibi rejects the 'clash of civilizations' theory and argues for the revival of Islamic humanism to help bridge the gap. Chapters expand on:

- intercivilizational conflict in global politics;
- dialogue between religious and secular, East and West;
- Western concepts of Islamism;
- Euro-Islam and the Islamic diaspora in Europe;
- Islamic humanism as a tool for bridging civilizations.

Shedding new light on the highly topical subject of Islam in politics and society, this book is an essential read for scholars and students of international politics, Islamic studies and conflict resolution.

Bassam Tibi is a Professor Emeritus of International Relations. Between 1973 and 2009 he taught at the University of Goettingen, and he was A.D. White Professor at Large at Cornell University until 2010. Between 1982 and 2000 Professor Tibi was parallel to Goettingen at Harvard University in a variety of affiliations, the latest of which is the Bosch Fellow of Harvard. In his 40-year-long academic career he had eighteen visiting tenures in the US, North and West Africa and Southeast Asia. His work has been translated into sixteen languages, and he has published a great number of books including *Islam's Predicament with Modernity* (Routledge, 2009) and *Islam, World Politics and Europe* (Routledge, 2008) as well as *Islamism and Islam* (Yale UP, 2012). The president of Germany Roman Herzog decorated him in 1995 with the Cross of Merits/first class, the highest Medal/State Decoration, for his 'bridging between Islam and the West'.

ISLAM IN GLOBAL POLITICS

Conflict and cross-civilizational bridging

Bassam Tibi

Routledge
Taylor & Francis Group

LONDON AND NEW YORK

First published 2012
by Routledge
2 Park Square, Milton Park, Abingdon, Oxon OX14 4RN

Simultaneously published in the USA and Canada
by Routledge
711 Third Avenue, New York, NY 10017

Routledge is an imprint of the Taylor & Francis Group, an Informa business

British Library Cataloguing in Publication Data
A catalogue record for this book is available from the British Library

Library of Congress Cataloging in Publication Data
Tibi, Bassam.
   Islam in global politics: conflict and cross-civilizational bridging/
   Bassam Tibi.
   p. cm.
   Includes bibliographical references and index.
   1. Islam and world politics. 2. Culture conflict – Religious aspects –
   Islam. 3. Islam and humanism. 4. Islamic countries – Relations – Europe
   5. Europe – Relations – Islamic countries. 6. Islamic countries –
   Relations – Western countries. 7. Western countries – Relations –
   Islamic countries I. Title.
   BP173.5.T53 2011
   303.48'2176704–dc23   2011017348

ISBN 978–0–415–68624–2 (hbk)
ISBN 978–0–415–68625–9 (pbk)
ISBN 978–0–203–80202–1 (ebk)

Typeset in Bembo and Stone Sans by
Florence Production Ltd, Stoodleigh, Devon

Printed and bound in Great Britain by the MPG Books Group

CONTENTS

PREFACE

The following pages unite seven heavily revised papers into a book of Islamology. What is the distinction between this approach and traditional Islamic studies? With a retrospective look at the past forty years of scholarship on the place of Islam in society and politics, as well as Islam's role as a cultural system in social and political change, I claim to have established a new field of study for which I have chosen the name: Islamology. However, the story of this engagement is much longer than the academic part of my study of Islam. It is the story of my life since my birth as a Muslim in Damascus in 1944. I was socialized in my family and educated at school in the related value system of Islam. In 1962 I went to Frankfurt and was fortunate to study with Theodor W. Adorno and Max Horkheimer. In my academic career I engaged in the daring venture of deviating from traditional wisdoms of established scholarship and paid for it dearly. In the course of my study of Islam my work received praise from some but, in contrast, it was tarnished, even subjected to defamations such as the accusation of 'Islam-bashing' and 'self-orientalization' as well as the use of other similar defamatory clichés alien to an academic culture of free debate and civility. It is intriguing to see some ideologically blinkered Western scholars siding with Islamists in these actions. The two books with which I end my academic career are this one, *Islam in Global Politics*, followed by *Islamism and Islam* (Yale University Press, 2012, forthcoming). Both were born in this charged atmosphere of politicized scholarship.

Some scholars believe that communism is being replaced by Islam in the new post-bipolar patterns of conflict in world politics. Originating from the Left, I go beyond the deplored politicization of scholarship and acknowledge the place of culture, religion and ethnicity in contemporary conflict studies, but with a grasp of related reality, which is different from established schools of thought. I am an International Relations scholar who wants to be free from the obsession with realism and neo-realism. Throughout the process of learning that is the background for establishing Islamology, I engaged in studying Islam in the way reflected in the seven chapters of the present book.

In view of my intention to end the scholarly part of my life with this book I acknowledge its special place. The radical shift that I underwent from socialization in an Islamic value system in Damascus to a new life and new thinking in Frankfurt, is a telling story. In the late 1960s I joined the student revolt in Frankfurt, parallel to an exposure to the critical Marxism of the Frankfurt School (Theodor W. Adorno, Max Horkheimer and Jürgen Habermas). In the context of this radical shift I switched from the conservative–traditional Islam that I had internalized in Damascus to the Marxist critical theory that I adopted in the course of my academic training in Frankfurt. This change in thinking I maintained from 1962 to 1975, ending with the publication of my Marxism inspired *Handbuch der Unterentwicklung* ('Handbook of Underdevelopment') that I co-edited with the German Marxist Volkhard Brandes. That handbook was published in the book series *Political Economy*.

From this background I turned to study Islam under the impact of the Durkheimian sociology of religion that views religion as 'fait social', that is as a social reality. In this context I recognized the tensions between the Islamic values and those of secular European Enlightenment labelled as cultural modernity. The tensions between the two value systems are not merely related to an academic inquiry, but to the lives of those Muslims that oscillate between both. The *Crisis of Modern Islam* is the title of the 1981 book that I published first in German and thereafter in an English (Utah University Press, 1988) edition. In that book I sowed the seeds for the study of the intercivilizational conflict not only in individual lives, but also in world politics. This venture has shaped my scholarly work ever since. The present book is the culmination of four decades as a university professor and a three-decades-long process of reasoning and research in Islamology (1980–2010). In short, Islamology is a social–scientific study of Islam and conflict, not of the scriptural faith of Islam and its practices, a field that I leave to scholars of the divinities and to anthropologists.

The present book unites my unpublished research papers on the subject matter in point, after radical rewriting and numerous revisions, to fit them into an integrated study that revolves around the theme of intercivilizational conflict. I study this conflict in the spirit of dialogue in the pursuit of bridging between civilizations as a peace strategy for the twenty-first century. In fact, this book is a collection of essays, rewritten to make them resemble a monograph. I may not have been successful in this pursuit, but I assure my reader that I did my best. I cut repetitions and overlapping phrases, but some of these remain and they may betray the origin of these chapters. I did my best to limit this as far as possible. I leave it to the readers to find out how successful this endeavour has been, while I remind them of the rule that an established scholar has the right to collect together his or her writings toward the end of an academic career.

On top of my scholarly aims, my intention is to establish a dissociation between analysis of the intercivilizational conflict in world politics and any 'Huntingtonization' of the issue, in which conflict is viewed through the late Samuel Huntington's rhetoric as a *Clash of Civilizations*. I argue against this view that a conflict is not a clash and hence avoid any polarization. In addition, I ascertain that no singling out of Islam is implied in the present analysis. The argument is that next to the West Islam is the only civilization that raises claims to universality. In contemporary history Islamism politicizes those claims in a strategy for a remaking of the world along a new interpretation of the related, mostly constructed, civilizational concepts. These claims are marked by a lack of pluralism. The new quest for a new world order is not only a counter-enlightenment but also a counter to pluralism. As a Muslim I know that the new Islamist International Relations language does not exist in classical Islamic doctrine and that Islamism is based on an invention of tradition. Neither the concept of an 'Islamic state', nor the concept of a world order exist in Islamic heritage. These constructions rather reflect a new Islamist ideology that fuels the intercivilizational conflict. Hence, the distinction between Islam and Islamism matters significantly to avoid any Islam-bashing. I refer in this context to the book *Islamism and Islam* that follows this one as it accounts in all details and on all levels for the distinction pointed at. That book was completed during my Yale tenure 2008/2009 and is due to be published by Yale University Press in spring 2012. The ideology of Islamism that determines the politics of Islamist movements fuels an intercivilizational conflict. The Islamist New Internationalism emerges from the politicization of Islamic universalism. This reference not only reflects the continuity of my work, but also serves as the foundation for two different books, even though they relate to one another in a chain of research and scholarship.

The major theme of the research papers united in a new shape in the present book is the study of civilizations with a focus on intercivilizational conflict. While this inquiry – as already mentioned – dismisses the clash rhetoric of the late Huntington it leans on classic and modern authorities. For me, Ibn Khaldun of the fourteenth century, author of *Muqaddima* ('Prolegomena') and Raymond Aron of the twentieth century (his *Paix et Guerre entre les Nations*) are among these authorities. Methodologically my work is close to historical sociology, as the present study views Islam and its civilization through a reasoning in which Islam is placed into an overall historical context beyond the existing claims to absolutism. True, I refer in Chapter 1 to some topicalities such as the transition in the US adminis-tration from a damaging polarization (G.W. Bush) to one of superficial bridging (Barack Obama). However, these references serve merely as a way to illustrate the issue. To be sure, this is not a book on US politics, nor is it restricted to the Middle East. It is based on a generalist approach to the study of contemporary Islamic civilization. Admittedly, only in one case the book refers to a concrete issue area: Islamic migration to Europe and the related conflicts. I cover this in Chapter 5 on European Islam not only because I live as a Muslim immigrant in Europe, but also because I share Francis Fukuyama's views expressed in his Lipset lecture, in which he argues that Europe has become 'the battlefront in the struggle between radical Islamism and liberal democracy'. However, unlike Fukuyama, I do not restrict this matter to an 'identity politics', but rather see herein an intercivilizational conflict.

In contemporary history Islamism revives – in, as Hobsbawm expressed it, an invention of tradition – collective memories of past Islamic glory to claim a return of history. In short: this book goes beyond those obsessions that prevail in the US, be it in the media, in scholarship or in politics. Do not be mistaken: Islam is not to be confused with 'Middle East politics'; it is about world history and world politics. The number of non-Middle Eastern Muslims in the world at large exceeds that of all Middle-Easterners – Arabs, Turks and Iranians – put together.

Transnational Islamism is poised to restore an imagined Islamic glory in a dangerous dream of the return of history. The structure of the present book reflects an effort at disenchantment and a demystification of that dream. In Chapter 1 I spell out what the notion of intercivilizational conflict means. Then in Chapter 2 I look for ways of conflict resolution and focus on global communication. Hereby I consider the intercivilizational dialogue as an avenue for bridging. Unlike the sociologist Niklas Luhmann who – in his system theory – puts the existing interconnectedness and international communication on an equal footing, I see in that chapter a simultaneity of globalization and fragmentation. This simultaneity undergirds conflict. I acknowledge that each civilization has its own value system that separates it from others, and infer that global communication between civilizations is underpinned by particular values. Hence, the need for a consensus over universal values. If this is missing, conflict looms. I argue that cross-cultural morality connects and dismisses the argument that global communication in itself leads to connectedness. Cultural fragmentation is a source of conflict.

In the third chapter I look at one dimension of the intercivilizational conflict carried out as a war of ideas. This is followed by an inquiry into the potential of a 'peace' of ideas in Chapter 4. The related insights lead to the theme of humanism. I argue that the heritage of Islam includes a tradition of humanism that was buried in the past by Islamic *fiqh*-orthodoxy, and it is suppressed at present by Islamism. In Chapter 5 I move to a concrete case, that is, to the theme of Islam in Europe. True, Islam *and* Europe have a long history both of conflict and of cross-cultural fertilization, but Islam *in* Europe is a contemporary history that relates to global migration. Thus, there is a great distinction between the two themes, Islam 'and' Europe; Islam 'in' Europe. In our time Islam has become a segment of Europe itself. In a project at Cornell University on 'Religion in an expanding Europe', I coined the phrase 'Europeanization of Islam or Islamization of Europe' as a way of depicting the conflicting options for Europe's future. The envisioned Europeanization of Islam (Euro-Islam) is an effort at bridging to counter what I have termed in a Stanford University based project, 'ethnicity of fear'. This fear grows from an intercivilizational conflict and the ethnicization of the Islamic diaspora in a counter-culture of parallel societies. A Europeanization of Islam would be a bridge and also a resolution of a conflict Europeans are reluctant to acknowledge, and therefore it is the better option with which this book sides.

In Chapter 6 I come back to the significant distinction between Islam and Islamism to ask the most sensitive question: why does the Left in the West – as well as some liberals – of today support the right-wing ideology of Islamism?

The chapter unveils a sentiment related to a new variety of uninformed Western Third World-ism as a romanticization of the cultural other in terms of *bon sauvage*. The chapter makes it clear that Islamism is neither a theology of liberation nor of anti-globalization. This is Western wishful thinking. Chapter 7 includes the conclusion and a summary of my thinking about civilization, conflict and peace. It originates from a keynote address to an intercivilizational dialogue held in Seoul/Korea, December 2009. To be sure, this book provides an analysis and aims at an enlightenment – not a demonization – about Islamism. I acknowledge the significance of Islamist opposition and argue for an engagement, but warn at the same time of a self-defeating empowerment of Islamist movements.

The list of people who supported my Islam research in the past four decades 1970–2010 is long and therefore I decline from adding a lengthy acknowledgement. One can find such a list in my three most recent books published 2008 and 2009 by Routledge and extensively in my book of 2012 to be published by Yale University Press. The only people I would like to thank by name are my staff assistant Elisabeth Luft, who helped (for a full decade, 2000–09) to transfer my research from repeatedly handwritten manuscripts (I am a pre-computer age writer) into clean, arduously and meticulously typed, chapters. In the two years ensuing my mandatory retirement 2009–11, the most important associate in my scholarly life has been my Ph.D. student and research assistant Thorsten Hasche. Earlier he worked closely with Elisabeth Luft assisting with several book projects; after my retirement Thorsten's assistance has been essential for the completion of this final draft. I also need to express my great gratitude to Joe Whiting. In close cooperation with Joe this is the third book I have published with Routledge. Two very fine ladies, Emma Hart at Routledge and Charlotte Hiorns at Florence Production, did a great job in the final copy-editing and production of this book, and therefore deserve to share this warmest gratitude.

With this book I end my forty-year-long academic career and leave the stage. I do this after teaching and lecturing in all five continents of the world and after the publication of a voluminous work written in Arabic, German and English that is translated into eighteen languages. In awareness that some dispute my work I leave it to history to assess this Arab–Islamic thinking that claims to be both enlightened and reform oriented. My reasoning about Islam and its civilization in a time span of forty years is based on the hope that 'Islamic revivalism' means a revival of the heritage of the Islamic rationalism of al-Farabi, Avicenna, Averroes and Ibn Khaldun, and is not to be confused with the political religion of Islamism and its drive for a shari'a state. Also with regard to this point this book differs from the understanding of 'revivalism' in many established Islamic studies. The invention of tradition by Islamism is no Islamic revival.

Vienna/Austria
February 2011
Bassam Tibi

1

INTERCIVILIZATIONAL VALUE-CONFLICTS AND BRIDGING IN THE PURSUIT OF POST-BIPOLAR PEACE

The point of departure is the insight that international relations and, consequently, twenty-first-century international conflict assume a new shape in the new world time of religionized politics. In the course of this development the return of religion to the public square becomes a basic feature that also affects world politics. All related issues pertain to incompatible value systems: on the one hand, religious and, on the other, secular. This is not a matter of an individual's conduct based on the underlying values. It is rather about values that relate to the order of the world, secular Westphalian, or religious (based on the concept of lex divina), that is, a law inspired and determined by religious precepts. That said, the issue is not what some may dismiss as a Huntingtonian 'clash of civilizations', but rather an inter- and intra-civilizational value conflict in a new Cold War of ideas about law, order and legitimacy.

Introduction

The change addressed in post-bipolar politics is general and global, but the prominence and significance of Islam in the new pattern of conflict is acknowledged. This pertains to the fact that Islam is, next to Christianity, the only world religion with a universal claim to its values to be disseminated through proselytization. The Islamic name for this claim is the obligation to *da'wa*. To be sure, there is no discriminatory singling out of Islam through profiling, since the return of religion is at first a global phenomenon that occurs in all religions. This return is also not about religiosity in terms of faith and the related religious practices – this is a basic human right – it is rather about politics. In my work I have coined a phrase to depict this reality, the term 'religionized politics'.[1] The return of religions to the public square is about a remaking of the world on two levels: first the state and then the international order.

There exists a distinction between those religions that are restricted in their claims to a local validity and those that claim universality for their views and value systems. Today, this distinction has attained a tremendous significance for post-bipolar politics. Hinduism and Judaism, for instance, have a limited impact, when they are politicized to a religious fundamentalism, since they do not claim a world order among their tenets, but Islam does. To address this is not to engage in a profiling or singling out of one religion. The debate on intercivilizational conflict focuses on Islam and world order, because this discerns a reality; one does not construct relations between Islam and world politics, but refers to facts.

There are different approaches for the study of religion. The one selected here is the sociology of religion. Those scholars who study religion in the tradition of Emil Durkheim as *fait social*/social fact, do not primarily deal with a faith, but with the place of religion in society. Islamist political movements are – in this sense – a social fact and they claim a *nizam* ('new order') for the state and for the world at large. In my capacity as a scholar of religion who happens to be a Muslim I do not view this claim as inherently Islamic; it is rather a constructed one and this construction is based on a reality of the politicization of Islam and to an Islamism as one variety of the global phenomenon of religious fundamentalism. In other words, I draw a clear distinction between *Islam* and *Islamism*.[2] Islam is not Islamism, because it is faith and culture, not a political religion. However, the shari'atization of Islam by Islamism transforms it into a political religion. This Islamist endeavour stands in contrast to the earlier buried traditions of Islamic humanism.

The study of the current international intercivilizational conflict dismisses the binary mindset such as the one of 'clash of civilizations'; since its identifying of the conflict intends to reach out to a conflict resolution. The term used for this concern is intercivilizational bridging. The present book aims to cover all these issues. I lay down the grounds for this task in this introductory chapter. To recap in a few phrases: the current international conflict is a value-system based conflict over the order of the world and over the concepts of law that underpin it. There is a solution to this conflict in the effort at an intercivilizational bridging. And finally, the focus on Islam is not profiling, as it relates to the political claim of an Islamic world order.

The foregoing phrases add to the approach of sociology of religion the one of international relations. Based on a four-decades-long professional life in international relations I argue that the paradigms of realism and neo-realism fail to explain conflict and war in the new world time of post-bipolarity. With a reference to Thomas Kuhn one can speak of a paradigmic crisis that compels one to think about change in the search for a new, more satisfactory, paradigm with a better explanatory capacity.[3] No doubt, post-bipolar international relations need a new paradigm that accounts for the changed international environment in which non-state actors arise and new issues (e.g. incommensurability of values) come to the fore. The unveiling of the value-based 'heterogeneity of civilizations' (a term coined by Raymond Aron[4]), earlier veiled politically by the bipolar system, brings back a suppressed issue to world politics, but should not be confused with Samuel Huntington's *Clash of Civilizations* (a book translated into thirty-nine languages and printed in millions of copies), thus with the related impact. The late Harvard scholar – with all due respect – distorted the issue, and therefore, this book dissociates its thinking from all sorts of a Huntingtonization of the issue in point. My book claims to rectify this by bringing back civilizations into international studies not only free of bias, but also with a concept of conflict resolution. In short, the world-politics related conflict between civilizations is not a clash. In contrast to a clash, a conflict can be subject for resolution and it does not focus on 'fault-lines' – as did Huntington in his essentialization of cultural difference. In addition, Huntington continued to be obsessed with realist thinking, as he believed that civilizations act as a block led by a core state. In fact, none of the three states he lists, Iran, Saudi Arabia and Turkey, are in a position to lead Islamic civilization. One adds to this the fact that intercivilizational conflict is basically a conflict on the non-state level. To understand this reality one needs to go beyond the state. The differences between cultural values and worldviews in a conflict over the future of world order can be subject to change. This change needs to happen within the civilizations. The example of Turkey, where Turkish Islamists and Turkish–Muslim secularists fight one another demonstrates the fact of an intra-civilizational conflict. As I argue in an earlier book on *Islam's Predicament with Modernity*, the inner-Islamic solution is 'Cultural change and religious reform'. In the relations among civilizations there is a need for a shared 'cross-cultural morality' for 'preventing the clash of civilizations' and to smooth the way for post-bipolar world peace (see note 4). This chapter introduces the related thinking that guides all chapters of the present book on the intercivilizational conflict and bridging between the civilizations with a focus on Islam in world politics.

In my view, the place of civilizational values in world politics, which has become one of the pertinent features of post-bipolar politics, has often been ignored. Afterall, values are not a novelty, as they have always been deeply rooted in history. I have always been among the harsh critics of the Bush administration, but believe it is wrong to view the intercivilizational conflict as a result of its distorted politics. Among the damaging burdens the disastrous Bush administration left behind as its legacy is the US response to the terrorist-jihadist assaults of 9/11, 2001. The US administration did not at all understand the related challenge of Islamism. When President G.W. Bush announced pursuant to 9/11 a 'crusade' in defiance he not only generated inflammatory responses, but also proved to be entangled in the same logic of Islamism: it religionized politics (see note 1). A day later, Bush was told by some advisors how damaging his pronouncement was. His declaration after 9/11 of a 'crusade' was made front-page headlines in newspapers throughout the world of Islam. The prevailing perception in Islamic civilization is that Islam is embattled, being under siege, encircled by 'Jews and crusaders'. To rectify his wrongdoing, Bush visited the precious Washington mosque, talked to its Imam in front of TV cameras and praised Islam in a lip-service as 'a religion of peace'. But the damage done could not be easily rectified. Not just that Bush's apology came too late, it was also the actions of his administration that belied what was supposed to be a benign statement. It may not have been the intention, but it was a reality of Bush's war on terror that almost every Muslim became a suspect and Muslim visitors to the US had to endure an often humiliating second inspection upon entry. I was in those years among the Muslims who suffered this and therefore it was most relieving to listen to the message of the following US president, Barack Obama, delivered in front of the Turkish parliament in April 2009: 'America is not at war with Islam.' Ever since, Muslim visitors to the US are also relieved of the humiliating 'second inspection'. Nonetheless, the conflict addressed in the present book continues to be in place. The Obama administration offers no solution to it; it is not even acknowledged, even though Obama addressed the basic tensions in his famous speech in Cairo. The flawed US policy did not have a proper response to the Arab Spring of 2011. When an uprising in Egypt took place geared for freedom and democracy but tainted by an Islamist attempt to take-over the contestation, the Obama administration proved in its policy a good will in its pronouncements but a very poor performance in its politics.

On top of the legacy of the Bush administration is the most disastrous Iraq war, formally ended by Obama, though turmoil and violence continue to prevail unabated. That war was launched without a clear post-Saddam scenario and also without a strategic pondering about the effects and the consequences. The damage that followed was great and it intensified the intercivilizational conflict. It is, however, recognized that the contested Iraq war removed, despite all odds, one of the nastiest dictators in the world of Islam. That was, as Fouad Ajami rightly put it, 'the foreigner's gift' of a liberation from Saddam's 'republic of fear' by the USA.[5] Nonetheless, the war contributed to a deepening of the existing anti-Americanism and also to a post-eventum upgrading of Saddam's legitimacy and of his person. He is placed today as a hero in the civilizational collective memory. For many Muslims and Arabs Saddam is viewed today, under the conditions of an intensified intercivilizational tensions, as a 'martyr'. These topical references serve as illustrations of a new conflict to be addressed in an in-depth analysis.

The theme of an intercivilizational conflict compels me to engage in a venture which is highly charged. Today it is quite risky to deal with the conflict between the world of Islam – addressed as civilization – and the West, and go unscathed. The Western memories of 9/11 have faded to the extent that scholars who are alert to terrorist jihadism that emanates from totalitarian Islamism are accused of Islamophobia and even of being close to the so-called 'neo-con'. The result is then to be dismissed on these grounds. While acknowledging the damaging legacy of the US administration under G.W. Bush and recognizing the merits of the promising presidency of Barack Obama, one has to be aware of the risks any candid analysis of the tensions between Islam and the West – viewed as civilizations – runs. At issue is not a mere political conflict, but also an intercivilizational conflict over the future of world order. Next to the analysis of the conflict one needs a proper policy for dealing with it. One has to go beyond the extremes of denial and polarization. The present book proposes bridging vs polarization in the relations between the civilizations. Bridging is not about shared – mostly dishonest

– public pronouncements of cordiality, but rather about thinking about the intercivilizational conflict in a mindset of peaceful conflict resolution. This book claims to help understand the conflict in place, which is a basic requirement for serious efforts at its resolution.

Obama and 'ending the clash of civilizations'

On the one hand there is the reality of a conflict between civilizational value systems that undergirds an intercivilizational conflict, and on the other the post-bipolar international environment itself. The pertinent question is about this environment in which Western politicians act and navigate in the troubled waters of competing civilizations. In the analysis of post-bipolar politics one has to address next to the overall issue of globalization the fact of cultural tensions that lead to conflict.[6] Given the centrality of Islamic civilization in post-bipolar politics, some political theorists have coined the notion of 'geopolitics of Islam' and suggested it be employed as a framework for discussing political theory.[7] This notion refers to the place of politicized religion in world politics in a return of the sacred (see note 20). The politicization of religion generates tensions and, in a step further, conflict. How can politicians act properly in this environment?

Let us look at the way US president Barack Obama handles pending issues. In his first visit to an Islamic country, Turkey, Obama rightly stated that the United States 'is not and will never be at war with Islam'.[8] This is an indication of a politics in a sea of change. The global edition of *New York Times* reported this and rightly commented in its editorial pages under the headline, 'Ending the clash of civilizations'. The change in viewpoint in this editorial is that Bush was accused of 'feeding fears that the so-called war on terror was really a war on Islam'.[9] The Bush administration gave every Muslim who entered the US the impression that the US was at war with Islam. I am a Muslim born in Damascus and I experienced this profiling when my German–European citizenship did not protect me from a 'second inspection' at a US airport. My own record as a Muslim staunch critic of jihadist Islamism did not matter, as did the fact that I am filed as a Muslim born in Damascus. This general unlawful and damaging profiling done in the name of better security fuelled the intercivilizational conflict and supported the Muslim perception of an 'Islam under siege'.[10]

Both in Ankara in April and in Cairo in June 2009 Obama knew well that he was navigating in troubled waters of conflict. That was intensified, but not created by the Bush administration. In Ankara, Obama did not refrain from praising the founder of Turkey, Kemal Atatürk, for having established a 'secular democracy' in Turkey – the first country of the Muslim world that moved towards secularization.[11] The AKP, unfortunately praised by the academic US–Islamic studies in a mindset of apologism for Islamism as a 'moderate Islamist party' has ruled Turkey since 2002. US politicians like to believe that the AKP is aimed at creating 'moderate Islamic democracy', and overlook the AKP politics of Islamization. In short, the AKP is not what it claims to be, namely an 'Islamic–conservative party'. It is rather an Islamist party. The 'creeping Islamization' of secular Turkey results from the AKP's politics of de-secularization.[12] Therefore, Obama's praise for Atatürk's 'secular democracy' implies a reference to a conflictual issue area combined with a preference for secularism against the ongoing de-secularizing Islamization.[13]

The New York Times/International Herald Tribune's already cited editorial 'Ending the clash of civilizations' is a very prudent commentary that ends with this phrasing: 'Obama . . . will have to acknowledge not just common ground, but important differences with many Muslim countries – including the issues of women's rights and freedom of religion – that are not easily bridged' (as note 9).

The cited, highly insightful phrases acknowledge an existing conflict value, which is neither to be confused with the Huntingtonian 'clash of civilizations', nor with Bush's 'War on terror'. The conflict in point relates also to those values pertinent to shaping the order of the world that is the theme of the present book. The issue is civilizational dissent over how to re-order the world in the crisis of its present order and this was addressed by Obama on 4 June 2009 when he continued his journey to the world of Islam.

It is highly encouraging that Obama dared to make a second step to address these value differences with the world of Islam when he, in Cairo, addressed the people of Islamic civilization in a historical speech in which he was not silent about existing disagreement. Obama listed seven areas of tension to be dealt with in the dialogue. The politicization of the dissent should be replaced by a dialogue in which value-conflicts can be addressed. In an age of overwhelming globalization people come very close to one another and in this closeness they not only need to live in peace, but also to accept the requirements heretofore. Among these is above all a mutual recognition that is not yet in place. This need is undermined by a variety of factors at the top of which is, as this book argues, the failure to reach a real bridging – beyond a rhetoric of peace. The laughable European agenda of 'alliance of civilizations' presupposes a convergence that does not exist. There is a conflict and what is needed is an intercivilizational, peaceful conflict resolution. One has to acknowledge some major facts to smooth the way in the search for conflict resolution. One cannot talk about 'ending the clash of civilizations' without addressing the conflictual crucial issues, of which I single out the following five:

First: humans are born as individuals, but are socialized in the worldview and values of local cultures and cross-cultural civilizations. Each of these entities has its own value system that is civilizational. These systems are not in line with one another. Civilizational difference is what makes people distinct from one another. Historians are aware of the fact that the history of humankind is a history of civilizations.[14] The highly negative response to Huntington's use of the notion of civilization in politics demonstrates that social scientists have a problem with the fact that humanity is subdivided along civilizational lines. It is fashionable in social science to talk about diversity, but scholars shy away from relating this notion to civilizations. One of the few exceptions is Cornell's political scientist Peter Katzenstein who acknowledges the place of civilizations in world politics.

In his already quoted masterpiece, *Paix et Guerre Entre les Nations*, Raymond Aron laid the foundations for the idea of 'the heterogeneity of the planetarian systems' (see note 4), that is based on a 'heterogeneity of civilizations'. Aron does this without overlooking the fact that these civilizations are 'embedded in the same system', which is the international system of sovereign states. As already quoted, Aron was aware of the fact that the 'heterogeneity of civilizations' was by then 'veiled' by the reality of a bipolar East–West conflict. Keep in mind that Aron published his book in 1962 at the height of that bipolar conflict and in the shadow of the Cuba crisis that led to a nuclear American–Soviet confrontation, and a crisis that could have almost developed into a war, but was de-escalated. Nonetheless, Aron was in his lifetime aware of the fact that 'the heterogeneity of civilizations . . . would be in the long perspective much more consequential than the inimical confrontation of two world blocks ever could be' (ibid.).

The implication is that an intercivilizational conflict – once veiled by bipolarity – not only comes to the fore in post-bipolar politics; it is also much stronger than the earlier formations of the East–West conflict. This process started to happen when the Berlin wall fell. It is amazing that Aron's book – like other major sources (e.g. Ibn Khaldun) – is not cited in Huntington's book. Aron's insight, and not Huntington's, guides the present book. Aron did not live long enough to see that his prophecy – that, if unveiled, the heterogeneity of civilizations would be a source of global conflict – is fulfilled and has become a world political reality. Post-bipolarity fulfilled Aron's prophecy.

Second: the post-bipolar unveiling of the reality of a conflictual heterogeneity of civilizations that shapes the twenty-first-century's world politics is a fact that belies earlier Eurocentric beliefs in one world civilization often identified as Western civilization.[15] It is true that European expansion generated a full-scale globalization. Nonetheless it failed to standardize the world as a project for a Westernization of the world.[16] In this chain of argumentation my second authority is a late scholar also of the calibre of Aron. The authority in point is Hedley Bull of Oxford.[17] The focus of his study was order and conflict in world politics. Long before the end of bipolarity Bull argued most insightfully that globalization 'brought societies to a degree of mutual awareness and interaction that they have not had before'. Nonetheless, this closeness 'does not in itself create a unity of outlook' as Bull argues.[18] The values of divergent people are different; the 'heterogeneity of civilizations' and their politicization leads to conflict.[19] These values are, as this book argues, civilizational and so is the related conflict, too. In other words, there is a simultaneity in the structural globalization in world economics and in international politics, and a fragmentation in cultural and civilizational values. This is one of the major areas to deal with in the present book, namely in Chapter 2.

Third: the twenty-first century heralds a major phenomenon that started in the late last century in which the assumption of a universal disenchantment of the world made by Max Weber, i.e. rationalization and secularization, is radically challenged. The phenomenon was first addressed by Daniel Bell as 'return of the sacred'.[20]

Some, even the bright mind Habermas, got it wrong, and believed this return implied a religious renaissance without understanding its major trait, namely the politicization of faith to political religions. Today, the return of the sacred is a drive guided by a world-political vision of a remaking of the world along religious – instead of secular – tenets.[21] This return of the sacred in a political shape generates 'the new Cold War' between religious and secular concepts regarding the order of the world.[22] Islamism claims a new world order based on Islamic tenets which is in conflict with the present one of a Westphalian synthesis. The substance of Islamism is based on this claim. The new Cold War in point takes place primarily as a war of ideas, as shall be argued in Chapter 3.

Fourth: the intercivilizational conflict in point is complex and multifaceted; it takes place on a variety of levels in which various actors are involved. Neither in Kashmir nor in Xingjian nor in Chechnya is the West involved. In these and in other places Islamic civilization faces other enemies. The conclusion is that not only the West, but also other civilizations are affected by claims of Islamism and the related conflict. In short, the major and global conflict in world politics is over the pillars of the international order: religious, or secular? In this meaning the conflict between Islamic religious and Western secular civilization[23] is a value conflict over a remaking of the world, it is not a war of religions.

Be sure, the addressed conflict is not between religions, as Islamists believe, and do not be mistaken in understanding the new Cold War of ideas fought by Islamists against secular values that underpin the secular world order. This challenge cannot be understood well by the wrong question Fewaz Gerges asks: 'Clash of cultures, or clash of interests?' This question not only reveals the sheer ignorance of this issue, but also reflects this scholar's misconception that ends up in an utter distortion of the issue itself.[24] Value-conflicts are not material conflicts of interest, but rather about the meaning of life and the order of the world. Gerges is not a Marxist nor does his book, which is a narrative of case studies, relate to any serious theoretical concept. Nonetheless, Gerges plays around with the slogan of 'clash of interests' and this reflects in an exemplary manner a vulgar Marxism. To argue in this manner at the expense of the moral order of the world and of the meaning of religion is to distort the issue.[25]

Fifth: it is pertinent to supply the argument of an intercivilizational conflict in world politics with evidence to protect this thinking from a looming suspicion of arguing for a clash of civilizations. The reader is assured that this is not the case. In this pursuit one has to achieve many tasks and this book claims to accomplish some basic ones among them. I single out three of these, first a bridging that replaces polarization; second a conflict resolution that replaces clash; and most importantly, third, an effort at overcoming the binary worldview of Islam vs West, or vice versa. I argue for a revival of the Islamic tradition of humanism in which rich diversity and borrowing from the cultural other were admitted. Such a revival would facilitate progress in the work on the tasks lying ahead.

Today, one speaks of 'Islamic revival' without any further specification. One has to ask first to what segments in Islamic tradition does this notion of 'revival' refer? And second, which Islam is meant? Virtually almost all references to Islamic revivalism point at political Islam, but not to other positive traditions. In this book I not only strongly disagree, but also propose an alternative. For instance, I repeatedly contradict Tariq Ramadan's Ph.D.-based book on the sources of Islamic revival, entitled *Aux Sources de Renouveau Musulman*, because the work of that author distorts the meaning of the notion of revival.[26] It is true that the nineteenth-century Muslim thinker al-Afghani was a Muslim revivalist, but Ramadan's grandfather Hasan al-Banna definitely was not. In fact al-Banna was the founder of jihadist Islamism, and for me this is not only not an indication of an Islamic revival, but is also a disservice to Islam.[27] If one is truly interested in bridging and in an honest 'peace' of ideas to replace the new Cold War, then one has to look for other sources in the heritage of Islam. In the search for cultural components that facilitate bridging I acknowledge the preference for medieval Islamic rationalism and to its tradition of humanism. The work of the related philosophers from al-Farabi through to Ibn Sina and from Ibn Rushd to Ibn Khaldun continues to be pertinent and it is more promising for a better future and also for conflict resolution. These Muslims have laid down a tradition of Islamic humanism.[28] In Chapter 4 on Islamic rationalism I give the notion of Islamic revival a different meaning to the one used by Tariq Ramadan in his *Renouveaux Musulman*. Those Western academics who have chosen to be involved in an apologism of Islamism and support Ramadan are no allies in the present venture. The renaissance of Islam needed is a cultural revival that has to be different from the one Ramadan's grandfather, Hasan al-Banna, had in mind wrongly presented as 'renouveaux Musulman'. The Islamic tradition of rationalist humanism is what has to be revived, not the Islamic *fiqh*-orthodoxy of Ibn Taimiyyah.

Competing globalizations: reviving the Islamic model

No one can deal properly with contemporary Islam without relating any of the chosen themes to the overwhelming globalization and to the challenges of modernity. The substance of Islam's relation to globalization is, however, not covered by those Western scholars who speak of 'globalized Islam'.[29] The new feature of Islam and of its civilization at present under conditions of post-bipolar politics, is not what Olivier Roy mistakenly presents to his readers. Let it be made clear at the outset, globalization is not a novelty to Islam. There always existed a connection between Islam, as a civilization characterized by universal claims, and the reality of the global structures Islam established in its ten-centuries-long *futuhat* expansion. Since its birth as a religion in 610 and the ensuing foundation of a new polity in 622, Islam presented itself as a vision for a global remaking of the world.[30] Beginning in 632 with Islamic conquests aimed at a global expansion named *futuhat*[31] Islam translated its claims into the first phenomenon of a globalization project in world history articulated in this Islamic *futuhat* expansion. Islamists reinvent this tradition in a trajectory aimed at a remaking of the world order under the present conditions in a reversed globalization.

If the term 'globalization' is employed in the meaning of a venture aimed at mapping the globe along the lines of one model based on one structure, then the vision of Islam to map the entire globe into one Islamicate called the global *dar al-Islam* could be viewed as the first model in world history for a pattern of globalization.[32] Therefore, world history in this global sense begins with the expansion of Islam, not with European expansion, as Eurocentric historians contend. For sure, Islamic expansion predates European expansion by almost one millennium. An acknowledgement of this fact while revisiting history, is to be seen as a contribution to overcome the Eurocentric conceptualization of global history. It is wrong to view European expansion as the sole source of globalization and the only historical example for it. This chapter contends the existence of competing models of globalization and this fact refers us to what the intercivilizational conflict is all about.

The concern of this chapter is not only to dismiss Eurocentric views of history, but also to argue that the Islamic contestation of modern globalization is a mere revolt against the hegemony of the West, since it is also driven by a centric view of the world: Islamocentrism. This revolt triggers effects that are becoming a major challenge posed by Islamic civilization in a bid for a return of history as a return to Islamocentrism. Thus, there is no 'End of history', but a vision of a return to Islamic glory.[33] The outcome is then a conflict. The vision of a restoration of Islamic glory to base the future on is an effort within the agenda of 'a return of history'. This is politically pursued by Islamist and Islamic–Salafist internationalism aimed at a remaking of the world along the provisions of a constructed shari'atized Islam. This is contemporary history and a new variety of Islam. The conflict in point relates to an utopia of a mapping of the entire globe into one *dar al-Islam* ('house of Islam'). The driver of this utopia is a vision of a new world order shaped by Islam.

Unlike the old globalization of classical Islamic civilization, modern globalization is based on the networking of the world through the means of modern technology.[34] Contemporary American hegemony is a continuation of the economic and political foundations of the West incorporated in the history of globalization. At present, the revival of the classical Islamic model of globalization may be viewed as an invention of tradition, not only to counter US globalization, but also to replace it by one's own model projected into the past.

Given the novelty of political Islam it is wrong to speak of an Islamic revival when the issue relates to Islamism. It would be more accurate to use the notion of 'invention of tradition'. Of course, Islamic history matters for understanding the present. Its pertinence matters to understanding Muslim collective memories that assume a new shape. The constructed memories relate to the way contemporary Islam is embedded in a global context. However, the self-assertion is not combined with any awareness of a construction, since a belief in a return of authentic history dominates contemporary Islamic perceptions.

The combination of the past with the present in the Islamist utopia being a vision for an alternative globalization revives collective memories fully shaped by the invention of tradition. This is a model inspired by a view of the world based on Islamic-religious precepts that should form a new order of the world. While acknowledging change and in avoidance of any essentialism, one can, though, state a persistent Islamic view of the world according to which Allah, in the course of the history of humankind, sent his revelations. These were transmitted to prophets. In the Islamic worldview Islam concludes this history of revelations in its 'final message' revealed in the Qur'an to Mohammed. This revelation is – as the Qur'an states – sent to Mohammed who is identified in the Qur'an as *Khatem al-Nabiyyin* ('the final of all prophets') (Qur'an, sure 33, verse 40). Thus, it is inferred that religion is by definition *ad-din 'ind Allah huwa al-Islam'* ('Islam') (Qur'an, sure 3, verse 19). The message of Islam aims at uniting humanity in one global structure determined by the Islamic definition of peace. This utopia is based on a binary worldview that divides the globe into *dar al-Islam* ('the Islamicate') and *dar al-harb* ('abode of war'). The contemporary term of the latter is *dar al-kuffar* ('house of unbelievers'), or *al-Gharb* ('the West'). This binary contradicts 'pluralism' of cultural modernity. For overcoming Islam's predicament with cultural modernity Muslims need to find a way to embrace pluralism not to undermine it in Islamist politics.[35] This is one of the aspects of the intercivilizational conflict.

One of the major sources for the new interpretation of the Islamic doctrine is the work of Sayyid Qutb. He translates jihad into 'Islamic world revolution' that claims to free the world from the West, perceived of as being at the brink while existentially crumbling: 'There is only one globe, it is Dar al-Islam, based on the Islamic state where shari'a prevails.'[36] In his writings Qutb engages in an invention of tradition while he presents his vision of a globalization as one based on classical Islam and claims that this is an authentic Islamic view. The novelty of the vision is that it is a grand strategy in which Islamic universalism is translated into an active Islamist internationalism. Again, at issue is a remaking of the world along the Islamic tenets as selected, redefined and reinterpreted by Qutb himself. Therefore, the reinvention of a classical Islamic globalization is one that generates international conflict as it challenges contemporary globalization. This is the meaning of the intercivilizational conflict.

The record of a globalization model in Islamic history and the reference to it at present in the Islamist global utopia is based on the belief in a religious dogma that claims universality. In this sense Islam has a mission for the entire humanity and prescribes action to implement it. In Islamic history Islamic universalism was practiced for one millennium. The collective memory of this history continues to shape the Islamic view of the world. From the seventh through the seventeenth centuries Muslims fought jihad wars combined with economic activities to spread Islam, not only as a faith, but also as a rule based on the doctrine of *siyadat al-Islam* ('supremacy of Islam'). Islam presents itself as the model of a world for a unified humanity. This global model of Islam addressed in the introduction, was first pursued in early Arab conquests and it was continued in the Turkish–Ottoman age. Jihad wars were not simply religious wars since they aimed at establishing political influence and drawing economic benefits in a global context. The practice of the implementation of a global model has been characterized by some historians as 'Islamic imperialism'. This reference to the past explains the problems of the contemporary world of Islam and makes clear the reluctance of Muslims to submit to the present world order dismissed as a *Pax Americana*. At issue is an attitude that has deeper historical roots that go to the subjection of the world of Islam to European expansion, ending in the pursuit of an Islamic globalization. It is more than anti-Americanism.[37] What is termed by some authors as an 'Arab Islamic awakening' is a term that has a broader meaning;[38] it is also the constructed revival of some historical memories that relate to a perception of the Islamic imperial past. The Islamic nostalgia begins with a response to contemporary globalization identified by John Kelsay as a sentiment of an outrage over the contemporary order of the world combined with the will to remake it along the prevailing Islamic prescriptions.[39] This is an effort to reverse development in a dream of a 'return of history'. This sentiment fuels the intercivilizational conflict.

The cultural schizophrenia of collective memories: torn between glory and humiliation

In the prevailing contemporary Muslim worldview modern history ends Islamic globalization. For Muslims this is a catastrophe that tips the balance in favour of the West. The subjection of the world of Islam is a deplorable reality, but responses to the change do not seem to be rational and they have been identified by the Muslim scholar Shayegan as 'cultural schizophrenia'.[40] In his view, these responses miss the point.

The world-historical background is the industrial revolution in the West that underpinned the techno-scientific 'military revolution'. This change made European armies more powerful and this is no conspiracy. At issue are social developments that contributed to strengthening the power of Europe within the framework of an 'industrialization of warfare'.[41] Islamic armies who were leading in the practice of globalization implemented through Islamic jihad were no longer in a position to withstand the new industrial standards of war. In consequence they lost one battle after another. The siege of Vienna in 1683 failed and it was the final expansive battle in the history of Islamic globalization. All following Muslim wars were defensive wars. The decline of the Ottoman Empire could not be stopped by the 'Importing of the European Army'.[42] In the course of the European expansion, Islamic global expansion was at first halted, then a military roll-back of the Islamicate existing in Europe took place followed by the European invasion of the world of Islam itself. Technologically powerful European armies were in a position to occupy Islamic territory in a shift from glory to humiliation. The results are a lasting wound in the Islamic soul that not only long predates the Bush administration, but also underpins the 'cultural schizophrenia' addressed by Shayegan.

The historical consequence of the process described is the mapping of the world of Islam into the new global structure dominated by Europe and later by the US.

It is this system that Islamic civilization is enduring to date. The historical root of this system is the European expansion. The process happened in two phases: first, colonial penetration, and second, de-colonization and the inclusion of the world of Islam in a process of nation-building into the Westphalian system of sovereign states established in 1648 that exists to date. Charles Tilly describes the process that followed the Peace of Westphalia in those accurate phrases:

> all of Europe was to be divided into distinct and sovereign states whose boundaries were defined by international agreement. Over the next three hundred years the Europeans and their descendants managed to impose that state system on the entire world. The recent wave of decolonization has almost completed the mapping of the globe into that system.[43]

One may add, the countries of the world of Islam were no exception. In their territory, the introduced nation state did not work well. The mapping of the world of Islam into the international system has two distinct characteristics:

First: most states in the world of Islam are nominal nation states that lack the necessary underlying structures and legitimacy. In the Middle East they have been qualified as tribes with national tribes.[44] Second: the modern global structure unified by international law brought about a frictional unification. As the late Oxford scholar of law H.L.A. Hart once stated,

> It has never been doubted that when a new, independent state emerges into existence . . . it is bound by the general obligations of international law . . . here the attempt to rest the new state's international obligations on a tacit or inferred consensus seems wholly threadbare.[45]

The Islamist shari'atization agenda can be viewed as a declaration of war against the existing international law in a war of ideas. This law is based on secular concepts. Islamism discards this secular universal law as an imposition on Islamic civilization.

The conflict and the Islamic revolt: an anti-globalization?

The mapping of the world of Islam into the system of sovereign states is a reality which is today contested by the spokesmen of Islamic civilization and therefore in crisis. Unlike most anti-colonial movements, the current global upheaval in the world of Islam against this system, as articulated by Islamism, is not a mere contestation of Western hegemony. At issue is a crisis also related to the global order itself facing a new challenge of de-secularization. As Hedley Bull describes this pattern

> The shrinking of the world . . . has brought together societies to a degree of mutual awareness and interaction that they never had before . . . [It] does not in itself create a unity of outlook and has not in fact done [so] . . . Humanity is becoming simultaneously more unified and more fragmented.[46]

The present structural globalization of the world is paralleled by a cultural fragmentation. There exists no consensus – neither over values, such as democracy, human rights and secularity, nor and most importantly, over the global order of the world itself. Islamism's agenda pursues an agenda of change in two steps:

1   to topple the order of secular sovereign nation states in the world of Islam;
2   to target the Westphalian system itself as an order for the world.

This is an agenda for a remaking of the world: first, the world of Islam, hereafter the world at large. This is pursued by Islamist movements legitimated by a new internationalism based on an imagined *umma* community in a reinvention of the tradition of Islamic universalism. These facts make it clear: globalization does not lead to a cosmopolitan worldview shared by a networked humanity; it leads to the emergence of particularisms and to contestation. The Islamic particularism is itself a universalism. An awareness of this tradition emerges in the context of global communication and its networking. Through modern means of communication, global travelling and global migration, diverse Islamic local communities communicate and interact with one another. They develop an awareness of a belonging to one *umma*, as an imagined community. This awareness underlies the perception of 'Islam under siege'. The classical Islamic tradition of universalism is translated in this context into a politically activist internationalism. In subscribing to this ideology, Islamist movements are driven by religious fundamentalism and pursue an agenda poised at a remaking of the world. Political Islam is an ideology of a new globalism; it is neither an anti-globalization, nor a liberation ideology as some, with Western wishful thinking, would like to believe.

The new globally imagined *umma* community

The reference to an Islamic history of globalization points at the construction of collective memories of the Islamic expansion practiced in the *futuhat* wars. These early global conquests were based on Islamic jihad. The related wars from the seventh through to the seventeenth centuries existed by then as the reality of spreading Islam by means of the sword. This is a historical fact, not an Islamophobic statement. In Islam *umma* was from the beginning a basic notion, but not to the extent of its significance today, as the internationally respected German student of Islam, Joseph van Ess, suggests.

Today the idea of the *umma* is most powerful. The notion refers to a cross-cultural comprehensive community and it is supposed to encompass beyond ethnicity all Muslims. The idea is based on the revival of the historical collective memories. The vision that this *umma* would be expanded to enhance all humanity united under the rule of Islam did not materialize. As shown, Islamic globalization declined to give way to Western globalization. The nineteenth-century's Islamic revolt against this subjugation of Muslim people and of their territory to European rule led to the earlier revival of the concept of *umma* in a new concept of jihad understood by then as anti-colonial jihad. The revivalist al-Afghani was the precursor. Unlike the global jihad of Qutb, the jihad of Afghani was restricted to an anti-colonial function.

At present, the second effort to reconstruct and to unite the *umma* imagined anew emanates from the ideology and action of Islamism. In this pursuit, the contemporary reference to the accords of Islamic history confuses the past with the present. In their call for a return of history as global history to be dominated by restored Islam, contemporary Islamists engage – whether willingly or unwillingly – in an invention of tradition. The meaning of any cultural effort qualified as an invention of tradition is outlined by Hobsbawm in this statement: 'Inventing tradition . . . (is) characterized by reference to the past, if only by imposing repetition . . . tradition is deliberately invented . . . in symbolism and ritual.'[47]

It is most interesting to see how modern technological means of globalization are employed to establish and underpin the new notion of an imagined *umma* in a new meaning. The *umma* is also a community of communication. The fighting of e-jihad is a variety of this communication pattern.[48] Indeed, there are many varieties of political Islam that compel to speak in plural of Islamisms. However, all of them are united by their approval of the instruments of modernity (modern science and technology) combined with a staunch rejection of the value system of cultural modernity. The imagined *umma* fights with modern technology united against the cultural values of modernity for the restoration of the glorious past. This empirical observation supports the view that structural globalization is paralleled by a cultural fragmentation. As shall be argued in Chapter 2, global communication contributes to cultural self-assertion of the *umma*, not to its integration into an international community. In short it thus contributes to the thriving of particularisms (see note 18), not to the desired bridging.

Collective memories, the *umma* and global communication

In the triangle of the world of Islam itself, the West (Europe and the US) and the Islamic diaspora, basically in Europe, modern technology facilitates high levels of global interaction and communication never accounted for before. Technological means are used to translate the religious notion of *umma* into a reality of a community not only based on the shared belief, but also on different cultural segments (inner-Islamic diversity), linked to one another by modern means of communication. In a yet unpublished case study by Claire Sisisky based on fieldwork it is argued that Muslims in Mauritius were integrated in a cross-religious polity beyond ethnicity with other non-Muslims in that island state. Global communication and ethnic interaction with peer groups in the cultural space beyond Mauritius have negatively affected the established consensus underlying the cross-ethnic religious polity and its fabric in that small state. The new global patterns of communication and interaction (media, internet, travelling etc.) have led to divisive identity politics. Even though Europe is a different case, some statements comparable with

Mauritius can be made. The Islam diaspora is yet not integrated in the societies of the host countries of the European Union. In their interaction with European states Muslim leaders claim to speak in one voice and ignore how divided diaspora Muslims are among themselves. The integration of Muslims in Europe is undermined by modern media technology. Turkish Muslims in Germany watch Turkish satellite TV and read the largest edition of the daily *Hurriyet* printed in Germany and distributed in the diaspora beyond Turkey. This global connection of the Turkish diaspora with the country of origin not only separates it from the host country, but also from co-religionists in the Muslim diaspora who are not Turks. It follows that global means of communication not only unite the *umma* and give a boost to identity politics, but also divide the *umma* itself. Therefore, identity politics is not always positive in its effects, as these are often divisive. In this context, Islamic identity politics unites culturally similar peoples and at the same time divides them from the cultural other on different levels.

Islamists claims to unite the 'Muslim we', to confront this entity with the 'non-Muslim they', in a politics of polarization that generates tensions that develop to conflict. This identity politics also divides the community of the *umma* itself along ethnic and sectarian lines. The notions of culture and globalization are therefore related to one another contextually in the study of conflict and tensions. The reference to this research (see note 6) and to its empirical findings underlies the notion of the 'simultaneity of structural globalization and cultural fragmentation' elaborated upon in the ensuing Chapter 2. There, the contention of a cultural standardization in a global village is refuted and the argument is elaborated upon.

Diversity is a blessing, but a specific kind of awareness of diversity in a process of globalization is not always positive, in particular when it divides in an identity politics that demonizes the cultural other. This is more than a global jihad against a unifying 'McCulture'. In fact, 'McCulture' is a simplistic notion that reflects the American perception of some 'pundits' about the world outside the US. This is a mere contention not an outcome of a serious analysis. There is a most important distinction between universalization and globalization. Universalization refers to values, globalization to structures. These are different issues. One speaks of the universal *not* of the global declaration of human rights. A universalization takes place when values that claim to be universal are accepted by peoples who belong to different communities. In contrast, globalization refers to structures, mostly imposed. In this understanding, the structure of the international system of states is global, as is the world economy. Modern technology also facilitates a system of communication. However, globalization does not move on along with universalization of modern values. These are two different processes that do not match with one another in their effects. The result is cultural fragmentation paired with structural globalization. This notion refers to the reality of different peoples united by global structures, but separated by adhering to culturally different value systems. Ethnic, religious and cultural particularisms are promoted by the global interaction and communication of the communities that adhere to them.

The simultaneity of globalization and fragmentation

There are scholars who – in wishful thinking – speak of a constructed world citizenship and ignore the opposed, but real ethnic-religious identity politics. In the Islamic worldview, the notion of globalization is not only generally discarded as a Western project, at times even vilified as a 'Jewish crusader conspiracy'; it is also challenged by a replacement Islamic vision of globalization. Therefore, Muslims and Islamists approve the notion of globalization if used in the understanding of a global Islamization. In most uninformed writings in the West about Islamic identity politics and the related search for authenticity, these issues are simply ignored. Authenticity and identity politics are dealt with positively and even approved. A closer look at the original writings in Arabic from Qutb and al-Banna in the past to Qaradawi and al-Jundi at present compels me to be critical. Research leads to the conclusion that the Islamist approach of de-Westernization is based on a mentality of purification from any alien impact originating from globalization. In the past, sentiments of a divisive fragmentation of this kind were alien to the ethics of Islam. Islamic civilization has a very rich tradition of learning from others in historical processes of cultural borrowing in a global search for universal knowledge. The history of Islam and Europe is not only a history of mutual conquests (jihad and crusade), but is also a history of cultural encounters in the course of which decisive processes of cultural borrowing took place on both sides.[49]

Today, the Islamists – in their totalitarian ideology – ignore these distinctions. True, the rejection of Western impact on the civilization of Islam happens in a context of Western hegemony. Culturally, there is a European mindset of orientalism rightly criticized by Edward Said. However, an orientalism in reverse is not the right response to dreadful orientalism, as it promotes cultural fragmentation.

The cultural opposition to structural globalization pursues an agenda of a purifying de-Westernization. This is not the right response to imperial Westernization. Earlier, Hedley Bull was quoted as rightly stating that the shrinking of the world does not lead, as assumed, to mutual recognition. The more people get closer to one another under conditions of globalization, the more tensions arise. Today, the worlds of Islam and the West need to learn how to come to terms with one another in a global civil society. Among the avenues for this venture is democratization in a global order based on democracy and cosmopolitain governance.[50] Another avenue is the establishing of a cross-cultural pluralism. In placing Islam into global studies, there are two approaches that run into extremes opposed to one another, while both share the feature of being based on normative rhetorics: the clash of civilizations contradicted by the other rhetorics of 'the convergence of civilizations'.[51] There are other ways of 'preventing the clash of civilizations' (see note 3) without an overlooking of the intercivilizational conflict.

There are also non-Western non-Muslims who have problems with Islamic claims to *siyadat* ('supremacy'). This is the case in south Asia and more in South East Asia. The right response to the discrepancy between globalization and fragmentation and the effects on Islam is the acceptance of cultural pluralism. In a global set up, diversity (between Muslims and non-Muslims and between Muslims themselves) is to be accepted, but also combined with universal standards of human rights, global civil society and democratization. In this understanding, diversity and universality in a global context complement and do not contradict one another. The incorporation of the Muslim *umma* in global–universal standards is the alternative to the approach of 'globalized Islam', as well as to the one of divisive identity politics. To avoid pitfalls one has to draw a distinction between Islam as faith, cult, ethics and cultural system as well, and Islamism as an expression of religionized politics. Islamism is based on a political interpretation of Islam, but still Islamism and Islam are different issues to be distinguished from one another.[52] If this distinction is ignored, the West would never be in a position to deal properly with the peoples and states of Islamic civilization.

The distinction between Islam and Islamism

The present book on intercivilizational conflict in world politics places Islam as a social reality, not as a faith in a geopolitical–global context. Some may contest this venture with the challenging question, 'Why on earth the singling out of Islam?' to come up hereafter with the accusation of Islamophobia. Now, Islam is a religious faith and a cultural value-based system; Islam is not a political system of government. Those Westerners who confuse the critique of Islamism with Islamo-phobia overlook the fact of politicization and dismiss any kind of inquiry of Islam related to world politics. True, the religious faith of Islam that assembles about 1.6 billion peoples of humankind imagined as a separate *umma*-community should be protected against prejudice. There is an Islamic entity in the world. Notwith-standing the great diversity of local Islamic cultures of Muslim peoples, all Muslims share with one another similar values and a worldview that unites them to one civilization. On these grounds the existing resemblance allows us, free of essen-tialism, to view all Muslims as peoples of one civilization. This is also what Muslims do when they speak about their entity as *umma*. Thus, we find in Islam cultural diversity within the unity of one Islamic civilization. In view of this cultural diversity, it is conceded that there is no monolith named Islam, despite the use of the notion of Islamic civilization. Add to this insight the inference that no Islamist has the legitimacy to speak for the Islamic civilization.

Therefore, it is a problem when existing Islamist movements of the twenty-first century claim to establish – at least perceptually – a kind of a monolith united by global links and called 'Islam'. Islamist internationalism is a world political reality, but it is not Islam. The reference to the threat of Islamism to world order has nothing to do with orientalism, not to speak of Islamophobia.

The question concerning the legitimacy of the reference to civilizations in the study of politics matters to international relations as a discipline for which the study of conflict matters a lot. In particular, since the deep transformation of the world around the end of last century, Islam occurs as a major factor in world politics. This occurrence can be stated on two political levels. First, on the level of the state: the Organization of the Islamic Conference (OIC) unites fifty-seven states with an Islamic majority population. Second, there are Islamic non-state actors (e.g. al-Qaeda and The Movement of the Muslim Brothers). These movements engage on all levels of politics, locally and globally.

The politicization of the religion of Islam leads to Islamism. This is connected with the claim that Islam is not only a faith, but also a constructed system of government. The idea of an Islamic state is based on shari'a law believed to be the constitution legislated by Allah for a divine order. This political interpretation of Islam makes out of this religion an ideology of Islamism that leads to inner conflicts within Islamic civilization. A political theorist, John Brenkman, addressed this issue as a 'civil war' within Islam (e.g. the fight between secular Kemalists and Islamists in Turkey). The spill over of this process to world politics assumes a geopolitical dimension with the related effects on world politics.

In a nutshell, the view that Islam and politics are interrelated justifies placing Islam in world politics. The politicization in point suggests a more complex relation between religion and politics on all three levels: local, regional and international/global. These complex issues can only be listed, and briefly discussed, but not analysed in this chapter. The major issue is that there is a return of Islam to politics that indicates the failure of the secularization process in the contemporary Islamic civilization. This failure is among other things related to the crisis of the secular nation state as a crisis of development.

In looking at the roots of politics in Islam in a process that transforms a 'cultural system' into Islamic politics one can state that this is no novelty. However, politicized Islam that serves today as a 'political ideology' is a device for the legitimacy of contemporary Islamist movements. This is the novelty. Islam's peculiarity is that this religion has a close relation to politics and war from its birth onwards. The novelty is, however, the recent phenomenon of Islamism and its idea of an Islamic state.

To understand the distinction one has at first to look at the past. Islamic revelation started spiritually at Mecca in the year 610. It was not until the creation of the polity of the *umma* (i.e. community, not the 'Islamic state', as Islamists today wrongly contend) in Medina in 622 that Islam was intermingled with politics. In that year Islamic history commences and therefore Muslims number in their calendar 622 as the year one. This is the Islamic *hijra* calendar. Therefore, *hijra* ('migration') has a specific meaning in Islam: a Muslim is supposed to migrate in the pursuit of the spread of Islam. In the year 622, the Prophet migrated from Mecca to Medina and engaged in politics for spreading Islam. For Muslims, this is a binding precedent. In his new location, the Prophet took political decisions and also fought wars. The late French scholar of Islam, Maxime Rodinson, characterized in his biography Mohammed as the Prophet of Islam, however, in a combination of 'Jesus and Charlemagne'. Nonetheless, it is a fact that neither the holy book of the Muslims, the Qur'an, nor the canonical tradition of the Prophet Mohammed, i.e. the scripture of *Hadith*, ever made any provisions concerning the polity. The term *dawla* ('state') never occurs in the scripture. It follows that there is no provisioned system of government in the authoritative scripture of Islam. In short, the idea of an Islamic state is a modern construction. After the death of the Prophet the system of the caliphate was established, but it should not be conflated with the 'Islamic state'. Islamists fight at present for an order that they have invented and that is not a part of Islamic belief.

Following the death of the Prophet in 632 the aristocracy of Mecca that was composed of the elders of the Islamized tribe of Quraysh powerfully established three tenets:

1   The Islamic ruler should be a successor, i.e. a caliph of the Prophet.
2   The caliph has to descend from the tribe of Quraysh. This requirement contradicts the Islamic provision that all Muslims create one community that transcends tribes into a transtribal *umma* to abolish herewith tribal affiliations.
3   The caliph has to be close to the Prophet and to the tradition he established. This *khalifat* ('the caliphate') system was based on selection on merits and descent in the formative years of Islamic rule from 632 through 661.

There were four Qurayshi leaders: Abu Bakr, Omar, Othman and Ali who were selected to rule as caliphs. Three of these *rashidun* ('righteous') caliphs including the last one, Ali, were brutally assassinated. Despite this bloody feature, the *rashidun* age is considered to date to be the model for emulation with regard to political rule.

Following the assassination of the caliph Ali 661, the Islamic *umma* community not only went through a violent shism in Sunna and Shi'a, but was also in the result dominated by one clan of the tribe of Quraysh. The Omaiyyads usurped the caliphate and established dynastical rule. In so doing, they transformed the caliphate from selective to a hereditary rule. They also shifted the capital of Islam from Medina/Mecca to Damascus. That was the first imperial rule of Islam named the Omayyad caliphate that successfully led global jihad wars. This Islamic expansion resulted in an Islamic empire that stretched from China to Spain. In Islamic history, there were two other such imperial caliphates to follow successively, namely the Abasside of Baghdad and the Ottoman of Istanbul. In this imperial history that lasted until 1924, Islam was not only a faith, practised in a great variety of local cultures that continue to be untied in a cross-cultural civilization. Islam had also served as a legitimacy for an imperial rule named the caliphate. This rule is considered to be the Islamic system of government. Muslims fought jihad wars from the seventh through the seventeenth centuries in pursuit of an Islamic expansion envisioned to map the entire globe into *dar al-Islam* ('abode, or house of Islam').

The real history of Islam did not follow the course that scriptural Islam prescribes. The fact is that the world – one millennium later – was mapped into another system, namely the Westphalian one of sovereign states established 1648. This system continues to date to be the basis of the modern international system that contemporary Islamism contests. This movement emerged in the twentieth century and is thriving in the twenty-first century as a revolt against this system in a bid to replace it with its own as a solution for its crisis.

The end of Islamic expansion, the rise of the international system and contemporary Islamist nostalgia

Up to this point it is safe to state that the Peace of Westphalia affects Islamic civilization in the past and present. The roots for the launching of a competitive globalization project are associated with the rise of the West and its 'military revolution' (1500–1800). This rise interrupted the Islamic expansion and replaced it with its own European expansion that created to date the major problem that determines Islam and politics. In the past, the rise of the West halted Islamic expansion. At present, the Westphalian system of states maps the entire world of Islam. The Islamic revolt against the West is not only against this system, but also aims to reverse history.

Since the failure to capture Vienna in 1683 Muslim armies were in retreat and lost all ensuing wars. The process of 'importing the European army' did not remedy existing deficiencies. European powers not only stopped Islam from further invading Europe and pulled it back from Europe, they also invaded the world of Islam itself. The third and last global Islamic caliphate of the Ottoman Empire decayed. After a successful revolution, Kemal Atatürk abolished the caliphate in 1924 in an act followed by the declaration of the secular republic of Turkey. It is still the only secular republic in the world of Islam that enshrines secularism in its constitution. One year after the abolition of the caliphate, the Azhar scholar Ali Abdel-Raziq published in 1925 his book *Al-Islam wa usul al-hikm* ('Islam and the Origins of Government') in which he argues in this manner: 'In Islam there is no system of government. Islam is just a religious faith that was abused to serve as a legitimacy for a political rule.' This depoliticization of Islam provoked strong Muslim contestations. In punishing Abdel-Raziq he was fired from al-Azhar and his material existence was destroyed. Nevertheless, Islamic modern history followed basically what happened in Turkey, however, without a formal adoption of secularism. The transitory period of colonial rule in most of the former provinces of the Ottoman Empire ended in building independent secular nation states throughout the world of Islam. These states were mapped into the Westphalian system of sovereign states, thus becoming a part of the modern international system. This is the age of secular politics in the world of Islam. It lasted from 1924 to 1967. The Six-Days-War of 1967 launched, in effect, the return of Islam to politics. This process has been facilitated by the fact that the new secular nation states had a weak legitimacy and lacked the substance needed. This weakness was dismantled in the repercussions of the 1967 war. The introduction of the system of sovereign states to the world of Islam resulted in the formation of weak states identified as 'nominal nation states'. Some experts deride these states in the world of Islam as 'tribes with national flags'.

Under conditions of crisis a new claim for an Islamic state arises. Therefore, conflict and Islamic politics are related to one another. For properly understanding this development one is advised to look at the historical period between the abolition of the caliphate 1924 and the Six-Days-War of 1967. This is the best way to understand the background of both contemporary Islam and Islamism. This period is characterized by two opposite directions: a very superficial secularization and also the emergence of the Movement of the Muslim Brothers in 1928 in Cairo, engaged in an activity of de-Westernization. Secularism prevailed in a variety of ways in most Muslim countries, of course not in Wahhabi Saudi Arabia, but in the staunchly secular republic of Turkey. Also, the pan-Arab Egypt under Nasser had a secular legitimacy, as had the largest nation of Islam in South East Asia, Indonesia, under the rule of the secular Ahmed Sukarno. The wind of change in favour of political Islam started with the watershed of 1967. The overall repercussions of the shattering Arab defeat in the Six-Days-War led to a predicament and to a delegitimation of secular regimes, first in the Middle East and followed by spill-over effects in the rest of the world of Islam. Among the consequences were the ascendancy of political Islam (Islamism) moving from the fringe to the core of politics. For a number of reasons, the effects of this process spilled over from the Arab Middle East to the rest of the world of Islam. One of the factors that promoted spill-over effects is related to the proven fact that the Arab part in Islamic civilization is recognized as the core. It generates cultural–religious influence over the rest of the world of Islam. For instance, the Middle East affects South East Asia in the interaction and not the other way around. It is Egypt (population of 70 million people) that affects Indonesia with a population of 235 million and not the other way around. This is a political reality based assessment, not driven by any Arabocentrism. Still and despite the impact referred to, the problems of 'Islamic legitimacy in Asia' are much different from those of the Middle East.[53] In the West one has to understand Islam beyond the Middle East.

The connection between Islam and politics is established today by the Islamist movements that reclaim a *nizam Islami* ('Islamic order') for the state and for the world at large. Therefore, the claim is not only restricted to the world of Islam. At present, it is Sunni Arab Islam and not the Shi'a revolution in Iran that generates (a) jihad in the new understanding of an Islamic world revolution; (b) shari'atization of politics, based on a new understanding of Islamic law; and (c) call for the return of history (i.e. the restoration of Islamic glory), not the end of it, as believed often after the breakdown of communism. The end of the East–West conflict smoothes the way for the new post-bipolar intercivilizational conflict that results from the revival of jihad and shari'a in a new shape combined with a claim of a return of history.

The return of Islam to the fore in a political shape parallel to the end of bipolarity is combined with conflicts. These are also related to Islam's predicament with modernity. Islam is a civilization undergoing a politicization of its values that happens also – in terms of world politics – as a politicization of the 'heterogeneity of civilizations' (R. Aron, note 4). This is the substance of the intercivilizational conflict.

The reader is again and again reminded of the distinction that a conflict is not a 'clash'. The pertinence of Islam and Islamism to the study of conflict in international relations is related to the fact that religion and politics have become intertwined in the countries of Islamic civilization in the age of post-bipolar politics. In this context, politicized religion is among the new sources of conflict. The articulation of pending issues in a religious language generates at first real cultural tensions that become later on political. The overall context is the predicament of Islam with modernity (see note 6) that develops to a source of conflict. There are many levels in this conflict. The first level is an inner-Islamic conflict over the secular nation state. Under conditions of globalization this conflict within Islam (e.g. Turkey) is then extended to an international one (e.g. Iraq, Pakistan and Afghanistan). The conflict escalates along the rise of powerful Islamist movements that challenge the existing nation states in the world of Islam with the aim to topple their order to replace it by an Islamic state. To wrap up, the Islamist claim leads to tensions and conflicts, which first occur within Islam, and then through spill-over effects reach the international and intercivilizational level. The inner-Islamic and international levels intermingle with one another.

To be sure, the call for an Islamic state is not to be conflated with the aim of the restoration of the caliphate, as some pundits contend. There is a novelty, next to the fact that politics is becoming religionized and religion is subjected to a politicization which is the idea of a *nizam Islami* ('Islamic order') that reflects the claim for an Islamic state. This novelty and the particularism on which it is based promote tensions and ignite conflict and it is articulated in religious terms.

In short, the 'Islamic state' is not the Caliphate since it is based on an invention of tradition. Thus, the continuity alleged in the formulation put forward by the Harvard professor Noah Feldman, *The Fall and Rise of the Islamic State*, ignores all facts on the ground and is therefore simply wrong.[54]

It cannot be repeated enough that conflict becomes intractable when it is religionized, because beliefs are not negotiable. Some students of Islamist politics fail to understand this reality. They argue that these Islamist Muslims are virtually secular, because they allegedly use, or abuse religion for non-religious, i.e. social and political ends. It is also fully wrong to see in Islamist leaders 'reformers' or 'revolutionaries'. Fieldwork shows that the Islamists act in good faith as believers. Their 'good faith' is never to be confused with cynicism. Profane Westerners seem to fail to develop a proper understanding of the place of culture and religion as sources of values in post-bipolar politics.

There are basic issue areas that determine the relationship of Islam and politics. Religionized politics emerges in the context of secularization and de-secularization. Political scientists are expected in their study of Islam to beware of and to avoid the way of debating that prevails in Islamic studies, in which the accusation of one another of 'orientalism' replaces a scholarly analysis of the pending issues. It is a fact, not an orientalism, to state that cultural tensions related to Islam lead to a political conflict shaped by civilizational values.

The study of religion and politics matters to all religions, but the pivotal place is given to those religions with politicized universal claims. In this understanding Islam of today is a politicized universalism related to the following issue areas:

- First, the ability of Islam as a religion to invade the public sphere teaching that the primary unit of society is the *umma*, the international brotherhood of believers.
- Second, Islam forces people to follow shari'a laws. If this law is elevated to state law in a process of shari'atization of politics, then conflicts based on a religious component are ahead.[55] These are much harder to solve. The involvement of religion in politics adds to the complexity of conflict and makes it virtually intractable.
- Third, political Islam has a great centrality to post-bipolar world politics through the transformation of Islamic universalism – in the course of a process of politicization – into a politics that leads to a religion-based internationalism. From here emerges the claim of a new world order based on Islamic tenets. This reference may be presented as an explanation for 'Islam's geopolitical war' that some political theorists contend in their linking of 9/11 to post-bipolar politics.

The contention that there is a model of an Islamist state matters to political science. In international relations of post-bipolar politics the competition of different cultural models generates tensions that develop domestically, regionally and internationally to a political conflict. Islam's problems with cultural modernity are central in this context. The ignited tensions not only occur among Muslims, but also in their relations to the 'non-Muslim other' in an international environment of crisis.

In concluding this point of Chapter 1 it is stated that civilizational encounters also include conflict to be studied from the point of view of conflict resolution, not of clash. Islam has a central place in this study committed to dismissing the damaging rhetoric of a clash or of convergence of civilizations that has entered academia and politics. However, any 'preventing the clash of civilizations' (see note 4) cannot dispense with the study of intra- and intercivilizational conflict addressed in this chapter. A conflict can be peacefully resolved in a negotiation process that could assume the shape of a dialogue between civilizations, whereas a clash is based on an essentializing view, and it suggests fault-lines that imply polarization. A bridging based on conflict resolution is a better option.

The reference to the place of jihad and jihadism in world politics needs to consider 'Democratic Responses to Terrorism' to replace the lawlessness of the war on terror pursued in the name of security.[56] The political interpretation of jihad as a 'world revolution' (S. Qutb) allows – as jihadism proposes – the resort to violence in an irregular war. This is also among the areas in the study of Islam, Islamism and conflict in post-bipolar politics that justify the proposition of the political theorist John Brenkman quoted earlier that, 'Islam . . . is in the midst of a civil war . . . There is something more underway, since the upheavals in the Muslim world are also geopolitical conflicts . . . Islam is embroiled in a geocivil war.'[57] Then he boldly ascertains the 'uncomfortable truth that . . . most of the dangers are coming from the Muslim world' (ibid.). Today, such views are often qualified as an expression of orientalism, but the concern articulated in the quoted statement is not this negative sentiment. The statement matters to the study of Islamism and conflicts in world politics. At first, the conflicts are among Muslims themselves, on the one hand, but then with the West on the other. There are also states like India, China and Russia, which are concerned. The cultural analysis of political conflict is not a culturalism. The conflict within Islam is ignited by political Islam, which not only uses in its Islamist movements Islam for their legitimacy, but also as a concept of order. Muslim peoples are advised to endorse the combination of Islam and democracy; the resolution of intra- and intercivilizational conflicts on a secular basis that separates religion from politics as ways for a better future. The study of the issues listed is a scholarly concern. Political religions aim to remake the world and assume the shape of religious fundamentalisms. These are not the ways to be recommended for Muslims.

Religion, fundamentalism and world politics

In this final section I draw on the concept of 'fundamentalism', deplorably knowing that this useful category for political theory in its dealing with the place of religion in politics has become contentious. This happens for a variety of reasons. Despite the fact that prominent scholars have worked and published on this subject within the framework of a big project chaired by Martin Marty and Scott Appleby at the American Academy of Arts and Sciences, the related findings published in five volumes are ignored. [58] This kind of research on fundamentalism is seldom quoted, and in fact simply overlooked. For an exemplary case I refer to Robert Lee who in a footnote states: 'The word fundamentalism has generally been applied . . . I side with those who do not find this term helpful.'[59] No argument is presented.

In a similar vein, opinion leaders and policy makers practice negligence with regard to published research and avoid the use of the term 'fundamentalism'. At a major conference of the Rand Corporation in Santa Monica, CA, attended by representatives of major federal US departments, including the Pentagon, one of these politicians pronounced in public the decision not to use the term 'fundamentalism', because it is considered to be offensive to Muslims. If this were true, why then does the prominent Islamist, the Cairo philosophy professor Hasan Hanafi, choose the formulation *Al-Usuliyya al-Islamiyya* ('Islamic fundamentalism') as a title for one of his major books?[60]

The scholarly analysis of political Islam is often charged with the accusation of orientalism. There is also the blame that the focus on Islam in the fundamentalism debate ends up in Islamophobic connotations. The term 'Islamophobia' is often employed by Islamists themselves in their war of ideas. They do this to defame their critics and to undermine the study of religious fundamentalism that includes Islam. These views that invalidate and discredit 'fundamentalism' as a significant analytical category in the social sciences are to be dismissed as ideologically blinkered.

The phenomenon of religious fundamentalism started to occur on a global level in the twentieth century. It heralds the interrelation of religion and politics. Religious fundamentalism is a response to challenge in the context of exposure to cultural modernity. Without considering this context, there would be no proper understanding of religious fundamentalism. Cultural modernity is secular and constitutes a challenge to all religions. In all religions the response to modernity could be done in a variety of ways. These are either cultural change with religious reform, or fundamentalism. The challenges arising from cultural modernity and its disenchantment with the world are the background for the emergence of this phenomenon that becomes central in post-bipolar world politics.

The discourse of modernity is also a political one. In substance it is secular in that it relates to the process of secularization of modern societies. Earlier in this chapter the return of the sacred (see note 55) was addressed not only as a response to cultural modernity, but also as a challenger. A process of de-secularization follows. This is the agenda of religious fundamentalist movements legitimated by their often totalitarian ideologies for countering cultural modernity and are thus a counter-enlightenment.

Islamism is a variety of the global phenomenon of religious fundamentalism. True, the origin of the phenomenon is to be traced back to American protestant fundamentalism, but it is today a global one.[61] This understanding has been established in research. Martin Marty and Scott Appleby state 'fundamentalists see themselves as militants . . . they react, they fight back . . . next they fight for . . . they fight with particularly chosen repository of resources . . . they fight against others . . . they also fight under God.'[62] All varieties of fundamentalism claim to be a revival of religion, but despite this claim these are not an indication of a religious renaissance. At issue is something else: an invention of tradition in the course of a politicization of religion and religionization of politics. Fundamentalism is therefore not only a defensive cultural response to modernity, but also at foremost an indication of a political phenomenon aimed at a remaking of the world. The result is not a 'post-secular society', but rather an intercivilizational conflict.

The fundamentalist is regularly a male who acts as a political man opposing Rousseau's popular sovereignty as sovereignty of the people entitled to determine government and politics. Fundamentalists act as the 'Defenders of God'[63] and argue – as is it in the Islamic case – for an 'Islamic World Revolution' (S. Qutb) for the restoration of *hakimiyyat Allah* ('God's rule'). Islamists are religious fundamentalists who believe that only God is the one who is the sovereign! Their rejection of popular sovereignty results in a rejection of the secular nation state and of democracy that rest on this principle.

The overarching context of fundamentalism is the reality of a world time of globalization. In fact, each civilization is based on a particularism of its own time documented in its own calendar. Additionally, one can speak of pre-modern civilizations while avoiding evolutionary thinking. There are also civilizations that are not secular and therefore religion-based. The historical root of contemporary and modern globalization is the process of European expansion. The related processes are viewed as an expansion of the international society established in the aftermath of the Peace of Westphalia 1648. This globalization is a secular process that results in the mapping of the world into the system of secular nation states. It was believed that this mapping was also a part of the universal process of Westernization and secularization. Today, the religious fundamentalisms uprising in non-Western civilizations against the West belie this assumption. Anti-Westernism is, for instance, the substance of Islamist fundamentalism as the vision of a restoration of a religious order against secularity and the West. As well, of course, there is also the protestant fundamentalism that also contests modernity. However, there are great differences with the other non-Western varieties of political religions in Asia and Africa.

The theoretical concept of a simultaneity of structural globalization and cultural fragmentation developed in my earlier work and introduced at length in the ensuing chapter refers to the effects of 'European expansion'. It launched a process that generated global structures that are today mapping all civilizations in one 'civilizing process'. This process, analysed in the magnificent work of Norbert Elias, is not paralleled by a process of a universalization of Western values.[64] In short, cultural universalization does not match the successful globalization of structures. Therefore, it would be wrong to infer that the 'civilizing process' led to the emergence of one civilization identical with humanity. The tensions that arise from a simultaneity of globalization and fragmentation lead to the emergence of religious fundamentalisms that also indicate an intercivilizational conflict. Here again I draw on Raymond Aron's notion that bipolarity 'veiled the heterogeneity of civilization' (see note 4). Following the end of the Cold War the return of the sacred in the shape of various religious fundamentalisms has been the foremost salient feature of post-bipolar politics. The binary worldview referred to is not mine, but rather the result of the religionization of politics.

The challenge posed by religious fundamentalism to secularization engages not only in a revival of religion, but also in a politicization of its values. This is the foremost aspect of the new phenomenon and basically what all fundamentalisms share. The remaking of the world with regard to government and politics is the basic concern of any fundamentalist agenda. In the course of religionized political, economic and social conflicts a civilizational dimension occurs in world politics. In Islam civilization is defined by a religious view of the world.

The Islamist's vision of a de-secularization as a starter for a remaking of the world on religious–political grounds is a particular case of religious fundamentalism because it is an internationalism. In a way, the 'holy terror' of September 11, 2001 revived the implementation of the approach used in the study of religious fundamentalism, but it also created obstacles to referring to this approach at the same time.[65] Since then it is considered to be politically incorrect to look at political

Islam in this way and to relate it to 9/11 as a threat to international security. Instead of more enlightenment these biased scholars turned round the binary worldview of jihadism to use it as an accusation against those who criticize Islamism. Islam and Islamism have been confused and this continues to be the case. Critics have also been accused of being trapped between myth and reality, not to speak of the accusation of 'orientalism'. Nonetheless, the focus on the Islamic case in the study of religious fundamentalism and in the media coverage relates to a reality. Next to Christianity Islam is the only religious faith that is based on a universalism. The politicization of this universalism results in a political internationalism expressed in the ideology of Islamism. This is a fact, not a distortion.

While acknowledging the place of Islamism in the war of ideas, I concede, of course, that it is wrong to reduce the political impact of fundamentalisms simply to the spread of ideas. For sure, religious fundamentalisms do not fall from heaven and do not come from nowhere. There is a structural underpinning. All fundamentalisms also arise from a crisis situation. On the one hand there is a crisis of meaning and on the other a crisis related to political and socio-economic constraints, i.e. a structural crisis. Some suggest that fundamentalisms are a passing phenomenon and present again the example of Islamism as the Islamic variety of fundamentalism believed to be declining. Nevertheless, that fact of a double crisis in the meaning addressed refers to what is underlying the phenomenon itself. If these constraints are still looming it seems not likely that a decline of the phenomenon is to be expected. In addition, fundamentalisms that grow also from a predicament with modernity are not something like a day-to-day politics. The global intercivilizational conflict related is expected to last for some decades to come. The contention of a post-Islamism is based on self-deception.

As argued throughout this chapter, the end of the East–West conflict smoothed the way for the already existing return of religion to world politics. Clearly, all religious fundamentalisms predate post-bipolarity, but they gain prominence in the process of the transition from polarity to post-bipolarity. Islamism is one significant variety of religious fundamentalism and it has a dual character: it is political and religious at the same time.[66] Religionized and ethnicized politics is a sign of the prevalence of culture, religion and ethnicity in post-bipolarity.

Conclusions

In the course of inflaming cultural tensions that fuel the post-bipolar intercivilizational conflict Islamism transforms traditional Islamic religious universalism into a political internationalism. The new ideology resembles more world communism than traditional Islam. In this transformation one special case of religious fundamentalism pertinent to world politics emerges and it underlies an intercivilizational conflict. In the fight in the world of Islam between democracy and authoritarian regimes Islamist movements meddle in a bid for power. The West, equally the US and the European Union, had neither a policy, nor a vision for a better future when this scenario of the fall of authoritarian regimes occurred at the beginning of 2011.

Under conditions of local conflicts (authoritarianism and state power), regional conflicts (Palestine and the Middle East conflict) and the global conflict over the order of the world the issue is religionized politics. The pertinence of the phenomenon can be identified in a checklist of issue areas. With one exception – the idea of an order for the world based on religion (Islamism) – all of the following features exist in all varieties of the global phenomenon of religious fundamentalism not restricted to the Islamic civilization and its core region the Middle East:

- political religion and the challenge of cultural modernity;
- politicized religion, secularization and de-secularization;
- religion and political order on the level of the state and the international system;
- religion and political legitimacy;
- religion and law;
- religion and political pluralism.

Politicized religion functions, as discussed in this chapter, as a contestation of the existing political order. It also aims at a remaking of the world. In this way it covers all of these listed issue areas. In this book it is argued that Islamism being one variety of religious fundamentalisms religionizes politics and inflames an intercivilizational conflict in global politics.

Even though I argue that Islamism is political ideology, not to be confused with the religion of Islam, it is certainly not a secular ideology; moreover: this ideology grew from an interpretation of Islam and it is based on the divine in contrast to the secular. Therefore, the comparison of Islamism with fascism and communism viewed as political religions is wrong, as these are secular ideologies. Nonetheless, the totalitarian character is shared. What matters here is that religious fundamentalism in Islam is an opposition to the secular nation state and herewith to the Westphalian synthesis of the international system. This secular order is envisioned as being replaced by a new order believed to be the true government of God based on divine precepts. This competition between religious and secular order underpins an intercivilizational conflict in world politics. There is an Islamist challenge. The prevailing Westphalian order of sovereign states that emerged in the aftermath of the Peace of Westphalia 1648, is questioned today as the state system imposed on the entire world. Since the wave of de-colonization a mapping of the entire globe into the Westphalian system took place.[67] This secular political world order is threatened today by all religious fundamentalisms in their drive for a remaking of the world. In particular, the Islamist internationalism, a variant of this threat,[68] confused by ill-informed scholars with pan-Islamism,[69] is a bid for a remaking of the world.[70] The confusion is not only dismissed for scholarly, but also for political reason: pan-Islamism (e.g. Afghani) is about uniting Muslims to on *umma*-entity. In contrast Islamist internationalism (e.g. Qutb) is about a world order for mapping the globe under Islamic rule.

The new global intercivilizational conflict that leads to a 'new Cold War' (see note 22) undermines the efforts for an intercivilizational peace that should emerge in a process of bridging between the civilizations. This is the theme of the present book. The normative driver of all ensuing chapters is to engage in a venture of a peace strategy for preventing the development of the conflict in point to a clash, also how to manage existing tensions to prevent their unfolding to a conflict shaped by religionized politics. The needed intercivilizational bridging in the service of peaceful conflict resolution can be promoted by referring to an Islam of a different tradition from the one claimed by Islamism. In the past, there existed a tradition of Islamic humanism that was buried by the establishment of the *fiqh*-orthodoxy. This tradition is worth being revived: it would be an authentic Islamic revivalism.[71] If this revival could materialize, then one would be in a position to truly speak of good conditions for a start aimed at bridging within the framework of a cross-cultural morality. However, if this morality in which a liberal Islam can be incorporated in the foundations of 'a peace strategy for the twenty-first century' cannot be established, then no peace of civilizations can be within reach.[72] The reality of multiple civilizations has to be combined with a cross–cultural legitimacy for a political culture of pluralism shared by all civilizations. This combination of diversity with shared values is the culture of pluralism that one needs in order to avert any binary based on a centrism, regardless of being Western or Islamic.[73]

2

INTERCULTURAL DIALOGUE AS A GLOBAL COMMUNICATION IN PURSUIT OF BRIDGING

Cultural particularisms and value-conflicts among the civilizations

When people of different cultures communicate with one another under conditions of globalization, an encounter between strangers takes place. Globalization establishes a networking, but not the cultural standardization required to generate some closeness. Therefore, the need arises for cross-cultural bridging to bring culturally different people close to one another. In this pursuit, dialogue is one of the avenues for a peaceful dealing with conflicts, on the top of which one faces the intercivilizational value-conflicts. Put differently intercultural dialogue is a means for conflict resolution in the pursuit of preventing a clash of civilizations.[1] However, for a promising bridging, fruitful communication is required to address the pending issues.

The parties involved in the search for conflict resolution are civilizations, but these are non-state actors. Who is supposed to be the representative of these competing civilizations? Next to required mutual recognition and respect as prerequisites for a promising communication, the cultural discourse of communication is a basic issue. (This book proposes cultural modernity[2] as a framework for global communication.[3]) The levels of the interaction among the representatives of cultures and civilizations need to be fixed. At first, this interaction involves both conflict and fertilization. In an exposure to the cultural other under conditions of globalization one can either engage in a cultural borrowing, or in defensive cultural identity politics that lead to conflict. Then, there are the two levels, one of which is the inter-state negotiation and the other is the communication between groups of civil society.

Different local cultures and cross-cultural civilizations do not only have different languages, but also different ways of thinking manifested in their own distinct discourses and also different ways of communication determined by values. If related to substance and to cross-cultural fertilization global communication could become an instrument for bridging. Here, however, the acceptance of shared knowledge and a common discourse is necessary to facilitate a mutual understanding. Nonetheless, this need continues to be missing despite intensifying globalization. Why? It is a fact that people of different cultures not only differ over values, but also do not share the same meaning of the notions used when they communicate with one another. For instance, Muslims refer to a different meaning that is distinct from the one Westerners use when they talk about peace and tolerance. The result of the rival meanings is a value-conflict. Links and networks generated by an instrumental global communication cannot change that reality of dissent. There is, nonetheless, a trend to belittle this conflict in viewing disagreement as a misunderstanding. This is, however, not the case, because conflict over values is a reality and no misunderstanding. The issue can be exemplified on the rule of law that could either be based on divine shari'a or on legislative, i.e. secular man-made law. These are different understandings of law, not the same and thus there is no misunderstanding, but rather a conflict between two rival concepts is in place.

Scholars who conflate world society and global communication while they dismiss intercultural tensions generated by rival value systems not only miss the point, but also fail to provide an inquiry for identifying the conflict in place. Each civilization has its own religious–political discourse. This fact ultimately separates and creates fault-lines that can only be overcome by a secular discourse. When religion is a part of the problem it cannot be a part of the solution, as Scott Appleby wrongly argues, ignoring the findings of the fundamentalism research project that he once led and significantly helped to shape. Another scholar, Stephan Stetter, who goes to the other extreme and believes in value-free communication, is as wrong as Scott Appleby.[4] Culture, civilization, ethnicity and religion matter, but they disconnect. The issue is not to admit these factors, or to dismiss them, but rather to understand their place in the conflict.

What is global communication?

Introductory deliberations

The communication that takes place as an intercultural dialogue is supposed to come close to the ideal view of intercultural interaction based on accepted universal standards. This ideal should be more than wishful thinking. Furthermore, it is more than a value-free function that the system theory suggests. The existence of an intercultural exchange during the high days of Islamic civilization between the ninth and twelfth centuries displays the fact that communication has to be based on a shared philosophy. In that age of a flourishing Islam, Muslim rationalists vowed to universal standards of knowledge and engaged in learning from others. Today, in view of closing the Muslim mind and the resulting attitudes, a defensive culture prevails. Therefore there exists an urgent need to revive the buried tradition of an open Islam. This seems to be most pertinent to promote an international society that shares values to avert an inflaming of the intercivilizational value-based conflict which is *not* a 'clash'. This would be a true Islamic revivalism. Do not be mistaken: militant Islamism is not an Islamic revival, but rather an invention of tradition that distorts Islam. There is a need to repeat the insight that there is no clash, but rather a conflict that can be resolved in a discursive dialogue, if this were designed as a means for conflict resolution. The hypothesis of this book to be tested in this chapter is that there are value-conflicts. These are placed in the context of a simultaneity of structural globalization and cultural fragmentation. The reality of this simultaneity is a major concern in the study of the intercivilizational conflict and the place of global intercultural communication in this setup. Reality is no construction!

No doubt, there are cultural particularisms that confront one another on a global level. This is an area of global communication and therefore the major theme of the present chapter. The common sense understanding of globalization that believes this process leads, in a global village, to peace is challenged. This wishful thinking is contrasted today by a reality of tensions, conflicts and wars of narratives. These are shaped, of course not caused, by religion and ethnicity. This reality belies the belief in a cultural standardization (e.g. McCulture[5]) expected to result as a major feature of globalization.

There exists a world time. However, the assumption of a 'world culture' is belied by all realities. The late Oxford scholar Hedley Bull enlightens about the fact that 'The shrinking of the world . . . has brought societies to a degree of mutual awareness and interaction that they never had before', but this globalization, he adds, 'does not in itself create a unity of outlook and has not in fact done' with the result that 'humanity is becoming simultaneously more unified and more fragmented'.[6] Based on this valuable insight one may recognize the effects of globalization and at the same time acknowledge an existing cultural fragmentation. In fact, the real structural globalization fails to contribute to a unifying cultural standardization of the world because cultural diversity maintains the pressure to conformity. The inference is that processes of globalization of structures do not match with processes of universalization of values (e.g. the culture of democracy) that are suited to be universal.

In short, the so-called 'global village' is nothing other than a mere intellectual construction. The fact is that this assumed 'village' is an imagination that does not reflect the reality of diversity. The present chapter aims in its inquiry to achieve two tasks to enlighten about the subject-matter.

First, the chapter provides an analysis of the existing cultural fragmentation that not only accompanies – as a preexisting set up – the processes of structural globalization, but also generates intensified side effects that lead to conflict.

In a second step I inquire into the cultural tensions that emanate from the disparity between individual cultures and an overall globalization.[7] On these grounds it is asked whether it is possible to establish a real discursive global communication between cultures in view of the outlined constraints.

The major question is: how could one mitigate the tensions and contribute to mending the fences? The potential for bridging between different local cultures, as well as between the rival cross-cultural civilizations under which these cultures assemble, depends on a successful intercultural discursive communication. Is this feasible?

Throughout the chapter, as well as in the entire book, the focus is on Islam and the West as civilizations with universal claims; both are linked to one another in a situation of tension from which an intercivilizational value conflict emerges.[8] Without falling into the trap of any centrism, both civilizations are placed at the centre of world politics. This can be explained with a simple reference to the fact that both civilizations are the only ones that claim universal validity for their own values. It follows that both are competing with one another.

Do not be mistaken and do not confuse: the reasoning on global communication that is supposed to bring peoples closer to one another in a process of bridging deals with values not with communication technologies. The latter provide instruments or means for communication, but are not in themselves the substance of a discourse. Put differently: the use of contemporary global communication technologies generates divisive, assertive and defensive cultural identity politics.[9] A technology does not unite nor does it generate mutual recognition and respect. Today, the pattern of self-assertive, defensive culture dominates global communication that assumes the shape of an exchange.[10] In this context, the awareness of the cultural other happens in the negative sense of creating fault-lines, not the respect and recognition needed. The binary of 'we' versus 'them' (e.g. the perception of Islam under siege) prevails.

The prevalence of instrumental technologies affects two channels for communication. One of them is virtual, that is the Internet and the exposure to global media, while the other is physical as it happens through encounters and interactions related to travelling across the borders of cultures. The first channel is facilitated through modern communication technologies while the latter is as old as civilizations are.[11] Today, both channels have become a major avenue for the unfolding of patterns of identity politics not always favourable to the needed intercivilizational bridging. An acknowledging of the cultural other as an equal partner is often rather questioned than accepted. Today, travelling has become a part of the trend towards global migration.[12] The related interaction among cultures that occurs in most big cities in the world is a conflict-ridden pattern. This conflict is illustrated by the fact that the incoming communities of immigrants are rather characterized by segregation (e.g. ghetto-Islam in Europe) than by integration into polity and society. The newcomers live outside the polity and civil society. They create ethnic communities of their own as happens in the process of an ethnicization of Islam in Europe that results in a gated diaspora.[13]

For presenting a strong example of the lack of a common discourse of reason-based thinking (rationality), needed to supplement intercultural communication, I cite the invective of an 'epistemological imperialism' put forward by a British Muslim academic, Ziauddin Sardar, to characterize Cartesianism.[14] This British Muslim academic with a migratory background seems to speak with authority for diaspora Muslims living in Europe because his views are popular. The implications are horrible, because cultural entrenchments are the result. Any mediation between diversity and universality runs counter to this kind of identity politics, because the latter is exclusive. The rampant globalization does not contribute to sharing a common thinking (e.g. the rational discourse of modernity), but instead it furthers divisive identity politics. The outcome is the stated cultural fragmentation. The rejection of Cartesian rationalism as an epistemological imperialism is a case in point.

To be sure, no substantive communication can grow with the mere assistance of the instruments that facilitate an interaction. There is a need for shared values for bridging to be based on a consensus that is not yet in place. What happens under these conditions? Is it realistic to envision global communication as means of conflict resolution? For answering these questions one needs to engage in an effort to identify the pending issues in order to also determine what we are precisely talking about. The pivotal issue is the place of cultural values and discourse in global communication and the central question pertains to cultural diversity of people in their interaction with one another. How do they define the self and also perceive the other? To test the hypothesis of the bridging function of global communication one has to juxtapose the model to the reality of tensions and conflict. Therein lies the puzzle that one is challenged to make sense of.

The overall context of the issue is determined on the one hand by the locality of cultures and on the other by the global framework of a structural set up in which these cultures are unwillingly embedded. This is a puzzle and it points out the most intriguing aspect in the present world time. In the past years I have developed the notion of a globalized world characterized by a simultaneity of globalizing structures and fragmenting cultural particularisms. This insight is paired with an effort to conceptualize the outlined reality. Phrased differently: it is a hallmark of the present world that it is shaped by the simultaneity of globalization and fragmentation in a pendulum between culture and politics. Contemporary Islamic civilization enjoys an unquestioned centrality – this reference is not related to profiling – to the extent that the present inquiry is best exemplified on this case. Therefore, the accusations of 'orientalism' and Islam-bashing made by some – because of this focus – are baseless. A Muslim need not be an apologetic and he or she can engage in a critical venture without ceasing to be a Muslim. In the past Muslim rationalists demonstrated that this is possible and the present analysis emulates this classical heritage of Islam.

The underlying issues of the simultaneity of globalization and fragmentation

In a global setup, communication between local cultures and their civilizations takes place under economic and political constraints. There is a reality of a world time based on the global age of the twenty-first century that undermines all cultural particularisms. These are challenged, but they consistently resist the pressure of unifying structures on a global scale. Against all odds, those culturally different people who are involved in this process are reluctant to share cultural commonalities. In international relations the late Oxford scholar Hedley Bull elaborated these different notions: he states on the one hand a value-based international society that unites and on the other speaks of an international system limited to interaction.[15] For sure, culture and religion divide, and hence the resulting fragmentation. Religio-cultural divides are expressed in identity politics of 'we' vs 'them'. In the civilization of Islam the perception of Islam under siege prevails also among Muslims who are not Islamists. In this perception the processes of globalization are viewed as a threat. Thus, there is no accepted cultural standardization. Could global communication help overcome – or at least mitigate – the intensifying divisive awareness of the self and of the other? I would never doubt that cultural diversity is a blessing, but nevertheless I relate this favourable assessment to the requirement of bridging. If this fails, then diversity generates tensions and even contributes to a binary.

Therefore, cultural diversity has to be dissociated from cultural relativism. The perceptual imagery of the self contrasted with an imagery of the cultural other exacerbates existing problems and contributes to digging trenches. This happens for instance in the imaginary confrontation of what is called *gharb* ('West') confronted with *dar al-Islam* ('the abode of Islam'). The growing networks of interaction on global grounds do not promote bridging through cross-cultural, i.e. shared values. The peoples of different cultures can be enriched, but also be separated by their cultural diversity. I positively acknowledge this diversity but limit it, however, for instance by placing democracy above cultural difference.[16]

Values are, as all other social components, subject to change. Cultures are always in flux. Of course, cultural change takes place in an interplay with social change, and both processes are embedded in politics in an overall context. There is, however, no mechanical or reductionist link between the changing segments of society. The argument for cultural change acknowledges that cultural values are neither to be essentialized – the one extreme – nor to be automatically viewed as a reflection of social conditions – the other extreme. Cultural values do not mechanically accommodate to the patterns of social change. Islam is the best case in point for this reality. The religious doctrines of Islam claim immutability and are thus an expression of essentialism. Therefore, the effect of structural globalization does not automatically generate parallel cultural change. In Middle East scholarship the unexamined view prevails that this Islamic essentialism is simply a prejudice. Add to this the fact that the tensions between the local and the global affect the development and even hobble the cultural accommodation. In my research in a variety of places in Islamic civilization I encountered this outcome. Under such adversarial global conditions one may ask whether civilizational bridging can be accomplished through global communication. Could the discourse of cultural modernity be shared as a means for global communication as proposed in this chapter?

There is an assumption that people of different civilizations could engage in the course of global communication in a kind of cross-cultural dialogue to reach consensus over core values based on a universal morality. The assumption implies the thinking that if this consensus, being a prerequisite, were feasible and to be accepted – despite existing inequalities, the lack of justice and existing power asymmetries – then shared discourse were possible, to make communication based on a mutual understanding possible at all.

The idea of an intercivilizational pluralism acknowledges diversity and is also related to acknowledging the other as equal. Candidly stated this is a problem in Islam and there is no misunderstanding, as some evade the point. If Islam were to become a significant part of an avowedly plural world – instead of being the source of a 'geo-civil war', as it is at present[17] – Muslim people would have to abandon the neo-absolutism of their cultural system that is revived in a political shape by contemporary Islamism and orthodoxy. In a global communication with the cultural other the notion of Islamic supremacism, *siyadat al-Islam*, has to be reconsidered by Muslims and I propose a full-scale abandonment.

Under the prevalence of the rules of political correctness non-Muslims may be denied the liberty to address the issue as candidly as I believe that I can do as a liberal Muslim. I am free of orientalism and Islamophobia and claim the liberty to freely ask uncensored questions. There is a need for an honest intercultural dialogue that acknowledges sources of tensions. In his address to the peoples of Islamic civilization US president Barack Obama took the liberty to list in a spirit of bridging seven 'sources of tensions' in the Islamic–Western relations. Putting the pluralism of cultures and religions on an equal footing is a taboo in the established dialogue. So what is the rationale of this kind of global communication that ignores sources of tensions that develop to a conflict?

What is needed is a dialogue not hampered by the politicization of religious beliefs related to cultural symbols in which tradition is invented. The present state of the art gives rise to the following questions: is the current cross-regional re-politicization of the sacred a positive indication? Is it justified to unfold patterns of an assertive identity being the expression of a revolt against West? Is the target of 'the return of the sacred' only Western hegemony, or is it more, that is, a de-secularization?[18] Is a reversing of the disenchantment of the world the goal? These questions are the drivers of the present inquiry.

The reference to Manuel Castells' term of 'resistance identity' for depicting the response of people 'stigmatized by the logic of domination' is not an indication of any essentialism.[19] At issue is the reference to a pattern of identity politics that is purely and simply an expression of a nostalgic romanticism. This is a kind of regressive and defensive cultural resistance to the ongoing rapid change on a global scale and an indication of a lack of willingness to communicate with the cultural other. Two Muslim scholars speak in this context of nativism and of cultural schizophrenia.[20] This debate gives rise to another question: could people stigmatized by inequality and domination engage in a global communication with those perceived as dominators? In other words, is global communication only possible when injustice and asymmetries generated by globalization are overcome?

There exists a culture of self-victimization that is not only not favourable to a discourse of global communication, but also undermines it. The defensive cultural response of an Islamization is an example of a response to real or perceptual domination which is not helpful. All that such a response accomplishes is just to turn the table round. In contrast, the vision of a democratic peace seems to be more promising in the search for a conflict resolution. The Peace of Westphalia went along with a process of secularization and this should not be reversed. For a discursive global communication there is a need for secular grounds for the interaction. Religion in politics generally establishes divides. Therefore, the religion-ization of politics leads to an intensifying of the conflict, not to its resolution. What is an absolute truth for the one party – as is the case in any religion – is a threat to the other. Therefore, the secularism of the Peace of Westphalia is worth being maintained against the Islamist threat despite all of its acknowledged shortcomings. Peoples of different religions cannot debate their faith, but they can do this with regard to secular values about ways for living together in peace.

Despite its focus on culture, the chapter dissociates all of its arguments from the views of any essentializing culturalism often discarded as orientalism. There is an interplay between cultural values, economic structures and politics. The institutions in society are the bedrock of reciprocal relations between these. Thus, the constraints that underly cultural change are multifaceted; hence this statement implies a dissociation from all kinds of essentialism or reductionism. In view of this interplay culture is upgraded and its development is placed next to the economic in development and also to political variables. I refer to this interplay in the outlined sense – when I speak of 'developing cultures'.[21] This is a rejection of reductionist thinking that places economy at the top of the variables and reduces to it all other variables. It is deplorable that many Western scholars have great difficulties in adequately understanding the hardships growing from cultural tensions. The discrepancies between social and cultural change emanate from an interplay between the underlying constraints. In short, it is professed that in this study of intercivilizational conflict culture is acknowledged. Global communication is given the same significance as pending economic factors.

The problem in the study of global communication and intercivilizational conflict is that the deplored reductionism prevails in the dominant research. This happens to the extent that analysts overlook the politicization of religion and ethnicity, as well as religious or ethno-fundamentalism that results from this. In all religions and ethnicities ethno-fundamentalists have an exclusivist mindset and therefore cannot communicate with the culturally ethnic other due to their exclusivist mindset not due to structural obstacles. It is therefore not helpful to deal with processes of modernization the way Roland Inglehart does.[22] This sociologist unspecifically employs the term of 'postmodernization' with the result that he fails to be specific. In pondering about the substance of the pending issue, one may ask: how could pre-modern, not yet industrialized societies be postmodern and postindustrial? Inglehart believes that processes of change lead straightforward to secularization. This is not happening, so why isn't the reality in line with the model? Today, the issue in point is rather de-secularization. It is a social fact that the present processes of de-secularization are arising from the current modernization crisis, as a crisis of development. This fact is downplayed by Inglehart in his suggesting that we view this issue simply as an 'impression' that the 'mass media tend to convey'. This phrasing not only reflects a very poor conclusion, but also an entirely wrong analysis. De-secularization and the revival of religions in world affairs are cultural phenomena that need to be taken most seriously. They matter in the present context, because they charge global communication and undermine the positive aspects of it outlined earlier.

The overall context of the return of the sacred underlies empirically a global trend toward religious fundamentalism. There is solid research on this subject ignored by Inglehart and many others; he contends that this phenomenon is represented by 'a dwindling segment of the population' and fails to explain why the fundamentalist challenge is most appealing and thus a popular choice.[23] The available data provide evidence for identifying fundamentalism/Islamism as a major stream of opposition. This phenomenon is not only restricted to contemporary Islamic civilization, but can also be observed in the world at large. Therefore, one can speak of a global phenomenon. The problem is that one needs to be inclusive with regard to this opposition, without overlooking the fact that fundamentalists themselves are not discursive; they even cannot talk to one another in their own community. The obstacles in point include therefore religious fundamentalism as an obstacle to a global communication based on shared values and on a rational discourse. Thus, political religion intensifies existing cultural tensions being the source of fragmentation.

The hypothesis of a reciprocal relationship between socio-economic and cultural change is central to this book and it shapes the arguments of an intercivilizational conflict. Those who virtually reduce culture to 'economy' and, most disturbingly, Islamic revival to 'oil-wealth' – as Roland Inglehart does – fall into the trap of the criticized reductionism. Inglehart most mistakenly states: 'Islamic fundamentalism remains an alternative model insofar as oil revenues make it possible to obtain many of the advantages of modernization without industrializing; but we would not expect this model's credibility and mass appeal to outlast oil reserves.'[24]

The present analysis suggests going beyond this kind of simplistic and reductionist thinking and it aims not only to dissociate global communication from the bias named 'oil wealth', but also from the view that a functional communication – regardless of the value system that underlies it – is in itself a bridging 'as communication orders'. The present analysis of global communication does not leave important issues such as cultural values unchecked. The 'impression' by Inglehart that Western media are the sole source of existing images is based on a simplistic view. Also the belief that global communication in world society stands for itself is wrong.[25] In contrast, the distinction between local cultures and regional civilizations is a promising approach.

Those scholars who focus on the impact of petro-dollars or on functional analysis end up in a crude reductionism. To relate modernization to global communication in the twenty-first century cannot be a promising effort at bridging if the acknowledgement of intercivilizational conflict is missing. Scholars like Stetter (see note 25), who suggest going 'beyond civilization' in a de-bordering of the Middle East in order to be able to 'rethink peace and conflict' in the Middle East, end up in failure. They fail to explain anything.

Intercivilizational conflict and global communication

One cannot repeat enough the fact that people are socialized in civilizational value systems that determine their worldview and their behaviour. The related thinking is neither determined by 'oil' nor by system functions, but rather by a discourse based on cultural values. In stating this, I am wary again of essentialism and maintain that the Islamic worldview changes, but this does not happen automatically as a reflection of a change in the social and economic constraints. True, this worldview is based on principles (e.g. immutable divine revelation) in which people believe. Nonetheless the world of Islam and its values are always subject to change and are thus in flux. The 'believers' do not allow this kind of thinking. In their belief these *al-usul* ('essentials') are universal. They refer to the ultimate and immutable divine revelation based on verbal inspiration viewed to be valid for the entire human-kind. Islamic values claim with this legitimation to stand unquestionably above time and space. It is not this author, but orthodox Salafi Muslims and Islamists them-selves who essentialize Islam in this manner. They support this thinking with a reference to the quoted doctrine of *usul* ('essentials') believed to be immutable. If this set up is presented as grounds for the communication of people of Islamic faith among themselves and with the non-Muslim other, then obstacles for global communication arise. One should not evade this observation in the name of political correctness. The statement made refers to an understanding of the 'essentials' of the Islamic doctrine that as a matter of fact compels me to ask: why is it so?

Muslims of today view global communication not the functional way Stephan Stetter does, but rather in this manner: the *umma* ('community') is in Islam the unit for communication; it recognizes neither limitations nor exclusivity. Any person who converts to Islam becomes a member of this *umma*, while Christians and Jews are allowed to live as *dhimmi* ('protected minorities') under Islamic supremacy. The tolerance of Islam is that it admits Christian and Jewish monotheists, but the problem is that it denounces all non-monotheist others as *kafirun* ('unbelievers'). The related cultural tensions are placed in a binary based on the revival of holistic and parochial worldviews (e.g. the splitting of the world in *dar al-Islam* and *dar al-harb*). This revival creates great obstacles for a mutual understanding. The global communi-cation between peoples of different faiths leads to conflict not to a recognition of the cultural other.

Today, the Islamic civilizational model of an *umma*-based community of *dar al-Islam* vs the rest of the world no longer reflects any reality in the contemporary world. It can be safely stated that this model of *umma*-unity never reflected any unity in classical Islamic history, as well. Nonetheless, the scriptural doctrine has never engaged in any revising of this binary worldview.[26] Twisted in this inherited tradition contemporary Islamic worldview continues its own constructed dichotomy. Even though it is not in line with reality, the binary worldview remains dominant. Of course, there have been some adjustments to changed circumstances, in particular to legitimate the adoptions of science and technology. The Islamic *Weltanschauung* represent the cultural commitment of many religio–political groups in this period of re-politicization of Islam. In the ideology of political Islam, the structure of disparity in the existing worldwide North–South gap is referred to in religio–political terms to present the call for the awaited *sahwa Islamiyya*,[27] that is the awakening of Muslims as the 'underdog' of the world order, being dominated by the West, i.e. by Europe and the United States. Global communication promotes this awakening, as it happens among Muslims across continents. It is justified to be critical of Western hegemony as an obstacle to a comprehensive global communication among equals. The problem with political Islam is, however, the mentality of self-ghettoization that cannot be reduced to existing asymmetries. The exposure of the people of Islam to global structures is a reality and self-ethnicization, as a sentiment, is another one. To avoid a severe misunderstanding it has to be noted that Muslims in their history had a rich tradition of cultural borrowing and interaction with non-Muslims. The worldview of Islamic rationalism facilitated this opening in the past. Islamic *fiqh*-orthodoxy in the past, and political Islam at present, have never demonstrated such an open-mindedness.

In the nineteenth century's revivalism Afghani continued to maintain that the primary characteristic of Islam consists of its claim to 'dominance and superiority'.[28] It follows that the leaders of Islamist movements criticize the Western dominance from a civilizational, not from a political viewpoint. In general, they are not committed to any egalitarian and pluralist concept of global communication. Their concern is rather to reverse the current hegemonic power situation in favour of Islam. At issue is not the 'end of history' as Fukuyama once maintained, but rather 'the return of history'. There is a 'hopeless dream'[29] for shifting the centre of power in a process of decentring the West for paving the way for a global dominance of Islam. Islamist internationalism is engaged in this hopeless dream. The Islamists envision an Islamic world order that they still cannot achieve. Instead, they are in a position to generate a world disorder.

The intercivilizational conflict is not constructed, but rather reflects the reality in which Islamists claim a dominance for Islam in a negation of diversity and pluralism (see note 17). From the point of view of bridging, any criticism on Western hegemony is shared. What is rejected is the drive to substitute one hegemonic structure by another one, regardless of whether it is an Islamic one or not. The revival of the collective memories of the classical Islamic conquests of the world in a new perception does not promote global communication. The pursuit of global communication between people of different cultures cannot be accomplished on the grounds of the sacred. For establishing equal grounds secular commonalities are needed to establish a consensus over shared core values.

One of the articulations of the intercivilizational conflict in the contemporary world of Islam is the ideology labelled as *al-hall al-Islami* ('the Islamic solution'). This is the core idea of Islamism that is one variety of the global phenomenon of religious fundamentalism. This ideology is exclusive and therefore viewed as an obstacle to intercultural communication. The acceptance of equality among people of different cultures undergoing processes of modernization is hampered in the crisis of development. In Western civilization, specifically in its heartland Europe, the industrial revolution took place within a cultural and structural context in which modern science and technology have determined a radical change in the worldview of the European people. The mastery over nature, which is no longer explained in religious terms, is one of the essential features of the industrial societies. Hence, rationalization is a process addressed by Max Weber as 'the disenchantment of the world' (*Entzauberung der welt*). This thinking is challenged today by Islamism being a powerful expression of the return of the sacred.[30]

The pervasive rationalization of all spheres of society has been facilitated by a shift in the European worldview from a medieval to a modern, rational and secular one. This secularization analysed by Franz Borkenau had great effects on the modern Western worldview.[31] In contrast, the Islamic *Weltanschauung* continue to be defined in pre-industrial, religious and theocentric (*tawhid-*) terms. This feature both of Islamic and other non-Western civilizations affects the intercultural communication and other interactions that take place in our globalized world. Is the interfaith dialogue, as a kind of communication, an exit strategy? Is it a substitute to secular–rational global communication? The dialogue-activity launched by Saudi Arabia, first in Madrid, then under the umbrella of the UN, was a mere ceremonial event management. This is in fact a non-starter because that event lacked all of the features of a real, open-minded, free dialogue. In contrast, the project *Encountering the Stranger* that was pursued as a trialogue at the US Holocaust Memorial Museum in Washington DC in 2007, was a promising effort.[32]

For understanding the value-based intercivilizational conflict one is reminded of the different but interrelated notions of the international system (based on interaction) and international society (based on shared values). The lack of shared values is a major source of a cultural fragmentation that undermines the trans-formation of the international system into an international society. The present global system embraces segmentary structures and cultures of various levels of development and, of course, it brings people of different norms, values and worldviews to interact with one another more closely. This interaction is not a communication in itself. In view of the existing cultural fragmentation an intercultural communication could only take place on equal footing between peoples of radically divergent values and worldviews who agree to acknowledge the cultural other and to share without ambiguity one understanding of peace. These peoples are forced into one structure. There is an inequality between the centre cultures that are technological–scientific and the periphery non-industrial cultures that lack these means of power. Despite this acknowledgement, I refuse to reduce the emergence of Islamism, which is a variety of religious fundamentalism, to this context of inequality. Therefore, the assessment of Islamism as a liberation theology is utterly wrong. Islamist ideology undermines a cross-cultural communication in the pursuit of peace.

The source of the distinction between 'international system' and 'international society' is the work of the late Oxford scholar Hedley Bull. The contemporary international system is based on the 'Westphalian synthesis'. It is 'a system composed of states that are sovereign'. Due to the 'interaction between them sufficient . . . we may speak of their forming a system'.[33] In contrast to this system, a society of states is more than an interaction. An international society would only exist 'when a group of states, conscious of certain common interests and common values form a society in the sense that they conceive themselves to be bound by a common set of rules in their relations with one another'.[34]

In a later publication focused on the non-Western revolt against the West, Bull distinguishes between the earlier just anti-hegemonial decolonization and the contemporary revolt against the West as a revolt against European values. 'The struggle of non-Western peoples to throw off the intellectual or cultural ascendancy of the Western world as to assert their own identity' is not only 'against Western dominance', it is also 'a revolt against Western values as such'.[35]

Already in Chapter 1 it was made clear that this understanding of value-based intercivilizational conflict determines the conceptual framework of the present book. Hereby it is professed that all value-conflicts are underlain by structural and normative constraints. In this understanding the contemporary 'Revolt against the West' relates to value-conflicts and it religionizes these to the extent that they occur in the shape of a re-politicization of the sacred. That process takes place today in Muslim societies and brings them into conflict not only with modernization in a drive towards a de-secularization, but also hampers discursive global communication. To be sure, contemporary de-secularization does even more: it also becomes an obstacle to interfaith dialogue. Functionally and technically, the global system promotes communication, but a mutual intercultural understanding is something else. In a predicament with cultural modernity Muslims of today are not only under-achievers in scientific knowledge, but also in knowledge needed for an intercultural communication. The result is an intensification of conflict.[36]

The global set up and the new players: the civilizations

To place the conflict in the context of secularization and de-secularization is to challenge the traditional wisdoms in the study of international conflicts. The challenge is also represented by a new approach that admits the study of civilizations into international studies.[37] To be sure, culture, as a domain of anthropology is not to be confused with civilization. In my work I distinguish between local cultures and cross-cultural civilizations. The latter assemble on the grounds of shared values and worldviews. In this process local cultures relate to one another. Development and communication need to be discussed within this framework. The intermingling of religious culture and of secular politics charges global communication. The integration of the study of culture and intercivilizational conflict into international studies has to be connected with global communication as a means for peacefully negotiating conflicts. Therefore, the terms negotiation and communication are related to one another in a process of intercultural bridging.

Next to the methodological needs one is also challenged to overcome Eurocentric bias in the Western hemisphere, where development is conceived as a transfer of the model of European social systems to the non-Western world. However, the attitude of a particular ethno-cultural authenticity that emerges among non-Westerners in response to Eurocentric bias is questionable as well. The illusion of a restoration of the pre-colonial past involves a romanticizing of development. The communication between those affected by Eurocentric bias and others dominated by the perception or an imagery that prevails in anti-Western ideologies of *tiers-mondisme* (Third World-ism) is not promising at all. Eurocentrism and *tiers-mondisme* opposed to one another are obstacles in the way of establishing the rational knowledge required for global communication. One example of this is the mindset of orientalism responded to by a reversal of the prejudice, i.e. by an 'orientalism in reverse'.[38] The reference to cultural constraints of underdevelopment in the world of Islam and elsewhere is not an expression of orientalism in development studies. Those who dismiss cultural analysis either in favour of the flourishing discipline of political economy or functional analysis engage in a counter-productive activity. They overlook the fact that culture matters and close the door in their prevailing misconceptions to a proper understanding of the intercivilizational conflict. The reference to this conflict is based on hard facts and is no construction. Neither are the terms 'pre-modern' and 'pre-industrial' constructed. Their use is free from the implications of evolutionist and 'culturalist' bias. The suspicion of an evolutionist determination of the concept of modernity ought to be defused. Industrialization and rationalization are related to historical choices and they are not determined in an evolutionary unilinear development. Global communication can be affected by tensions that arise from this set up. For instance, Islamic–Western tensions that arise from value-conflicts hobble efforts at mutual understanding. The related civilizations need bridging, neither a denial of their existence nor a rhetoric of 'clash'.

There are also misconceptions that concern the focus on the socio-cultural dimension of underdevelopment which lead to charging the shift to culture with culturalism, a term often used as synonymous with essentialism. The related suspicion implies that the cultural analysis overlooks the structural constraints that – in contrast – political economy could unravel. I do not replace the monocausality of economism by the one of culturalism. This one-dimensional cultural analysis is dismissed as a mere 'culturalist' approach. The argument is that any attempt to interpret reality needs to be multidimensional and able to cover all aspects in society. An interdisciplinary approach facilitates a dealing with economics and politics interconnected with culture and social structures. Given the focus of the present chapter on global communication, the structure of underdevelopment is seen to have political, socio-cultural and economic dimensions. These are not to be reduced to one another.

The focus on culture is chosen, because the needed discourse of communication in the service of bridging is a cultural one. However, the cultural analysis is not pursued in its own terms and there is no culturalism. Instead, the analysis is integrated into a more general framework. The focus on culture is not charged by explaining everything through the reference to culture. In short, culture is only one level of the analysis. Cultural analysis is an effort to bring this domain back, however, in a new design, into international studies and the study of global communication. In other words: despite the narrowing of the scope of my analysis to focus on cultural issues, I continue to keep the overall context of global communication in mind. Therefore, I view the European expansion as a global conquest of the world for restructuring it into an entity dominated by the European centre. This is the structural context of globalization.[39] Eurocentrism is a combination of an imagery and of the realities of a domination.[40] Earlier, and still today, this Eurocentrism has been dismissed in the romanticizing Third World-ist responses to it. Global communication requires an open-mindedness among the involved parties and an unbiased acknowledging of the other. This is the true meaning of cultural pluralism that is supposed to be much more than a simple acknowledgement of cultural diversity. It adds to this acknowledgement a consent over core values and it refrains from a discourse of self-victimization as a response to the developmental disparities.

The present analysis acknowledges the place of civilizations in world politics and relates civilizational tensions to different worldviews. These value-conflicts are embedded in structural realities, but are not a reflection of them. This fact displays the increasing significance of culture and civilizations for global communication. The reader is reminded that cultures and civilizations are not the same. Cultures are local, civilizations are cross-cultural. I repeat the major premise of this chapter: if people of different cultures in a situation where there is need for a common discourse, engage in sharing the universal discourse of cultural modernity, not only the culture of blame and accusation would subside, but also identity politics – a source of conflict – would become superfluous.

Global communication among civilizations as a dialogue

In this chapter, global communication is seen as dialogue between the civilizations. This venture is, however, not often honest. For instance, it has become a lucrative business of event management. Therefore, conflictual issues and the potential for their resolution go out of the window. For the understanding of civilizations the theory developed by Norbert Elias in his work *The Civilizing Process* (see note 37) is highly pertinent. Also Ibn Khaldun's *ilm al-umran* ('science of civilizations') continues to matter and should not be forgotten.[41] When it comes to the European conquests of the world one can see that these were based on a highly developed civilization in a process of European expansion that affected other civilizations tremendously. The phenomenon was addressed as the 'civilizing process' identified in European history by Norbert Elias. It spilled over and created global standards, but tensions as well. This European expansion that started in the sixteenth century was preceded by processes of Islamic expansion between the seventh and the seventeenth centuries.[42] Today communication is related to civilizational standards that can be shared, in contrast to those of expansion to be dismissed.

With respect and admiration I refer to Norbert Elias without being silent about his ignorance about another model of civilization not well conceived of in the West. The universalism of Islamic civilization legitimated the related *futuhat* ('expansion'), once bound to a vision of Islamizing the world. The Islamic expansion mentioned above was a successful pattern, but it failed to achieve its goal on a global scale, i.e. the global Islamization, as did the expansion of Europe in its venture of Westernization. Why? Elias is in a position to provide us with an explanation: in its endeavour to establish its own 'civilizing process', Europe achieved this:

> What lends the civilizing process in the West its special and unique character is the fact that here the division of functions has attained a level, the monopolies of force and taxation a solidity, and interdependence and competition an extent, both in terms of physical space and of numbers of people involved, unequalled in world history.[43]

The spill-over effects of the European 'civilizing process' have taken place in the context of the European colonial expansion. It is argued that Europe not only 'exported' a structure to the rest of the world, but much more. The pattern of socio-economic complexity and competition has been associated with cultural components. In the view of Elias this process was 'the last wave of the continuing civilizing movement that we are able to observe',[44] and he adds: '[T]he contrasts in conduct . . . are reduced with the spread of civilization; the varieties of nuances of civilized conduct are increased.'[45] With a reference to this globalization of the civilizing process I discuss differing variants of cultural patterns to establish the distinction between globalization and universalization that is missing in the literature.[46] Globalization relates to structures, while values spread via universalization. This is not the same. A communication between people of different cultures is affected by both processes. To be sure, the reference to Norbert Elias for pointing out the universalizing and globalizing effects of the European expansion in a civilizing process is also accompanied with the critique that there is not one single civilization, but rather multiple civilizations. The mindset of one civilization could be good or bad. Those who identify 'civilization' with the West are charged with Eurocentric bias,[47] others who use civilization to denote one humanity that respects one standard of ethics have good will. This is a naïve thinking.[48] There exist many civilizations different from one another in all aspects.[49] The fact that cultures and civilizations interact and communicate with one another in globalized structures does not undo the existing diversity and the related contrasts that end up in cultural fragmentation. The conflict between industrial and non-industrial societies has a cultural dimension. It is wrong to address it in terms of a 'clash of civilizations'. This is a rhetoric not an analysis. To be wary of the related flaws is not to overlook the pending intercivilizational conflicts.

The place of identity politics as a civilizational self-assertion in global communication: sources of fragmentation

The mapping of the world into one international system through globalization creates a system, but not a world society. This argument by Hedley Bull adopted earlier – acknowledging that all parts of the world are linked to one another – is a process that originated in Europe, but this globalization does not utter the heterogenity of civilizations characterized by diversity. Global communication compels peoples of different civilizations to mutual awareness, but this is not yet an acknowledgement of the cultural other. The cultural self-assertion in a 'revolt against the West' is best exemplified in the case of contemporary political Islam. This ideology emerges from a re-politicization of religion in Islamic civilization that characterizes the contemporary return of the sacred in a political shape.

It is wrong to ignore the cultural symbols employed in pursuit of political ends and just focus on what is viewed as the 'political'. The revolt in point is not only a mere upheaval against Western dominance, as it is also enhanced to become a dismissal of European values and a challenge to their claim to universality, to be replaced by another, Islamic one. The related identity politics is reflected in an articulation of a civilizational awareness of the self directed against the cultural other in a binary worldview of 'we' versus 'them'.

When it comes to identity politics, globalization and the use of modern means of communication contribute to upholding an imagined Islamic *umma* rebelling against the West. Thus, globalization promotes identity politics not a standardization to one 'world society' as Stephan Stetter (see note 25) contends. This view is also supported by Paul Lubeck as he observes, 'ironically globalization . . . increased communication . . . for the . . . Muslim communities of the global umma'.[50] The belonging to this *umma*-community in an assertive articulation of a civilizational awareness of the self is an identity politics that reflects a cultural fragmentation. These are articulations of once challenged peoples who in their responses advance the self to challengers.

The present pondering by a scholar who migrated from West Asia (the term the Middle East – east of Europe – expresses Eurocentric geography) to Europe is directed by a sceptical attitude vis-à-vis proclamations of *tiers-mondisme* in all of the variations involved. Of course, I continue to admire Frantz Fanon's critique and share the way he despises the ideology of négritude as a response to European racism. I view this identity-politics as anti-racist racism. Fanon dismissed the glorification of 'blackness' as a response to the dehumanization of Africans as 'negro'. Fanon argued that the response of négritude remains entangled in racist logic, or better 'unlogic'. This colonial issue continues to be topical and it matters to contemporary postcolonial identity politics entangled in a defensive culture that it does the same as the claim to a négritude did earlier. Today one is inclined to compare the defensive cultural function of négritude with that of Islamism to place both in one Western tradition of *tiers-mondisme*. There is also Western orientalism that turns the tables in an orientalism in reverse, resembling the response of négritude to European racism. This kind of identity politics is praised as an articulation of a postcolonial 'liberation' and refers to Islamic values in an invention of tradition.

In contemporary identity politics religion assumes a central place. The meaning of religion in processes of global communication remains, however, without any convincing explanation. The unaccomplished task remains. One has to investigate the politicization of Islam in the process of cultural and social change without reducing its system of meaning to social realities. There is an interrelation between the cultural system and the particular societal structure. The critique of ideology pursued in the context of cultural analysis needs to be placed in a careful scrutiny able to disclose identity politics in contemporary global communication as a source of cultural fragmentation.

A proposition: cultural modernity to be a shared discourse for global communication

What is cultural modernity?[51] In the context of cultural and social 'change' not only social structures, but also belief systems are supposed to change. Why does the notion of cultural identity matter to Islam and why the talk about change? In any religion this raises the suspicion of an involvement in heresy. If 'belief' were immutable based on a *wahi* ('verbal inspiration'), then there would be no space for change. In fact, change is problematic for every religion, not only for Islam. Underlying this attitude is the idea that religion – being the incorporation of the absolute – should not be subjected to change because the result would be in itself a heresy. In going beyond this scriptural understanding one sees religion is embedded into social reality. All societies are subject to social change. And how about cultural change? Religion is a cultural system embedded in social realities. But religious symbols expose meaning and are not simply reflections of these realities. These symbols are fixed in the scriptures of the particular religion. Therefore, it is as wrong to see in religion merely an ideological form of articulation of reality, as it is wrong to look at religion as untouched by change in social reality.

Operating on the assumption that these premises are right, I see a role for religion in the process of socio-cultural change that takes place in a context of global modernization, but I propose to separate religion from politics and to reduce secularity to this function. The argument for a secular global communication is based on the understanding of secularization as a process that is a byproduct of cultural modernity. I believe that secularization facilitates communication with the religious other of other cultures. Earlier, Westernized intellectual elites of non-Western civilizations were particularly affected by the acculturative contact. Despite all discontent arising out of the existing social tensions, these elites shared values in communication channels and means. In contrast, the contemporary counter-elites tend to de-Westernize their views and to ideologize religion by resorting to it as the imputed 'moral order'; they believe that this order had existed prior to this situation of Westernization in a colonial context and is now to be restored in a pattern of identity politics aimed at exclusionary authenticity. There are enlightened Muslim scholars who characterize these protest movements in non-Western civilizations in Western social–scientific terms as nativist or as imbued with 'cultural schizophrenia' (see note 20). The concern is the quest for objective knowledge that underpins intercultural communication. This runs counter to an agenda of an 'Islamization of knowledge',[52] as well as to the indiscriminate functional understanding of global communication that omits culture and overlooks the fact that the interaction between people of different cultures is based on different value systems. They turn a blind eye to this reality. The grounds for global communication have to be both secular and intercultural; no religion can be shared by all humanity, not even Islam that presents itself as the sole religion for all humans. Do not be mistaken, to establish secular grounds for a dialogue is not to dismiss Islam. Nonetheless, the missionary claim of *da'wa*, i.e. Islamic proselytization, is not to be confused with dialogue over sharing values.

There is another misconception to be cleared up. The preference for a secular discourse based in cultural modernity is not a support for outdated modernization theories. In his comparative social historical studies, Reinhard Bendix has overcome and gone beyond the old, almost scholasticized debate on the dichotomy of traditionality and modernity to impressively demonstrate that the concept of 'modernization' is vague, but still a useful one. This usefulness is retained only if one manages to know how to avoid 'confusion between scientific constructions and actual development'.[53] On these grounds the insight is established

> that modernization does not necessarily lead to modernity. Moreover the modernization process itself is neither uniform nor universal, for the economic and political breakthrough made at the end of the eighteenth century in England and France has put every other country in the world in a situation of relative backwardness.[54]

The overall context of contemporary value-conflicts is the introduction of cultural modernity. This issue cannot be understood in evolutionist terms nor, of course, in ways of reducing cultural, social or economic change to one another. The transition in point is not a repetition of the process that has already taken place in Europe. It is true, the distortive rapid social change in non-Western societies, as exemplified in Muslim societies, was triggered by European expansion and the Western mapping of the world. But the solution to the problems cannot be a ghettoization. Again, one is asked not to confuse reality with scholarly constructs (e.g. dependency theory) manufactured at the desks of the academe. For dealing with processes of rapid social change taking place in Muslim societies since their mapping into the global system, one needs proper knowledge about the political and cultural conflicts created by that change in these societies. As Bendix tells us, each of these is faced with

> the problem of fusing its historically handed-down structure and typical
> tensions . . . with the effects of ideas and techniques coming from outside
> . . .. Each one must bring the gravitational pull of the developed societies
> into harmony with the values contained in its own traditions.[55]

Bendix made this statement in a paper presented at an international sociological
congress back in 1966. At that time, it was still believed that evolutionary
modernization consists of the wholesale adoption of basically Western structures.
The collapse of the Iranian modernization experiment under the Shah and also the
failure of other experiments have contributed to questioning the approach of
Westernization.[56] There is a need for learning new perspectives to grasp the failure.
It is, however, very flawed to go into the other extreme of postmodernism. This
is exactly what happened in Western scholarship. This postmodernism is a cultural
relativism, but fails in its approval of Islamism to grasp that the latter is both: a
neo-absolutism and an anti-enlightenment.

In the recent past of Western scholarship there has been a move from the bias
of evolutionist modernization theory to that of cultural-relativist postmodernism.
In this process one flawed concept has been replaced by another equally flawed. As
earlier evolutionists believed that change leads to modernity, globalists believe that
the effects of globalization are irresistible and shall result in a kind of standardization
emanating from global structures that lead to a 'world society'. This wisdom is
challenged in this chapter by presenting the fact of a cultural fragmentation
simultaneous to the other fact of a structural globalization. If this is not well
understood, then one is left to the belief in an over-whelming 'world society', thus
ignoring the distinction that Hedley Bull taught us about the cultural fragmentation that emerges from two dimensions of globalization: the overall international
system (interaction) and the restricted international society (shared values).

The universal knowledge implied in Max Weber's notion of *Entzauberung der
welt*, understood as secularization, compels us to ask: is this process possible in
Islam? There is no escape from this perennial question! Among the attempted
escapes are the references to authenticity and particularism of Islam. In terms
of facts, Islamic civilization is torn in the twenty-first century between secularization and de-secularization. This chapter argues that this competition matters to
the needs of global communication. The introduction of secularism and modernity
to the world of Islam took place in a historical process of the dissolution of Islamic
order and forceful mapping of Islamic civilization into a world order of nation-
states created by Europe. This is a historical context different from the one of
Weberian rationalization of culture and politics that happened in Europe. In the
classical heritage of Islam there existed a synthesis with rationalism established by
Islamic medieval philosophers who combined Islam with the Hellenism of Aristotle
and Plato. This Hellenized Islam promoted an Islamic rationalism as a promising,
but not lasting, tradition in Islamic history.[57] This reference runs counter to
overstretching the notion of Islamic peculiarities. In the past, Muslim rational
philosophers set an example for intercultural communication and for rationalization

in the context of cultural borrowing. In contrast, Muslim *ulema* scribes have always been reluctant to admit the notion of change into Islamic doctrine. In modern times Muslims were and continue to be challenged to deal with changed conditions. Their adherence to a cultural system that is viewed as unchangeable is challenged as well. To be sure, the Qur'an includes this wisdom 'Allah does not change people unless they change themselves'. And the Prophet recommends, 'to seek for knowledge even in China', so why not also in the West? Why not borrowing from cultural modernity as did Muslims earlier from Hellenism?

The present study has been at pains to communicate the idea that in inter-cultural global interaction people not only deal with one another, but hereby may also learn and change. People of different civilizations have in each case their own cultural system that underpins one's cultural beliefs and the related worldview. What happens when rapid change takes place in society? Would the respective cultural system promote or hinder changes and learning from the other in a process of global communication? There is a predicament and it cannot be solved functionally. On the one hand reality is in flux, but on the other religion claims to be immutable! This predicament gives rise to the question: how do Muslims perceive this predicament and how do they accommodate social change culturally? The predicament is also one with cultural modernity.

The reasoning over these issues is often not welcomed and therefore there is a need to ask in free speech about the linkage between secularization, modernity and industrialization. For the plea of embracing modernity I have been accused of 'self-orientalization'. Most of these US scholars who make this accusation are not only outsiders to Islamic civilization, they also fail to see the overall context of modernization and secularization. They do not distinguish between secularism, being an ideology (e.g. Kemalism), and secularization, being a social process; they also do not understand the tensions that arise from different value systems. In the past Westernized secular elites were not successful, because they ideologically espoused secularism with no parallel efforts at secularization in society. These needed, but still missing, efforts not only pertain to structural, but also to cultural secularization.

Conclusions

Global interaction takes place today under conditions of a return of religion to the public square. The implications are a politicization of religion and a de-secularization of society and polity combined with an agenda for a remaking of the world. This process undermines a global communication based on shared core values; no religion can be shared on global grounds. Today the problem is that the earlier accepted 'secularization', regarded as a universal phenomenon, is now under fire. This premise of cultural modernity is challenged by what is wrongly named Islamic revival, which is in fact an invention of tradition. Cultural fragmentation receives a boost in this process. One may criticize the misfortunes of secular modernity, but the outcome needs not to be a denial of the existence of what is being criticized. To point out the limitations of modernity is not to abandon secularity in favour of a post-secular society. Do not be mistaken: the deliberations have nothing to do with the phased-out dichotomy of modernity versus tradition. The issue is of much greater complexity. In an earlier book, *The Crisis of Modern Islam* (1988), I interpreted secularization as a by-product of a process of functional differentiation of society affecting the religious system. Two decades later, in my *Islam's Predicament with Cultural Modernity* (2009), I continued to argue that religion is a part-system within a given society as a whole, but add in the light of new research for separating religion from politics. Fruitful dialogue and good communication can only be pursued successfully on the grounds of pluralism. Students of religion are aware of the fact that all religions, in particular the monotheist among them, claim the absolute.

To place the analysis that has been undertaken in the present chapter in context it is imperative to further differentiate the concept employed by making these two points:

− First, there is a correspondence between the sacred and the political in political Islam. The need for de-sacralizing politics in an effort at rationalization is not a functional problem. The intensifying cultural fragmentation stresses the importance of values and cultural analysis.
− Second, one needs to address the potential of an Islamic accommodation of technological–scientific accomplishments in a way that goes beyond the tensions attributed to modernity vs tradition. An adopting of items of modernity, i.e. instruments decoupled from their underlying values and the overall context results in an illusion of semi-modernity.[58] In the course of unfolding Islam's predicament with cultural modernity the notion 'Islamic particularism' religionized the issue and this distracts from all ethical and cultural implications embedded in a process of de-sacralization understood in the Weberian sense. The result is a cultural fragmentation that inevitably leads to conflict articulated in a regionalized politics.

From a point of view of cultural pluralism it is asked whether a global communication could contribute to alleviating this conflict potential? To pin these hopes higher it is asked, how can Muslims embrace secularization and pluralism to contribute to a better shape for their relations to others? This matters not only to the West, but also to Asia and Africa, where non-Muslims are affected by cultural fragmentation and the recognition of pluralism is urgently needed.[59]

In the present chapter I had to argue against many other approaches and set straight what communication means and what it could accomplish. This chapter, as the entire present book, conceptualizes the world of Islam as a distinct civilization based on a shared value system and worldview.[60] The reference to Islamic civilization happens consistently in light with the insight concerning diversity within Islam, as there exists no Islamic monolith. Therefore I have coined the formula that Islamic civilization is simultaneously characterized by unity and diversity. To avoid essentialization I add to this insight the other emphasis on change.[61] Another emphasis, the embedment of culture in an interplay between economy, society and politics (see note 21) illustrates that I do not fall into the trap of culturalism. In this sense communication is placed in the outlined broad setup.

In the main, the present analysis takes pains to overcome two extremes: at first an orientalism that explains Islamic civilization – and its core: the Middle East – merely by cultural essentialized notions. There is not only the other extreme of an orientalism in reverse, but also of scholars who abandon cultural undercurrents and even the notion of civilization, removing them altogether from the analysis. In a recent study globalization is not only reduced to a rampant 'worldwide interconnectedness', but also – by and large – limited to the systemic function of 'connective communication' in which 'chains of interconnected communication' are supposed to grow.[62] This view abolishes all cultural distinctions of Islamic civilization and of its core in 'conceptualizing the Middle East as a placeless spatial attractor which is constituted on the basis of (political) communications . . . on worldwide scale'.[63] This thinking that suggests to go 'beyond Orientalization and civilization' in order to argue that 'communication generates all social orders, actors and social processes'[64] is worse than any orientalism could ever be. I refer to this study just to maintain that communication is not merely a function in a system. Communication is also a substance in that it takes place on the grounds of cultural values and worldviews that may not be compatible with one another, thus it disconnects and does not connect. These values are incommensurable and this is a challenge not a fault-line. Communication could help connect, if a consensus over core values and a shared discourse is within reach. This is the task of bridging. Otherwise, communication fragments and results in tensions and a war of ideas. The outcome would be an intercivilizational value conflict in place.[65]

One example of tensions that arise in contemporary global communication is the Islamist's drive towards de-secularization and the rejection of cultural modernity. Moreover: Islamists view secularization as a result of a 'Jewish conspiracy'.[66] The Islamists' awareness of secularization is overly ideological and reflects cultural fragmentation; no 'global interconnectedness' whatsoever.

The critique of religion-based cultural fragmentation is in no way an argument against religious culture per se, it is rather a plea for a de-sacralization of politics in Islamic civilization to facilitate a kind of communication that really connects and helps bridging.

As is the case in any political religion, political Islamism is a variety of exactly this kind of politicized religion not favourable to global communication in a secular context of pluralism that acknowledges the religious–cultural other. In contrast, a kind of religious ethics that accepts the religious diversity of humanity is more positive about global communication that can be pursued in interfaith dialogue.

In short, global communication is not a function of a system but rather a dialogue that requires de-sacralizing politics. It is based on secular values with a disenchantment of the world for resolving conflicts. Religion should be preserved as an ethical answer to the questions of human existence. Diversity should be honoured in any intercultural communication. A thriving of a culture of positive diversity presupposes the acceptance of the political culture of pluralism. In Salafist unreformed Islam there is a missing commitment to civilizational pluralism and this disturbs the pursuit of a global–democratic peace. To come to terms with this impasse an absolving of internal social tasks by Muslims themselves is needed to facilitate a cultural accommodation of the change. This is required for decoupling religion, as a belief and a cultural system, from politics in a process of cultural change and religious reform in Islam. In its oscillation between culture and politics contemporary Islam needs a cutting edge of secularity combined with an authentic legitimation for an acceptance of democracy and the values of civil society. This is a challenge to Islamic civilization in the new millennium in its predicament with cultural modernity and it affects Muslims in their communication with the non-Muslim other. The challenge also illustrates the perils of the dichotomy of structural globalization and the kind of cultural self-assertion that leads to cultural fragmentation.

Next to the dismissal of reductionism one has to dissociate the intercivilizational conflict that emanates from the simultaneity of globalization, and cultural fragmentation from the rhetoric of *Clash of Civilizations*.[67] The required peace strategy for the new millennium needs to avoid this flawed thinking. Precisely, one should not trade the rhetoric of 'clash' with the rhetoric of 'convergence' between civilizations.[68] There is also the nonsense that maintains a Christian–Islamic civilization and worse: to abandon the notion of civilizations altogether.[69]

For a bridging between civilizations in the present conflict-ridden interaction a positive pattern of global communication could help to ensure peaceful resolution of conflicts. However, global communication in itself does not bridge. On the contrary, it could be a source of cultural fragmentation, tensions and conflict if a cross-cultural morality is not in place.

Intercultural fertilization is the foremost bridge between the civilizations. Therefore, one needs to establish a cross-cultural morality in order to facilitate shared cross-cultural discourse. This does not grow functionally from a global communication, but has to be promoted in a politics of an honest and issue oriented intercultural dialogue. The target is a consensus over core values to be shared whole-heartedly. Again: all communications are based on values and if this insight were to be left out of the analysis then no contribution to bridging could ever be promising. The Hellenization of Islam in medieval times is a precedent for emulation.[70]

3

THE NEW INTERCIVILIZATIONAL COLD WAR OF IDEAS AND ALTERNATIVES TO IT

The core feature of the intercivilizational conflict of our world time assumes the shape of a *harb al-afkar* ('war of ideas'). The conflict emerges from values–related tensions independently from Islamism. However, Islamists articulate the tensions in a defensive cultural manner in a perception of Islam being under siege.[1] The overall context are the conditions of post-bipolarity in a new Cold War between the 'sacred' and the secular. The rivalry in point is one between politicized religious and secular value systems. To be sure, religionized politics[2] that today affects the international environment of post-bipolarity is not about the basic human right of freedom of faith. In a cultural–religious rivalry that transforms worldview – and values-related tensions into a political conflict an intercivilizational conflict unfolds.[3] This emerging conflict revolves around the order of the world and the values that are expected to undergird it, and it is not about spiritual values of faith. Therefore, I hasten to add that religion and religious culture are not by themselves a source of conflict; they are not addressed here in terms of faith, cult and cultural system, but rather in their function as tools in an ideology of religionized politics. It follows that the conflict is not between religions, but inherently between concepts of world order, and it is about an envisioned remaking of the world.

Religion in its capacity as a faith and as a cultural system deserves to be respected. Religious practice in this meaning is also honoured as a part of human rights being entitlements in the context of acknowledging diversity. In contrast, politicized religion is a body to be named 'political religion'. Islamism is a case in point that generates an intercivilizational conflict. In our case, the conflict is not between Islam, Christianity and the West, but rather between Islamism, secular modernity and its open society, as well as the 'synthesis' of the Westphalian system, on which the present world order rests. However, Islamists cloud in an invention of an Islamophobia these issues to blur the debate in a war of ideas to defame their critics as 'enemies of Islam'. To be sure, a progressive Islam is better as a negotiating partner because it accepts participation in the pursuit of a democratic peace and allows bridging between the civilizations. This chapter argues for bridging as an effort at a peaceful conflict resolution. This book promotes a revival of the tradition of Islamic rationalist humanism to create a potential for a 'peace' of ideas viewed as the alternative to the new Cold War of ideas. In contrast, a propaganda war is waged by Islamism, which is a political Islam.[4] A consensus over the values of cultural modernity would help avert what some name 'a clash of civilizations'.

In short, the war of ideas in point revolves around values and, thus, is an expression of a value conflict. Of course, Christian, Western-secular and Islamic values are not the same, and they can be in conflict with one another. Such a conflict does not, however, relate to the religions of Islam and Christianity themselves, but rather to the incorporation of these world religions in a process of politicization of faith to a political religion. The conflict relates also to what is viewed as religious set in tension with what is secular. In this kind of religion-based politics contentious issues are articulated in religious terms and politics becomes religionized. The term 'religionized politics' coined in my work refers to a combination of a constructed religion and real politics. It is deluded to belittle the significance of a constructed and politicized religion embedded in world politics when some believe this issue is limited to an instrumental use of religion. The truth is that Islamists, as an example, do not refer to Islam as a pretext that camouflages otherwise secular concerns. It is not only wrong to engage in such an assumption, but this thinking is also misleading. The activists of 'political religion' believe themselves to act as 'true believers' in a war of ideas and perceive themselves to be the 'defenders of God'.[5] The most prominent case in the contemporary global war of ideas is Islamism. For sure, the term 'war of ideas'[6] that has been used after 9/11 is in its origin not a Western coinage; it existed for long in the Islamist writings as *harb al-afkar*, thus it predates 9/11.

Introduction

This chapter resumes the debate on the contemporary intercivilizational conflict discussed in Chapter 1 and elaborated upon in the context of globalization and communication in Chapter 2. This happens throughout in a spirit of bridging. The major assumption is that the conflict in point is between secularism and political religion. This is the substance of the war of ideas in a quest for a remaking of world order. This is, therefore, not an intellectual debate. The war of ideas indicates a 'return of the sacred' in a political–conflictual context. The related subject matters become religionized and this leads to a conflict. Despite prevailing misconceptions no religious renaissance whatsoever is in place. Instead, at issue is rather a rise of political religions and the conflicts they generate in the context of post-bipolarity. To be sure, the main concern of the war of ideas is not democracy vs jihadism, as has been often argued after 9/11. The conflict entails much more than a 'missionary crusade for democracy' as the one waged by the former

US president, G.W. Bush. The fact is that the war of ideas is embedded in a bid for a remaking of the order of the world.

The contentious issue of democratization in a war of ideas is not merely a Western 9/11-based concern since the institutional direction of political Islam pretends to be a pro-democracy direction. It is, however, a fact that the thinking of the godfather of Islamism, Sayyid Qutb, and – in his footsteps – his contemporary followers embodied in the Islamist movement are the source of the inter-civilizational conflict between the West and the world of Islam. In their view, the conflict is neither in its nature social–economic, nor political, but rather a battle fought 'between the ideas of believers and those of the infidels' (Qutb). Put in his own phrasing, the issue revolves around an uncompromising fight addressed in this phrasing:

> It is a battle between believers and their foes. It is in substance about a dogma/idea (*aqidah*) and it is absolutely about nothing else . . . (In other words) the battle is neither about politics nor about economic interests . . . if it were so, a conflict resolution would be feasible. Since it is in substance a war of religion-related ideas (*ma'rakat aqidah*) at issue is belief/*Iman* against *kufr* (infidelity/unbelief). The options are therefore: either Islam prevails, or a setback into *jahiliyya* (pre-Islamic ignorance/unbelief) takes place . . . The enemies of believers have tried to deceive in presenting the battle/war (*ma'rakah*) as a polit-ical, economic or racial one. It is not. Believers should dismiss this deception . . . done by world crusaderism (*Salibiyya alamiyya*) . . . [7]

Qutb's quote reflects a textbook-like definition of religionized politics that occurs in a return of the sacred. This happens under circumstances of this war of ideas in which jihad is fought in the new interpretation provided by Qutb. The terms used unveil clearly Marxist–Leninist origins, in particular when Qutb speaks of a 'world revolution'[8] and replaces the proletariat with an imagined *umma*. Qutb makes clear that Islamic claims are not negotiable and thus leaves no space for dialogue or debate. His standing precludes appeasement and determines the conflictual matter in terms of war. Therefore, Islamism is to be excluded from the agenda of bridging. To be sure, the comparison of Islamism with Marxism–Leninism should not distract from the fact that religionized politics is not secular; it is a political religion. If this point is not well understood then the war of ideas between the secular and the sacred in an intercivilizational conflict would not be understood either; it would remain beyond comprehension.

Islamism and the West: why is this war not a controversy?

The Islamist war of ideas includes an effort to shape the relations between Islam and the West in an intercivilizational conflict.[9] Islamism contests the existing secular order of the world. From this point of view the following four issue areas are pivotal.

First is the legitimation of the use of the notion of war to identify the competition between secular and religionized concepts of world order. Islamists themselves use the notion of war in a different meaning from the one established in the study of international relations. In this context Islamism reinvents Islam by adding to it a concept of world order to allow political Islam to fight an ideological war on its own terms often viewed as jihad. Islamism translates traditional Islamic universalism into an activism of a new political internationalism. Why is this competition between ideas/concepts viewed in terms of a war and not simply seen as a debate or even a hot controversy between rival parties that adhere to different views competing with one another? The answer is that Islamists fight against the Westphalian world order in a belief that they wage a war against *kufr* ('unbelief') and therefore they have no inclination to engage in 'a debate', nor in a competition. As the Qutb quoted statement clearly reveals, Islamists act as 'true believers' fighting war guided by I-win-you-lose thinking: either Islam, or *kufr* and nothing in between. In this way of thinking Islamists claim 'to fight', not to debate, or to compete. Qutb says the 'West' is finished and it is now the time for Islam to take over, period. No debate. Qutb's prose reveals this mindset expressed in its absolutism:

> Today, humanity stands at the brink . . . bankruptcy . . . is the most obvious feature of the West . . . democracy is finished along this bankruptcy . . . The leadership of the West is about vanishing . . . It is Islam – and nothing next to it – that possesses the necessary values (to save humanity) . . . It is now the time for Islam to take over in this time of crisis and turmoil . . . There is a need for the restoration of the supremacy of the umma to make Islam resume its expected leadership of humanity . . . This is the meaning of Islamic revival/ba'th Islami.[10]

Qutb's thinking with regard to what is named Islamic revival reflects a claim of a 'return of history', understood as a return to *siyadat al-Islam* ('Islamic supremacy'). This drive to turn back the clock seems obviously not to be a sign for the victory of Western values, as Fukuyma once argued.[11] The drive is the hallmark of a powerful transnational movement. After the breakdown of communism there was no 'end of history', but rather a rise of Islamism which claims to do exactly the opposite: return of history. Again, Islamism is a powerful transnational movement, and not as some pundits ignorantly state, just '*takfiri*-jihadi pockets', that is, insignificant extremist subgroups supposed to be acting at the fringe. Some believe they can be chased and brought to court. This is a self-delusion and a consequential one when it comes to security.[12]

In their war of ideas Islamists concede that the West once launched a *Ghazu al-fikri* ('invasion of ideas') in a war against Islam to be countered today. In their imagery they fight a war against the crusaders (*salibiyyun*) who act as 'proxies of world Jewry'.[13] As envisioned by Qutb, it is now the turn of Islam to reverse the existing balance of power. Muslims are called upon to combat 'Western value systems' through de-Westernization. On these grounds Islamism envisions restoring the supremacy of Islam. In an inflammatory combination of anti-Americanism and antisemitism a sentiment of a war declaration is reflected;[14] this is not the spirit of conciliatory dialogue, nor of a debate aimed to deal with tensions in a spirit of bridging. Therefore the term 'war of ideas' is justified and authentic by Islamist standards.

Next to the justification of the notion of a war of ideas the second issue pertains to the conflict over the order of the state followed by a conflict over the shape of the international system itself. The war of ideas is a part of the war in which an intercivilizational conflict is carried out over a remaking of the world. In this regard John Kelsay rightly asks the pertinent questions:

> In the encounters between the West and Islam, the struggle is over who will provide the primary definition to world order. Will it be the West . . . or will it be Islam? . . . The very question suggests a competition between cultural traditions with distinctive notions of peace, order and justice . . . [15]

In a book by Kelsay published two decades later he points at the revival of Islamic shari'a reasoning to address this option of a remaking the world through jihad.[16] Unlike Kelsay, who views the issues as they are in reality, there is a mushrooming literature on Islamic divine law by a community of self-pronounced 'Islam-pundits' who lack this well-informed standard of scholarly knowledge. They write about the revival of shari'a, without knowing shari'atized Islam is based on an Islamist invention of its tradition. This is what the issue is all about. Classical shari'a and the reasoning based on it deals with right conduct and at times is about just war, but traditional shari'a is never about the world order. The Islamist venture opposes the values of cultural modernity in a war of ideas waged in an aggressive tone that reveals a very uncompromising spirit poised for remaking world order. Though the war of ideas is against outsiders, it unveils a predicament within Islam which revolves around its relation to modernity.[17] Thus, in the Islamist war of ideas the issue is not only about a civilizational binary worldview that divides humanity into 'them' and 'us'. Entrenchments are also created within Islam itself in an inner civilizational crisis.

Third, in a debate, even in a furious controversy, and also in any competition, as tough as it might be, one can think of a dialogue. Its goal could be bridging to reach at least a truce, if not an accord that facilitates an enduring system of living together in peace. An assumption of this kind presupposes, however, the acceptance of the civic culture of pluralism. The Islamists are self-righteous and put their views forward in the spirit of an uncompromising jihad against those viewed as enemies of Islam. Therefore it seems to be that no accord between Islamist jihadism and the Kantian concept of democratic world peace is possible. Honest Islamists who do not play games in doublespeak preclude dialogue. The Islamists Sharif and Zaibaq are honest and they write for instance:

> The idea that establishing an approximation among religions based on reason is supposed to generate a truce between Muslims, Christians and Jews is an

idea that emanates from Orientalism. Such a dialogue can only take place at the expense of Islam, because Islam is the only true religion . . . To abandon this claim as a requirement for the dialogue is to do a great damage to Islam.[18]

There is another more prominent Islamist, Anwar al-Jundi, who also argues in this direction and even warns of the 'trap of dialogue' installed by 'world Jewry'[19] to weaken Islam. In awareness of these binary sentiments this chapter proposes an exit strategy to avoid polarization in an effort at bridging. I recommend at first an engagement in a distinction between Islam and Islamism.[20] Second, is a plea to revive the heritage of humanist Islam for establishing common grounds. This concern is the subject matter of Chapter 4 in the present book.

The fourth issue is the Islamist perception of the war on terror. This perception is fuelled by the ill-designed policies of ex-president, George W. Bush as a war on Islam that has led to a sweeping anti-Americanism. The new US president, Barack Obama has done his best to rectify the damage. He acknowledged the Islamist jihadist threat, did not confuse it with Islam, though he continued to speak of Islam in general with no further specifications. Unlike some pundits, such as John Esposito, Obama did not confine himself to cordiality, but also listed in his historical speech in Cairo on 4 June 2009 seven 'sources of tension' between Islam and the West.[21] The averted assaults of al-Qaeda to blow up a US plane short of landing in Detroit in December 2009 seem to have derailed Obama's fine approach.

Unlike Bush, Obama does not supply Islamists with ammunition for their war of ideas, but rather disarms them. An established Arab newspaper, *Al-Hayat*, qualified Obama, with no irony, a 'caliph of Muslims', because he aptly and appropriately quoted form the Qur'an in Cairo. What can the West learn from the blunders of the Bush-administration? And how could Obama avoid the trap of going into the Bush-avenue? In the following six deliberations, I provide grounds for proper answers to these questions.

1   Among the most consequential flaws of the Bush administration was its failure to distinguish in the war of ideas between Islam and Islamism, on the one hand, and between jihad and jihadism, on the other. In the Western–Islamic dialogue envisioned by Obama one has to acknowledge basic distinctions. Back in 2002 in Jakarta I defended the US in siding with the attending US ambassador against the defamation voiced there, that the 'war on terror is a war against Islam'.[22] This accusation was made in Jakarta not only by furious Islamists, but also by incensed ordinary Muslim participants. I am sad to state that it did not take me long to realize that I was wrong. Under the Bush administration I was consistently reminded of a racialization of Muslims every time I entered the US when I had to go through a humiliating second inspection. The simple reason is that I am a Muslim born in Damascus, as indicated in my German passport. My ethnic German blond wife received a better treatment in that she was relieved from this ordeal. The European citizenship that I share with her did not protect me from being profiled as one of the people from 'countries of concern'. This profiling made clear to me that the

Bush administration did not care about loss of friends and allies among Muslims. As a liberal Muslim I admire American democracy, but saw it damaged through the way Muslims were treated in the 'war on terror'. I am aware of the fact that this racialization of Muslims is not the primary cause of anti-Americanism, but the related facts have been used by Islamists to inflame an already existing anti-Americanism in their war of ideas.

2   The Obama administration is challenged to learn soon that the best way to fight jihadist terrorism is to dissociate these jihadists from ordinary Muslims for winning the hearts and souls of those Muslims, who are not Islamists. This task can only be accomplished if one distinguishes between Islam and Islamism. I have misgivings that the new administration may go into the other extreme namely in an illusionary appeasement of Islamism, again making the same mistake, but in reverse, while overlooking the distinction between Islam and Islamism. I missed this distinction in the otherwise superb and outstanding speeches delivered by Obama in Ankara and Cairo as an effort at bridging to Islamic civilization by the West.

3   The blind 'crusade for democratization' the Bush administration pursued lost its vision and acted with no compass. In this way it − directly or indirectly − helped Islamists to come to power in the name of democracy.[23] This happened through the ballot box. Islamists were able to come to power in Iraq, Gaza and also in Turkey. Of course, policy makers are challenged, not only to distinguish between Islam and Islamism, but also to make distinctions within Islamism itself. There are jihadist Islamists committed to jihad, understood in the mind of S. Qutb as 'Islamic world revolution'. One cannot talk to these Islamist terrorists (e.g. Taliban). There are, however, those institutional Islamists who agree to participate in the game of democracy and who go to the ballot box, but their claim to be moderate cannot be taken at face value as some misguided US pundits do.[24] To play games in doublespeak is not a sign of moderation.

One should keep in mind this fact: the so-called 'moderate Islamists' share with jihadists the refusal of the values of cultural modernity, above all those of political pluralism, religious freedom, secularity and power-sharing. With some restrictions and for convenience one may do business with them, but one has consistently to be wary of the delusion that they are allies. They are not. The AKP of Turkey is not as it presents, itself a conservative−Islamic party; this is a delusion. The AKP is clearly an Islamist party. Therefore, the Islamist rule in Turkey[25] cannot serve as the model for the world of Islam, above all not for Egypt where the Islamist Muslim Brothers are waiting to take over after the fall of Mubarak hoping for a US blessing. In the war of ideas the AKP fights on the anti-Western front and also supports Hamas. President Obama needs advisors who do not conceal this from him, as was the case with Bush who was ignorant about the issue. The US president has to be protected from the consequential naïveté that for instance the Muslim Brothers represent an 'Islam without Fear' compatible with democratic solutions.[26] This is not consonant with facts on the ground. No doubt, in a democracy one needs to engage with Islamist movements, but an engagement is not to be confused with empowerment.

4   In their war of ideas Islamists also employ the instrument of *iham*, meaning wilful deception. This new Sunni-Muslim term was coined along the Shi'i one of *taqiyya* ('dissimulation'). Among the ways of *iham* is the doublespeak. In Europe, Tariq Ramadan is accused by Caroline Fourest of this double-speak, but he had succeeded, though, to become a member of the task force summoned by Tony Blair when he was then Prime Minister.[27] Ramadan consulted Blair in his dealing with Islam. In my view, doublespeak conceals the intercivilizational conflict.

5   The conflicts in Palestine, Kashmir, Chechnya etc. are not a cause for Islamism, however, their rekindling gives a boost to the thriving of Islamist movements. In the war of ideas these conflicts are abused to promote the perception of an Islam under siege (see note 1). In substance, the Bush administration did nothing that contributed to a conflict resolution in this field to de-escalate the war of ideas. The new president as well as his successors could do better, if he disarms Islamists in their war of ideas in demonstrating a US approach for bridging, as he did in Ankara and Cairo. Cooperation and conflict resolution should replace the earlier politics of confrontation that did great harm to US relations with the rest of the world. It also nourished an anti-Americanism that shall continue to thrive for some time to come.

6   The final concern to be considered is that the war of ideas is not restricted to Islamism fighting the West. The Hindu ethno-fundamentalists also act as challengers – even worriers – as Islamists do. Not only to preempt an impending discard, but also for analytical reasons one cannot repeat enough that the intercivilizational conflict is a reality: it is neither a constructed 'clash' nor an inflamed polarization. A clash can be averted; it is avoidable. Conflict can be solved.[28] In a double-strategy one can combine dialogue with a security approach.

Islamism is the value system for a remaking of the world

Unlike Islam which is a faith established in spiritual belief, Islamism is a religionized political ideology. It can be traced back to 1928 when the *al-Islam al-siyasi/* ('political Islam') was established along with the Muslim Brotherhood.[29] Islamism is a twentieth century contemporary phenomenon continued in the twenty-first century and heralds the return of Islam to world politics in a new shape.[30] The assumed depoliticization in the aftermath of the abolition of the caliphate is challenged by political Islam. The re-politicization of religion is related to a historical background embedded in the context of local, regional and international developments. It was veiled by bipolarity and is now unveiled in post-bipolarity.

Ever since the abolition of the Islamic order of the Caliphate back in 1924 and the ensuing disintegration and fall of the last Islamic empire[31] the world of Islam has been reshaped and subdivided into secular nation states to be integrated on these grounds into the Westphalian international system. Given these facts and in view of the secular Kemalist revolution in Turkey it was believed that Islam has been restricted to a spiritual faith, thus has ceased to matter to world affairs. Underlying this belief was the reality that the former provinces of the Ottoman Empire, as well as other parts of the territoriality identified as *dar al-Islam* ('abode of Islam') were mapped as 'new states' into the international system. The former Ottoman provinces went through a transitory period of colonial rule and then emerged formally in terms of international law as nation states based on popular sovereignty, i.e. on secular foundations. In the twenty-first century this is changing. In the world of Islam the secular nation state is undergoing a double-crisis. One is a legitimacy crisis while the other is a crisis of development. Islamism emerges from this context of the crisis of the secular nation state and it fights a war of ideas against this order in favour of establishing the Islamist shari'a state. This targeting of the secular nation state happens in the context of the return of Islam in a political guise. The secular nation state is accused of being a failed state. The alternative presented to it is the Islamic shari'a state. The order envisioned is totalitarianism. Therefore it is a misconception to present Islamism as 'Islam without Fear'. To be sure, Islamism is not only against Western hegemony, but also 'against Western values as such'.[32] In Bull's view, this contestation is best 'exemplified in Islamic fundamentalism'. This makes 'clear that in matters of value the distance between (Islam) and Western societies is greater than in years of national liberation or decolonization' (ibid.). This is a major dimension in the ongoing war of ideas. The issue is complicated by the fact that Islamism is not a passing phenomenon. Those pundits who claim to see a 'fin de l'Islamisme' ('end of Islamism') are fully misled.[33]

The re-politicization of Islam matters to world politics and it breeds life into the war of ideas. In the aftermath of the 1967 war a crisis of the nation state emerged and it gave a great boost to political Islam. Islamism predates this development in that the Movement of the Muslim Brotherhood was founded in 1928 in Cairo.[34] However, the height of the process of politicization of Islam was the post-1967 crisis-ridden situation. The result is a movement based on transnational religion combined with the claim to de-secularization which is the Islamist response to it. In the Arab part of the Middle East the secular nation state slipped into a crisis related to the de-legitimation of pan-Arabism after the crushing defeat in the Six-Day-War of 1967 and its severe repercussions.[35] Political Islam thrives in the context of the de-legitimation of the nation state in a severe crisis of Arab politics.[36]

The earlier foundation of the Movement of the Muslim Brotherhood in Cairo heralded a new political stream. That was by then unfolding, but yet still on the fringe. The 1967 war was a watershed moment for Islamism that was upgraded to a mobilizatory ideology that called for *al-hall al-Islami* ('the Islamic solution').[37] This is what 'Islamist politics' is all about. This solution preaches a political theology of *din-wa-dawla* ('unity of religion and state'). Within this context, Islam is interpreted by Islamism as *nizam* ('system or order') which governs all aspects of life with no separation between what is public and what is private. This is a true totalitarianism. Uppermost we face the claim: it is only Islam that determines how the state is to be shaped. The new call has been framed as a political Islam that challenges the secular nation state in presenting an alternative to it, namely the *nizam Islami* ('Islamic order'), based on *Hakimiyyat Allah* ('Allah's rule'). This is the opposite option to popular sovereignty and it contradicts the civic culture of pluralism and its provision to power sharing. All this happens in the new drive toward de-secularization. It is argued that only Allah is the true sovereign and thus it was concluded that the Western concept of popular sovereignty on which the nation state rests is an import from the West decried as *kufr* ('heresy') leading away from true Islam. This is not only the core issue in the development of political Islam; it is also the core issue in the war of ideas as a new Cold War between the legitimacy of the existing nation states in the world of Islam, and is constructed as an 'Islamic state' based on shari'a.

The source of the idea of *Hakimiyyat Allah* ('Allah's rule') is the work of the rector spiritus of political Islam, namely Sayyid Qutb, who reinterpreted jihad in the new meaning of an 'Islamic world revolution'.[38] This global jihad is to be waged not only as a new irregular war fought by non-state actors, but is also *harb al-afkar* ('war of ideas'). Therefore it is utterly wrong to view these Islamists who forgo violence as a means in their political action as moderate since Islamism is not about violence, but rather about remaking world order. In a nutshell, the agenda of the present Islamist movements based on a transnational religion in a new variety of internationalism is to establish a new order for the world in which the Islamic claim of *siyadat al-Islam* ('Islamic dominance') materialized in a return of history.

Islamism combines the idea of *Hakimiyyat Allah* with the one of global jihad as a framework for achieving the envisioned order. This happens in a war and it is not an intellectual debate in an academic set up. Qutb borrows Marxist–Leninist vocabulary and speaks in the context of the cited 'Islamic world revolution' of an awakening of the *umma* that replaces the proletariat. The impact of the ideas of Qutb on contemporary political Islam and Hasan al-Banna's jihadism continue to prevail. One may also add to this list the name of the Pakistani Abu al-Ala al-Mawdudi. Unlike classical Islamic jihad both scripturally and historically the new pattern of jihadism is rather based on a new interpretation of this Islamic doctrine to legitimate in view of Islamic weakness the new kind of irregular war against the militarily superior West. Only in this understanding, jihadism is a modern variety of terrorism, fought also in a war of ideas.

In concluding this section it can be safely stated that jihadist Islamism in world politics is a new totalitarianism. Hannah's understanding of totalitarianism both in the meaning of a movement and as a rule has been applied to Islamism.[39] European fascism and Stalinist communism were the earlier patterns of totalitarian rule in the twentieth century. Jihadist Islamism is at present a movement, not yet a rule, but it can be viewed as the new totalitarianism of the twenty-first century. The Islamists, both the institutionally active ones and the jihadists create a challenge to Muslims themselves. The contemporary predicament of Islam with modernity is a feature of the current Islamic civilization in its positioning at a crossroad, torn between the appeal of the mobilizatory ideology of jihadist Islamism and the need to join the world community on the path of democratic peace.

In going beyond the problems of Islamic civilization in order to look at the competing concepts for a new world order one comes across three issues in world politics. First, the increasing significance of non-state actors in international politics; second the cultural turn that gives transnational religion and its political culture a significant role in world affairs; and third the ascendance of irregular war, both by arms and propaganda. In this overall context political–religious ideas could have – as value systems – trickle-down effects to become as a mobilizatory ideology a powerful factor in the conflict over a remaking of the world.

The place of the war of ideas in the twenty-first-century's post-bipolar politics

The major difference between bipolarity and post-bipolarity is also one between the old and the new Cold War. These differences matter to the understanding of the war of ideas in point. The bipolar age was determined by the existence of two quasi-rival empires, the United States and the Soviet Union. Both powers were embedded in the pre-existing global structure of the international system of states that was not of their own making. In earlier pre-modern times, there also existed real empires, but at those times no global structures were in place. The pre-modern world was characterized by a diversity of competing civilizational empires, structurally not greatly linked to one another. In contrast, the modern system maps the entire globe.

Despite the lack of a global standard in pre-modern times there existed earlier a global history of civilizational empires. In the time span between the seventh and the seventeenth centuries several Islamic empires succeeded one another and all fought successful jihad wars to dominate major parts of the world.[40] It is a fact that in this time span of ten centuries, three caliphates succeeded through their Islamic conquests to partially globalize the model of the Islamicate beyond *dar al-Islam*. In the light of these historical records one is inclined to argue that the Islamization of the world in that time was a variety of globalization that predates the Western one. Islamic globalization was successful within limits. It was superseded by the European expansion that generated the modern project of globalization, one underpinned by the 'military revolution' that took place in Europe. The rise of the West was based on modern science and technology. The addressed military revolution smoothed the way for the emerging West being the new civilization that not only challenged Islam, but also has been successful in accomplishing what Islam had failed to achieve, namely the mapping of the entire world through one globalization process into one structure. In the course of the past five centuries Western globalization (1500–2000) has dominated the world. To be sure, bipolarity was just a half-century-long interval in world history. Since the Second World War, the ensuing age of bipolarity as well as since the end of it, the core of Western civilization, as perceived by the non-Western others, has been the USA; no longer Western Europe, the birthplace of this civilization. Nevertheless, Western globalization has been truly launched by the European expansion. At present, all aspects of this history are challenged in a war of ideas paired with the claim to turn back the clock in an imagined return of history of Islamic glory. The war of ideas is a war of historical memories.

The European conquests launched processes in the context of which the world of Islam had an encounter with Europe: the exposure to colonial rule. The revivalist al-Afghani called for jihad against the West in that time. That was a defensive cultural anti-colonial jihad aimed at deterring the European expansion.[41] Unlike the earlier expansive and aggressive jihad fought between the seventh and seventeenth centuries, the nineteenth-century anti-colonial jihad was purely defensive. In the twentieth century jihad became jihadism. It is continued in the present century. The new jihad is neither the classical one nor the defensive anti-colonial one. The new jihadism is not only about violence it is also a war of ideas in post-bipolarity. To understand this new pattern named jihadism one should not confuse it with a simple terrorism. To know more about Islamism, its place in a religionized post-bipolar world politics and its global jihad in the age of post-bipolarity, one has to deal with the West and the existing world order. The values against which global jihad directs its war of ideas are values on which Western civilization and the Westphalian world order rest. This is the substance of the intercivilizational conflict. What kind of bridging is needed between the civilizations under these conditions?

Islamism is the Islamic variety of the global phenomenon of religious fundamentalism, it does not bridge, it wages a war by all means including a war of ideas combined with a violent irregular war. Prior to the end of the old Cold War this jihadist war was successful against the Soviet troops; it weakened the Soviet empire to the extent of being the decisive beginning of its fall; by then it also enjoyed the support of the West. Contemporary Islamists believe this decline can also happen to the US empire as a result of the challenge posed by global jihad. This is the future envisioned not only by al-Qaeda, but also by what is named 'moderate Islamism'.

The war of ideas is a war over the future of the world with a cultural dimension not well understood in international relations analysis. In particular the significance of Islam to world politics in the twenty-first century is left to traditional Islamic studies that fail to grasp the meaning of global jihad and have a poor knowledge about it. Islamism transforms jihad into jihadism and bills its Islamist views as democracy.

The questions that relate to knowledge, in particular those about war and peace, and how the non-Islamic humanity could understand how Islamists operate are important; they touch on all the approaches to an Islamization of knowledge.[42] Is there a specifically Islamic knowledge? As much as I contest the call for global jihad, I rebuff the mindset of political Islam as a *Weltanschauung*, which is believed to operate on its own pattern of knowledge of the world in its waging of a war of ideas.

In studying Islamism and Islam I operate with an awareness that there is no overall 'Islam' as a monolith. This is what Islamists pretend. In reality, the world of Islam is sub-divided within itself along (among other things) sectarian lines (Sunna and Shi'a etc.). It is also characterized by a tremendous cultural diversity that I have seen on the ground. These dividing lines also apply to the call to global jihad and to the related war of ideas. However, this diversity corresponds with a unity within Islamic civilization, as well.

In its origin, jihadism is a Sunni-Arab movement, as currently run by non-state actors in the context of transnational religion. The Islamic Revolution in Iran of 1979 presented a new jihadist dimension as a Shi'i internationalism, which is oddly based on a nation state. The Islamic Republic of Iran views itself as the centre of the world,[43] and aims to export its model of an Islamic revolution in pursuit of jihad, but it is still, though, a nation state, and this runs counter to its ideology. Still, the Sunni and the Shi'i Islamisms are different branches of Islamist internationalism. Both wage their own war of ideas, but nonetheless share the challenge to the West and to Western educated secular liberal Islamic elites. The Islamist counter-elites contest cultural modernity as an import from the West that derails Muslims from *sabil Allah* ('the path of God'), but Islamism adopts at the same time the techno–scientific instruments of modernity. This is a worldview of semi-modernism.

In going for an Islamic embracing of cultural modernity and, consequently, of the idea of democratic peace to replace tensions related to the Islamist war of ideas I seek to establish a cultural underpinning for this plea to promote its accept-ance by Muslims. It would be wrong to impose any alien concept on Islamic civilization, because it would then lack legitimacy. This effort only makes sense when one explains – as will be done in the course of this chapter – that the core issue is Islam's predicament with modernity. The tensions between global jihad and democratic peace – as two competing options – are a general concern of international politics. Muslims themselves are also challenged to engage themselves in religious reform and cultural change. In Chapter 4, on Islamic humanism, I shall draw on medieval Muslim rationalists who succeeded in incorporating the legacy of Hellenism into Islamic heritage to better demonstrate traditions in Islam.

To stick to the present it is noted that the Islamist idea of *Hakimiyyat* is among the issues of secularization and de-secularization.[44] To open the door for demo-cratization in Islamic civilization, the education of Muslims in secular democracy is an agenda that runs counter to the present Wahhabi institutions engaged in an education in Salafist Islam.[45] This pattern of education contributes to intensifying the war of ideas that alienates Muslims from the rest of humanity as the non-Muslim 'other'. In the West these issues are not well understood due to the lack of better knowledge. One further needs conceptually oriented case studies of the mechanisms of the Islamization of conflict in a war of ideas in order to understand the religious dimension that closes the door to a peaceful conflict resolution. The politicization of religion becomes an ideology of conflict based on a neo-absolutism.

When conflictual issues are religiously articulated they become non-negotiable, because Islamist neo-absolutists admit only one truth which is theirs. A case in point is the second intifada in Palestine. It articulates the political conflict in a religious language. This 'Islamic politics'[46] in Palestine contributes to the emergence of new conditions under which it becomes difficult to engage in any solution. The first intifada was secular and it was possible to end it with the negotiations with the secular PLO that led to the Oslo Peace. The second intifada is religious–Islamist and Hamas refuses any compromise.[47] When conflict becomes intractable under these conditions of a war of ideas, the disciplines of international relations and conflict studies are challenged to cope with the new reality and to rethink the existing approaches. The prevailing approaches in US Islamic studies do not contribute to a better understanding of the new place of Islam as a transnational religion in the twenty-first-century's international politics, nor do they help understand the ongoing war of ideas. Instead they prefer to continue to be obsessed with orientalism while they in fact are entangled in an orientalism in reverse. In the past I engaged in proposing a new sub-discipline in international relations enriched by cultural studies and sociology of religion. I name this approach 'Islamology' as a social–scientific study of conflict with regard to Islamic realities. In this venture I faced great obstacles and cornering.[48]

In conclusion I state that the under-theorized Islamic studies in the West need to obtain a real international relations perspective and a sociological perspective as well. Throughout my academic career I have been arguing for a study of Islam that goes beyond scriptural orientalism and the narrative of anthropology. Islam is a transnational religion. Today, the political shape of Islamism is a source for contemporary conflicts to be dealt with using the social–scientific tools of Islamology. A proper understanding of the ongoing war of ideas cannot be reached in the way Islam is dealt with by most US anthropologists. Their understanding of 'Islamic politics'[49] is highly wanting and needs major corrections.

A war of ideas for the 'return of the sacred'

The topicality of culture and religion in post-bipolar international relations compels me to reconsider the way Islam is dealt with in US Islamic studies and to recognize the need for admitting social science, in particular the discipline of International Relations and sociology into the study of the 'return of the sacred'. Religious fundamentalists in contemporary Islamic civilization are at work as non-state actors and they act as soldiers of Islamism/political Islam. Today, Islamism is the most significant variety of the global phenomenon of religious fundamentalism.[50]

In fact, 'political Islam' (i.e. Islamist fundamentalism) wages a war of ideas on the secular international system to facilitate the return of the sacred. The present order is legitimized by the principles of the Westphalian peace of 1648. Islamism is a challenge to the authority structure of the present international system. The al-Qaeda attacks are incorporated in this context.

In Islamic civilization the rise of Islamism is related to a global phenomenon of the politicization of religion in a 'return of the sacred' which is not a renaissance of religion. The challenge is directed to the secular worldview underlying the Westphalian foundations of the international system, as underpinned in Western societies by cultural modernity. This challenge is pursued in a war of ideas that further promotes a process of politicization of religion that targets the secular order of the state and of the world. This happens in the context of religious articulation of international conflict (e.g. jihad against the West). This pattern of religious fundamentalism cannot be simply reduced to a variety of fanatism or extremism. At issue is a concept of order based on divine foundations.

It is regrettable that the findings of the *Fundamentalism Project* of the American Academy of Arts and Sciences did not find their way either to established Islamic studies or international studies and their journals. Only a few journals accept submitted articles on political Islam in the context of the post-bipolar crisis of world order in which it is acknowledged that culture matters for the study of the changed environment in a war of ideas that replaces the old Cold War.[51]

The related values matter to international politics. The late Oxford scholar Hedley Bull introduced in this regard the distinction between international system and international society. In Bull's view:

> a *society of states* (or international society) exists when a group of states, conscious of certain common interests and *common values*, form a society . . . bound by a *common set of rules* in their relations with one another . . .
>
> An international society in this sense presupposes an international system, but an international system may exist that is not an international society.[52]

An international 'peace' of ideas seems to be only feasible on the grounds of shared values on which a shared understanding of peace can be based. If not, then the contemporary Islamist global jihad for an Islamic peace – regardless whether pursued by peaceful means, or violent – shall continue and disorder the world. To be sure, democratic world peace is not compatible with the values of war and peace represented by Islamism. At issue are different understandings of these issues that lead to a conflict. It is wrong to address this conflict as a 'clash of civilizations'. The addressed different understanding of war and peace can be found in Sayyid Qutb's book on *World Peace and Islam*. Qutb rephrases the Islamic classical claim to enhance the Islamicate to map the entire globe, but gives this understanding a modern shape in the pursuit of an Islamic world order.

When Qutb acted, the earlier – 1928 – established Movement of the Muslim Brotherhood was still marginal. In the aftermath of the 1967 war a radical change took place in the course of which Islamism has become a 'mobilizatory ideology' that undergirds a 'mobilizing Islam'. The context has been the crisis of the existing secular nation states. This process inflamed the war of ideas. Islamists contend an infection of Islam with a Western virus and envision a de-Westernized world of Islam, hereafter the world at large. Purity and authenticity are basic in this identity politics located in a war of ideas against the West. The traditional Islamic universalism is revived in a crisis-ridden situation, but it is given the shape of a political internationalism that opposes the ideas of an international society based on pluralism and democratic peace.[53] Islamic civilization could embrace a pluralist perspective of civilizations if it overcomes the illusions of Islamism. Muslims are challenged to engage in overcoming Islam's predicament with cultural modernity.[54]

The new war of ideas is taking place under the conditions of the 'return of the sacred'.[55] In the context of post-bipolar world politics there is a war between three competing options: First, Pax Americana based on the US-hegemonic unilateralism that the Bush administration pursued. Second, the vision of a Pax Islamica, which presents the other extreme. It should not be played down as an Islamist rhetoric, or the illusion of a single person (the late bin Laden) and some minor jihadi pockets that adhere to al-Qaeda. This rhetoric is much more; it is a political religion in action. Third, the option of a democratic peace being really pluralist, i.e. neither based on the dominance of the West, nor on an alleged Islamic moral supremacy, but rather on an option of living together with mutual respect and recognition. This goal requires sharing the core values of freedom, democracy and individual human rights with the non-Muslim cultural other. This is a prerequisite for bridging as this book suggests.

In the present war of ideas, postmodernists, who are cultural relativists and who reject the universality of cultural modernity, refuse to side with universal values. Secularity is a societal reality, not a constructed formula. The cultural relativists overlook the fact that in Western societies Christianity underwent a real social process of secularization. In this context, religion ceased to have an immediate impact on politics. In fact, cultural modernity is intrinsically secular and therefore the West and Islamic civilization can share its values. The leading Western philosopher and previously mentioned theorist of cultural modernity, Jürgen Habermas, refers to the sociologist Max Weber to identify modernity with secularization while borrowing the Weberian formula of 'the disenchantment of the world' (*Die entzauberung der welt*).[56] Weber, and in his footsteps Habermas, see in the separation of the worldly from the divine a basic accomplishment of cultural modernity. As Habermas puts it: 'Weber described . . . as rational the process of disenchantment which led in Europe to a disintegration of religious worldviews that issued in a secular culture.'[57] Is this a specifically Western or a universally valid knowledge on which modernity rests? Could this knowledge underpin an option acceptable to non-Westerners? These questions were addressed earlier as they relate to a war of ideas in which Islamists employ the aggressive term of 'epistemological imperialism' for denouncing modern rationality and its knowledge.[58]

Modern rational knowledge has precedents in the heritage of Islamic rationalism and it can serve for a bridging between civilizations to end the war of ideas. In earlier periods of history of intercivilizational relations one can see cultural borrowing and cross-cultural fertilization that happened on the premise of universality. The medieval Hellenization of Islam is referred to as a classical venture to be revived in the context of the contemporary war of ideas. Islamic humanism (see note 73) provides a potential for bridging between the civilizations. Therefore, I not only suggest a revival of this heritage in Chapter 4, but also an emulation as a prospect for avoiding the binary Islam vs the West.

At this juncture the focus continues to be political Islam and its contemporary war of ideas. At first it can be safely stated that the prediction of a 'decline de'Islamisme' by Gilles Kepel (note 33) proved to be a wrong one. In this context, one can rather state that the return of the sacred heralds a challenge. The Islamic variety of it is related to a model for a new international order. This is not a passing phenomenon of daily politics, and it shall continue to be with us as long as its constraints prevail. In addition, there is a war over the universality of values. It is for this reason that I call for a revival of classical Islamic rationalism, which once affirmed universal knowledge. A revival of the political philosophy of al-Farabi could help suggest some foundations in international politics that constitute a 'peace' of ideas, not war of ideas. Only when this happens – along with solved structural problems – then Islamism would decline. It is not in sight that the war of ideas would end any sooner. The fashionable formula of a 'post-secular society' tolerates the return of the sacred in the illusion that it heralds a religious renaissance. This notion dilutes the values of secular modernity.

The reader is reminded of the major idea elaborated upon in Chapter 2. It is about the tensions between the normative claim of universalization and real structural globalization. In that chapter the issue is addressed in terms of a 'simultaneity of cultural fragmentation of norms and values and structural globalization'. The contended simultaneity of globalized structures and the missing cultural underpinning for this globalization – as needed to render them legitimacy – creates the world-historical context of the current crisis of the secular nation state in the non-Western world. The abode of Islam (*dar al-Islam*) is a particular case in point. All states in this part of the world are nation states, however, only by the legal definition of international law, not in reality. The institutions and the values that undergird the nation state are not in place. In this regard, I coined the term 'nominal nation-state' to explain the crisis of the nation state in the world of Islam. In a 'revolt against the West' Islamism not only contests the political hegemony of the West, but also its core values including those of the 'Westphalian synthesis' that underpins the present world order. Underlying this revolt is a legitimacy crisis of the international order reflecting an international system (interaction), but lacking the commonalities needed for establishing an international society (rules, norms and values). This challenge of global jihad is often wrongly reduced to a matter of 'terrorism'. It is much more than that, as it is a politicized return of the sacred that leads to an emerging world disorder.

The Islamist option that is currently wrongly named as an Islamic revival invents as a concept Islamic peace, the order called *Hakimiyyat Allah* ('Allah's rule'). This term was coined by Sayyid Qutb.[59] He rejected the subdivision of the world of Islam into nation states, as well as the secular world order they are embedded into. It is imperative to take a look at these views to understand that the idea of 'World Peace and Islam' formulated by Qutb aimed 'to defeat any power on earth that prevents the mapping of the world under the call to Islam/*Da'wa*', and separates Muslims from others. This is the definition of Islamic proselytization as related to jihad. Therefore, Qutb continues in concluding: 'Islam needs a comprehensive revolution . . . being a *jihad* prescribed on Muslims to lead this revolution to success for establishing the *Hakimiyyat Allah*/rule of God.'[60]

In short, we read him summarizing the argument,

> *jihad* envisages a world revolution/*thawra alamiyya* . . . for the realization of (Islamic) peace . . . for the entire humanity . . . These are the outlines for world peace in Islam . . . This does not mean to avoid war/*qital* at any price . . . Islam is a permanent *jihad* which will not cease until Allah's mission rules the world.[61]

The quotes indicate a declaration of global jihad understood as a war against the present world order. The religious name of it is *da'wa* ('invitation'), verbally pronounced as a message of peace, but it is transmitted clearly in the language of war. This is an Islamist inconsistency. Qutb's ideological 'permanent *jihad*' has been promoted to a dangerous '*global jihad*' practiced by a variety of jihadist movements on top of which we see al-Qaeda. The idea of jihadism becomes the Islamist irregular war of the twenty-first century. This is a correlation between the war of ideas and the jihadist war; both are features of political Islam that indicate a powerful variety of the return of the sacred in a political guise that guides the Islamist agenda of a remaking of the world.

The conclusion is that Islamism continues to be on the rise as the return of the sacred in the world of Islam. At issue is a political religion that aggravates difference and prevents an accommodation of Islamic civilization to the global environment in a globally democratizing world.[62] The competing choices in a war of ideas between jihadism and democratic world peace are related to cultural concepts of the sacred and the secular. This is the reason why I place secular cultural modernity at the hub of my reasoning and introduce it to the study of world politics. If the people of the Islamic civilization were to embrace cultural modernity, abandon global jihad and the shari'atization of politics[63] in a sea change of the mind and the heart, Muslims would put themselves in a position to overcome their predicament and join democratic world peace. This should be the substance of dialogue, to replace any war of ideas between Islam and the West into a 'peace' of ideas under conditions of bridging. The related thinking compels me to spell out the argument of the predicament of Islamic civilization in its exposure to modernity in order to clearly see what obstacles stand in the way.

Islam's predicament with modernity: the issues, options, illusions and obstacles

Often one hears modernity criticized for being European in origin and imposed on others, and then the values of cultural modernity are discarded with arguments grounded in cultural relativism. Is this the reason why the revolt against the West has become a revolt against the values of cultural modernity? When the secular organization of the United Nations was founded, there was no contestation or rejection of Western values on which its charter rests. The authority structure of the peace of Westphalia that underpins the international system was by then accepted. Currently, the return of the sacred in the guise of political religion is changing this consent. Underlying the contemporary rejection of secular modernity on which the present world order rests, is a contestation described with a reference to Bull as 'The revolt against the West'. The opposition to the order of the secular nation state indicates what Mark Juergensmeyer has labelled as 'a new Cold War'. It is a war of ideas between the religious and the secular. World peace, most desirable for the twenty-first century, cannot be attained under the present conditions of the return of the sacred in a political guise. Politicized transnational religions engender regional conflicts that assume a religious shape and become intractable. The drive towards de-secularization is not only based on a worldview, but also on a political agenda that targets the Westphalian foundations of the present world order.

Cultural modernity is a secular project as are the foundations of the present world order. With Bull I argue that the Islamist revolt against the West is a revolt against the values of modernity. It is not only directed against the hegemony of the West, but also articulates a wholesale rejection of secular Western values and the rational worldview on which cultural modernity rests. Islamists not only preach a prescription and bill their views as a strategy for the future of Islamic civilization, but also envision a new order for the world. In a different phrasing, putting the issue in an international relations language: the Islamist revolt against the West is a global jihad against the present world order and the secular authority structure it is based upon. This global jihad is not only the violence of the jihadist irregular war, it is also a war of ideas waged by Islamism most successfully. Even in the West it has become risky to criticize this agenda and remain unscathed.

The reader is reminded of the fact that the Kantian idea of eternal 'democratic peace' (*Ewiger Friede*) emanates from cultural modernity. The vision is secular in that it implies the separation between religion and politics. How could peoples of different religions be in a position to come to terms with one another and live in freedom and peace, if not on a secular basis? The Islamic idea of world peace presupposes a submission of non-Muslims. Today, this is as unacceptable as it was in the past. People need to share a common understanding of peace and order beyond religion. Islamism is not only a variety of the politicization of religion, but also a forceful one that runs counter to this need. It envisions a totalizing shari'a–based Islamic divine order. With a reference to the Islamic universalism Islamists claim universality for the neo-Islamic order. They fight their global jihad for it in the name of freedom of faith. The definitely fundamentalist concept of *Hakimiyyat Allah* ('rule of God'), as developed by Qutb and his supporters is thought for entire humanity. One cannot escape foreseeing that three-thirds of humanity, which does not belong to the Islamic civilization, would not succumb to the call for an 'Islamic world peace' based on a global enhancing of *dar al-Islam* to map the entire humanity on the grounds of the divine law shari'a. This is the Islamist vision that originates in Sayyid Qutb's work. Millions of Islamists act in adherence to an Islamic order and are, thus, in conflict with other millions of Muslims who do not wish to live under a political system of *Hakimiyyat Allah*, as they prefer (on the grounds of the values of cultural modernity) to live under conditions of a secular democratic peace. An incorporating of the world of Islam into the rest of humanity is a liberal–Islamic agenda. Underlying this position is the view that only a cross-cultural morality can be acceptable to the entire humanity. To act in this line one needs a dialogue in which not only global jihad and its neo-absolutism, but also the unilateralism of the West, is to be dismissed.

Stated in a nutshell, the critique of political Islam and its war of ideas is not driven by an a-religious position at all. In contrast, religious ethics are admitted. The commitment to secular modernity expressed here is restricted to decoupling religion from politics. Religion can be related to politics in ethical terms, but it should be dismissed in the meaning of a concept of political divine order. Parallel to the criticism advanced, religion is admitted as a source of ethics for a cultural underpinning of modernity. Earlier, I referred to the precedent for this thinking in the Hellenized tradition of Islamic rationalism. Based on this premiss I argue that religion – as ethics, *not* as a concept of order – could be incorporated into a cross-religious and cross-cultural morality that contributes to bridging between Islam and other religions, as well as cultures. However, this task is not fulfilled by the contemporary resurgence of religions arising in a political shape, for all of these political religions aim at a re-making of the world along their own concept of order. Therefore the politicization of Islam results in the combination of a religio–cultural neo-absolutism with a new political variety of totalitarianism not acceptable to others nor to democrat Muslims. Hence, the war of ideas.

In an analogy to Karl Popper's call to defend the 'open society' against its 'enemies', I argue in the spirit of Islamic enlightenment in favour of an 'open Islam' against global jihad to overcome any civilizational binary.[64] This position is compatible with the tradition of Averroes who put Islam in harmony with the rational worldview of Hellenism. I am at pains to establish an analogy between Hellenism and cultural modernity to provide legitimacy for the spirit of cultural innovation and religious reform. As much as medieval Islamic rationalists[65] were receptive to the Hellenization of Islam, contemporary Muslims could embrace cultural modernity to give its values an Islamic underpinning. Such an effort would end their predicament with cultural modernity in line with reviving the heritage of Islamic rationalism. The issue is not only such an enlightenment, but also the Western hegemony that should be put on the table. The Islamist jihad alienates Muslims from the rest of humanity. With respect to this war of ideas, jihad provides the needed legitimacy. Islamists do not fight against imagined shadows. Western hegemony and the oversized power of the West are realities. One should not be silent about this component. Otherwise the analysis would not be sound. The talk about bridging implies that there is a real structural gap. The value conflict does not emanate from it, but it helps legitimate the revolt against the West.

Islamology as a study of conflict and war of ideas

At this point I come back to my criticism of the traditional Islamic studies that evade dealing with most of the issues addressed in this chapter; they ignore conflict in politics and prefer to discard critical analysis as 'orientalism'. To rectify, Islamology is proposed as a study of conflict, however, in a discursive-communicative, hermeneutical manner. This study is guided by the spirit of conflict resolution and bridging in a better and critical understanding of Islamic societies and their problems. Islamology resembles the earlier Sovietology as a study of global conflict, but it dismisses any Cold War mentality and focuses on bridging between the civilizations.

The discipline of Islamology for the study of Islamic realities in a global conflict is a pertinent new approach. The background of the new discipline is that neither the classical orientalist study of the scripture of Islam nor the cultural–relativist narrative of culture pursued in US anthropology are helpful for the study of contemporary Islam in the religionized post-bipolar politics. It is a fact that philologians, historians and cultural anthropologists dominate the field in Islamic studies. There are only a few political scientists who are in a position to professionally study Islam and international conflict. The need for a combined historical and social–scientific study of Islam – not as a faith, but as a political reality – is not fulfilled. The narrative of local culture that anthropologists provide ignores the fact that these cultures assemble in one Islamic civilization in a world globally shaped and networked by the instruments of modernity. All Islamic local cultures share a common view of the world determined by Islamic universally related values essentialized on the belief that they are revealed by Allah. In contrast to the mindset of established Islamic Studies, Islamology acknowledges that Islam is a civilization to be placed in an inquiry on the behalf of international relations into global conflict. The Swiss university of St Gallen established in a pioneering manner in 2003/2004 the position of a 'visiting professor of Islamology' that stood, by then, in contrast to traditional Islamic studies. I was the first incumbent of this professorship. When I left it was not continued. At the German University of Goettingen where I established Islamology as a social–scientific study of Islam and conflict in international studies the chair was abolished parallel to my retirement 2009. Unfortunately, the prospects are not promising for this kind of study that contradicts traditional wisdoms.

The de-politicization and equally a de-militarization of the Islamic concept of jihad, or even its abandonment altogether remain a requirement academia is reluctant to address. The same applies to Islam's predicament with modernity. Until that day comes one needs Islamology. Islamists reinvent the tradition of Islam and silence their critics with the suspicion and accusation of Islamophobia and Islam-bashing. This is also a part of their war of ideas.

The Islamological study of the shift from classical jihad to jihadism is not a simple study of terrorism within the framework of a security analysis. Instead it deals with cultural fragmentation that reflects a predicament of Islam with modernity that creates one of the major sources of conflict and war of ideas. Unlike traditional Islamic studies the Islamological approach grasps the issue and places the subject matter in the discipline of International Relations as a civilizational issue. Again: the war of ideas is not about clash, but about conflict. Long before Huntington set the most controversial debate on this issue, Raymond Aron acknowledged aptly the pertinence of civilizations to world politics.[66] By then, no one contested Aron's scholarship. Today, politically correct-minded students defame Huntington and use the dismissive reference to his work to overly turn down the study of civilizations as such. Well, I agree with the dispute against the book by Huntington on this subject, but a blunt rejection of any research on civilizations is questionable. Therefore, I propose to replace Islamic studies with Islamology to guide the thoughts of the study of Islam and conflict in post-bipolar politics. To be sure, an orientalism in reverse does not overcome the Huntingtonian bias, nor orientalism itself. As Robert Spencer puts it, 'the issues here are too important to be relegated to politically correct silence, wishful thinking, or lies of intimidation or politeness. It is incumbent on us to look squarely at the truth.'[67] In fact, these requirements are essentials of scholarship, but often ignored by the establishment of Islamic studies and therefore there is a need for change. The methodology *and* the mindset of Islamology not only admit the study of the war of ideas, but also promise enlightenment to end this war in a 'peace' of ideas. It is, though, not welcomed in the field.

The proposition to introduce the study of Islam into international relations within the framework of Islamology has been supported by three world political events in the recent past in a time span of about a quarter of a century. The rise of political Islam wrongly addressed as 'Islamic revival' in a crisis-ridden situation is – as repeatedly argued – related to a predicament of that civilization with modernity that leads to the politicization of Islam. The result is a political religion that is not a revival. The overall phenomenon of religious fundamentalism touches on a cultural system, not on Islam as a religion and a belief. At issue is the place of Islamic civilization in world politics. I maintain that most problems occur in this context. The approach of Islamology is proposed for studying these problems and the conflicts they engender. Among my eight books published in English the major one among them deals with the subject of a predicament that generates conflict.[68] Now let me list the three world political events pertinent to the theme in point:

At first was the Islamic Revolution in Iran 1979; it was academically speaking the beginning of the study of Islam in world affairs, however, mostly not in a professional International Relations manner.[69] Among the reasons underlying the world-political pertinence of that revolution was the pronouncement of its leaders to export it to the rest of the world of Islam and also its claim to have a universal place in history at large. This happened in emulating the universality, but not the values of the French Revolution. The leaders of the Islamic Revolution of Iran claimed a vision for re-making the world along Islamic lines. This is the challenge of Islamic fundamentalism to world order. It fights a war of ideas that greatly matter to Islamology. The Iranian president, Ahmadinejad, is in this context one of the most furious warriors in the war of ideas.

Next to the Shi'i Islamic revolution a Sunni-driven world political event took place when al-Qaeda in its jihadist action of September 11, 2001 assaulted major targets in New York and Washington. That was a symbolic attack on the only remaining superpower, after the Afghan Mujahideen in the first Afghanistan war brought the Soviet Union to its knees. In a way 9/11 was a watershed in world politics. The Islamist internationalism has claimed a place in world politics. Here Islamology reminds one of Sovietology. However, one should over and over again keep the difference in mind: that Islamology studies the significance of transnational religion in post-bipolar politics focused on Islam not with a spirit of Cold War, but rather of bridging. This third event is singled out in its significance to legitimate Chapter 5 on Islam in Europe and bridging.

The third event in the addressed chain of a universal 'Islamic Revolution' aimed at establishing a divine world order to replace the existing one is not well received in the US. The event is a combination of assaults in Madrid, Amsterdam, London, Paris and Copenhagen in the years 2004–06. This phenomenon of an incremental jihadization of parts of the Islam diaspora in Europe has not been well received by European opinion leaders either; they are most reluctant to acknowledge the new war.

All of these three world political events are also a war of ideas that Islamists wage legitimated by a universal, i.e. non-sectarian, Islamic clothing. Despite this claim, the war of ideas also takes place within Islam. The Islamic revolution in Iran clearly has Shi'a confines that limit its appeal as a model to the Sunni majority (ca. 90 per cent) of the Islamic *umma*. Nonetheless, no one can ignore the earlier demonstrative spill-over effects of the revolution; they are undeniable, but they do not eliminate the Sunni–Shi'a rift.

Sunni Islamism was taken by surprise by the Shi'a Iranian revolution. In the first war in Afghanistan the incursion of Soviet troops contributed to mobilizing Sunni Islam. In the fight against the 'infidels' combined with an importing of an Islamist variety of Wahhabism to central Asia and later on to the introduction of al-Qaeda, a competition between the Sunni pattern of irregular war of global jihad, on the one hand, and the terrorism of the Iranian Revolution, on the other, came to light. There are Sunni and Shi'a competing varieties of global jihad, but both represent the world-political phenomenon of Islamist internationalism.[70]

The study of the religion-based political internationalism in world politics needs the interdisciplinary methodology of Islamology. This is a cross- and inter-disciplinary approach enriched by historical sociology. Historically, there is a double exposure to the West. In an earlier stage of this process Islam was at first exposed to the superior military power of Europe and, second, to cultural modernity. One should not confuse these two different levels. Muslims had to deal with a new power structure and also with challenging values of cultural modernity. The outcome is the already addressed predicament for Islam and for its believers. To be sure – and this is to be repeated – there exists no monolithic body of Islam since Muslims belong to a great variety of local cultures. However, and despite this great diversity, all Islamic local cultures are united in a family resemblance and, on the grounds of shared values and worldviews, constitute a grouping named Islamic civilization. In so arguing I am not essentializing Islam, nor am I falling into the trap of viewing Islam as a monolith, in an orientalist manner. I am simply stating the simultaneity of a civilizational unity and a local-cultural diversity within the Islamic civilization. If this is denied then there is no proper understanding of Islam in place. There are divergent responses to the crisis of Islam in an age of the return of civilizations to world politics and of the revival of the sacred. In this regard there are also common patterns among Muslims. The established historical study of civilizations has become pertinent, because civilizations are competing for a new world order. Do not be mistaken and do not use the terms culture and civilization interchangeably, this would be wrong, because the terms have different meanings.

This is also pertinent for the understanding of the war of ideas in the context between secular democratic peace and Islamist jihadism. This civilizational competition is the subject matter of Islamology. The war of ideas is a part of this subject and it draws distinctions between the numerous local cultures and the cross-cultural civilization of Islam.

There are various levels for the study of the war of ideas between Islamism and the values of cultural modernity. There are two civilizations involved, each of them subscribing to different worldviews but claiming universality for its model. There are other civilizations (Hinduism) that simply do not do this, because they are not universalistic. In this understanding, Islam and Christianity are viewed as transnational religions. At issue is a history of equally mutual conquests and admiration, covering about fifteen centuries. This tradition is continued by the West as secularized Christianity. In the present, Islamic migration to Europe and the drive of AKP-Islamist Turkey for accession to the European Union bring Islam back to Europe. As John Kelsay suggested in this situation one can no longer speak of 'Islam *and* the West, but of Islam *in* the West'.[71] The existence of al-Qaeda cells throughout Western Europe (see note 70), as well as other Islamist movements brings political Islam to the heart of the old world. This process includes a specific component of the war of ideas. It is a war between the needed values for an integration of Muslim immigrants to citizens and the culture of the new 'Islamic enclaves', that separate this diaspora from Europe.[72]

It is basic for Islamology to understand that the war of ideas as suggested is not a war between the West and Islam. Hence there is no clash, but a conflict. As a liberal Muslim, I refuse to accept the suggested invincible character of these alleged fault-lines between Islam and the West, regardless of their source, be it Huntington or the Islamists themselves. Therefore the Islamological study of world politics that describes a conflict is guided by other incentives. Among these is the drive to establish a consensus based on shared ethical foundations. Such commonalities help overcome the fault-lines in a competition between global jihad to democratic world peace. In this context I envision an intercivilizational dialogue which is also a part of Islamology that is not only a study of international conflict, but also an exploration into a peaceful conflict resolution. Viewed in this manner, a real dialogue would contribute to ending the war of ideas. To be sure, these Islamists who insist on replacing the existing order with theirs cannot be trusted in this venture of bridging.

At this junction I come back to the historical precedent of the experiment of bridging in the history of Islam. The precedent is the Hellenization of medieval Islam that, as a strategy for bridging between the civilizations, is proposed for emulation in the twenty-first century.

War and peace of ideas

Between history and the present: Islam, Hellenism and reform

This book includes a chapter on the tradition of medieval Islamic humanism. That tradition is viewed as compatible with cultural modernity and with rationalism as an acceptance of primacy of reason. This may not be always acceptable to Muslims of today, but in the past it was essential in the heritage of their civilizations. Instead of constructing fault-lines – as does Islamism – an effort at bridging is to be done. This has been undertaken in this book in the belief that this venture is more promising. The classical Greek heritage is considered to be one of the pillars of modernity in the West and it was so for medieval Islamic civilization as well. Today, Islamists suppress the fact that this Hellenist heritage was essential for the classical heritage of Islam and for its tradition of rationalism. I claim that there existed a secular humanism in Islam based on the adoption of the heritage of Hellenism.[73] In this context Chapter 4 will discuss the pending issues. They are pertinent to the war/peace of ideas-problematic, but I shall take pains to avoid repetition here and there.

Today, Islamists associate Western civilization with the Christian 'infidels'. The idea of the West is not based on Christianity, but on Hellenism; it is one of the sources of secular Western civilization that was established on a reason-based view of the world. In this capacity Hellenism was also accepted by medieval Muslim rationalists such as al-Farabi, Ibn Sina and Ibn Rushd up to Ibn Khaldun from the ninth through the fourteenth centuries. This process was described as the Hellenization of Islam. A revival of the related historical records matters to the international relations of our present, because it helps to revive the tradition of Islamic rationalism and the secular political philosophy of the state established by al-Farabi.[74] In this regard, I draw on Leslie Lipson's formidable comparative study of civilizations, to adapt from it two major arguments and related insights pertinent to a peace of ideas.

1   The introduction of Hellenism to Europe took place via the rationalist line of Islamic civilization. Lipson informs us that,

> Aristotle crept back into Europe by the side door. His return was due to the Arabs, who had become acquainted with Greek thinkers . . . Both

Avicenna and Averroës were influenced by him. When the University
of Paris was organized, Artistotle was introduced there from Cordoba.[75]

2   With the assistance of Hellenism, Christendom that determined the civilization
of Europe was secularized to smooth the way into a new civilization named
'the West'. Ever since, European–Christian civilization has been transformed
into the existing one which is secular. As Lipson states,

> The difference in the West before and after the Renaissance . . . can be
> summarized in one sentence . . . The main source of Europe's inspiration
> shifted from Christianity back to Greece, from Jerusalem to Athens,
> Socrates, not Jesus, has been the mentor of the civilization of the
> West.[76]

These references to history shed a better light on Islam in the present war of
ideas and they support (with justifications) the view that in the history of ideas
there were bridges for a 'peace' of ideas between civilizations. Given the fact that
Muslims in the past were capable of accommodating Hellenism to incorporate it
into the heritage of Islamic rationalism, one is compelled to ask why this cannot
also happen today? Are the Muslims of today ready to accommodate in a similar
manner and mindset cultural modernity to end the war of ideas?

Historically, the Muslim adoptions from Hellenism reflect a positive civilizational
encounter and create a precedent for cross-cultural fertilization pertinent to our
age. The revival of this humanist legacy could serve as a cultural underpinning
for embracing modernity and its vision of democratic peace in world politics. The
contemporary Islamic rationalist Mohammed Abed al-Jabri rightly argues that
for people of Islam a promising 'future can only be Averroist'.[77] By this, the late
al-Jabri means that a true Islamic revival can only be established on a reason-based,
i.e. rational, worldview in contemporary Islamic civilization. This Islamic-
enlightened mindset is supportive to the peace of ideas, but it is unfortunately not
reflected in the mainstream, as Islamism is.

In summing up the argument, it is argued that Muslims, instead of waging global
jihad could, if they wanted to, engage in reviving the tradition of Islamic rationalism
which flourished in Medieval Islam. An establishing of a rational worldview would
help smooth the way for the acceptance of democratic peace that includes a 'peace'
of ideas. In medieval Islam the rejection of rationalism came basically from
the *fiqh*-orthodoxy (sacral jurisprudence), as it comes today from Islamism. In the
past, the *fiqh*-orthodoxy prevented the institutionalization of the scientific view
of the world established by rational Islamic philosophy. Without a process of
institutionalization in society no cultural innovation can be enduring. The Salafist-
orthodox effort at undermining cultural innovation took place in the Islamic institutions of learning in which this orthodoxy prevailed. The introduction of the
reasoning of Islamic philosophy into the curriculum was prevented. The tradition
of darkness, not Islamic humanism, is being revived today by political Islam in an

alliance with Wahhabi orthodoxy, which does the same job. Oil-rich Wahhabism provides funds for waging a global jihad, certainly not for the spread of democratic Islam. What are the repercussions from the point of view of the need to incorporate Islamic civilization into an international society on the premise of democratic peace? Can we draw on the classical heritage of Islam (science and philosophy) to present a better Islamic perspective for the future? How can we bridge between Islam and the West within the framework of an international secular community?

The questions asked touch on major issues, but I profess not to have a recipe, even less a panacea. These questions support the plea for an agenda of research to promote an international relations focused Islamology. The intercivilizational conflict in which the war of ideas is embedded is the subject matter in point. The spirit of a 'peace' of ideas stands in contrast to Islamist jihadism. Islamic humanism is a thinking of cross-civilizational bridging against religionized politics that shall be further elaborated upon in the ensuing chapter.

Conclusions

War of ideas, cultural modernity and world order

The fault-lines that I dismiss in the present work are related to the tensions between global jihad and a cross-cultural international morality. In principle there are no fault-lines between Islam and the West. The plea for a cross-cultural bridging which is not merely restricted to an intellectual undertaking, argues for a cross-cultural consensus over values in a venture to reform world order that ends constructed binaries. The late Oxford scholar Hedley Bull placed the issue of order at the centre of his reasoning. Seen from this perspective, post-bipolar world politics is characterized by a competition between two concepts of order, one is secular the other is based on religionized politics. Without knowing the work of Bull, John Kelsay in his book *Islam and War*, phrases the problem in asking who will determine the future of world order. The question is not a rhetorical one, it is about the agenda. John Kelsay expresses the intercivilizational conflict over the order of the world in this phrasing:

> Much of the contemporary return to Islam is driven by the perception of Muslims as a community . . . having a mission to fulfill. That this perception sometimes leads to conflict is not surprising. In encounters between the West and Islam, the struggle is over who will provide the primary definition to world order. Will it be the West, with its notions of territorial boundaries, market economies, private religiosity, and the priority of individual rights? Or will it be Islam, with its emphasis on the universal mission of a transtribal community called to build a social order founded on the pure monotheism natural to humanity? The question for those who envision world order, then, is, 'Who determines the shape of order, in the new international context?'

The very question suggests a competition between cultural traditions with distinctive notions of peace, order, and justice. It thus implies pessimism concerning the call for a new world order based on notions of common humanity.[78]

In short, the twenty-first century heralds a competition between two visions of order for the future of humanity: either the expansion of *dar al-Islam* (Islamicate) pursued with the means of the revived jihad to map the entire globe in one order according to the visions of Sayyid Qutb; or an ordering of the world along the concept of a 'democratic peace'. This concept is based on reviving the views of the greatest philosopher of European Enlightenment, Immanuel Kant, on *Ewigen Frieden* ('perpetual peace'). The idea of a perpetual peace is an expression of cultural modernity. Therefore, the pivotal subject matter is not 'Islam or the West' – this phrase expresses not only a clash, it is also too general and therefore inappropriate – but rather an intercivilizational conflict. It takes place between the worldview of cultural modernity and the one of global jihad for the world order of *Hakiymiyyat Allah* ('rule of God') as an order of the Islamicate in a new understanding. The present analysis supports the hypothesis that most of the problems of Islam derive from its predicament with modernity. The pending choice is: either Muslims subscribe to a world of religious pluralism based on cultural pluralism and thus accept a pluralist perspective to intercivilizational relations, i.e. the cultural others are equals to them; or they engage themselves in the ongoing political articulation of the well-known *da'wa*, i.e. proselytization. Underlying this *da'wa* is the vision of a global *dar al-Islam*. In other words, Islamic civilization is at a crossroads with competing options. Viewed from this angle, an embracing of cultural modernity by Muslims would contribute to embracing a view of a pluralist world. Then, jihad would be viewed as a legacy Muslims could and should dispense with for a better future based on intercivilizational bridging.

While recommending an Islamic embracing of cultural modernity I hasten to add that modernity cannot be reduced to items to be adopted from instrumental modernity, for it is also a rational worldview based on secular values. At the crossroads there are options other than the extreme choice between Islamization and Westernization. Kemalism and similar varieties of equating progress (*tarakki*) with Westernization not only failed, but also have paved the way for the rise of Islamism in contemporary Turkey.[79] In learning from this experience, we need to seek other options. I refuse to see in the drive toward de-Westernization the necessary conclusion of the failure of Westernization. It is worth mentioning that the Egyptian Islamist Hasan al-Sharqawi refuses Kemalism as a strategy of Westernizing the world of Islam, but is keen to adop Western weaponry for fighting jihad against the West. For him there is no contradiction in arguing this manner, as he blatantly states: 'Our goal cannot be to Westernize, but to learn from the West how to deal with modern weapon systems, and even more: to produce these systems by ourselves to be in a position to defeat the West as our enemy.'[80]

This Islamist author engages himself in reviving the nostalgia of Islamic growth. The mindset of Islamic nostalgia combined with political jihadist Islam is not simply an expression of cultural self-assertion – as some Western scholars believe – but rather a dream of restoring *Pax Islamica* as the proper Islamic world order. In this regard, the work of Kelsay is worth being quoted again at length:

> it would be wrong . . . to understand the contemporary call for revival among Muslims as simple nostalgia . . . Some authors long for the glory of the past . . . (and) have argued that the ascension of European and North American civilization in world affairs has been based on a failure of leadership in the Islamic world and on the Western willingness to shamelessly exploit, in the name of profit, the human and material resources of the developing countries. The mood of such writers is not nostalgia but outrage over the state of the world, in particular the state of the Muslim community.[81]

Clearly, at present the Islamists committed to the outlined mindset of a constructed nostalgia – wrongly named Islamic revival – do not engage in a religious renaissance; their concern is to topple the existing order, but they are not in a position to accomplish this goal; they destabilize, however, through their action of global jihad. One should be concerned about a 'new Cold War' between the secular world order and the Islamists order of *Hakimiyyat Allah* ('Rule of God'). The Islamists have the illusion to be able to remake the world for a global mapping of the world in an enhanced *dar al-Islam*.[82] The present analysis supports the two hypotheses that Islamism wages a war of ideas related to order – the nation state and world order – and thus the conclusion that political Islam and its jihadism matter to international and security studies. This thinking also supports the need for dialogue with one another on what might be accepted by both as the right order. Dialogue should be viewed as a variety of conflict-resolution in peace, not merely as a forum for rhetorical pronouncements. The event-management, so-called 'Christian–Muslim understanding', alleged to happen as an indication of good will, is not an effort at conflict resolution. This ceremonial venture falters at the bedrock of the reality of conflict. People of good will avoid acknowledging this reality.

This chapter on the war of ideas suggests in its conclusions a revival of the heritage of Islamic rationalism established by Muslim medieval philosophers committed to reason. Contemporary Muslims could emulate their ancestors who were able to learn from Plato's concept of the state and the Aristotelian logic of politics. In the next chapter I shall seek to legitimate a peace of ideas based on secular humanism with such a reference. If contemporary Muslims were willing to look back to their Islamic heritage, and to revive it instead of engaging in an Islamist illusion of a remaking of the world, then there would be a way to come to terms with the non-Muslim others. In my view, al-Farabi's classic *al-Madina al-Fadila* ('The Perfect State') is also acceptable to the non-Muslim parts of humanity; it is the rational order of the *Madina al-Fadila* as a perfect polity supposed to be led by a philosopher as a ruler. This ruler is understood in the Hellenistic sense, not as an Imam complying with the shari'a, but with rational principles of good governance for a polity. In contrast, any imposition by the Islamists of a *Hakimiyyat Allah*, which is – by the way – neither mentioned in the Qur'an, nor in the Hadith, would be perceived by non-Muslims as a jihad/declaration of war on them for coercing them to accept their subordination to an Islamic order alien not only to non-Muslims, but also to truly democratic Muslims committed to bridging.

Ethical integrity compels me not to conclude this chapter without the confession that the propositions made here are not yet a popular public choice; they are only shared by a minority of contemporary enlightened Muslim thinkers such as al-Jabri and Arkoun among others. To admit that the vision of a civil Islam is not among the current popular public choices in the world of Islam and its diaspora in the West is not to belittle 'The other Muslims', who are 'moderate and secular'.[83] They are not an insignificant 'slice', as a US-political scientist favourable to Islamism thinks.[84] These 'other Muslims' may not represent the dominating public choice, but they are the promise of cultural change in the world of Islam. If one writes them off for the favour of Islamist policies then a rethinking of Islam would stay out of the door. If Muslim opinion leaders continue to ignore the need for innovation and cultural change necessary for successfully coping with a changing world in terms of coming to terms with Islam's predicament with modernity, then the war of ideas will continue unabated. If Islamists dominate the 'Arab Spring', it would become a dark Arab Winter. The tensions Islamism ignites would lead to a most consequential conflict.

My last conclusion is that the ongoing war of ideas is not only related to a cultural war, but is also interrelated to issues of security. For accomplishing a democratic peace and for moving away from global jihad, there is also a need for a security approach combined with a dialogue. Among the findings of this chapter is the insight that post-bipolar politics is also affected by culture and religion – major themes for the combination of dialogue with concerns of security. To be sure, this security has to be a joint Western–Islamic venture if one wants to avert a development that helps make the scenario of a clash of civilizations become a self-fulfilling prophecy. The ongoing intercivilizational war of ideas is a basic part of this story and therefore it deserves a grater attention.

4

WHICH ISLAM FOR BRIDGING?

The heterogeneity of civilizations as a background for the plea to revive the grammar of Islamic humanism

President Barack Obama has been more conciliatory than his predecessor G.W. Bush as he aims at bridging the divide to Islamic civilization, albeit without any further specification of 'which' Islam he is speaking of. In a similar vein the then acting German president stated in his speech on the commemoration of German re-unification on 3 October 2010 that 'Islam is a part of Germany'. What do these politicians mean when they speak of Islam? Is there one Islam? In the need for the emphasis on bridging in a world of multiple civilizations one has to underline humanism as the best cross-cultural tradition in the history of humanity. In the historical context of the twenty-first century a geopolitics of Islam emerges as a new factor in world politics. This geopolitics has taken clear shape and has become visible to everyone as a source of conflict in post-bipolar politics in the past decade. The years of the intensification of the intercivilizational conflict were inflamed, but not caused, by the disastrous effects of the policies of the George W. Bush presidency, but a scholarly analysis does not accept the blame for replacing analytical thinking about the development addressed with beliefs based on unchecked assumptions. It is more serious to address the conflict in place and to inquire into its structural constraints. There is also the related normative orientation paired with a binary worldview that underlies the conflict. In short, neither the politics of polarization, nor the other extreme of unspecific conciliation are helpful. One not only needs to admit that there is a conflict, but also be specific (which Islam?) when one deals with Islamic civilization. The 'war on terror' declared by the then US president George W. Bush contributed significantly to an intensification of the interciviliza-tional conflict in point, but it did not invent this conflict. However, the promises of the following president Barack Obama did not yield any noticeable positive outcome. President Obama visited two major Islamic countries in 2009. In April in Ankara he proclaimed the end of the 'clash of civilizations'. Thereafter he went to Cairo in June to propose that peoples of Islamic civilization establish a dialogue.

In a positive manner Obama did not shy away from addressing seven 'sources of tension'. However, the ensuing policies did not take account of this thinking. Aside from the good will Obama's new policy has generated, it has been dominated by insignificance and a lack of distinction. The major flaw has been Obama's ignoring of the existing distinctions within Islam. While talking about Islam he failed to state which Islam he was thinking of. This is the most disasterous blind spot in Western policies. Thus, Obama consequentially had no clue about the partner needed in the envisioned dialogue. Obama wrongly reduced the unfavourable facts in Islamic civilization to radicalism, or extremism; he not only spoke of a positive Islam in general, but also erased Islamism. But what is Islam?

This chapter uses the reference to the outlined background in contemporary history to launch a deeper debate about Islam rich in nuances and distinctions. No doubt Obama's new policies promised a change in the international environment. Therefore, in 2009 after only nine months in office Obama was awarded the Nobel Peace Prize. The justification provided said that Obama had 'created a new climate in international Politics' (*International Herald Tribune*, 10–11 October 2009, frontpage). In response to the honour he was given Obama said, 'I will accept this award as a call for action' (ibid.). I refer to this event as a starter for the debate on bridging which should not be flawed by an evasion. As already stated, a cross-cultural humanism is the foremost bridge between civilizations. In Ankara and Cairo Obama did not talk about the need for a revival of Islamic humanism. I am not sure whether he, or his advisors had knowledge about this tradition in Islam. Moreover, Obama again failed to make clear distinctions within Islam.

In theorizing about tensions between civilizations the fact is acknowledged that the history of humankind has always been a history of competing civilizations and that Islam is not only a religious faith but also a civilization with its own history.[1] For educated people this statement may sound like a rehash of a common sense. Today, it has become quite a risk to address humanity as a history of competition of civilizations and to add to this insight the notion of conflict. The issue itself has been tainted by the biased and damaging debate on 'clash of civilizations'.[2] In Chapter 1 it has been made clear that a conflict is not a clash. A conflict can be solved while the rhetoric of a clash essentializes tensions and thus contributes to a polarization. In earlier times there were better debates on these issues. When the French Sorbonne was still a university of world class carried by giants, there were genius scholars among its faculty that no one can replace today. In those times, these great scholars engaged in promising debates. One of these intellectual giants was Raymond Aron at the Parisian Sorbonne. Back in 1962 Aron articulated the idea of a 'heterogeneity of civilizations'[3] in a major book on *Paix et Guerre entre les Nations*. This happened long before the late Huntington in a most controversial article published in 1993 pronounced from Harvard the pertinence of the study of civilizations in world politics. He made the right reference, however, in a most odd and even damaging manner. In 2010 the Cornell scholar of International Relations, Peter Katzenstein, made an effort to rectify the damage. Nonetheless, he endorsed the pertinence of 'civilizations' to the study of international politics, but he, too, fell victim to the dominating culture of political correctness that forbade an outspoken reference to tensions and conflict.[4]

This chapter goes beyond the outlined extremes. The first is the one of a clash, and the second is its reversal to the 'convergence/alliance of civilizations'. There is also the nonsense related to the allegation of an 'Islamo-Christian civilization' (see note 2). Instead, I prefer to draw on Aron's already quoted major book published 1962 at the height of bipolarity. Aron rightly believed that the source of conflict in world politics, namely, the cited 'heterogeneity of civilizations', had been veiled by the then existing rival blocks. He noticed that the veil was not a lasting one and he was right about this prediction. Indeed the end of bipolarity unveiled the real subdivision of humanity in rival and competing civilizations. Today, civilizational awareness assumes the shape of identity politics and it becomes a source of conflict. In contrast, the revival of a tradition of humanism could tame dangerous intercivilizational tensions. Under conditions of post-bipolarity Islamic civilization is placed at the core of global conflict and hence the need to revive Islamic humanism in an effort at cross-cultural bridging. President Obama who qualified his acceptance of the 2009 Nobel Peace Prize as 'a call for action' was supposed to continue the effort at bridging between Islam and the West as civilizations, but he failed to do so. What are the lessons to be learned?

Introduction

The theme of this book is conflict, but the present chapter sets out the fact of a classical heritage of Islam in which processes of intercultural fertilization existed. By then, Muslims engaged in a cultural borrowing that is seemingly not well-known or ignored in the recent debate. One also notices a lack of knowledge about the work of the founder of *ilm al-umran* ('science of civilizations'), Ibn Khaldun, of the fourteenth century. In his masterpiece *al-Muqaddima* ('Prolegomena') Ibn Khaldun laid the foundations for this new discipline. Today, Ibn Khaldun's approach is most pertinent. In addition to the ongoing revival of civilizations one needs to engage in a cross-cultural bridging without overlooking the inter-civilizational conflict.[5] Here it is suggested that there is a grammar of humanism that can be shared in many ways by all multiple civilizations. It is proven that this grammar is an essential part of the classical heritage of Islam.

In medieval Islam, Muslim rationalists established values that were shared with the non-Muslim cultural other on universal grounds. The tradition of Hellenism lived forth in medieval Islam and it continues to be pertinent for the present. If one wants to prevent both the Huntingtonian self-fulfilling prophecy of a clash between the civilizations, and the related Islamist 'war of ideas' analysed in Chapter 3, then one is challenged to look for alternatives. In this venture it is, however, most pertinent to ensure that the critique of the rhetorics of 'clash of civilizations' cannot be overcome by going to the other extreme of convergence mentioned above. It is also wrong to contend that there is an 'Islamo-Christian civilization', thus denying all existing conflicts. The silly notion 'alliance of civilizations' is also meaningless.

Conflict is not the focus of this chapter, the concern is rather the grammar of humanism viewed as a bridge between the civilizations.[6] The fact of a mixed bag of diversity of cultures and civilizations is acknowledged. In the literature, the two terms of culture and civilization are often used interchangeably, even though this is wrong, as both terms have a different meaning. If this is ignored, then confusion would be at work that not only relates to a wrong use of terms, but also to consequences of blurring and diluting the meaning. The resulting confusion may affect the analysis and the related policy implications.

There is another flaw that indicates Western ignorance paired with arrogance or Eurocentrism. This occurs when scholars speak just of one civilization, as William McNeill did in his powerful book *The Rise of the West* (1963). McNeill talks about humanity, but means the West.[7] This view is contradicted by an ascertainment of multiple civilizations that is combined with a major stream of diversity. In contrast to the pure diversity of conflicting cultural values, there is a humanism that bridges and tames cultural tensions that may lead to conflict. In a nutshell: in an age of a simultaneity of structural globalization and cultural fragmentation, differences based on diversity become a major source of tensions and lead to conflict.[8] Under these conditions there is a need for shared humanist values. Cultural relativists deny this value universality – as well as value-conflicts. They inadvertently close the door to the venture of bridging.

The framework of this chapter is based on the reference to the heterogeneity of civilizations, combined with an inquiry into the resulting conflict and into the potential of a cross-cultural bridging, as mediation to alleviate the culture-based conflicts. The conflict between what is named Islam and the West (Europe) has centuries-old roots that also include war (jihad and crusades). But there was also a cultural fertilization (Hellenization of Islam and Islamic impact on European Renaissance). The contended grammar of an Islamic humanism is placed positively in this overall context of intercivilizational relations.

The idea of a humanism shared in the past between Europe and Islam in common traditions presupposes the acceptance of a universality of core values. The implication is to challenge the damaging confinements maintained today by cultural relativism. It is scandalous that cultural relativists do not even shy away from dismissing the universality of individual human rights. In contesting this mindset, I dismiss the contemporary postmodern European nihilism that deconstructs every notion, including the one of humanism. This happens to the extent of ending up in rubbles disguised as a process of epistemological deconstruction. In a similar vein, I argue against the absolutism of political Islam (Islamism), being in fact exactly contrary to Western cultural relativism. To be sure, these two mindsets of cultural relativism and neo-absolutism collide head-on with one another. Therefore, it is quite intriguing to see Western postmodernists and Islamists – acting as relativists and neo-absolutists – as strange bedfellows that are at times united in the furious rejection of the universality of European values of humanism.[9] The human- or individual-centred view of the world, which is the substance of humanism, is uppermost of these values. The present argument emphasizes that the humanist worldview is rooted in Hellenism. In cultural modernity the 'principle of subjectivity'[10] discussed by Habermas refers to the process Max Weber identified in his formula of *Entzauberung der Welt* ('disenchantment of the world').[11] This is another phrasing for secularization. Cultural modernity is a rationalist modernity. Therefore, the combination of rationalism and humanism links the history of ideas of Hellenism and modernity to one another. The uneasy Islamist–postmodern alliance referred to as one of the strange bedfellows united a new variety of Third World-ist romanticism (see Chapter 6) is not positive about this combination. The late Ernest Gellner argued in favour of a Western and Islamic enlightenment based on humanism. Therefore, he dismissed the stated alliance in some derogatory phrases, as he argues:

> Logically, the religious fundamentalists are of course also in conflict with the relativists . . . In practice, this confrontation is not so very much in evidence. The fundamentalists notice and despise the . . . relativism so pervasive in Western society, but they do not take much interest in its philosophical rationale. The relativists in turn direct their attack at those . . . non-relativists within their own enlightened tradition, but play down . . . religious fundamentalism.[12]

This chapter defends the tradition of Enlightenment and its humanism in the present venture of bridging, but also takes a stand against cultural–relativist post-modernism in favour of a universalist humanism. In the discipline to which I belong one reads for instance in an International Relations theory article in an established encyclopedia the following phrasing on this issue: 'Postmodernists reject . . . the assumptions of the French Enlightenment about . . . modernity . . . More subversively, postmodernists reject the idea that modernity . . . is necessarily the best or only one way to order things.'[13] In this manner postmodernists also dismiss the major assumptions of a universal humanism, as well as its continuation in cultural rationalist modernity. Therefore, humanist thinking that can be traced back to classical Hellenism once embraced by Muslim rationalists of medieval Islam stands not only in contrast to religious fundamentalism, but also to postmodernism. In contrast to both, this chapter argues for shared values based on a humanism that approves cultural modernity and the claims of its values to universality. If this venture is not possible, then no real bridging could ever be feasible. Period.

While operating on the assumption that the intercivilizational conflict between Western and Islamic civilizations can be resolved through sharing a humanism in a process of a cross-cultural bridging, I unfold the idea of an international morality. I trace humanist morality back to see it in the classical heritage of Islam. I maintain that it is possible to find in this heritage seeds for an Islamic humanism that emerged in the context of the Hellenization of classical medieval Islam. I do not stand alone, as there are other students of Islam who confirm with substance the evidence for a humanism that existed in Islam. For instance, Joel Kraemer states:

> by renaissance of Islam I refer to a classical [. . .] flowering within the soil
> of Islamic civilization [. . .] the principle expression of this renaissance was
> philosophical humanism that embraced the scientific and philosophical
> heritage of antiquity . . . equivalent in many ways of its nuances to Greek
> paideia [. . .][14]

It is also a fact that the tradition of humanism was suppressed in Islamic history through the *fiqh*-orthodoxy. In other words, the heritage in point is not constructed, as it really existed. It is also a fact in European history that Europe adopted the Greek heritage as a Hellenism from Islamic civilization in a classical process of intercivilizational encounters and cultural borrowings. Stated in a nutshell, the classical heritage of an Islamic rationalism includes a cultural variety of humanism. The reference to this heritage should serve as a reference to a bridge between the civilizations of Islam and Hellenism. This tradition is worth being revived in the present age of civilizational conflict in world politics. This conflict is not to be confused with the 'clash' rhetoric of Huntington. Therefore, the grammar of humanism in Islam matters also to the West in the present conflict-laden post-bipolar world time. It is a fact that Islamism inflames the intercivilizational conflict while postmodernists indiscriminately speak of 'alliance of civilizations', also confusing different traditions within Islam.[15] To revive Islamic humanism would be a real Islamic revival. It is utterly wrong to qualify Islamism as 'revival'! A revival of what?

The contention that Islamism is another modernity in a set up of multiple modernities is dismissed. Islamism rather engages in a politics of polarization. Islamists contest in the name of purity and authenticity any bridging between the civilizations of Islam and the West. To counter this purist and exclusionary mindset, a revival of the tradition of Hellenism and Islamic humanism not only contributes to alleviating what is named 'Islam's geo-civil war', but also helps to prevent the underlying tensions that lead to this war stated by the political theorist John Brenkman. He coined the cited phrase in his dealing with the geo-civil turmoil caused by Islamism while arguing, it is

> an uncomfortable truth . . . It has to be faced: most of the dangers are coming
> from the Muslim world . . . Europe must learn how to deal with . . . conflicts
> generated within and between Muslim countries, and between radical
> Muslims and the West . . . The crisis of Muslims' relation to the West is
> condensed.[16]

As an International Relations scholar I share this assessment and argue that one should stop dismissing such references to a real world-political set up as 'orientalism', or even worse, as 'Islamophobia'. Those who do this undermine the needed debate. How could one bridge, if thinking about conflict is not admitted?

Another prevention of the debate in point is the accusation of a binary mindset. To dissociate the present analysis from any binary view of the world the reference to global conflict is combined with another reference to inner-Islamic conflicts that undergird 'the civil war of Islam'. This expands to the extent of assuming a geo-civil shape. There is also the highly disliked reference to Europe as battlefield. Europeans like to believe that their continent is not affected by the conflicts addressed. It is a fact that Islamism is based today in Europe abusing the diaspora as a shelter for its networks. The violence in Madrid and Amsterdam (2004), London and Paris (2005), and Kopenhagen (2006) that illustrate this fact is a warning of worse to come. This is a challenge to Europe[17] where the conflict in point carries with it a potential for an 'ethnicity of fear'.[18]

In a time of crisis and uncertainty a revival of a universal humanism is a strategy of bridging. This is also a way of thinking against postmodernism that promotes nihilism. The issue matters to the pending theme. It is therefore not a digression to state that the postmodern method of deconstructing ideas and concepts destroys finally and forever the heritage of humanist universal knowledge based on certainty. This tradition has been passed down to us in precious historical, cross-cultural developments and challenges the fashion of cultural relativism in the West that coincides with the rise of the religious neo-absolutism named fundamentalism in Islam.

By way of introducing my controversial subject matter I am inclined to report that I, back in 1994, witnessed a controversy between the debated cultural relativism and humanist universalism. That happened at an event that I place among the highlights of my scholarly life. It was the Dutch symposium of the Erasmus Foundation, and the controversy took place between two great scholars: the late Ernest Gellner and the late Clifford Geertz. Both were passionate about their views. The humanism of Ernest Gellner that claims a universal validity was contested by the cultural relativism of Geertz. The debate was published in Amsterdam under the title 'The limits of pluralism', subtitled by the formula 'Neo-absolutism and relativism' (see note 9). Humbly I joined that debate and confronted in Amsterdam the debating parties with the anti-humanism promoted by the counter-enlightenment of political Islam. With all the respect due to the late Geertz, I chose to side with the humanism of Gellner against the cultural relativism of his foe. I acknowledge, though, my indebtness to Geertz with whom I spent a year at Princeton and published in a German edition one of his books on *Islam Observed*. I learned from Geertz to understand local cultures. At a dinner in my house in Princeton I succeeded to get a confession from Geertz that his anthropology does not go beyond cultural particularisms. It has to be plainly stated: Gellner knew much more about Islam than Geertz ever did. In contrast to Geertz, the late Gellner was knowledgeable about the global environment of cultural particularisms.

Islam and the concept of humanism

The question that one should not evade is this one: is the venture in point a reading in an arbitrary manner of a European notion into Islam? What is humanism? Hellenism is the basic intellectual root of humanism. The concept means – of course, without questioning God – that humans are at the centre of the universe and that they can manage life on their own. Humanism attributes to man the capability of recognizing the world through human reason (episteme) and combines this knowledge with the ability of man to change the globe along with human needs. The German historian of Hellenism Christian Meier coined the notion of *Koennensbewusstsein* ('the consciousness of one's own capabilities') to depict both abilities of man.[19] This German notion coined by Christian Meier consists of the continuation of two words to address the ability of man/human to shape one's own destiny. This is an interpretation of the idea that rests at the centre of classical Greek thought. The combination of the German verb *Koennen* ('to be able') and of the noun of *Bewusstsein* ('consciousness') – that means a capability of an awareness/conscience – into the notion of *Koennensbewusstsein* covers this meaning: humans have the cognitive and physical ability to act as a subject of their own. The notion of *Koennensbewusstsein* rests on the combination of two classical Greek concepts: *episteme* (ability of recognition) and *techne* (technical capability). Humans, though created (in the thinking of believers) by God, are nevertheless in a position not only to recognize the world by their human intellect, but also to shape it by their *techne*; to make it meet their own needs. The meaning of the notion *Koennensbewusstsein* determines the substance of humanism. The combination of the humanist worldview and the artisan handicraft led to the emergence of modern science in Europe. In this process some borrowing of Europe from Hellenized Islam was involved. This tradition stands in conflict with the theocentrism of all religions, above all the *tahwid*-doctrine of Salafi Islam. The concept of humanism is therefore also rationalism and Enlightenment, and above all secular. It is, however, not atheist, but it replaces the absolutist mindset of a sweeping theocentrism, with a free understanding of religion reduced to spirituality.

In modern times humanism is embedded in cultural rationalist modernity that rests on the 'principle of subjectivity'. This Habermasian formula is not to be confused with subjectivism, as some reviewers did in the course of reviewing my work. Prior to his invention of a 'post-secular society', Jürgen Habermas engaged in deliberations on humanism for delineating the principle of subjectivity in this phrasing: 'Religious faith becomes reflective; the world of the divine was changed in the solitude of subjectivity into something posited in ourself.' This is in fact the exact meaning of humanism identified by Habermas as 'the principle of subjectivity that determines the forms of modern culture . . . The moral concepts of modern times follow from the recognition of the subjective freedom of individuals'.[20] It follows that humanism humanizes the universe in dissociating it from the sacred and from the divine, clearly without becoming an atheism. I contend that this humanism, understood as a secular cultural modernity, has seeds in the classical heritage of Islam's Hellenization. The new notion of 'a post-secular society' coined by Habermas is not only a misplaced effort for bridging between Islam and the West after 9/11 – as Habermas intends – but also detrimental to the identity of Europe based on secular foundations.[21]

In contrast to Habermas I defend Europe, also on the grounds of what I learned as a former student of Adorno and Horkheimer at the Frankfurt School of the 1960s. By then, I also attended classes with Habermas and learned a lot from him. In my thinking, I combine the capacity of a Muslim immigrant living in Europe with the humanism in Islamic history and thought with the civilizational idea of Europe. A decade ago I asked the intriguing question: *Europa ohne Identität?* ('Europe without Identity?')[22] In that book I also draw on the Amsterdam Geertz–Gellner controversy just mentioned to question the cultural–relativist view about Europe in the age of global Islamic migration and its identity politics.

Unlike the approach of a 'post-secular society' that fails to bridge, an effort at an incorporation of the thought of humanism into the present debate is more promising. The existence of this concept in Islam (see note 14) predates the emergence of the humanist discourse in the West. In Hellenism one finds the roots of humanisms that were adopted by Islamic philosophers since the late ninth century. This tradition was then transmitted to Europe through borrowings from Islamic civilization. The tradition of *falsafa* ('rationalism') was suppressed by the *fiqh*-orthodoxy and today by Islamism. It is a hypocrisy when Islamists boast that Europe engaged in borrowing from Islam while they overlook the commonalities in the grammars of European and of Islamic humanism.[23] This humanist tradition is threatened today by the emerging alliance of the strange bedfellows: Islamists, who are neo-absolutists, and multiculturalists, who are cultural relativists. In contrast to these people, the theorist and historian of civilizations, Leslie Lipson, established in an amazing manner the view of a continuity between European and Islamic humanism existing in a historical context. Both traditions share a universality of rationalist view of the world and the related philosophical thought based on universal knowledge, which is identified here as humanism. Today, a decade and a half after the cited Amsterdam Erasmus controversy (note 9) over universality of values vs cultural relativism I prefer to combine this reference with the argument that there existed a shared tradition of Hellenism between Europe and Islam. I repeat: this is pertinent for today's needs. Underlying this pertinence is the fact that this tradition provides common civilizational roots in the Mediterranean. Those scholars who produce literature about civilizational convergence focus on Mediterranean identity.[24] However, the heritage of rationalism dismissed by Islamists today, and also ignored by others, is a heritage of a universal humanism that originated in Hellenism. This is not taken into account. Worse are those scholars who write off civilization altogether.

The reference to the Hellenist roots of humanism is based on the research of the foremost German historian of classic Greece, Christian Meier.[25] His already cited research supports with strong historical evidence the idea that the roots of humanism are to be found in the Hellenist heritage. Islamic humanism rests on these roots in the context of historical borrowings and adoptions in a time when Muslims were open-minded and receptive to others.

The substance of humanism is enlightenment which is the worldview that a human is, as a subject, capable to determine the self. This is viewed as a 'principle of subjectivity' (Habermas) which is utterly secular. Habermas makes no reference to the work of Christian Meier, and also – in his turn – ignores the fact that the tradition of Hellenism built up the roots of cultural modernity. In his revisionist concept of 'post-secular society', the same Habermas revokes his earlier views in a belief that this helps to bridge to Islamic civilization in the aftermath of 9/11. It is unfortunate that Habermas' poor knowledge about Islam is most consequential to his deliberations. Among the consequences is the failure to distinguish between *fiqh* ('orthodoxy') and *falsafa*-rationalism as rival traditions in Islam. There is no 'one Islam', since diversity is the hallmark of this civilization.

There is a legacy that matters to the intention of bridging. In the past the Hellenization of Islam, as well as the entry of Hellenism to Europe via Islam at the eve of the Renaissance, constituted such a legacy which is pertinent for our present.[26] Unfortunately, the Islamic tradition of humanism was not a lasting one. The conflict between *fiqh* and *falsafa*, which was understandably also a conflict between humanism and theocentrism in Islam,[27] ended with the defeat of humanism in Islamic civilization which was – as stated – a short-lived tradition. When it waned, Islamic civilization declined too in a process of civilizational decay to enter an age of darkness. Parallel to this process of decay, humanism thrived in Europe in the historical context of the Renaissance. On these grounds, Europeans navigated Europe from Jerusalem to Athens. Lipson describes this process succinctly in this most impressive phrasing:

> The difference in the West before and after the Renaissance . . . can be summarized in one sentence: . . . the main source of Europe's inspiration shifted from Christianity to Greece, from Jerusalem to Athens. Socrates, not Jesus has been the mentor . . .[28]

Ahead of making this statement Lipson engages in describing in a poetical manner the Arab Muslim part of this story of European humanist Renaissance:

> Aristotle crept back into Europe by the side door. His return was due to the Arabs, who had become acquainted with Greek thinkers . . . Both Avicenna and Averroes were influenced by him. When the University of Paris was organized, Aristotle was introduced from Cordoba.[29]

This statement, though it sounds poetical, is, nonetheless, based on an historical evidence. It is the reality of humanism shared by Islamic and European civilizations. What Muslim rationalists achieved in the past in their borrowing from Hellenism could be done today with regard to cultural modernity. European and Islamic grammars of humanism might differ, but they share in substance the same humanism and its reason-based worldview. This presentation of the concept of humanism combined with the contention that this tradition is highly pertinent to world peace in the twenty-first century argues in favour of restoring universalist thinking against the one of cultural relativism and its confinements. Rationalist modernity of the Enlightenment is more promising than postmodernity that could be put in the service of counter-Enlightenment.

Unlike medieval times, the modern age heralds a mapping of the world by structural globalization. The values of cultural modernity and the reality of one world time that establishes beyond particularisms (e.g. Islamic *hijra*-calendar) one calendar valid for the entire humanity creates new conditions for all. In this set up, the contemporary Islamic civilization is exposed to rival options concerning the design of its future. In this situation, Europe and Islam are caught between neo-absolutism and cultural relativism. Today, peoples of Islamic civilization come to Europe via global migration and they bring rival Islamic traditions to Europe.[30] Some of them claim validity for these traditions and get support from multi-culturalists. The Islam-diaspora of about 24 million Muslim immigrants builds up a kind of an enclave within Europe. The shift of Islam from the Mediterranean border to the heart of Europe will strongly affect the future of Europe in terms of the competing scenarios: Europeanization of Islam, or Islamization of Europe.

It is not the place to discuss here the positive scenario of a Europeanization of the Islam-diaspora. This shall be done in the next chapter to support a sharing of the values of cultural modernity that stands in contrast to the neo-absolutist Islamization scenario. Islamists make full use of cultural relativism in an instrumental manner. The bridging needed in the twenty-first century requires establishing common foundations. The values that humanism delivers under conditions of the heterogeneity of civilizations is what humanity needs to avert the negative aspects of diversity.

Which Islam in our world time? Islamic humanism, or shari'a-Islam?

It is absolutely correct to criticize the preconception of 'monolithic Islam', but such an effort would be useless, if one shies away from specifying what are the many divergent Islams and what they, nonetheless, have – despite diversity – in common. If this were missing then flawed thinking would be the result. The salience of globalization relates to the creation of one world time valid for all civilizations and their cultural particularisms. Even though every civilization - also Islam – has its own calendar (e.g. the *hijra*-calendar) as an indication of one's own civilizational time, this world time links all peoples to one another in a context of global com-munication. This is not only bridging since inter- and intra-civilizational conflicts are also generated. Nevertheless, there are Europeans and Muslims who, in a similar manner, share distorted views about these conflicts. In the past 'jihad and crusade', and at present a 'war of ideas' between humanism and shari'a are to be viewed as unfavourable to bridging. The related construction of collective memories leads to a perceptual 'war of civilizations'. Some want to counter the misperception of a 'clash' by going to the other extreme of viewing Muslim–European relations in an uninformed rhetoric of 'convergence': it is a venture that ignores the basic historical facts.

For illustrating this distorted thinking I refer in an anecdotal manner to the following experience made on the occasion of presenting the Italian edition of my book on *Euro-Islam* in Rome 2005 (see note 30). I was honoured to be part of a book presentation alongside two prominent speakers. These were the then acting German and the Italian Ministers of Interior Affairs. At that event, the German politician Otto Schily made a benign statement that, next day, created the major media headlines. Schily said: 'We must rewrite our history and add Islam to the sources of European culture.' The then minister talked in a general manner and did not specify 'which Islam?' he meant. This is the question asked in the heading of this section that most policy makers prefer to ignore. President Obama is no exception: in 2009 in Ankara and Cairo he spoke in general of Islam and shied away from specifying to 'which' Islam he aims to bridge.

In the course of the Rome debate I did all I could to intervene, to ask the question asked in the heading. Even though I was, as the author in that book-launch, the major speaker, I was denied the possibility to specify. The correction of the misconception expressed by the German Minister of Interior Affairs is essential. Westerners need to learn that there is no one Islam. It follows that Islam has many traditions; one of them is the *falsafa*, the tradition of humanism. Again, there exists no Islam in general. The other tradition is shari'a-Islam of the *fiqh*-orthodoxy which Kelsay identifies as shari'a reasoning. Only *falsafa* rationalism inspired Europe at the eve of Renaissance; it was Islamic humanism and not the shari'a reasoning.[31] In order to rectify this version of distorted history I tried at the ensuing dinner in Rome to humbly pass to the minister my story of distinction, but he – despite all respect – seemed not to be receptive or interested in knowing more about the issue. This politician insisted on his ignorance and played the specification down by blatantly stating: 'This is an academic and a professorial matter, not a political concern.' I lost composure and shouted out my dismay: 'No, it is not, it is a civilizational issue that touches on the very identity of Europe as based on humanism.' This chapter is a part of an academic study that keeps in mind Ernst Haas' notion 'Knowledge is power'.[32] This insight is not only restricted to academicians. Humanism is a case in point and it is sad to see politicians dismiss this knowledge 'as an academic concern'. They operate then on the grounds of unspecified, at times even false, knowledge on Islam. This is most consequential.

Knowledge about the world time in the politics of the twenty-first century as a time of geopolitics of civilizations is the point of departure. Europeans and Muslims alike must specify and also make clear what they are talking about when they indiscriminately refer to the impact of Islam on Europe. Today, Islamists use the argument of an Islamic impact on Europe for promoting their own agenda of an Islamization of Europe within the framework of their shari'atization of Islam. I always read this agenda when I encounter the project of Islam in Europe in terms of 'Islamic mission', as pronounced for instance by Tariq Ramadan in the title of his presentation at a conference in Sweden back in 2006. The Islamist project introduced here is not compatible with the civilizational idea of Europe, nor is it in any way an effort at bridging between two competing civilizations. In contrast to Islamism, a revival of the grammar of Islamic humanism could contribute to a true Europeanization of Islam. No doubt, Islamic humanism rests on the tradition of a Hellenization of medieval Islam. To revive this tradition is a different agenda from the one of the Islamist project of an 'Islamic mission for Europe'.

Greek humanism was embraced by Muslim *falsafa*-rationalists and for this reason they were in conflict with shari'a Islam. This conflict in medieval Islam between humanism and the *fiqh*-orthodoxy maintains its pertinence throughout history up to our present. Today, the conflict assumes the shape of one between reform- and shari'a-Islam at home, and one between Euro-Islam and Ghetto-Islam in the European diaspora.

Humanism is undermined by the civilizational fault-lines of politicized religion. The foremost thinker of political Islam (Islamism), Sayyid Qutb, greatly contributed to the establishment of such fault-lines. He did that ahead of Huntington. Qutb maintains 'it is out for Europe' and he adds that Islam is ready to take over. Qutb's prose sounds, as the following quote suggests like a declaration of a civilizational war on Europe, not like a bridge, as once Islamic humanism was:

> Today, humanity is at the brink ... Western Europe lost its values and democracy is in a state of bankruptcy ... The leadership of the world by the West is about to vanish ... Under these conditions only Islam is in possession of the values needed ... It is the turn of Islam to take over.[33]

The Islamist entrenchments established by Qutb are continued today by his heir, the Muslim Brother Yusuf al-Qaradawi, dubbed 'the global Mufti', because he speaks out his *fetwas* almost weekly in the incitement television al-Jazeera. The latter is celebrated by some as the alternative to the official Arab television stations of propaganda. The difference between both is, however, not the 'propaganda', but rather its direction and content. Al-Qaradawi revives the shari'a based anti-humanist tradition in Islam against what he labels as the '*hulul al-mustawradah*' ('imported solutions').[34] The usurpation of Islam in a shari'a-based 'Islamic solution' presented by Qaradawi rejects democracy with the argument that it is alien to Muslims due to its Greek–humanist sources and thus not acceptable to Islam. The global Mufti al-Qaradawi ignores, or even erases in his war of ideas a three centuries' old tradition of Islamic humanism based on the Hellenization of Islam being the precious classical heritage of Islam.[35] Muslims of today are challenged to present an alternative and to revive the classical Islamic heritage of humanism. In this context the unspecified notion of an Islamic revival needs again and again to be combined with the repeated question: 'Which Islam is to be revived?'

Do postcolonial studies provide an answer to this question? There is a British Muslim named Z. Sardar who pursues postcolonial studies in a mindset of enmity to the idea of Europe and views Cartesianism for instance as 'epistemological imperialism'.[36] One is inclined to be more accurate and to identify this approach in the light of its attitude as 'anti-European studies' paradoxically taught at British universities. In contrast to the postcolonial dismissal of Cartesianism, which is one of the pillars of European humanism quoted as 'epistemological imperialism', I question the equation of postcolonialism with the rejection of the idea of Europe itself. At issue is an attitude that seems to reflect one of the varieties of civilizational self-denial in Europe itself. Humanism bridges between Islam and Europe, in contrast to a postmodernism that creates trenches in the name of cultural relativism. Instead, one needs today commonalities to prevent the existing cultural fragmentation between the civilizations from becoming a source of conflict.

In avoidance of an entrenching misconception it is repeated that the reference to inter- and intra-civilizational conflicts has nothing to do with the rhetoric of a clash of civilizations. In contrast, the concern is here 'preventing the clash of civilizations' through bridging.[37] The talk about prevention clearly implies the acknowledgement that there is something existing that needs to be prevented. At issue is the civilizational conflict over values that could assume violent forms. This conflict is ignored by nihilists. Humanism established as a universality bridges between cultural particularities and seeks commonalities. Postmodernists fail to see that humanism has been for centuries the civilizational identity of Europe, and also that this identity is – in the model – inclusive, not ethnic. For a limited period of time this humanism existed in Islam as well. The valuable epoch of Hellenization lasted in Islamic history for some centuries, basically from the ninth to the twelfth centuries. By then, Islamic humanism thrived, but then waned, and along this process Islamic civilization itself declined. In contrast to that time, today there is only one world time that affects the question 'Which Islam for the world time of the twenty-first century?'

Islamic humanism is the variety of Islam that should be revived to become the link that underpins the commonality needed. Unlike humanism, shari'a creates fault-lines. A prominent contemporary Moroccan philosopher and humanist, the late Mohammed al-Jabri, called for a revival of the Islamic rationalism of Avicenna and Averroes as the humanist tradition in Islam. In this pursuit al-Jabri states with the strong phrasing of 'to be or not to be' that the future of Islamic civilization depends upon its capability to breathe life into this forgotten Islamic heritage of humanism. As al-Jabri ascertains: 'Contemporary Arab-Islamic thought . . . ill-poses the problems . . .' For him, the way out of this impasse is 'the survival of our philosophical traditions . . . it can only be Averroist'. Throughout his lifetime, al-Jabri argued, classical Islamic humanist rationalism is characterized by 'universality and historicity . . . The Averroist spirit is adoptable to our modern era, because it agrees to . . . rationalism', i.e. to humanism'.[38] This is an authentic Islamic option that competes with shari'a-Islam, not only in the world of Islam, and in the Islamic diaspora of Europe, but also in the world at large. At issue is the shari'atization-inspired vision of a remaking of world order and the alternatives to it. The traditions of humanism in Islam are consonant with rationalist modernity, the basic foundation of Enlightenment. Unlike shari'a-Islam a humanist Islam shares the values of cultural modernity that would help best to prevent a clash of civilizations.

In awareness of the Eurocentric bias of the European concept of humanism I have coined the term 'cross-cultural international morality' (see note 37) for the purpose of bridging. This concept ensures the recognition of diversity in the sources of humanism. The first and great political philosopher in Islam, al-Farabi is among the pillars of this heritage of Islamic civilization.[39] Well-informed scholars are also familiar with the high ranking Aristotle once enjoyed in Islamic tradition and they also know that al-Farabi was given the distinguishing title *al-Mu'allim al-thani* ('the second master'), ranked only second to a non-Muslim. The ranking of *al-Mu'allim al-awwal*, was reserved for Aristotle.[40] For enlightened Muslims Farabi was the foremost source for his rational political philosophy in Islam; he lived between 870–950 and he was ranked second to Aristotle. Similarly, Europeans value the Muslim philosophers Ibn Sina/Avicenna (980–1035) and Ibn Rushd/Averroes (1126–1198). Their humanism was the substance of the transmission of Greek legacy in an Islamic shape to Europe. In this context, the epistemological accomplishments of Muslim philosophers such as, for instance, Ibn Rushd's teaching about the '*Haqiqa al-muzdawaja*' ('double truth') were shared by the European Renaissance. This Ibn Rushdian insight differentiates between philosophical, i.e. reason-based knowledge and religious beliefs based on divine revelation. This idea paved the way for establishing modern rationalism, also in Europe on which humanism rests.

The inference to be drawn from this reference to the history of ideas is combined with another one: it is to the already introduced notion of world time. Islam and the West are – in this world time – related to one another. Earlier, they shared a human-centred view of the world that replaced theocentrism by a humanism. If one honestly wants to avert a clash in a world time of a geopolitics of civilizations resulting from 'Islam's geo-civil war' (see note 16), then one needs to revive the Islamic grammar of humanism. Contemporary binary Islamism engages instead in an invented tradition of jihad and shari'a that is not consonant to humanism, and also contributes to a polarization, not to bridging.

This section concludes in stating that there is one world time, but no one Islam. Shari'a-Islam is only one tradition that stands in contrast to the other tradition of *falsafa*-rationalism with its humanist implications. For shaping the relationship between Europe and Islam under conditions of world time one needs to revive the positive elements of humanism in order to present it as an alternative to a shari'atized Islam. The latter is entering Europe with the tacit support of postmodern multiculturalism in the name of diversity. In a world time of the simultaneity of the unsimultaneous, Islamist neo-absolutists and European cultural relativists are strange bedfellows, who nonetheless share a dismissal of the universality of the tradition of humanism.

The revival of humanism is the true Islamic revival

The prudence of the intercivilizational humanist discourse lies in its shared universality by rationalisms of all civilizations. There existed an Islamic humanism, as a part of the legacy or a heritage of classical Islam that is today almost absent in the contemporary world of Islam. The reader is asked to recall the cited preeminent historian of civilizations, Leslie Lipson, in particular his cited reference to the intellectual Islamic impact on the emerging West at the eve of the Renaissance. This reference supports the argument of cultural borrowing between the civilizations of Europe and Islam. The late Islamologist Maxime Rodinson addresses the attraction of Muslim Cordoba and Toledo to the West in terms of '*La fascination de l'Islam*'.[41] It is this very spirit of Cordoba that inspired the Holocaust survivor and the preeminent British publisher Lord George Weidenfeld to invite major opinion leaders to that city to engage in a trialogue there. It was launched in February 1998 and continued until 2000. Due to the second Islamist intifada, this Europe-based trialogue declined. However, it has been pursued in the new century by a US institution, The Holocaust Memorial Council in Washington DC. In October 2007, Jews, Christians and Muslims met at the Holocaust Museum and pledged in the name of a cross-religious humanism that the crimes committed should never ever occur again. 'Encountering the stranger' is the name given to this new endeavour committed to the substance of humanism viewed as the core value in a pluralism of cultures and religions. This trialogue can be assessed as an effort to revive the tradition of humanism on cross-religious grounds. If this tradition is cross-culturally accepted, then the 'stranger' is no longer perceived as a threat. This is also a dimension of a cross-cultural tradition of humanism shared by civilizationally divergent communities.

In Cordoba and Washington I argued for dealing with conflict between the civilizations in a shared discourse. This is a requirement for the search for means of peaceful conflict resolution that has to be based on humanism.[42] In a similar understanding the contributors to President Herzog's volume on *Preventing the Clash of Civilizations* (see note 2) argued for peace. In my contribution to that volume I maintained that the revival of the tradition of Islamic humanism helps establish a reason-based dialogue in the pursuit of conflict resolution. The positive heritage of Islamic humanism is viewed here as a bridge in the search for ways for a peaceful conflict situation. I take the liberty to place this kind of thinking in the biographical background of being a person with an Arab-Muslim upbringing combined with an academic training in Germany and research activities in the United States. To live in the West as a Muslim immigrant creates a specific pattern of a *conditio humana*. The question asked is, could a Muslim in Europe accept the choice of becoming 'a citizen of the heart'?[43] The answer is yes, if cross-cultural foundations of humanism were to be accepted. Today, I see in my daily life more differences than commonalities between Western and Islamic civilization and, therefore, ask further: are these tensions of a temporary political character, or do they have some deeper cultural underpinning? In arguing for a tradition of humanism and simultaneously stating a conflict, I also have to refer to an absence of humanist tradition in today's political Islam. The plea for a humanism as a cross-cultural bridge seems to reflect simply wishful thinking. What can be done to make the commonality of humanism a strategy worth being pursued and, moreover, is it feasible?

The reference to the Islamic awareness of Aristotle paired with the high ranking attributed to his philosophy serves at present as a reminder of a positive precedent of a shared humanism. It demonstrates that Muslims of that time were open-minded, not gated or even closed-minded as they are today: with the perception of Islam under siege they like to cultivate in a sense of self-victimization. Today, sharia'tized Islam promotes a kind of a 'clash'-mentality and is not favourable to the prevention of polarization.[44] In contemporary Islamic civilization these sentiments are coupled with strenuous rejection of any cultural borrowing from the West beyond the adoptions of techno–scientific instruments of modernity.[45] It is wrong to address this instrumental adoption as the 'other modernity'. Those who do this overlook the fact that universal humanism is pivotal to modernity. It cannot be reduced to an 'instrumental reason' (Horkheimer). The already cited 'principle of subjectivity' is among the pillars of any humanism. For a positive interaction between civilizations in the post-bipolar age at the beginning of the new millennium, humanism is essential. One should, however, distinguish between realism and wishful thinking and, therefore one is compelled to ask questions about the potential of a revival of the grammar of Islamic humanism. One can safely argue that the present conditions promote the mindset of Islamism that is not favourable to this project of a universal enlightenment based on rationalist modernity.

The outlined bleak perspective for a positive intellectual encounter between Islam and Europe in the spirit of humanism – beyond instrumental dialogue – leads to the question of the meaning of a dialogue. When the peoples of the civilizations of Islam and of the West talk to one another, they have to address the pivotal question: 'How to deal with the differences?'[46] Based on two-and-a-half decades long experience in the dialogue business, I pinpoint several areas of 'difference' that generate tensions and underlie the present conflict. One of the basic issue areas is the democratic secular nation state versus the totalitarian divine order of *hakimmiyyat Allah*. Among the other areas, one finds individual human rights versus religious duties (*faraid*) and the place of humanism in the prevailing worldview of contemporary Muslims. The dialogue – or trialogue – not only needs to go beyond instrumental pursuits, but also beyond moralizing benign pronouncements. Instead, it has to stand in the service of peaceful conflict resolution after addressing the issues in honesty and candour. If this task can be completed, then there can be a rational dealing with the challenge of 'how to deal with the differences'. A mindset based on humanism could help cross the dividing fault-lines. In the spirit of establishing commonalities based on reason and a human-centred view of the world, the heritage of Islamic rationalism based on the Hellenization of Islam ought to be revived by Muslims themselves. This is a repetition, but the statement in point cannot be repeated enough. It is also not well received.

The focus on the values of humanism is not driven by an illusionary mindset. A combination of values and power is acknowledged. In the first domain of values, value-change is thinkable. In Islamic civilization the values related to humanism unfolded by the rational *falsafa* were not enduring. Islamic rationalists lacked the power to institutionalize their school of thought against the *fiqh*-orthodoxy. The *ulema* had power over the educational system (the *madrasas*) and therefore were in a position to prevent the spread of the opposed values of humanism. Cultural analysis teaches that new ideas and worldviews cannot be enduring if not related to a cultural institutionalization.[47] This is a power problem. In the past the *fiqh*-orthodoxy had the power to prevent this process. At present this undermining is happening again. An education in humanist democracy is hampered by the power of political Islam/Islamism that dominates the educational system, even though it is not yet in position to seize political power.[48]

Today, the alternative to Islamism is the value-system of Islamic humanism. Given the fact that values determine the civilizational worldview of peoples I argue for the values of humanism that bridge and counter the divisive political ideologies of religious fundamentalisms. These undermine any cross-cultural morality based on humanist values and on rationalism. Put in a different phrasing: unlike religionized politics, humanism is the foremost avenue to prevent a 'clash of civilizations'. Therefore, it is pertinent to understand the grammar of Islamic humanism and to place it in the context of Islamic–Western relations. Europeans need to be concerned about the incompatibility of some Islamic choices and not to be indiscriminate.

The diversity of cultures and civilizations challenges the earlier prevailing evolutionist schemes of change from tradition to modernity. The theory of modernization assumed a smooth transition from traditional and modern societies.[49] In this thinking, values were considered to be either traditional, or modern, or those of the passing societies. There was no place for the concept of a universal humanism in this discourse. Today, under conditions of the cultural fragmentation that is taking place along the processes of globalization one can state with Hedley Bull that: 'the shrinking of the globe . . . does not in itself create a unity of outlook . . . humanity is becoming simultaneously more unified and more fragmented'.[50] What can one do to bridge under these adverse conditions?

The balance statement is that the model of Westernization and modernization did not work. The spokesmen for this model were caught in an evolutionist mindset and never cared for a culture of humanism for bridging cultural tensions that uneven developmental standards generate. Helmuth Plessner drew attention to the fact that it was not humanism, but rather an instrumental reason that dominated the export of the European model to the non-European world. This unfavourable pattern continues to affect Islamic–European relations. The humanism of Hellas was accepted in medieval Islam in contrast to the present in which the idea of Europe is rejected. Why? The explanation is to be sought in the different settings of cultural borrowing. Culture is meaning[51] and it neither can be exported to a different environment, nor can it be reduced to tradition or modernity. Plessner wrote his book on Germany, *Die Verspäetete Nation* (*A Nation in Delay*) while living in Dutch exile to survive the Nazi barbarism. He makes the following precious statement: 'In a mindset of Europeanism (*Europaeismus*) Europe conquered the world . . . The European expansion was based on the instrumental use of science as an apparatus, not on the humanism and its ethos that Europe once unfolded.'[52]

Under these conditions anti-hegemonial Muslim attitudes are confused with an anti-humanism. This happens in contemporary Islamic civilization while its own tradition of humanism is superseded, or even suppressed in the name of purity wrongly named *asalah* ('authenticity'). The result is that the cultural modernity of

Europe is perceived negatively as a threat in an encounter dominated by collective memories of colonialism. Even after the decolonization, there are constructed collective memories about the colonial legacy that shapes Muslim perceptions and drift from the reality. To be sure, technical modernity of science and technology and a cultural modernity of values are different segments. Despite their anti-Westernism Muslims are positive about science and technology which they are willing to adopt, while they reject the second segment of cultural modernity that rests on humanism. Today's semi-modernity in Islam is characterized by an approval of an adoption of techno–scientific instruments from the West, but this is paired with vehement rejection of the related humanist values.[53] This is exactly what Plessner dismissed as a mindset of *Europaeismus* that is determined by instrumental reasons. There was never an honest will or venture aimed at a substantive Europeanization of the world.

Raymond Aron was among the very few scholars who acknowledged cultural diversity and I agree with his contention that the persistence of the cultural value systems against the standardization effects of globalization happens in a process of a 'shrinking of the globe'. This is not to an emerging 'global village'. There is no global culture in sight. Aron addressed the issue of cultural diversity in terms of 'heterogeneity of civilizations'.[54] He argued that the fact of this heterogeneity was superseded and superficially veiled earlier by the then existing international structures of bipolarity. At present economic globalization continues this job of veiling. Aron was quite sure that the veil imposed by bipolarity would not be a lasting one – and in this forecasting he was right. History sustained his prediction. The new century heralds the return of civilizations to centre stage, yet in a different shape and, of course, under radically different conditions. A revolt is at issue.[55] Huntington has been the one who brought the issue – albeit in a distorted manner – to the fore, but certainly did not invent it, as his foes contend. His distortion of the issue has been a charge to the debate on the civilizations. Let it be stated: their return is the return of history, not the end of it.[56]

Why are these issues referred to in this chapter on humanism? Is this an indication of a digression? The present debate on humanism as a *Weltanschauung* relates for sure to the fact that every civilization has its own worldview. Civilizational *Weltanschauung* is regularly based on the values of the people whose belonging to a civilization is fixed in these worldviews as well as the related values. Values are different from one another and their incompatibility generates an inter-civilizational conflict. Under these conditions, humanism can serve as a bridge in a value-conflict. This argument justifies the allusion to the matters addressed and related to the return of history as a return to the conflicting worldviews of civilizations.

In this context, humanism connects, while the politics of instrumental reason geared at Westernization disconnects.[57] A revival of Islamic rationalism would be a revival of humanism that connects in an age of intercivilizational conflict. Humanism is human-centred and recognizes only one rationality to be shared by all. In short: rational knowledge is universal and connects in an age of civilizational conflict. Today, it is phased out to view values in an evolutionist manner either as 'modern' or 'traditional', not to speak of a reduction of culture to socio-economic constraints as vulgar Marxists often do. In contrast, I argue that there exists an interplay between cultural, socio-economic and political change. Men and women are embedded in these intricate processes, while they have their culturally deter-mined perceptions. Cultural perceptions are not always mechanical reflections of an objective reality inasmuch as they themselves – though imagined – could shape existing realities and affect them as well. For this reason, the study of values in the context of a debate on humanism in the twenty-first century needs to be embedded in a pursuit of an intercivilizational dialogue. I view this dialogue as a strategy for averting the clash of civilizations. This pattern of cultural diplomacy is a soft power guided by the will to transform the war of worldviews waged among the civilizations in post-bipolar politics into a peace of ideas.[58]

Humanism – European and Islamic – revisited

Globalization and the competing options: Westernization, Europeanization and Islamization

European and Islamic humanism are historically related to one another as docu-mented in the historical records of cultural borrowing. To state this is not to overlook the fact that Western and Islamic values are quite different. These differences are exacerbated today in the cultural responses to structural globalization. One may cite the view that the twentieth century was, as Eric Hobsbawm puts it, an 'age of extremes'. This is continued to a higher degree in the twenty-first century that is an age of value-conflicts between civilizations. The plea for a revival of human-ism is proposed as a peaceful solution to the conflict.

European expansion, which took place in the pursuit of economic goals, was legitimated in an ideological manner by European powers with the claim to cul-turally Westernize the world. This Westernization was equated with modernization. The reader is reminded of the reference to Helmut Plessner which helps to understand that the 'Europeanism' – the term was coined by Plessner – exported to the rest of the world was not European humanism, but an instrumental reason that justifies conquest and explanation.

There is the evolutionist assumption that in a process of modernization non-Western parts of the world would also adopt Western values in the course of a transition from tradition to modernity. This has been belied by a new revolt against the West. This revolt is not restricted to contesting hegemony, since it is also directed against European values believed to be valid for the entire world and all of its civilizations. In this understanding, European expansion has been related to claims and processes of modernization, acculturation and Westernization. All of these three concepts were hitherto willingly or unwillingly used interchangeably in a bundle. For this reason non-Western peoples – aside of diplomatic courtesies – are distrustful when asked to join a dialogue with the West about common values. Often the argument is made that power asymmetry is an obstacle. Given this obstacle, it is wise to acknowledge that dialogue is not a swift and untroubled business. At any rate it is argued that cultural diplomacy is – despite all asymmetries – a feasible avenue.

In the Western debate some basic insights were blatantly missing. In the first place, as already referred to, the conceptualization of culture in terms of tradition, and modernity as well as the perception of processes of change in terms of unilinear development directed towards more progress were based on a Eurocentric misconception. The claim to universal validity of all Western assumptions has been an impediment in the way of better, i.e. accurate knowledge about non-Western civilizations. An accurate understanding is needed. As Aron put it, people belong to cultures and civilizations with their own worldviews and values. This insight underpins my idea of the simultaneity of globalization and cultural fragmentation resulting from processes of modernization on a global scale. The existence of cultural and civilizational diversity does not disappear through the shrinking of the world into an assumed global village. In fact, this process has led to an unprecedented mutual awareness and interaction among peoples of different cultures and civilizations, but it could not 'in itself create a unity of outlook and has not in fact done so' (see note 50), as Hedley Bull rightly argued. The mutual awareness on global grounds has not led to cultural standardization, but rather to the opposite: an awareness of being different. Thus, the result has been an assertive awareness of the values of one's own civilization that takes the shape of identity politics that disconnects. Instead, values and norms of humanism would bridge between East and West in an effort to resolve the intercivilizational conflict.

It is well known that leaders of the early anti-colonial revolt against the West made full use of Western concepts (e.g. popular sovereignty and the nation state) to legitimize the drive to national independence and nation-building. In contrast, the present 'revolt against the West' is directed – as already pointed out – against Western values as such and above all against their claim to universality. This rejection includes the values of humanism. In view of a war of ideas I earlier coined the formula *Krieg der zivilisationen* ('war of civilizations') (note 58) in a book on this subject matter published 1995. Since 9/11 and since the assaults of 2004–07 in Europe the 'war of civilizations' assumes a dimension of violence in an irregular war. To be sure, civilizations have no armies and cannot revolve around a core state to compete for the position of a world power, as Huntington contends. My research interest revolves around worldviews and values with the argument of value-conflicts. Therefore my search for grounds for value-sharing is a concept about bridging. The tough question is how to do this? I believe the answer is to be found in humanism as a grammar comprehensible for all mankind. There is a variety of this humanism in Islamic history that Muslims could revive if they wanted to end 'Islam's geo-civil war' that is burdening the international society and alienating Muslims from the rest of humanity.[59] This war creates cultural entrenchments. When violence is involved in an irregular war often confused with terrorism then Islam and the West could establish a joint-venture of security. This is another dimension of dialogue.

The findings and some future prospects

In a step further to analyse the conflict and to inquire into the potential of bridging, this chapter is at pains to revive a tradition of common grammar shared by European and Islamic humanism. My earlier strongly misconceived coinage of 'war of civilizations' does not refer to a war fought by armies, but rather to one waged as a war of ideas and worldviews as shown in the previous chapter. Given that there can be no single and discrete civilizational universalism imposed on all, a humanism with different grammars could be the grounds for a consensus, but is not a holistic concept for the entire humanity. Humanism is instead a concept of international morality based on cross-cultural and also cross-civilizational grounds. It serves as a platform for a consensus over basic values. To be sure, this international morality is not the self-gratifying 'world ethos' belief coined by the catholic theologian Hans Küng. In my view, there exists in reality no such thing: the related thoughts of Hans Küng are based on Eurocentric wishful thinking. To be sure, a Eurocentric Christian theology presented as 'world ethos' is unacceptable. In reality, each civilization has its own ethos underpinned by a respective worldview. Since there exists no 'world civilization' there can be no 'world ethos'. Instead, the grammars of humanism can be shared, because they are rational, not religious, and also based on assumptions acceptable to peoples of different religions.

The need for humanism under conditions of a simultaneity of globalization and cultural fragmentation analysed in Chapter 2 requires some degree of universalization of values. This is not the trap of acculturation and of a Westernization of the world within the framework of Western universalism. The interaction has to take place in a two-way street. The contemporary other extreme of counteracculturation and de-Westernization compels me to seek other solutions. Hereby, there are two points to underline:

First, despite existing distinctiveness, the awakening of pre-modern cultures, believed to be 'parochial', and of the traditional civilizations – such as Islam, Hinduism, or Confucianism – is embedded in the very same global context. It is a context for which the established terms 'world time' and the 'global village' have been coined. However, globalization is basically different from universalization. The distinction between the two notions is not merely an academic concern of differentiation. It is much more than that. The bottom line is that the unfolding of global structures does not lead to the acceptance of universal values; it also does not correlate with an alleged cultural standardization, as shown in Chapter 2 on globalization and fragmentation.

Second, structures originated in Western civilization have been globalizing. In a time span of five centuries the European expansion established a framework for a globalization. At the same time the values of European civilization have not been successfully universalized simultaneously. Unfortunately, this distinction between globalization and universalization seems not to be well understood in the literature of the field. Therefore, it seems that the simultaneity of structural globalization and cultural fragmentation, i.e. the co-existence of global structures and particularisms in a dissent over values has to be recognized.

While keeping in mind the conditions of a simultaneity of unifying structures and separating outlooks addressed as a fragmentation, I see a decline in the consensus. This affects a shared humanism. The existing heterogeneity of civilizations compels me to engage in a mediation between these often conflicting entities. It is imperative to avert a clash for the sake of a world peace based on humanism.

The plea for a shared humanism is based on the search for common values and for the establishment of a value-consensus in terms of international morality. This process is addressed as a shift from universalism to an effort of cross-cultural underpinning for bridging between competing and rival and, thus, potentially clashing civilizations. My work on individual human rights and democracy in Islamic civilization in the pursuit of a cross-cultural bridging presents an alternative to a sweeping Western universalism.[60] An Islamic grammar of humanism would underpin this indigenization of individual human rights that have emanated from European humanism.

Shared humanism contributes to reducing the ever-increasing cultural fragmentation in the international society. At this juncture it seems useful to me to introduce a basic differentiation used in the study of international relations for understanding the structural unity and paralleling disunity or fragmentation in the realm of values. The systemic linking of the different parts of the world to one another in the context of the globalization of the European institution of the nation state has resulted in the emergence of the *international system of the states*. This system is, however, no more than a systemic interaction between the different units creating its whole. Unlike this international system of formal interaction, an international society, i.e. a society of states, 'exists when a group of states, conscious of certain common interests and common values . . . conceive of themselves to be bound by a common set of rules in their relations with one another'.[61] No prudent observer would deny the existence of universal rules in the international system even though the relations between the states forming this system are more or less based on formal interaction. It follows that our world is a mixture of an interactive system and a norms- and values-centred society, even though both cannot be equated with one another.

The findings of the present analysis can be summarized in stating that there are different grammars of humanism based on diversity. Nonetheless, these resemble one another in many ways to the extent that it is justified to speak of universality underpinned by a cross-cultural international morality. One can connect the international system of states to an international society that shares common values in a changing world of tensions and conflicts. This bridging between the system and society on the grounds of humanism could bring people of different civilizations closer to one another. The imperative of honouring the natural and historically developed subdivision of humanity into local cultures and regional civilizations leads in the realities of international relations to viewing groups of states as civilizational state communities. In so doing, I do not follow Samuel Huntington who replaces the earlier existing state blocs of the bipolar world by the envisaged new state blocs of civilizations. It is extremely difficult to identify one or more core states in each civilization eligible to function as a leading power. In Islamic civilization this is quite impossible. Civilizations are too diverse in their inner relations and thus may not allow such a structure as that envisaged by Huntington. However, in their external relations civilizations emphasize their common values.

In post-bipolar world politics there are value-conflicts between civilizationally divergent communities not to be identified by the dichotomy of modernity versus tradition. These value-conflicts affect post-bipolar international relations and can be resolved in an intercultural and intercivilizational dialogue. This can also be pursued as a cultural diplomacy.

This chapter proposes to view humanism as an international morality based on cross-cultural, i.e. mutual, not imposed universalistic grounds. In the pursuit of democracy and human rights this cross-cultural approach seems to be more promising than any imposed universalism.[62] To be sure, humanism is universal, even though it is expressed in a variety of cultural grammars. At first, the two statements are not in contradiction. And second, the diversity of cultural grammars of humanism is not to be confused with the particularisms. The 'heterogeneity of civilizations' is a reality that should not be developing to a clash. If the idea of a core of values based on humanism that leads to a consensus can be accepted by humanity, then heterogeneity and consensus could be put in line with one another.

For pondering on the prospects for the future, the reference to some international projects seems to be useful. The approach of cross-cultural human rights is based on humanism. The idea of human rights is established on a cross-cultural, instead of a universalistic underpinning. It is also related to the concept of humanism that is related to another one: the concept of an international cross-cultural morality. This reasoning was developed at the Wilson Centre in Washington DC, at the Norwegian Institute for Human Rights in Oslo and it is also related to a Dutch project in Amsterdam on the grammar of humanism.[63] This concept provides a cultural underpinning for democracy and human rights in the world of Islam. This is a strategy for bridging between the civilizations that concedes that an ethical potential of humanism is available for an agreement on basic values to be shared.

The assumption of cross-cultural bridging acknowledges the differences between local cultures and regional civilizations. Political correctness and cultural nihilism, in contrast, deny these realities. In fact, these political correctness-driven attitudes of blinding oneself vis-à-vis cultural differences are a highly risky and self-defeating way of dealing with realities in which cultures and civilizations are moving to centre stage. I have already referred to the very important Islamic–Western dialogue run in Karachi (see note 46) where the basic formula for the dialogue was, 'How to deal with the differences?'. In order to further pursue this goal, one needs first to be in a position to acknowledge these differences. To find ways to deal with them is the substance of the dialogue being an instrument to avert a clash of civilizations. It follows that any denial of differences not only results subsequently in damaging the potential for a fruitful dialogue, but also undermines efforts at establishing a cross-cultural humanism in a pursuit of bridging.

Conclusions

The analysis of an intercivilizational conflict is done on the grounds of an awareness of inner-civilizational distinctions. In this understanding there are different Islams. One of them is contemporary shari'atized Islam that generates cultural tensions. These could lead to a political conflict that unfolds under conditions of globalization. The result is the great challenge that one faces today; it compels me to rethink old wisdoms and to develop new insights. The idea of an Islamic grammar of humanism points at another positive 'Islam'. This grammar is supposed to exist also in a variety of civilizations. For instance, Islam and Europe not only could provide some convincing answers for the pending tough questions, but also help bridging to one another with the help of humanism. Values are related to cultures and civilizations and they differ from one another. To argue for a cultural relativism would be the wrong conclusion to draw from this fact. The universal value-system of humanism could serve as a connect in this adverse situation. It is possible to establish universality on cross-cultural grounds. This is the better conclusion.

Radical and rapid change is a basic feature of globalization, but it is a fact that change of values does not follow from the economic change launched by intensifying structural globalization. The centrality of Europe supported by the fact that it is the historical location of modern globalization has led to a Eurocentrism. With the current demise of Europe the prediction of a shift of the centre gains strength as some non-Western countries (e.g. China and India) are moving to the fore. One has also to deal with the American belief in a standardized 'McWorld' culture. In the minds of some Americans there is a world which is 'McDonaldizing', i.e. culturally standardizing along US lines. This is not only clearly based on a misperception; it also implies that the American culture of consumption holds in itself a meaning. A popular culture of items (e.g. music and clothing) does not provide meaning. Therefore, it is silly to view the revolt against the West as a 'Jihad versus McWorld'.[64] There is a need to overcome simplistic thinking and to acknowledge the reality Aron addressed in 1962 as 'heterogeneity of civilizations' to seek on these grounds an international cross-cultural morality based on values. In fact, this is the substance of humanism in our time. A 'McCulture' could not impede this heterogeneity developing into a source of conflict. Again, no 'McCulture' relates to cultural value-systems based on meaning. Instead, one needs grammars of humanism. Islam connects to the European variety of humanism and even shares with it a common history of an adoption of Hellenism. This is something other than the assumed 'McCulture' and the effects attributed to it.

In short, globalization is ill-conceived by some as a 'McDonaldization'. Those who do this overlook the fact that a fragmentation in values and a conflict result from this process. The evolving awareness of the self as civilization (identity politics) ends up with the drive towards peoples of different cultures and civilizations constructing the self in the process of identity politics and re-imagining not only a community, but also one's own history is an invention of tradition. Islamism is a case in point. In the search for a solution I argue for an intercultural and intercivilizational dialogue over values based on a grammar of humanism. This option is more promising as an avenue for a proper coping with pending challenges. The political correctness-driven silencing of this debate by postmodernist Europeans is a prohibition of free speech about differences at a time when fundamentalists are developing these differences into trenches among humanity. Both parties are inflicting damage on the culture of humanism that has the right to claim universality.

In a world-political situation of competing and rival civilizations the reference to the earlier positive encounters between Europe and Islam, as based on humanism, would be a promising venture that needs to be coupled with a policy dimension. To point out a 'common heritage' of both civilizations is to provide a good starter for a dialogue that should not be fearful of addressing points of difference as sources of tensions. These have to be acknowledged. However, difference should not be essentialized. In addition, some universal core values stand above cultural differences. For instance, in my dealing with the competition between two visions: a Europeanizing of Islam or the Islamization of Europe,[65] I coined at Cornell University the formulation, 'democracy vs difference'. Here I add a new formulation: universal humanism vs cultural difference of particularisms.

Put in a nutshell, humanism could accommodate diversity, but if 'difference' contradicts the related cross-cultural universal values, then humanism needs to have the right to veto any cultural difference. In Islamic tradition there existed a heritage of humanism that was suffocated and buried by the Islamic *fiqh*-orthodoxy.[66] At present, the ideology of cultural relativism is a self-defeating venture that cannot combat the unfolding Islamist neo-absolutism. The prevailing Islamist claim to revive the glory of Islamic jihad conquests creates tensions and conflict. In contrast to this Islamist drive, the plea included in this chapter for a revival of the grammar of Islamic humanism for the twenty-first century in the present post-bipolar age is the best way to deal peacefully with the intercivilizational conflict. Thus, the answer to the question asked in the heading of this chapter: 'Which Islam?' is: the Islam of humanism and rationalism. There is no one Islam, but a great diversity within Islam that includes a variety of Islamic options not compatible with one another. Those scholars, opinion leaders and policy makers in the West who announce bridging need to acknowledge which Islam and which options they are ready to embrace: Islam of humanism or Islamism.

5

EURO-ISLAM AS A VISION FOR BRIDGING

A liberal and secular Islam for the Islamic diaspora in Europe

In the twenty-first century, intercivilizational conflict takes place on different levels. In the preceding chapter it was argued that the level of the world order is the core issue, given the Islamist bid for a re-making of the world. There are, however, two further levels to be accounted for: one within Islamic civilization itself (e.g. the conflict in Turkey between Islamism and secularism[1]), the other in the West itself, in particular Europe. Islamic migration to Europe is not recent, however, though this phenomenon has intensified significantly since the second half of the twentieth century. The rocketing statistical figures support this statement. Today, more than 23 million Muslims live in Western Europe next to about 12 million Muslim Europeans in the Balkans. True, the relationship between the Muslim southern and eastern Mediterranean and Europe north of it is as old as Islam and Europe as civilizational entities. In the light of Islamic migration to Europe and in contrast to the past, one is compelled today to speak of Islam *in* Europe, not only of Islam *and* Europe.[2] Therefore, currently, intercivilizational conflict is placed in Europe itself. In the context of Islamic migration to Europe one finds in the academic literature a benign, but naive assessment that contends that Europe is the place where Islam and the European culture of democracy meet.[3] Those well-informed scholars who are not experts on Islam, but are able to acknowledge a civilizational value-conflict know well how wrong this assessment is. Of course, the Islam diaspora in Europe could become an engine of democracy, if one works on this, but this compatibility does not happen by itself, it does not come from the blue. The 'givens' do not support the cited assessment.

Among the insightful authors who observe the intrusion of Islamism into Europe is Francis Fukuyama. He knows well how 'dysfunctional' the contemporary world of Islam is – being in a European international environment – and he contends,

> however that the more serious long-term challenge facing liberal democracies today concerns the integration of immigrant minorities – particularly those from Muslim countries – as citizens of pluralistic democracies.[4]

As one of these immigrants I know well that Europe not only has failed to do so, but worse, continues to be reluctant to acknowledge not only this failure, but the problem itself. The venture of a Europeanization of Islam – as a venture of bridging – is not in sight. In general there is a marginalization of Muslims in Europe that generates resentment among those immigrants and even contributes to radicalization. I am one of them and I do not hate Europe and like the idea of Europe as an ideal, but I do not see that European ideals are reflected in realities. Therefore, I claim what the European dream promises, but not delivers. There are Muslims, primarily the Islamists, who come to Europe not only to enjoy democratic freedoms and civil rights fleeing persecution in the world of Islam, but also to build up Islamist logistics in the West. The Movement of Muslim Brotherhood is a prominent case.[5] Knowing this, Fukuyama acknowledges that 'Europe has become and will continue to be a critical breeding ground and battlefront in the struggle between radical Islamism and liberal democracy.'[6] This statement contradicts the cited naive assessment of Europe as 'meeting point'.

On the grounds of social data one can speak of an ongoing ethnicization of Islamic diaspora in Europe. There are two scenarios for the future of Europe. One is based on the vision of a Euro-Islam. The other is the unpromising consequences of the mentioned ethnicization: ethnicity of fear.[7] This chapter presents a general study of the civilizational conflict within Europe guided by the spirit of bridging between Islamic and Western civilization.

Introduction

World historians know well how old is the relationship between Islam and Europe – as old as both civilizations are. However, the contemporary return of Islam to Europe – taking place since the late twentieth century in the context of global migration – is a novelty which is a phenomenon of a different shape. Among other things, there is in Europe today a demographic change in the composition of the populace in favour of a growing Islamic segment on which Islamists count in their agenda for the Islamization of Europe. Therefore Islamists are not positive about an integration.

The growing size of the diaspora of Islam in the West of the European continent is a phenomenon that not only correlates to a changing composition of the European population, but also creates a challenge to the identity of Europe itself understood as a secular civilization. The new immigrants bring religion back to the secularized Europe that – in the terms of Max Weber – underwent a process of 'disenchantment of the world'.[8] Europe is not only a 'battlefront' of Islamism, it is also the battlefront of the 'return of the sacred' in a conflict emerging from new claims of political religions in the public square.[9]

It is a fact that most leaders of the Muslim diaspora do not endorse secularity as separation of religion and politics, as they have other options in mind for the future of Europe. To be sure, the challenge is not one-dimensional since Muslims who move to Europe to make it their new home are challenged too. They are exposed to the need for cultural change, and have a more intense predicament with modernity.[10] Above all, the Islamic theocentric-absolute worldview challenges the culture of pluralism and is self-challenged. Europe as 'the old world', is no longer exclusively inhibited by ethnic Europeans. However, neither the Europeans nor the incoming Muslims seem to be – by and large – ready, willing and able to allow an open debate on these burning issues. Scholars like Jytte Klausen pretend that there are no problems and believe things are going well in dealing with the outlined new reality. Her book rhetorically uses the notion of challenge, but the intercivilizational conflict is flatly denied. Now, both parties, Europeans and Muslims are pressed to make choices and to face uncomfortable options. The present chapter deals squarely with this predicament and rejects a compliance with self-censorship, be it in the name of political correctness, be it what is called respect for Muslim sensitivity, or whatever. The matter is urgent and needs to be addressed with candour. No bridging would be possible if the conflict is ignored.

This chapter reflects my efforts as a Muslim immigrant with a European identity to establish a venture of a secular–liberal Euro-Islam. I have been involved in this endeavour since 1992 in an effort at bridging, but I find myself not only in opposition to the Islamist and Salafist agenda of the Islamization of Europe, but also in contrast to the self-defeating Europeans who deny the identity of Europe. At the end of this, the multiculturalist acceptance of an 'Islamic space' in Europe not only admits Islamist shari'a, but also a neo-absolutism that fuels the inter-civilizational conflict. This is not a European Islam, rather an Islamic 'counter culture' within Europe as critics note.[11]

In the outlined opposition to the absolutist Islamism and to the relativist multiculturalism the venture of a Euro-Islam subscribes to pluralism and views Muslims living in Europe no longer as aliens living in Europe as *dar al-shahada*, a new term coined by Tariq Ramadan. It is synonymous to *dar al-Islam* ('House of Islam') which is not Europe.

The benign jargon of viewing Muslims in terms of 'people of migratory backgrounds' features only superficially a better sentiment than the one of those Europeans who despise Muslims as intruders and cultivate clichés about them. In both cases Muslims are not viewed as citizens and are cornered, even marginalized. In all honesty and seriousness I have to admit that Muslims themselves mostly neither feel at home in Europe nor can identify with European values. They prefer to withdraw and ethnicize the self. In a compensation for the alienation of their diaspora Muslims establish their own diasporic ghettos in big European cities and legitimize this through identity politics that prevent Muslims from becoming European 'citizens of the heart' (see note 11). This behaviour becomes a political problem, and a great challenge to Europe when the emerging 'enclaves' are seen and used by active Islamists as an extension of *dar al-Islam* ('house of Islam') in Europe itself. It is proven that al-Qaeda has been recruiting its jihadists from these 'enclaves'. One can speak of these enclaves today as 'Turkey in Germany' or 'Algeria in France',[12] instead of addressing the involved immigrants as Turk-Germans or Franco-Algerians. The enclaves of this Islam diaspora become as parallel societies slowly a place for religionized politics that reminds one of the colonial style *amsar*-settlements in the classical Islamic *hijra*-migration for the spread of Islam.[13] These *amsar* were an indication of Islamic settler imperialism based on religion. Today, these ghettos, or enclaves are functioning as parallel societies in the West, but not of its civilization. In short, both parties, Europeans and Muslim immigrants, share responsibility for the present malaise.

The author of this book is a Muslim immigrant. Therefore there is no reason to shy away from a reference to one's own life as a part of the story in point.[14] I came to Europe from Middle Eastern Damascus in 1962 at the age of eighteen and I have retired in conjunction with the completion of this study in Fall 2009. In this time span of almost five decades I never succeeded – beyond lip-service paid to me – to be accepted in reality as a European citizen. I also have never had equality of opportunity in my academic career. I never had the same opportunities that an ethnic German normally enjoys, despite all of my professional accomplishments. Next to my achievements I embraced European civic values and even the civilizational idea of Europe. The production of twenty-eight scholarly books written and published in German and translated into sixteen languages never helped to get the pay-off an ethnic German is entitled to get. I was excluded from upward mobility in the German academe. In defiance, I do not shy away from stating that I have enriched German literature and culture by my writings and work.

These autobiographical asides can serve as grounds for generalization to refer to the discriminatory distinction between an immigrant who succeeded to be a legal European by passport – *Syrer mit deutschen pass* ('Syrian who holds a German passport') – and an ethnic European. Therefore I not only accuse Islamists of self-ethnicization, but also blame European liberals for the malaise of 23 million Muslims living in 2009 as aliens in the EU. In my life I experienced Europe as an exclusionary space and not as the place 'Where Islam and democracy meet' (see note 3). This cornering enforces the cultural drive of Muslim immigrants to act in a very self-assertive manner. This happens to the extent of ethnicizing the Islamic diaspora community. At the end of the day Islamists and European liberals legitimate the existence of the Islam diaspora and Europe as two different worlds. This is the European 'Migration story'.[15] It follows that the success story of integration told by the Danish professor Jytte Klausen who lives and teaches in the US is baseless; it is belied by the facts on the ground in Europe.[16]

In contrast to the wrong findings in the unpromising research of J. Klausen and other similar-minded scholars, the vision of Euro-Islam unveils the Islamist agenda of an Islamization of Europe (see note 7). To be sure, every Islamist is a Muslim, but not every Muslim is an Islamist. The most significant distinction between Islam and Islamism is not only the most important one in general, but also pertinent to the specific venture of an integration of Muslims living in the EU.[17] The failure of Europe to help migrant Muslims to become 'citizens of the heart' (see note 11) gives the identity politics of diasporic Islamism the greatest boost and enables its supporters to fish in troubled waters. Do not be mistaken: Euro-Islam is a concept related to migratory Islam in Western Europe, not for the world of Islam which has a different story and different problems. In addition: the Europeanization in point is not the old concept of Westernization.

Is the vision of Euro-Islam feasible and can there be hope for a change? I think there is hope and I borrow the language of Martin Luther King to state in my capacity as the founder of Euro-Islam that I have a dream of a European Islam. This is, however, not the dream shared with the grandson of Hasan al-Banna, Mr Tariq Ramadan. This person also uses the term I coined, namely 'Euro-Islam', without reference to its origin. Moreover, he gives the notion a different meaning as he pursues a different agenda. For sure, it is not the Europeanization of Islam;[18] Ramadan has been accused by liberal Muslims of engaging in the *Islamisierung Europas* ('Islamization of Europe'), which is viewed to be an agenda of political Islam in Europe.[19] In this introductory section the controversy with Ramadan over the concept of Euro-Islam is mentioned ahead of dealing with the issue in substance not because Tariq Ramadan is interesting, nor to unravel the politics of double-speak.[20] This is not the concern of this chapter. The intention is rather to set the record right: it is this author, who is the founder of the concept of Euro-Islam, as shall be documented, it is not Mr Ramadan, as some of his supporters contend. Clearly, he is not the source of the coinage. Do not be mistaken: the concern is not self-referential, but clearly is the issue itself. The original concept means no more and no less than a Europeanized Islam free of shari'a and of jihad. Euro-Islam is not a 'mission of the Muslims in Europe', as Tariq Ramadan himself states.[21] These different agendas are incommensurable and do not only radically separate the two persons involved, but also indicate two different visions for the future of Europe.

The core argument is this: if a European, secular Islam by reform is accepted both by Europeans and Muslims, then both parties may manage to live together in peace without any proselytization on both sides. The result would be bridging, not a 'Convergence of civilizations'.[22] This bridging would not only avert the cultural imperialism of an Islamization agenda, but also the potential for an ethno-religious cruelty that could develop into an ethnicity of fear (see note 7). The ongoing ethnicization of the Islam diaspora in Europe is becoming, as a peril, a source of violence, and possibly of a civil war in future, which might happen with the Kosovo model as a precedent.[23] Despite my fears of Islamism based on the exposure of all kinds of experienced harrassments and threats, I am not panicking, but rather outline a dangerous scenario and seek to enlighten with regard to ways to avert it. Therefore, this book is not only about the intercivilizational conflict, but also about bridging. The alert included in the prediction is a warning and also displays my anxiety about the bleak future prospects that could surely be averted. These are only avoidable if Islam in Europe were to be Europeanized to allow Muslims to become 'citizens of the heart' to identify with European democracies. This is not only a job for Muslim immigrants, but also for Europeans them-selves. If both parties want peace then they need to have the will to engage in bridging.

The first requirement in this venture is that people on both fronts need to stop 'ignoring predictions they dislike', as they do at present. I borrow this formulation from the front page headline of an article on the financial crisis published in *Financial Times* of 30 December 2008. The quotation above is supposed to be an answer to the question, 'Why is the crisis so unexpected?' Of course, the term 'crisis', as used by *Financial Times*, does not refer to Islam in Europe, but rather to the financial crisis of 2008 and to the disastrous ripple-effects it generated into 2009. I contend that there is a parallel here between the two themes: the same may happen in Europe in the foreseeable future with regard to Islam. There were many alerts beginning with Madrid, 11 March 2004, extending to the intifada of Paris, October–November 2005 and the earlier bombing in London in the same year. None of these alerts was received well. Instead of acknowledging an intercivilizational conflict, the alerts were overlooked and predictions ignored. European politicians and opinion leaders continued to engage in rhetoric of mutual understanding, qualifying tensions as misunderstandings. For instance, the Spanish government reversed the dreadful rhetorics of 'clash of civilizations' into the benign, but quite concealing and equally naive formula of 'alliance of civilizations'. Some scholars reverse the formulation 'clash' into a 'convergence of civilizations' (see note 22). In free France, not only the government, but also all French media and opinion leaders prefer to deny (in a spirit of self-delusion) the fact that the turmoils of 2005 have anything to do with Islam. The use of the term 'intifada' and the jihad slogan *Allahu Akbar* shouted by the perpetrator while torching thousands of cars, are either fully ignored, or simply played down.

The situation in the US is not much better. There are pundits who claim to be knowledgeable about Islam and Europe who join the prevailing self-delusions, using headings like 'Integrating Islam'.[24] These pundits reduce an existing problem to a minor one of social marginalization, again to deny the existing intercivilizational value-related conflict. Other pundits of this mindset declare Europe as the place 'where Islam and democracy meet' a misnomer quoted at the outset of this chapter. I recommend putting aside this kind of literature so that the issues can be addressed. It would be better to focus squarely on the reality. Those readers who are willing to listen and want to be properly informed about the real issues are advised to ignore such studies. To repeat the reference to *Financial Times*, Europeans need to be ready to be exposed to 'predictions they dislike'. The sentiment that the predicted fearful scenario could be halted can only thrive if a sea change is allowed. Unfortunately it is not in sight. Nonetheless and despite all odds, the present book and, specifically, this chapter, argues for a bridging knowing well that this venture requires such a sea change. To facilitate bridging in the existing intercivilizational conflict a combination of a sober analysis and a promising vision is needed.

The civilizational value-conflict

Between Islamization and Europeanization

Let us start with the analysis of the conflict and discuss two scenarios for the future of Europe (Europeanizing Islam, or the Islamization of Europe, see note 18) that emerge from the existing intercivilizational value conflict. The vision of a Euro-Islam aims at bridging and it shall follow the analysis. The notion of a Europeanized Islam is the starter. In this debate the civilizational identity of Europe is acknowledged; it is not an Islamic one. In contrast to Tariq Ramadan I state that Islam was never a source of European identity[25] and I dismiss as a non-starter 'the Muslim mission in Europe' pronounced by Ramadan to create a space for Islam in Europe of its own, that is on the grounds of non-European values.

The identification of Europe as *dar al-shahada* by Ramadan runs against the European civilizational identity, which is not Islamic. Clearly, the cited notion implies a religious imperialism, because the new term is only another one for *dar al-Islam,* which means the territoriality of Islam.[26] To date, Europe is not a part of this territoriality, and I hope – as a European Muslim – that Europe will never be mapped in *dar al-Islam,* because this would be clearly an imperialism. Unlike Ramadan who claims to be modern, Salafist Muslims continue to identify Europe as *dar al-harb* (' house of war'). To substitute this term with *dar al-shahada* does not indicate a shift of mindset towards more tolerance, as some naïve Europeans like to believe. The new notion indicates rather a mindset of capture and of taking over Europe in a peaceful conquest via migration. A Muslim author favourable to Tariq Ramadan summarizes his thinking in the following manner:

> Tariq Ramadan, a theorist of what he calls 'European Islam', argues there are five fundamental rights that are secured to European/Western societies:
>
> - The right to practice Islam.
> - The right to knowledge.
> - The right to found organizations.
> - The right to autonomous representation.
> - The right to appeal to law.[27]

Where these rights exist, he argues, that place should be considered an 'abode of Islam'. How European could this venture be? Obviously, the agenda outlined in this quote does not engage in making incoming Muslims Europeans at all. It is the other way around. Muslims are not supposed to become part of Europe. It occurs that the reverse is envisioned, namely that Europe should become a part of Islam, *dar al-shahada,* as Ramadan clearly states. Therefore Ralph Ghadban has described this approach as an agenda for the Islamization of Europe. One can place this future perspective for Europe in the history of Islamic expansion that lasted from the seventh to the seventeenth centuries in terms of *futuhat*-jihad wars.[28] However, the new venture happens peacefully and therefore its qualification is as 'moderate'.

I refer here to the critique of the approach of Tariq Ramadan, which is qualified by Ralph Ghadban as an agenda of '*Islamisierung Europas*' ('Islamization of Europe') (see note 19) to point out competing scenarios for the future of Europe. To be sure, Euro-Islam rests on the idea of a 'Europeanization'. Therefore it is legitimate to question Ramadan's use of the term Euro-Islam to qualify his agenda.

After all of these clarifications it is advisable to depersonalize the issue to the extent possible in order to focus on the pending issues themselves, however, not without making in short this conclusion: the civilizational value-conflict revolves around the two competing options: 'Europeanizing Islam or the Islamization of Europe' as scenarios for the future of Europe. The first option is grounded in my work, while the latter reflects a competing view.

The vision of a Euro-Islam for Europe based on a Europeanization of Islam is a perspective geared to the future of Europe. Its scope is restricted to the European Islam diaspora and is presented avowedly with a reference to my work as the original source of the concept of Euro-Islam. Some may dismiss this as self-referential. Therefore, I add that this personal story is told while asking for the reader's indulgence for resuming some autobiographical asides. As earlier mentioned, I came to Europe as a student who in his youth never considered staying in Europe as an immigrant. In my youth I belonged to the post-1967 Arab Left and engaged with Edward Said and Sadik Jalal al-Azm in thinking about a better Arab world in which I believed in the late 1960s to pursue my activities and to design my future.[29] My years of study at the University of Frankfurt under the intellectual influence of the Frankfurt School with great minds such as Theodor Adorno, Max Horkheimer, Jürgen Habermas and Iring Fetcher as my academic teachers were supposed to be limited to a venture of acquiring knowledge in my capacity as a Muslim traveller. However, the boost political Islam has received since the early 1970s in the course of a battle between Islamism and authoritarian secular neo-patriarchy diffused all of the illusion cultivated by the critical Arab-Muslim intellectuals. In this battle the Arab Left – including myself – was marginalized to the extent of becoming insignificant. Since the late 1970s (parallel to the victory of political Islam[30]) I decided to choose Europe as a permanent home. Along with that decision I started to care about Islam in Europe and to think about bridging without overlooking the conflict.

The thinking about a Europeanization of Islam received a basic impulse through experience gained in West Africa about Africanization of Islam. In the summer of 1982 I visited for the first time in my life an Islamic non-Arab cultural space. This happened in West African Senegal where I encountered a most sympathetic variety of a non-scriptural Islam with no veiled women, no shari'a and no gender apartheid.[31] There too, I watched on the side how Wahhabi orthodox Muslim Arabs were acting and employing all possible means – above all their petrodollar funds – to purify the wonderful African Islam from its most precious feature: being African. By then, I asked myself: how could Islam, which is a religion based on an Arab – not an African – culture alien to Africa, be able to strike roots there? The answer was: because Islam has been Africanized.

Ten years later, in November 1992, I was invited to join a historical process taking place in France: the abandoning of the French policy of 'assimilation' in favour of the concept of an integration limited to the acceptance of the civic values of the French Revolution and of its secular republic.[32] Of course, this is only the model in 'ethnic France'. In a short paper presented there I proposed my concept of Euro-Islam that emerged from the background outlined in West Africa. The term 'Euro-Islam' and its meaning were, in 1992, new. This is indicated in the report about the Paris meeting published in the *Frankfurter Allgemeine Zeitung* in December of that year. The publication of the Paris paper followed in 1995 in a French book that emerged from that project. These documents are the published evidence for the contention regarding the origin of the concept.[33] These references document the first public pronouncements of the vision of a Euro-Islam as a concept for the integration of Muslims in Europe based on Europeanization. What is the substance of this venture? The special issue on Islam in Europe published in *Time* magazine acknowledges the fact about the founder and the substance of the concept in this phrasing:

> Bassam Tibi . . . who coined the term Euro-Islam insists that the integration of Europe's Muslims depends on the adoption of a form of Islam that embraces political values, such as pluralism, tolerance, the separation of church and state, democratic civil society and individual human rights. The options for Muslims are unequivocal, says Tibi, there is not middle way between Euro-Islam and a ghettoization of Muslim minorities.[34]

Just one clarifying comment to this fine and accurate summary: those Muslims who demand a cultural space for Islam in Europe (e.g. Tariq Ramadan) end up in endorsing ghetto- not Euro-Islam.

While ignoring the Paris-based project as the origin of the concept, the term 'Euro-Islam' was later on used by others, not only with no acknowledgment of the source, and no reference to the story of its emergence, but also in an utterly different meaning that flatly distorts the concept. Among the people who engaged in this venture one finds not only Tariq Ramadan, but also Olivier Roy, alongside less well-known others. In view of this misconception, it was a great consolation that the University of California at Berkeley launched, in the late 1990s, a project inspired by my approach on 'Islam and the changing identity of Europe'. The findings of that project were published in the volume *Muslim Europe or Euro-Islam*. One of the chairpersons of the project who acted as an editor of the volume points out:

> Bassam Tibi attempts to rethink Muslim identity in Europe by devising a new form of Islam, one Tibi calls Euro-Islam . . . Tibi writes that the point of departure for the understanding of Islam in Europe is the recognition that Islam is . . . rich in cultural diversity . . . Tibi argues, Euro-Islam is the effort to devise a liberal form of Islam acceptable both to Muslim migrants and to European societies, thus accommodating European ideas of secularism and individual citizenship . . . Tibi points out that Euro-Islam is directed against both ghettoization and assimilation . . . Tibi advocates the democratic integration of Muslims into European society.[35]

The two quotes cited above reflect properly my understanding of Euro-Islam that caused the creation of a front against me and my work. There are a variety of critics who act as my enemies, undertaking all efforts to undermine my work, to the extent that gives the impression that there is no such thing as academic freedom of free speech in the West. In awareness of the hits taken that taint my reputation with all kind of defamations including accusing me as a believer-Muslim of Islamophobia. Despite all odds, I do not shy away from stating that the story of Euro-Islam is one of a personal journey undertaken by a Muslim between the Middle East, West Africa, Europe and the US. Today, as a professor emeritus I look back at this journey, considered to be an essential part of the concept itself, and believe it relates also to a venture that I view to be greater than the limited one of a Europeanization of Islam. It is the venture of bridging between the civilizations combined with another venture of dealing with Islam's predicament with cultural modernity. In a major book published in the year of my retirement, 2009, *Islam's Predicament with Modernity*, I present my life's work that deals with the latter venture most pertinent to the vision of a Europeanization of Islam limited to Europe.

One cannot deal with Islam in the Europe of today without engaging in some historical retrospectives and comparisons. Unlike earlier Islamic conquests this new one happens in a peaceful manner, however, without abandoning the claim of Muslim belief in a universal proselytization combined with a sentiment of supremacy (*siyadat*). Today, this happens at the home of Western Christendom where the secular civilization of the West emerged. This image of Islam of the self as superior creates a great challenge to Europe. Sadly, the aspect of terrorist jihadism that relates to 9/11 which is only a minor sideshow, has distorted every serious dealing with this subject. Therefore one should beware of distractions from the major issues. In short, the challenge is not terrorism, but rather relates to a questioning of the civilizational identity of Europe through a dream of an Islamization of the old world. The dream is based on a transnational movement of Islamism to be taken most seriously.

In looking back to history one is reminded of earlier Euro-Islamic encounters.[36] The Mediterranean was the borderline between the two civilizations. Today, Islam is situated through its diaspora within Europe. One may add to this fact another one, namely that not only ordinary Muslims come to Europe, but also persecuted Islamists who seek asylum and get it. These Islamists politicize Islam into an ideology in their dream of global Islamization. This is a hopeless dream of a return to history; as a return to the dominance of Islam (*siyadat al-Islam*).[37] In Europe Islamists seek to establish safe havens and they have been successful in this endeavour.[38] The competing scenarios of a Europeanization of Islam or an Islamization of Europe are the major topic, as placed in this context. The conflict between the two options is often blurred through the Islamist politics of doublespeak.

The present analysis of the civilizational conflict-ridden competition between Europeanizing Islam and the Islamization of Europe is, on the normative level, guided by an intention of bridging for 'preventing the clash of civilizations', in a kind of a dialogic conflict resolution.[39] Again, the presented option of a

Europeanization of Islam restricted to Europe that underlies the proposition of a concept of Euro-Islam aims at bridging in the existing intercivilizational conflict.[40] I cannot repeat often enough that Euro-Islam is based on the Europeanization of Islam and is proposed to be the alternative chosen to prevent the Islamization of Europe as envisioned by Islamism. The Islamists are not a 'crazy gang' (E. Said), but rather an organized powerful movement which is also strong in the European diaspora of Islam. Therefore, the issue has to be taken seriously and not played down.

Those who belittle Islamism as a 'radical Islam' of crazy minorities acting at the periphery of society also use ideological weapons – such as the disqualifying of an enlightening as panicking, or even worse, by defaming it as Islamophobia – undermine a serious debate. Knowing that there are Europeans who are prejudiced about Islam – and I combat this – I refrain, though, from using the term 'Islamophobia' for the simple reason that it has become a weapon in the Islamist war of ideas to undermine any criticism of Islamism. In a hearing on this issue organized by the parliamentarian council of Europe and held at the Danish parliament in September 2009 I proposed European parliamentarians replace 'Islamophobia' with the term 'bashing Islam'. To relate the statistical figures of an increasing Islam diaspora in Europe to security, if integration fails, is neither panicking nor 'Islam bashing'.

The figures are: in the year 1950 only about 800,000 Muslims lived in Western Europe, basically in France and the United Kingdom. At that time, the Islamic presence in Europe was related to the colonial legacy of these European states. At the turn of the twenty-first century, not only had the figure climbed to 15 million, but also the outreach of Islam had changed. In 2008 a figure of 20–23 million Muslims has been estimated, living throughout the European Union, including countries with *no* colonial past. This growth indicates that Muslims are now an increasing segment of the population in Europe. For a variety of reasons there are no verified statistics, that are in line with reality, but rather estimates are based on realistic numbers. Scholars who insist on the use of official statistics lag behind the facts. For example, they indicate the figure of approximately 13 million (instead of 23 million) to cover the Islam diaspora in Europe. This is simply wrong, to say the least.

One may add to these immigrant Muslims living in Western Europe the community of native European Muslims of the Balkans who amount to about 12 million people. I leave this aside, because the focus here is Western Europe. In this regard, the pertinent question is: how can these new immigrants be integrated into the European polity? The answer has to be free from wishful thinking and from prevarications. The quest for a reform Islam as a Euro-Islam is a part of the venture of an intercivilizational bridging in an existing value conflict.

Islamic parallel societies

It is a social fact that the majority of Muslim immigrants to Europe live in ghettos, named parallel societies or even 'enclaves' (John Kelsay). In an anecdotal manner

I illustrate the lack of integration of Muslim immigrants in Europe with a reference to a documentary broadcasted in January 2008 by the inter-European television station 'Arte'. It aired at length and verbatim the inflammatory speeches of incitement made by an influential Moroccan Imam acting at the major al-Quds mosque in Hamburg. It is well known that the Hamburg Cell of 9/11 frequented this mosque and used it for its meetings, as well as for the related indoctrination and recruitment. The arduous Imam engaged in alerting migrant Muslims to the exposure to Europeanization and warned his listeners of losing their faith. To avoid this he made provision that they should not interact with Europeans whom he defamed as dirty 'unbelievers' (kuffar). This happened in a major European city and it is no exception, but rather an exemplary case. In short, the message of the Imam is: Muslims who live in Europe should not live as Europeans, but keep their Islamic culture in demanding a space for Islam in Europe.

The demand that Muslims have the right to (a) found their own organizations; (b) have their own representation; and (c) practise their own law of shari'a, does not indicate a will of true integration in European societies following the televised documentary mentioned. A televised debate between pundits to discuss the notion of Euro-Islam took place. I was a participant and argued against that Imam in a plea for an integration of Muslim immigrants to European citizens. This would be the only way to keep them away from the networks of Islamism. In this context, I am reminded of the rioting of October–November 2005 in the French suburbs, labelled 'banlieues de l'Islam'. The rioters shouted jihad slogans and viewed their uprising as 'Intifada', but the opinion-leaders in Europe not only do not listen to 'predictions they dislike', but simply ignore all warnings and the related facts.

The radicalization of young people in the Muslim diaspora is not covered well by the media. The media also avoided reference to the uprising in France as an 'Intifada', as it was proclaimed by its perpetrators. This revolt of 2005 in Paris was remembered later in the fall of 2007 by Muslims shooting at the police in revenge for the deaths of two young Muslims. Most of the perpetrators were born in France and are therefore no longer immigrants, but legally European citizens. Why do they do this? What is the underlying issue? Why does this turmoil happen? And why do Europeans turn a blind eye and deaf ears to the issue in its relation to a politicized Islam? These questions compel me to engage in an effort to determine the pending issues relating to Islam and Europe.

The present study aims to enlighten about the risks related to Islamization and to inform about the potential of a conflict. At issue is a conflict determined by a mix of cultural and socio-political constraints and is thus in its nature not a religious one. True, it emerges from the social marginalization of most Muslim immigrants who constitute an ethnicized underclass in Europe, but these people articulate their contestation in religious–cultural terms. This happens neither in an instrumental manner, nor is religion used as a pretext. One has to mention that a tiny Muslim middle class is – very slowly – emerging in Europe, but it is not yet representative. Therefore the sample that is presented by J. Klausen in her earlier cited and disputed study is dismissed. If one looks at this very thin minority of a Muslim middle class within the Islam diaspora as grounds for generalization, then one ends up in wrongly generalizing the findings based on an extremely narrow sample with misleading conclusions as the result. The fact is that the statement of an 'integrated Islam' is based on a delusion, not on empirical findings. The reality is one of Islamic parallel societies. True, the social–political conflict in point is related to the majority social underclass of Muslim immigrants, but one is again reminded of the fact that the contestation is expressed in religious–Islamic terms. This gives the rebellion a religionized character, but – I reiterate – the conflict is *not* religious, but social in its character.

The lack of integration is clearly a social phenomenon, as well as the related conflicts. However, religionization of conflict does not happen on the surface. Conflicts underpinned by a religious legitimacy become intractable, because religious issues are not negotiable. The Europeanization of Islam has a secular dimension aimed at averting this already unfolding scenario of religionization. For this reason, the cultural concept of Euro-Islam has to be a secular contribution to facilitate the integration of Muslims living in Europe. The concept has also to be paired with a social policy that ends the state of marginalization. Based on my own experience as an immigrant Muslim who is among the very few who have succeeded in being sufficiently upwardly mobile to be appointed as a university professor, I state that the discrimination is not merely a matter of social class. It has also a cultural dimension that leads to an Islamic identity politics. The self-ghettoization of Muslims in parallel societies within the European cities implies an ethnicization of the diaspora as a cultural, not merely social phenomenon. The social seeds for Islamization grew on these grounds and are coupled with a combination of Islamic and Islamist challenges.

Parallel to the fact that the EU clearly lacks a policy framework for an appropriate European response, Islam is changing Europe, but most Europeans, in particular their politicians, are reluctant to deal with this issue, even to discern it. The worst is the drive to defame those who are willing to acknowledge the existence of the problem. The results are established taboos, well guarded against a free debate to the extent to cornering any person who does not comply with the defamation of 'trouble maker', or even 'right wing'.

There are people (primarily in the US) who present themselves as experts and claim to know about Islam in Europe. They not only doubt the figure of 23 million Muslims living in Europe, but also all related problems generated by the lack of integration of the Muslim diaspora in society and polity. Instead of analysing the sources of this problem, these 'pundits' speak of 'integrating Islam'. Others exaggerate to the extent of stating that Europe is the place where Islam and democracy meet. The authors of this kind of study prefer to escape all challenging realities, including the fact that Europe is the place where postmodern cultural relativism (self-denial) and neo-absolutism (Islamic assertive identity politics) meet.

For their part, Islamists accuse anyone who dares to address the issue of Islamophobia and promote the ideologically blinkered perception of Islam under siege.[41] Myself a devout Muslim and an immigrant in Europe I challenge those who speak of a successful integration, doubt this and outline the worst scenario, namely the one of an 'ethnicity of fear' (see note 7). The scenario of Euro-Islam based on a vision proposed here as a cultural variety of a Europeanized Islam not only promises a better perspective, but also a bridging in the pursuit of inner peace in Europe. It leads to a Europeanization that could make Islam compatible with the model of a religion- and ethnicity-blind secular civilizational identity of Europe. This compatibility is not pre-existing, but a mere vision that can be accomplished by Muslims through religious reforms and educational channels supported by European social policies. Europeans need to engage in this venture. As already stated, this Euro-Islam needs to be incorporated into a substantial policy for integration that is not yet in place. Even though I do not exclude the state as an actor, I argue basically that civil society should be the framework for transferring the vision of Euro-Islam into a social reality in Europe. An honest Muslim–European cooperation beyond the dishonest pronouncements of harmony and convergence and the covered action of *iham* ('deception') and prevarication is needed.

To be sure, Euro-Islam is a secular concept, but it admits religion as a source of political ethics; nevertheless it strictly separates faith from politics. This helps avoid any 'religionization' of conflict. Euro-Islam is also a policy to replace polic-ing. The message to Muslim immigrants has to be (in the long run) conciliatory and accommodating to avoid the perception and reality of exclusion in a state of 'Islam under siege' (see note 41). Therefore, the concept of Euro-Islam is both cultural and political and it promises, if accepted, to deliver a peaceful solution for the Muslim diaspora and for Europe. No doubt, this concept can only be success-fully pursued if it is combined with social patterns required as policies of integration and if it is accepted by Muslims living in Europe.

The reader is reminded of the fact that the contemporary presence of Islam as a diaspora in Western Europe compelled French decision makers to abandon the politics of assimilation in the understanding of total adjustment. The phased-out approach of assimilation is replaced by a concept of integration. It is most important to note that these two terms have quite a different meaning. Unlike assimilation, the new approach of integration is, for instance in France, restricted to the accept-ance of the civic values. Integration no longer demands a wholesale adjustment. In this context, the French were – even though extremely laicist – willing to admit some Islam, however, only on secular European grounds. In short: No to shari'a claims. As noted above, I was lucky to be included in that venture and to be given the opportunity to present in November 1992 my paper 'Les Conditions d'une Euro-Islam' at the Institut du Monde Arabe in Paris. As noted earlier, this paper was also published there a few years later (1995), and it is the origin of the concept of Euro-Islam as a vision for integration, not for the assimilation of Muslims in Europe (see notes 33 to 35). This original debate, as well as the related publications and the question of whether and how Muslim immigrants who live in their parallel societies could become Europeans as 'citizens of the heart' are issues that are fully ignored in the work of people like Tariq Ramadan and Olivier Roy.

This section on the Islamic parallel societies in Europe looks at these com-munitarian entities not only as ghettos in which people are more susceptible to

Islamism and to Wahhabi Islam, but also as 'enclaves existing in Europe, but not of its culture'.[42] This ugly social reality is often presented nicely as multiculturalism. Can this be changed, and if yes, then how? Among the necessary policies is one that halts the ongoing ethnicization of the diaspora of Islam in Europe. This process is related to the lack of integration and it even reinforces the negative related outcome. Do not be mistaken: a civic integration in civil society is not assimilation. The malaise of the suppression of a free debate contributes to these confusions. European and Muslim immigrants need a Euro-Islam to bridge between the separated communities, and a free debate on these issues.

At first, one has to state – like it or not – that Islam in Europe is a problem and not a theme for romantic fantasies or any ideology ranging from anti-globalization to class struggle. Therefore a free unbiased debate over the issues is needed. Instead, one encounters two extremes among those who deal with the pending topic of Islam and Europe. The first subscribes to a populist and unaccept-able Islamophobic view, while the other is multiculturalism in the understanding of 'anything goes'. Beyond these extremes of the Left and the Right no prudent person can turn a blind eye to the emergence of Islamic parallel societies, which are in fact social enclaves within Europe that create political, cultural, economic and social problems. The warnings repeatedly referred to in the recent past between 2004 and 2006 touch on what happened in Madrid, Amsterdam, London, repeat-edly in Paris (2005 and 2007), as well as in Copenhagen. These were not mere unrest, but rather an indication of severe conflict. In this context, well-informed politicians and experts acknowledge the need for a politics of integration that ensures inclusion to avoid worst-case scenarios.[43] In contrast, some postmodern scholars obsessed with multiculturalism deny conflict. To be sure, assimilation on the one hand and xenophobic exclusion on the other are extremes to be dismissed in favour of civic integration, in which consent to shared cultural values is also combined with an economic integration. To request that Muslim immigrants share some core values and live as citizens of civil society in peace and mutual recognition is not to be confused with assimilation. This undertaking also requires a social and an economic integration in the workplace (make no mistake: a migration into the welfare system – as commonly happens in Western Europe – is to be averted, because it creates social dynamite).

The reasoning about Euro-Islam revolves around the question: what can be done to take Muslim immigrants out of their parallel societies to make them true European 'citizens of the heart'? In response to this question and under the outlined conditions I developed the concept of 'Euro-Islam' that promises to provide the frame-work for an optimal integration. Salafist leaders of the Muslim community, as well as Islamists reject any notion of Euro-Islam, because it runs counter their agenda. There are also those racist Europeans who do not want to see any Islam in their 'old Europe'. Next to these strange bedfellows who reject integration you see those benign multiculturalists, who confuse apartheid with the right of cultural com-munities to autonomy. This creation of an Islamic space is a strategy that runs against the idea of Europe with a civil, open Islam, and it clearly upholds the existence of parallel societies.

In a debate about countering the trend towards building parallel societies of Islam in Europe, I was asked during the Dutch EU presidency in 2004 to propose a model for a reasonable integration that allows Muslim immigrants to feel like European 'citizens of the heart', in contrast to citizens by passport. The question, 'Europe. A Beautiful Idea?' was supposed to determine the guidelines for the expected reasoning. In the related presentations made in Rotterdam and later on published in Amsterdam[44] I argued for an inclusion that cannot be achieved by a multiculturalism of 'anything goes', nor by the communitarianism (space for Islam in Europe) that Tariq Ramadan wrongly names Euro-Islam. In the presence of the prime minister, Jan Balkenende, and top politicians of the European Union I made the case clear that, on the one hand, assimilation is neither feasible nor desirable while the inclusion of Muslims in Europe, on the other hand, is imperative; it requires a policy of integration that helps Muslims become 'citizens of the heart' (burgers van het hart). On the side of the Islam diaspora, their leaders are expected to be willing to engage in a reformist interpretation of Islam to abandon the obstacles of shari'a and jihad. The background of the whole story is Islam's predicament with cultural modernity.[45] One has to cope with this predicament with candour, and with vigour, as well.

The substance of the concept of 'Euro-Islam' with regard to a diaspora of Europe is the vision of a Europeanization of Islam to facilitate a secular view of the world that allows the embrace of secular democracy, individual human rights, pluralism, civil society and the enlightenment culture of tolerance. This task can only be accomplished, if religious reform and cultural change are to be admitted. On these grounds, a Euro-Islam is a reform Islam. It smoothes the way for Muslim immigrants to become Europeans. In this situation, there can be no half solutions. It is by no means polarizing to state that the prospects are: either to be European in a 'citizenship of the heart', or to be citizens by passport. If Muslims were to live their diasporic culture in their own enclaves, as Tariq Ramadan seemingly selects, then they would be deprived of becoming real members of civil society in Europe and thus never be addressed as Europeans.

To put the issue blatantly: any claim for a 'space for Islam in Europe' is an agenda for parallel societies that features a resistance to integration. The claim is also an endorsement of the existing enclaves and of the aims at establishing a territoriality of Islam within Europe. Clearly, this is an incursion, not a sign of bridging. This claim is nothing more than an effort to create a separate landscape outside of civil society. In contrast, the pursuit of Euro-Islam is understood as a venture for Europeanizing Islam to take Muslims living in Europe out of their enclaves of parallel societies to help them become European 'citizens of the heart'.

The substance of the notion of 'Euro-Islam' and the feasibility of the concept

Again, in this section some historical references are also needed for properly answering the questions to be asked about the substance of the vision and the feasibility of the concept. When Islam was born in the seventh century in an Arab environment, it was at the outset an Arab religion based on an Arab culture in that environment. In the course of the ensuing centuries Islam spread to Asia and to Africa within the framework of an Islamic expansion that can be viewed as an Islamic pattern of globalization. The cultural adjustment accomplished in this context sufficed in the past. In West Africa and South East Asia Islam was for instance incorporated into local cultures. In those non-Arab parts of the world of Islam, an adjustment, not a reform, took place. Today, in Europe more needs to be done. Why? Today, Islam is a pre-modern culture. This statement does not reflect an essentialization nor an evolutionism. Some Europeans say Islam is archaic, and it could never become European. I reject this view. Others go to the opposite extreme and speak of an Islamic modernity. Muslims for their part cultivate in their identity politics an essentialized, allegedly immutable Islam. I reject this, too. Some Imams in Europe seek to purify Islam from any European impact, and they claim at the same time a cultural–political space for Islam in Europe. These preachers do not allow an accommodation, not to speak of reform. In arguing against both parties I state, there is *no* essential Islam, and *no* essential Europe. Both can be brought together, however, only in a process of change and accomodation on the grounds of cultural modernity.

Europe is one civilizational entity, but it is characterized by diversity. Neverthe-less, the situation in Germany does not differ in a way much from the situation in the UK. My fellow Muslim in the United Kingdom, Hanif Kureishi, came to a similar conclusion based on experience worth being quoted at length:

> The mosques which I visited were dominated by arduous preachers, one follows the other in an engagement in inflammatory preaches. In an endless torrent, these Imams incite hatred against the West and the Jews . . . This does not only happen in mosques, but also in most religious institutions including the faith schools in which these ideas are disseminating.[46]

This sound report reminds me of the Hamburg Imam cited earlier. Multi-culturalists ignore these realities. For sure, this kind of inflammatory Islam alienates Muslims not only from Europeans, but also from other non-Muslim immigrants. One should keep in mind that Muslims in Europe range between 40–50 per cent of the immigrant community. There are other non-Muslim immigrants. A Wahhabi, or any shari'a-based Islam is not acceptable in Europe to all non-Muslims, as well as to liberal Muslims. Islamism and Salafism contradict the secular culture of democracy and civil society. They should not be admitted in the name of diversity.

The basic function of Euro-Islam is first, to promote the identity of citizenship; second, to allow the social and economic integration in society and its labour market; and third, the most difficult requirement of a cultural integration in Europe, to promote the cultural integration of Muslim immigrants, which is unequivocally the meaning of a Europeanized Islam. If these three requirements are fulfilled, then one can talk about real integration on the grounds of a resolution of the inter-civilizational value conflict. Unfortunately this is not the case.

For Europeanizing Islam, religious reform is needed to provide Muslim immigrants with an Islamic legitimation for the acceptance of five pillars of civil society to become Europeans. This legitimation is needed to underpin a Euro-Islam that is not yet in place. Muslim immigrants continue to be challenged to embrace:

1   Democracy: not only as the electoral procedure of voting (balloting), but rather as a political culture of civil society that entails the acceptance of the related core values.
2   The separation between religion and politics (secularity, not to be confused with the ideology of secularism): secularity does not advocate atheism and abolition of religion. One can be secular (a separate between faith and politics) and at the same time be a faithful Muslim. This is no contradiction.
3   Individual human rights in the understanding of entitlements: in Islam there are *faraid* ('duties'), no *huquq* ('rights'); one should beware of this confusion.
4   Pluralism of cultures and religions in society, that puts all religions on equal footing: Islam should not be placed above other religions, as Muslims commonly do.
5   The issue of tolerance: tolerance is referred to here not in the Islamic understanding of treating Jews/Christian monotheists as protected minorities or *dhimmi* (second class believers), but rather based on equality within the outlined requirement of pluralism. By current standards, the notion of dhimmitude in Islam is an expression of discrimination, not of tolerance, as Muslims would like to believe.

To be sure, there can be no reconciliation between Europe and Islam on the grounds of an Islam based on the three Salafist pillars of *da'wa* ('proselytization'), jihad and shari'a. If Muslims insist on these pillars and fail to embrace the five core values outlined above, and if Europe does not maintain its civilizational identity then Euro-Islam could never succeed as an option.

Islamists who view Islam as a system of government unveil themselves in this manner as religious fundamentalists aiming at a re-making of the world. Like all other varieties of the global phenomenon of religious fundamentalism the Islamic one is based on the idea of a political religion that envisions an order of state and government based on religious tenets. This ideology is an obstacle to the integration of Muslims in Europe. Therefore the notion of a 'moderate Islamism for Europe' is to be strictly dismissed. It provides a camouflage for a politics of Islamization. Islamism is the most recent variety of totalitarianism.[47]

No doubt, the way to a Euro-Islam in Europe is thorny. There are plenty of obstacles created by Muslims and Europeans alike. I place Islamism and European ethnicity uppermost of the obstacles to overcome on the way to establishing Euro-Islam. Islamism has been successful in establishing its networks in the existing Islam diaspora in Europe. In Amsterdam, after the assassination of van Gogh by the jihadist Islamist Mohammed Bouyeri, as well as in London in the light of the continued assaults since 2005, some vigilant Europeans engaged in discussing the issue of 'radicalization and society's response' at a variety of events. At some of these events I presented my concept of Euro-Islam as an exit strategy. For instance, the Dutch–Moroccan Islamist Mohammed Bouyeri, committed his crime against van Gogh in the belief he was fulfilling a religious duty (*farida*) against unbelief. This is also the thinking of those who torched cars in France 2005 and shot police officers in 2007. The letter of Bouyeri included the phrase: 'Europe! It is now your turn.' This pronouncement of a threat heralds a scenario of tension and fear to which both Muslims and Europeans are subjected. Unless Muslims and Europeans begin to de-ethnicize, the threat of an 'ethnicity of fear' (see note 7) continues to be in place. Do not forget the problem, namely that time is running out for Europe, while Europeans are falling asleep and not only ignoring the pending issue, but also all the predictions they dislike.

What is Europeanizing Islam all about?

To dissociate Islam in Europe from traditions of cultural imperialism one may make these comparisons: to Europeanize Islam in Europe resembles (in a way) the Africanizing of Islam in Africa. I visited and lived in some Islamic regions of West Africa and know what I am talking about and Europe is my chosen home. I have also lived in South East Asia and familiarized myself with the 'civil Islam' in Indonesia. It was earlier stated that Islam has been adjusted in Africa although no related reform was necessary. Clearly, African Islam is still very much different from Arab Islam. In Africa I was surprised by observations made there on these grounds and often asked: 'Is this really Islam?' adding, 'This is not the Islam I know.' The self-confident answer given to me was always: 'This is African Islam, this is our Islam.' The same happened to me later in Indonesia. The related indigenization process explains why Islam in West Africa, and Islam in South East Asia are at home. In contrast, Islam in Europe is completely alien, as revealed in the life of Muslims in Europe in enclaves of parallel societies. It would be unfair to put the blame exclusively on Europeans. Muslims have their share in the related problem. There are attitudes of a cultural othering on both sides and they reinforce one another.

The incentive received in West Africa was the beginning of my thinking about Euro-Islam. This allusion to the observations made in Africa where Islam has become part of the African culture is in my mind every time I think about Europe and Europeanizing Islam. Nevertheless, it was also made clear that Africa and South East Asia do not provide a model for Europe. Why? As earlier stated, Islam is by origin an Arab religion when it came to Africa. Islam became, in Africa, an African culture accommodated to *adat* ('traditions') of local cultures. In Indonesia and in South East Asia a similar accommodation took place. In contrast, Islam is still utterly alien in Europe, because it is not yet accommodated. It is professed that this admission is more difficult than in the South East Asian cases. If Muslim immigrants were honestly willing to become European 'citizens of the heart', and if Europeans were also honestly willing to be inclusive, not only in theory, but also in practice, then an Islam that comports with the values of cultural modernity would be feasible. But the realization of this vision of a Euro-Islam requires still some homework. It is made more difficult by the experience that Europeanizing Islam seems not to be welcomed by Muslims and Europeans. Even though multiculturalism is a dead end it is preferred by Muslims, because it allows the shari'a that amounts to legal apartheid; it would be wrong by all means to qualify multiculturalism as a cultural pluralism. It is not.

To continue this outline on Europeanizing Islam I am inclined to draw on an American way of challenging people who like to talk, but have no clear message. Under such conditions the question is often expressed, 'What are we talking about?' It is well suited to challenge the debate on Islam in Europe. This debate is, though, of extraordinary importance to the future of the continent, and is most wanting in Europe, because of the Europeans themselves who evade predictions they dislike. They do not like to hear that Islamism has established its networks in the diaspora of Islam in Europe.

Euro-Islam is a democratic–civil Islam and therefore opposed to all varieties of Islamism. This is a totalitarianism that creates a challenge to Europe and to a tolerant Islam. I state the contradictions between Islamism and open society and see great obstacles in the way of Europeanizing Islam; the major one of which is Islamism and its politics of Islamization.

The references to 'Europe and Islam', as a centuries-old relationship, and a contemporary one, 'Islam in Europe', carry themes highly distinct from one another. History is the best source to learn lessons for shaping a better future. Therefore, I engage in a reference to Henri Pirenne's thesis 'No Charlemagne without Mohammed' to explain the roots of the relationship between Islam and Europe.[48] What the cited historian Pirenne states is that without the challenge of Islam, Charles the Great's Christian Occident would never have come into being the way it did. Pirenne shows that both of these civilizational entities – Europe as Western Christendom and Islam as a religion-based civilization – have a shared historical record.[49] From the very beginning onwards this relationship consisted equally of challenging one another through jihad and crusade and in contrast to cultural fertilization. This cross-cultural fertilization was better than the threat of jihad conquests. These historical records of an intercivilizational relationship between Islam and Europe are revived today also in the context of the massive migration of Muslims to Europe and the revival of collective historical memories in a constructed manner. What are the implications of this for the present and for the future? And why do the addressed historical records matter to the venture of Europeanizing Islam?

The reference to Henri Pirenne, and to the inspiration his work generates, supports an interpretation of the relationship of Islam to Europe as one of a century-long mutual 'Threat and fascination' (*Bedrohung und faszination*). Each of these two civilizations has threatened the other, be it with jihad conquests and crusades in the past, or colonization and jihadism in modern history. At the same time both have enriched the other in cultural and civilizational terms. This is documented in medieval Islam's borrowings from Hellenism or the influence of Islamic rationalism on the European Renaissance. These processes are continued to the present. One may place the diaspora of approximately 23 million Muslims living in Europe today in this history. The overall context continues to be determined by threat and fascination. As cited earlier in the arguments of John Kelsay, these Muslim newcomers to Europe build up 'Islamic enclaves' that exist in Europe, but are alien to its civilization. Now, is it possible to find a way of bridging between the two entities, as did Europe and Islam in the past? As a 'reform Muslim' I propose bridging and think it is feasible. The concept of Euro-Islam presented in Paris in 1992 is a venture for a Europeanization of Islam in today's Europe. This could be based on a precedent: the Hellenization of Islam in medieval times. The Islamic *fiqh*-orthodoxy undermined the institutionalization of that Hellenization of Islam. Will Islamism at present be also successful in undermining the Europeanization of Islam? Do multiculturalists – of course unwittingly – assist in this Islamist venture of Islamization?

It is deplorable to state a severe problem at present in Europe regarding the debate on 'Europeanization versus Islamization'. These issues cannot be discussed freely in public due to the taboos established in the name of political correctness. This culture promotes prevarication and all kinds of ways for evading the pending issues. Despite all odds I acknowledge that it has been possible to enjoy greater freedom of speech in the US than in Europe. It was at Berkeley and Cornell (between 1998 and 2006), later on at Stanford and at Yale where I was able to further develop my concept of Euro-Islam in the context of an understanding of a Europeanization of Islam seen as an intercivilizational bridge. It was also in the US where a project on 'Ethnicity in Europe' could be run at Stanford University. There, I warned of an 'ethnicity of fear', if a Euro-Islam were beyond the reach. In contrast, in Germany my Euro-Islam was ostracized – for instance, by an orientalist in the *Süddeutsche Zeitung* who defamed this proposed vision as the 'one man sect of Professor Tibi'. What's this all about? Does it make sense to carry on in a time in which US scholars and Europeans alike celebrate people like Tariq Ramadan and Olivier Roy who – in my view – distort the meaning of the concept of Euro-Islam? And how far do some carry on with the false argument of 'Islamic sensitivities' to undermine the freedom of speech and academic research? The practice of censorship dictates with the power of intellectual hegemony that eyes are closed so that it is not possible to see how shari'atization of Islam pursued by Islamism not only reaches Europe, but also finds acceptance in the name of multiculturalism.[50]

Citizenship versus collective identity politics: Islamic enclaves as *insertion communitaire*

Citoyenneté is a French term adopted in the concept of Euro-Islam; it means much more than legal citizenship. In 1992 at the Institut du Monde Arabe in Paris I was engaged in reasoning about the competing concepts of assimilation and integration. That French debate was documented in a book that heralds the French abandonment of the earlier politics of assimilation founded on a concept considered as a prerequisite for *citoyennité* (see note 33). Already by then 'assimilation' was buckling under the huge influx of new immigrants from the Islamic world. Unlike the earlier immigrants who were quite successfully assimilated, the newcomers are insisting on holding onto their cultural collective civilizational identity. In their related identity politics they demand to be recognized as a collectivity entitled to rights in this capacity within Europe. In awareness of this change, the summoned experts suggested in Paris in 1992 that assimilation should be replaced by the newly drawn-up concept of integration. As explained earlier, integration does not demand cultural surrender of the self through total conformity, but merely the participation in public life along with the acceptance of civic values of the civil society's system.

Unlike assimilation, integration is limited in its scope to the adoption of a citizen identity within civil society, it focuses on the rights and duties of the *citoyen* as an individual defined in religion – and ethnicity – blind terms. On these grounds, a question was asked in 1992 in Paris, with this phrasing: 'Integration ou insertion communitaire?' (see note 33). The heading of this section refers to the subtitle of the 1995 book on Islam in Europe, edited by Robert Bistolfi and François Zabbal in which my paper, 'Les conditions d'un Euro-Islam' is included. This paper is the origin of the concept of Euro-Islam that I presented in Paris 1992 in which the term was used for the first time.

The reader is reminded of my references to the Africanization of Islam based on experience in Senegal and later on in South East Asia, particularly in Indonesia. The pertinent and recurrent questions that come to my mind while discussing the competing options are: what is needed to be done to make Europeans of Muslims in Europe? Is the comparison drawn between African Islam in Senegal and South East Asian Islam in Indonesia relevant to Islam in Europe? Earlier, in the present study, I argued that the indigenization of Islam in Asia and Africa was an easier process of adjustment. I remind the reader of the underlying two reasons for this. At first: in Europe, it is clear that Euro-Islam is impossible without cultural change involving religious reforms. It is not a simple cultural adjustment, as has been the case in West Africa. The other reason is that Muslims in Europe – unlike West African Muslims – are immigrants, not local people. Not only Islam itself, also the Muslims themselves are aliens.

Due to the distortions that seem to be imposed on the concept it is most unfortunate that the notion of Euro-Islam is becoming increasingly meaningless and just a buzz word. In the writings of Tariq Ramadam I see an unreformed, i.e. a Salafi orthodox Islam, and it is infuriating to see this understanding being presented not only as Euro-Islam, but also with terms like 'radical reform' and 'liberation'. I fail to see any of these features.

To sum up, there seems to be an agenda for an Islamization of Europe through *da'wa* and *hijra*. From here stems the conflict not only with the basics of cultural modernity (democracy, individual human rights, civil society), but also with Euro-

Islam that embraces pluralism and secular democracy. There can be no place for Islamic enclaves in Europe in the name of a European Islam. If Muslims were to become *citoyens* in Europe, then their Islamic value-system has to be Europeanized going beyond proselytization of an 'Islamic mission for Europe'. Euro-Islam is egalitarian in the sense of pluralism of religions and it therefore dismisses Islamic and Islamist religious–cultural supremacism.

Euro-Islam and the ideal of an inclusionary European identity

Unlike the earlier universalist European ideology of Westernization that replaced missionary Christianity, the vision of a Europeanizing of Islam is not related to any universalism. The venture is limited to Muslims who are settled in Europe, as well as to countries (like Turkey for example), which want to become full members of the European Union. In this understanding Muslim immigrants are expected to recognize that Europe has its own civilizational identity, as well as the right to preserve it. This statement is not directed against Muslims, because the idea of Europe is supposed to be inclusive. Respect for the identity of immigrants has to be coupled with a respect for the identity of Europe. One is entitled to expect immigrants to have the will to be integrated and to make their identity compatible with Europe. This is not a contradiction. The same applies to countries that want to join the EU. The Islamist AKP that has ruled Turkey since 2002 and is de-secularizing the Kemalist state disqualifies that country for EU membership through its dismissal of integration and Europeanization.[51]

It is not only strange, but also beyond comprehension when some Europeans – such as Timothy Garton-Ash – confuse the demand for a reform of Islam in Europe with the demand for Muslims to give up their faith. A reform of Islam is simply an effort at rethinking Islamic values in a changed world time in order to come to terms with cultural modernity. This reformed Islam is able to overcome incommensurabilities and to be compatible with European identity. In my view as a Muslim immigrant, Europe doesn't need Europeans who do not stand up to European values that are challenged by Islamic proselytization which is a cultural incursion. There is a value-conflict in place that I, a Muslim, acknowledge and I profess that the idea of Europe is more appealing to me than any Islamism or Salafism. By this identity pattern I mean the inclusionary model – unfortunately not always in the reality – and not an 'Ethnic Europe'.[52] I know the European reality is not always consistent with Europe's claim. As a Muslim, I learned to appreciate the idea of Europe as an 'island of freedom in an ocean of despotism' from my Jewish teacher Max Horkheimer who was a survivor of the Holocaust, and thus deeply familiar with the other very ugly side of Europe.[53] However, this ugly face of Europe should not distract from the freedom and Enlightenment of the other Europe that stands in contrast to totalitarianism and racism. Therefore it is a shame when some people use the Frankfurt School in a Third World-ist manner to legitimate Islamism.[54]

Along with Horkheimer I dissociate myself from the Europe of totalitarianism and refer to the Europe of freedom, individual human rights, democracy, pluralism and civil society. These traditions are that what makes of Europe a beautiful idea, one that can also be shared in a cultural synthesis with non-Europeans, including Muslims. Euro-Islam is an attempt to make the idea of a 'European identity' palatable to Muslims in the form of a cultural synthesis with Islam. I avoid the term hybridization because I dislike postmodern fashions. Muslim immigrants could become European 'citizens of the heart' by appropriating European values into their value system. In the context of a Euro-Islam, migrant identity could be shaped by multiple identity patterns, that entail simultaneously European and Islamic components. This is much more than a hybridization.

In the context of this discussion the distinction between Islam and Islamism (see note 17) is most pertinent. Islam is a religious faith as well as a cultural system, while Islamism is a totalitarian ideology. This distinction matters a lot. Islamism contests the European universalism of values that is neither ethnic nor religious, and thus consequently inclusive, in favour of Islamist universalism. Therefore, Islamism is, in contrast to Euro-Islam, a threat to the civilizational identity of Europe.

Despite allegations to the contrary, the European identity is not Christian: it is secular. This distinction is highly important, because European identity can only be in this secular feature inclusive. Among its sources is humanist Hellenism. At the highpoint of Islamic civilization, the same Hellenism was among the sources of medieval Islamic rationalism. These historical facts point at the historical record of a bridge linking the two civilizations and therefore it needs to be revived. In principle, a Muslim or a Jew can be European without being Christian, and also without having ethnic roots in Europe. In the model, the sole precondition for sharing European identity is the adoption of the European civic values of the Renaissance, the Reformation, the Enlightenment and the French Revolution. And if you do that, you can remain Muslim, and wholeheartedly become European citizens. This embrace cannot be done, however, without reforming and rethinking Islam to overcome its predicament with cultural modernity (see note 10).

The Islamists nestled in among the Islamic diaspora, reject the venture of a Euro-Islam and propagate the idea that the integration of Muslims in Europe is a camouflaged Christian proselytism. The Islamist prime minister of Turkey, Erdogan, condemned integration as a crime against humanity. Clearly, Islamists aren't after integration, because it thwarts their vision of an Islamized Europe. The introduction of the shari'a in the name of multiculturalism matters more to them. The problem is not only Islamism, but also European opinion leaders. These pay lip-service to the idea of Europe in pronouncements that are not to be taken seriously. For instance, they propagate inclusion, but words are not followed by deeds. As stated above, European inclusiveness is a model to be achieved, not yet a reality – similar to the vision of a Euro-Islam. In other words: to bring Islam and Europe together on European soil, both Muslims and Europeans are challenged to engage in a sea change.

The civilizational European identity in the above outlined sense and the historical records of cross-cultural fertilization should be the grounds of the encounter between Islam – not Islamism – and Europe. For non-Western peoples it is a positive sign, when Europeans abandon their former Eurocentrism. It is, however, unfortunate that this happens in a trend to renounce European core values. The debate we are concerned with here, in which the Enlightenment has been written off and defamed as a sort of fundamentalism, is a debate that not only demonstrates intellectual confusion but also a lack of value orientation. Postmodern value-relativism is not the opening that Europe needs to open itself to others. The vision offered by Euro-Islam stands in contrast to the value-relativism of today's Europeans, first and foremost regarding the EU as a value community.

In addition, one has to state that European values are not shared by Islamism. The moderate Islamist Hasan Hanafi correctly recognized that Europe is in a crisis and suffers from a lack of orientation. And what is his solution? In 2004 he suggested publicly in Madrid that Europeans adopt Islam as the solution! Is this Islamization the solution that will bind Europeans and Muslims? I fear not! Therefore I repeat the notion that emerged from a Cornell project chaired by Professor Peter Katzenstein published as, 'Europeanizing Islam, or Islamization of Europe'. This formulation is meant to counter those Muslims who are demanding that *dar al-Islam* ('The house of Islam') should be extended into Europe. Orthodox Islamic doctrine prescribes that *hidjra* ('migration') should serve the worldwide dissemination of Islam. The emergence of parallel societies is related to the admission of shari'a. It is a step in this direction and it must be possible, notwithstanding the rules of political correctness, not only to discuss this openly, but also to contest this Islamization agenda. If Europe is addressed in the way Tariq Ramadan does it, namely as *dar al-shahada*, that is implicitly a part of *dar al-Islam* making Europe an Islamic territory, then the implication is clear: Europe undergoes an Islamization. This is not the goal of Euro-Islam I envision as a founder of the concept.

The Euro-Islamic thinking introduced in this chapter is not shared by the leader of the Islamist Turkish Justice and Development Party/AKP, Tayyip Erdogan, who claims membership of his country in the European Union. The Islamist AKP has been in power since 2002. Prime Minister Erdogan speaks of a 'shared value community' with Europe and at the same time rejects the universality of European values; he even goes further and condemns the Europeanization of Turks in Germany – as already cited – as a 'crime against humanity'. Is this a European, or an Islamist approach? The Islamist AKP divides secular Turkey.[55] The AKP also assaults European identity, but European politicians turn a blind eye to this assault. I do not subscribe to Oswald Spengler's view about the decay of Europe as 'Untergang des Abendlandes', but feel reminded of his prose when I see the way some European opinion leaders respond to the challenge of Islamism in a self-defeating mindset. To understand this mindset I prefer to draw on Ibn Khaldun's *asabiyya* (*esprit de corp*). Ibn Khaldun thinks a weak *asabiyya* is a sign of a weak civilization that no longer stands up to its values.

Conclusion

The conflict and the plea for a Euro-Islam in the pursuit of bridging

It is a fact that the massive Islamic migration to Europe is changing the 'old continent'. The phrase 'Islam and the changing identity of Europe' was the title of an University of California, Berkeley, project of the late 1990s that addressed this issue. Within that framework my Paris-1992-concept of Euro-Islam was first introduced in the US. The result was the UC Berkeley's book *Muslim Europe or Euro-Islam?*[56] The title of that book clearly expresses the options available, discussed at length in this chapter. There is a conflict and the options are: either Europe Europeanizes Islam, or Islamism Islamizes Europe. The worldviews of two competing universalisms collide head on. Europeans unfortunately respond to this challenge based on a competition of models either with a political correctness-driven silence, or with a self-defeating censorship. Politicians, like the German president, Christian Wulff, state (as quoted at the outset of Chapter 4), 'Islam is part of Germany' without knowing what they are talking about. Whether we like it or not, the conflict in place remains not only in this way unresolved, but also intensifies. Those European sentiments – provoked by the financial crisis and addressed at the beginning of this study – namely to discard 'predictions they dislike' also prevail in the debate on Islam in Europe.

Ahead of drawing conclusions and based on experience I repeat my statement preemptively that the notion of a civilizational value-based conflict should not be confused with the rhetoric of the clash of civilizations. I pride myself on having contributed to the book *Preventing the Clash of Civilizations* co-authored with the former German president, Roman Herzog.[57] We, the contributors to that book, take issue with Samuel Huntington. In this line of reasoning Europeans are expected to respond to the existing challenge with a proper policy of Europeanization not with improper prevarications. There is nothing fearful about the concept of Europeanization limited solely to bringing European values and standards to bear on Europe itself, within the territory of Europe. The concept of Euro-Islam is opposed to the Islamist, as well as to the Salafi orthodox Muslim view of Europe becoming part of *dar al-Islam*. As a Muslim living in Europe I acknowledge that Europe has its own non–Islamic identity and this fact needs to be respected by Muslim immigrants. If this applies, where are the Europeans who defend Europe against the claim of Tariq Ramadan that Europe has become *dar al-shahada*? Where are those peace researchers who thrive for peaceful conflict resolution, but fall into the trap of doublespeak, of a convergence of civilizations, and thus overlook the intercivilizational conflict?

I am a Muslim and therefore leave it to Europeans themselves to answer these questions; it is their business, not mine as a Muslim immigrant. Here I prefer to confine myself to drawing conclusions. The concern is how to manage a living together in Europe in peace and democracy. This includes the need for a mutual respect that Muslims and Europeans have to share. When I argue for a cultural synthesis that includes a Europeanization of Islam in its European diaspora I engage in a reasoning that presupposes that any inclusion of Islam in the political culture of the EU requires a 'Europeanization'. Today, people from all over the world live in the territory of the EU and they need to share a value system that promotes peace and harmony in a democratic civil society. The proposed Europeanization separates identity from religion and ethnicity and links it solely to the values of cultural modernity that consist of secular democracy, individual human rights based in civil society as reflections of the principle of subjectivity that Jürgen Habermas argues for in his book on cultural modernity. I believe that this is a universal, not a Eurocentric project, as has been amply illustrated in the example of the possible synthesis of Islam and Europe to a Euro-Islam. Secular Muslims embrace the concept and are receptive to the idea of a Europeanization implemented as criteria not only for accepting the Turks of the diaspora as European citizens, but also Turkey in the EU. If this proposition were not acceptable to Turks and to Turkey, the Turkish magazine *Turkish Policy Quarterly*, based in Istanbul would not have published my 2004 plea for a Euro-Islam, repeated in 2010 in the book of the Turkish–American scholar Zeyno Baran.[58]

In the search for an Islamic basis for the concept I relate Euro-Islam to a concept developed by the last great philosopher in Islam, Ibn Khaldun. This great Muslim thinker died more than 600 years ago (1406), and left to us his *Muqaddima* that includes the notion of *asabiyya* (*esprit de corps*, or 'better collective civilizational identity'). I draw on it as a reference in the face of self-defeating Europeans. For Ibn Khaldun the state of *asabiyya* helps measure the related civilizational awareness of the self to assess strengths and weaknesses of a civilization. In this sense, it is asked: how strong is the European *asabiyya*? Only when Europeans go for the Europeanization of the newcomers to help make Muslim immigrants Europeans, then Europe may succeed in unfolding a democratic response to the Islamic and Islamist challenge. In this case one could speak of a strong European *asabiyya* in Ibn Khaldun's sense. The opposite case is self-defeatism, certainly not an opening of the self to other cultures. To be sure, Euro-Islam is not a concept for assimilation as I draw a distinction between this and integration.

Today, it is a positive sign that Eurocentrism is put into question. To integrate Europe itself as a continent of the old world and also as a civilizational entity into a pluralistic world at large is not tantamount to abandoning European civilizational identity. This open identity is Europe's own *asabiyya* as a clear determination of the self. It needs not be exclusionary to have a civilizational self-awareness if this spirit is integrated into a pluralistic perspective. Today, intercivilizational relations can peacefully manage value-conflicts.[59]

The incorporation of immigrant Muslims through a politics of Europeanization is a civilizational project for Europe that is more than an economic or business community, not to speak of a common space for housing. Europe is a community of values worth preserving as a civilizational 'beautiful idea'. Europe is a model of a community of values based on cultural modernity. I know that this is not reflected in the realities of 'ethnic Europe' in all walks of life.[60] The concept of Euro-Islam suggests an Islamic participation in this project of a new Europe. In the twenty-first century Europe can no longer afford to pronounce an ideal not honoured in European realities. Similarly, the idea of Euro-Islam is still a mere vision, but it could become a political concept approved in the European diaspora of Islam. The task of preserving Europe with Islamic participation is viewed as a peace project for the twenty-first century. The opposing concept of the Islamization of Europe is to be dismissed as a recipe for repeating in Western Europe at large what happened in Kosovo as specific to the Balkans. Liberal Muslims and democratic Europeans are expected to thwart this Islamist agenda through conflict resolution in a civilizational bridging between Islam and Europe within the territoriality of the European Union. As a European Muslim I acknowledge the civilizational identity of Europe and dismiss the expansionist notion of Europe as *dar al-shahada* ('abode of Islam'). In my view no one can approve this Islamization agenda and be at the same time favourable to Euro-Islam. The first perspective is a religious imperialism (see note 13) while the latter goes for intercivilizational bridging. These two perspectives are incompatible with one another and reflect incommensurable worldviews. It follows that there is a conflict. The solution for this intercivilizational value conflict is a cross-cultural morality. In Europe Euro-Islam is a case in point.

Immigrants and Europeans could live together in peace and mutual recognition if both parties accept the idea of an open civil society and of its values that need to be shared. In the thinking about a Europeanized Islam the problem of bridging is not only related to Muslims, but also to the ethnic Europeans themselves with regard to their most unpleasant tradition of Eurocentrism often imbued with cultural arrogance and even racism.[61]

Liberal European Muslims claim that the idea of Europe promises to fight the ugly, real face of some exclusionary Europeans. Today most Europeans are confused, like a pendulum swinging between arrogance and self-denial. Against all odds, I hold to the idea of Europe, because the legal structure in that old continent guarantees my freedom, and also the freedom of 23 million Muslim immigrants more than any of the 57 Islamic states does. Even the minority of the totalitarian Islamists who find shelter in Europe benefit from the freedom of civil society that protects them although they are enemies of 'open society'. In this mindset I embrace the idea of Europe for bridging and argue not only against Islamists, but also against those racist Europeans who prefer to have no Islam and no Muslims on European soil. In the year 2010 it was appalling to Muslims living in Germany to watch how a book written against them by the former Secretary of Finance in the city of Berlin, Thilo Sarrazin, *Deutschland schafft sich ab* ('Germany abolishes itself') was well received and even became a bestseller (1.2 million copies sold, printed in 17 editions). Sarrazin implicitly views Muslim immigrants in biological terms as people who supposedly share the same genes and are damaging Germany.[62] These biased European views are shared in a reversed manner with Islamists despite all divides being 'the enemies of the open society'. As a European Muslim I refer with admiration to Sir Karl Popper and credit it to his insight that it is not the substance of tolerance to be tolerant vis-à-vis intolerance, regardless where it comes from: racist Europeans or totalitarian Islamists. The argument that Muslims share the same genes is laughable, because the 1.7 billion big *umma*-community of Islam is composed of Asians, Africans, Europeans and Americans. Whatever the truth is, Muslims and Europeans may not share the same 'genes', but in historical records they share the universal grammar of humanism.[63] This unites them against all enemies of 'global open society' based on this cross-cultural foundation. My vision – and dream – of a European Islam (Euro-Islam) is part and parcel of this cross-civilizational humanism.

6

INTERCIVILIZATIONAL CONFLICT, BRIDGING AND CRITICAL THEORY

The Western Third World-ist romanticization of Islamism and beyond

Any effort at bridging in a situation of an intercivilizational conflict has to account for the distinction between the earlier revolt against colonialism in a process of de-colonization and the present one. The postcolonial revolt against the West and its civilization is anti-Western, not merely against hegemony. The distinction points at two conflicts different from one another. In the past, anti-colonial leaders were not anti-Western; they had no problems with borrowing European concepts of freedom, sovereignty, the nation and the related nation state, as well as other European ideas, and using them for legitimizing the contestation of colonialism. They saw no contradiction between this borrowing from Europe and their anti-colonialism.[1] They were against European hegemony, but not against European values. Therefore, the early de-colonization did not herald any intercivilizational conflict over values, but rather a political conflict over power, hegemony and rule. Unlike this early de-colonization, which – as Hedley Bull put it – was 'not a revolt against Western values as such',[2] the present revolt is precisely against Western values and their concept of a secular order of the state and the world.

One of the writers on this kind of postcolonial studies who teaches at a British university goes to the extent of defaming Cartesianism as Western 'epistemological imperialism'.[3] This is simply outrageous! This mystification also thrives in the West itself in a state of disorientation and in a mindset of guilt that confuses what is good and what is bad about Europe and Western civilization. The old Third World-ism is reborn as anti-globalization that romanticizes non-Western cultures and embraces anti-Western ideologies such as Islamism. Why is it so?

In the past, as well as at present, the progressive Left in the West was susceptible to the old cliché of the *bon sauvage* in its articulation of sympathy vis-à-vis non-Western self-assertiveness. For the old and the new the Third World-ist view is in substance a Eurocentric view of the world in reverse. The Western Left of today cultivates this mindset and views Islamism through its lenses as anti-capitalist anti-globalization. When the old bipolar polarization of the world ended, Anthony Giddens recommended that we go 'beyond left and right'.[4] Neither, the Left nor the Right heeded this advice. The new central topic in the ideologically shaped public debate in the West is Islam and its place in the world at large. On this subject, both the Left and the Right have their own myths. The Right practises Islam-bashing (I recommend the use of this term to replace the charged one of Islamophobia) while the Left romanticizes Islamism confusing it with Islam.[5] Today, the earlier accusation of anti-communism has been replaced by the current defamation of anti-Islamism (Islamophobia). Both ideological notions distort the potential for deliberations over the new global value-conflicts addressed in terms of an intercivilizational conflict to be combined with an effort at bridging. My work in the past decades focuses on Islamism in a clear distinction from the religion of Islam. Those who romanticize this ideology and the movement that embodies it end up with wrong conclusions.

This is a feature of Third World-ism revived in the dealing with Islamism. The present criticism is not only put forward by a liberal Muslim with a leftist background, but is also by all means against conservatism. My biography, referred to from time to time, moves next to my Islamic socialization in Damascus and my life in the Frankfurt School. In the 1960s my academic teachers were Max Hork-heimer, Theodor W. Adorno and Jürgen Habermas, all of the Marxist Frankfurt School, who by then shaped my mind.[6] With the power of the arguments of Max Horkheimer I contradict the Left of today discussed in the example of the work of the Cornell professor Susan Buck-Morss. Her views about 'Islamism and critical theory on the Left' reflect a Third World-ist upgrading of Islamism that seems to overlook the fact of a totalitarian ideology at work.[7] In contrast, I argue that the political legacy of Max Horkheimer compels me to reject the new Islamist totalitarianism. The Third World-ism of the Left reflects a predicament of a mindset that idealizes non-Western parts of the world in the tradition of the *bon sauvage*. Islamism, which fuels the intercivilizational conflict, serves in this chapter as a case in point. To be sure, this intercivilizational conflict is not related to any class struggle of the suppressed poor of the South against the suppressor-rich of the North. The Islamist revolt against the West is not about capitalism, but about cultural values and the order they underpin. There are on the Left in Europe and in the US many confusions, among which one finds many wrong views and misperceptions about political Islam/Islamism. These are mostly characterized by a general ignorance over the issue itself, intensified by ignoring the basic distinction between Islam and Islamism.

In the tradition of Max Horkheimer I see in the politicization of the religion of Islam into an ideology of Islamism a new totalitarianism. This is also the ideology of an intercivilizational conflict in post-bipolar politics. This interpretation leans on the critical theory, as well as on Hannah Arendt's work and it stands in con-trast to some authors of the Left who upgrade Islamist thinking to an ideology of liberation. This chapter seeks to establish some clarification on this disputed issue to give enlightenment about totalitarian Islamism, and draw conclusions about

Islamist ideology as a political religion. The assessment of Islamism in a critical dispute with some parts of the contemporary Western Left places the following issue into the theme of this book: intercivilizational conflict and bridging.

Introduction

The point of departure is the belief of some theorists of the Left that 'Islamism is a creative space for political articulations of protest against present inequalities.'[8] These people think 'Islamism is not a religious discourse, but a political one. It is a debate about modernity.'[9] Other theorists of the Left believe that there is a contestation of capitalist globalization pursued by Islamism.[10] They attribute to Islamism a progressive character, but overlook in their misconception the empirical fact that Islamism is a variety of the global phenomenon of religious fundamentalism. There is no progressive movement at work acting under this name. The leftist interpretations cited are presented by respected scholars of the Left. With all respect due to the Cornell professor Susan Buck-Morss who knows the critical theory well, I question her support of Islamism based on unchecked assumptions.

The endorsement of Islamism by the Left and by some liberals stands against the legacy of Max Horkheimer. As one of the former students of this great scholar I contradict these views strongly and view, in the tradition of critical theory, Islamism as the new totalitarianism. Hereby I follow Horkheimer's view articulated in his will that supporters of his critical theory are obligated to counter totalitarian ideologies, regardless of their origin and shape. In this chapter I do not want to engage in any polemics. Instead, I shall review the position of Horkheimer and use it as grounds for interpreting Islamism as the new totalitarianism that undermines bridging in post-bipolar value-conflict between two major civilizations.

The reference to a text considered to be the expression of the will of Horkheimer is made here in the pursuit of reviving the related legacy. Already in my early academic career I engaged as a member of the Left in a strong critique of the romantics of Third World-ism. Today I go a step further to argue that Islamism, though a Third World ideology, is the most recent variety of totalitarianism. The greatest flaw is that capitalism seems to be mistakenly identified by the Left of today with the cultural idea of the West itself, as well as with its humanism. Some leftists believe that one has to be anti-Western in order to be critical of capitalism. The argument against this view which is a mere misconception of the Marxian critique of the capitalist system is based on the fact that Karl Marx was truly a European humanist, as Max Horkheimer himself was, who stood in the same tradition. At issue is the defence of a cross-cultural humanism against totalitarian Islamism legitimated by misguided leftists and liberals. The contemporary Left seems no longer to endorse the tradition of Western humanism.[11] In Chapter 4 of this book an effort has been made to revive the tradition of Islamic humanism that shares crucial roots with Western humanism. This cross-cultural minded reference, and not anti-Westernism, serves as an effort at bridging.

Let it be also stated that Islam/Islamism is today the source of a new Islamist antisemitism.[12] So how could one stand in the tradition of Islamic and European humanism and argue positively about Islamism? Jewish thinkers like Maimonides were part of the tradition of Islamic humanism. The romanticism of the 'Third World' is ignorant about these positive traditions best suitable for bridging.[13] In fact, postcolonial developments dealt a blow to the illusion of a universal liberation by Third World-ism. The postwar development in Vietnam and also the records of dictatorships legitimized by a third-world-ist ideology in Africa (e.g. Idi Amin and Robert Mugabe) or Asia (e.g. Pol Pot and others) as well as in the Arab world (e.g. Qadhafi in Libya until 2011) did not compel the Left to reconsider its positive assessment of Third World-ism. Some leftists compared the Islamic Revolution in Iran positively with the French Revolution, overlooking its totalitarian character. The Left did not learn from these facts to rectify its errors. I believe that a revival of the legacy of Max Horkheimer combined with an analysis of the Third World-ist political ideology presented in the example of political Islam could help to provide some guidance in this world time of disorientation and of uncertainty exacerbated by the cultural relativism of the value-free postmodernism.

In the spirit of bridging that guides this book, I draw on the legacy of my academic teacher Horkheimer to revive his ideas in the search for value-orientation. This revival is proposed by a Muslim immigrant living in Europe whose mind is shaped by a cross-cultural combination of a relationship to Horkheimer and an identity based in Islamic civilization. This background provides solid credentials against any accusation of orientalism or Islamophobia. Furthermore, the years of study spent with Horkheimer protect me from an orientalism in reverse, i.e. from a mindset that prevails today among the supporters of Edward Said on the postmodern Left to be qualified as a Saidist variety of Third World-ism. In order to protect critical theory from abuse in the search for an endorsement of totalitarian Islamism one has to outline the humanist substance of critical theory. Susan Buck-Morss is fully wrong in her use of critical theory to endorse Islamism. The reverse would be correct, as done in this chapter, namely to engage in a reference to Horkheimer precisely to dismiss Islamism and unmask it as a variety of totalitarianism. This dismissal is at the same time a contribution to bridging.

Horkheimer, the 'Third World' and the Left

The pending issue can be best illustrated by a reference to some memories of the 1960s. By then, at the height of the Vietnam war and the protest against it, we, students of the Frankfurt School at the University of Frankfurt at that time, were organized in the *Sozialistischer Deutscher Studentenbund/SDS*. This was an organization that represented the (then) new critical Left based on the thinking of the Frankfurt School. Some of us went to our highly revered teacher Max Horkheimer and asked him to endorse with his signature our pro-Vietcong and anti-US declaration. He politely turned us down, and in response, we were impolitely not only outraged, but also highly disappointed. The great philosopher for whom we had the highest reverence, Horkheimer, failed us and refused to support our Third World-ist agenda. Horkheimer made it clear that he, on the one hand, shared with us the opposition to the Vietnam war, but on the other hand, neither endorsed our admiration of the Vietcong and respectively of other ideologies of the 'Third World', nor our anti-Americanism. In that communication Horkheimer supported his reservations not only with reports published in the press according to which the Vietcong practised torture, but he also argued in a general manner against the Third World-ist mindset. It was most obvious that Horkheimer was dismayed by our Third World-ist and anti-Western views that he rejected in clear and unequivocal terms leaving no ambiguity. Horkheimer's dismissal of the leftist Third World-ist romantics was combined with his commitment to the idea of the West.[14] For him the tradition of humanism in the West as 'the free world' was an essential part of his legacy. Horkheimer made it clear that the notion of Western humanism is not to be identified or confused with the system of capitalism. What dismayed Horkheimer most was the way the Left dismissed Western humanism altogether in a wholesale rejection of the West masked as anti-capitalism.

Horkheimer acknowledged his preference for European ideals that were put in contrast to any romanticization of non-European cultures in the shape of a third worldism. This romanticization would be a reviving and an upgrading of the old ideology of the *bon sauvage*. The people of the Third World serve the Left in a Eurocentric manner as the new *bon sauvage*. I am sorry to state this, but feel it as a non-Westerner.

To make the long story a short one: we, the Left of 1968, did not appreciate Horkheimer's thinking. Another disappointment followed when in the same year Horkheimer joined the celebration of the US Day of Independence while we were – in contrast – simultaneously shouting furious anti-US slogans on the streets. Today, four decades later, it is clear to my mind that I – though a non-European – was unwittingly participating in an old tradition of European anti-Americanism culturally alien to me. Professedly, I was also subjected to the romantics of the *bon sauvage* cultivated by those Frankfurt leftist students. Today their successors admire Islamism. In Europe, leftists and some liberals continue to cultivate this myth of the 'Third World'. Tariq Ramadan seems to enjoy this upgrading. I admit, in the 1960s I felt flattered, in those years of ugly racism, by being upgraded by that romanticization, from an 'inferior Arab' (*Araber von unten*) to a 'theorist of the Third World'. Today, I admit shamefully that I was among those who resented the behaviour of Horkheimer, and repent.

The kind of thinking criticized as 'leftist Third World-ism' was underpinned by two major intellectual sources on which we, the Left, drew to support our romanticism. One of these sources was the book *The One-Dimensional Man* by Herbert Marcuse. It was a kind of bible against the West, which included an idea put in the form of this question: could the Third World in its upheaval against the West be the source of inspiration of the revolution needed? Herbert Marcuse wrote off the proletariat as the subject of revolutionary change in Europe. In his search for an alternative he discovered the 'Third World'. Even though Marcuse's thinking was flawed, his phrasing was more careful than ours. His phrase deserves to be quoted at length. After his acknowledgement of failure and despair Marcuse states:

> Another alternative seems possible. If industrialization and the introduction of technology in the backward countries encounter strong resistance from the indigenous and traditional modes of life and labor ... could this pre-technological tradition itself become the source of progress?[15]

We, the Left of the late 1960s, translated this question into a firm belief in upgrading the anti-industrial rhetoric of Third World-ism to a new strategy for liberation. It is no longer the proletariat, but the Third World that shall liberate humanity, including the West itself. Today Islamism is appealing to the Left liberals who perceive this totalitarian ideology as a promise of liberation. Today, in Islamist ideology the Islamic *umma* replaces the proletariat.

In the 1960s nothing went well. We destroyed tradition, but failed to establish a new one against the ills of capitalism. At that time, we – students and other marginal groups – were quite presumptuous, but not to the extent to imagine that we could be the subject for the envisioned revolution needed for the transformation of society towards the realization of our ideals. I put the criminal Baader-Meinhof sect aside which, along its *Rote Armee Fraktion*, fell to this illusion. We, the mainstream, believed in the 'Third World' and also in its capability to deliver, hence our unrestricted *tiers-mondist*, Third World-ist romanticism.

The other source of Third World-ist thinking in point was Frantz Fanon's book *The Wretched of the Earth*, a truly inspiring text. However, the phrasing of Fanon is quite inflammatory:

> Let us waste no time in sterile litanies and nauseating mimicry. Leave this Europe where they are never done talking of Man, yet murder men everywhere they find them, at the corner of every one of their own streets, in all the corners of the globe. For centuries they have stifled almost the whole of humanity in the name of a so-called spiritual experience. Look at them today swaying between atomic and spiritual disintegration ... We today can do everything, so long as we do not imitate Europe, so long as we are not obsessed by the desire to catch up with Europe. Europe now lives at such a mad, reckless pace that she has shaken off all guidance and all reason, and she is running headlong into the abyss; we would do well to avoid it with all possible speed ... When I search for Man in the technique and style of Europe, I see only a succession of negations of man, and an avalanche of murders.[16]

Unlike Marcuse, who was as a philosopher very careful, therefore, to put the issue in the form of some questions, Fanon used a strong language to simply write off Europe and the West altogether. Fanon contends that he sees Western civilization 'running headlong into the abyss'. Despite the different mindsets, one finds the very same phrase in Qutb's book *Signpost along the Road*, a text that is the bible of the Islamists today. There are multiple Third World-isms. They do share something: the attitude of anti-Westernism.

The promise of a liberation of humanity by the Third World did not materialize, but it is still alive. Today it is resumed by Islamism that grows from a failed development. However, the flaws of postcolonial developments cannot be reduced solely to the ills of capitalist colonialism. If so, then why does a country like Yemen, which was never subjected to colonial rule, have the lowest standard of development while a former colony like India has sky-rocketing development expected to lead the country to becoming a superpower of the future?

The comparison of Yemen and India is solely made to dismiss the reference to colonial rule as the sole source of explanation. My argument is that there are other internal constraints in 'developing cultures' concealed in the worldview of Third World-ism.

Today, forty years after the reported disappointment with Horkheimer, I, as a Muslim who fled from 'Oriental despotism',[17] or the authoritarianism of Middle Eastern dictators (call it what you want) to Europe, read Horkheimer anew through different lenses. In the light of knowledge about Islamism, I am concerned about the misconception of this ideology by the Left. I cannot join the Left of today in its romanticization of political Islam as a 'theology of liberation'. In the past, this Third World-ism led to nowhere and it will continue to do so in the fore-seeable future.

Based on the decades-long research on Islamism,[18] I am not only fearful of it as the new totalitarianism, but also very much concerned about its intrusion to the West via global migration. It is a fact that Islamism has been successful in establishing itself in the diaspora of Islam.[19] As shown earlier Islamist movements benefit from the marginalization of Muslims to Europe which enables them to recruit in the diaspora for supporters of its agenda. Keep in mind: what comes from the 'Third World' has not been what Frantz Fanon once promised in his dismissal of Europe. In the light of these facts, I rediscover Horkheimer's legacy against totalitarianism. In the preface to his collected essays on *Kritische Theorie*, published in 1968 under this title, Horkheimer made abundantly clear that he stands up to the West as 'free world', however, not uncritically.[20] It is possible to com-bine the approval of the idea of a 'beautiful Europe' with a criticism of racist fascism and communist dictatorship. In Horkheimer's thought, this no contradiction. There is no one monolithic in Europe.

There is no doubt, despite his commitment to Western humanism, Horkheimer was highly critical of the West. Horkheimer makes it clear that he subscribes to the notion of the West itself (*Begriff*), not to the practices that may stand contrary to the idea of Europe and the West. In substance the message is this: Western policies are to be criticized, however, not to be confused – neither associated – with Western humanism (see note 11). There is another concern that Horkheimer cared about, namely the ideology of anti-Americanism, which is not only a variety of anti-Westernism, but also of antisemitism. The view of Horkheimer deserves to be quoted in full:

> America, regardless of its motives, saved Europe from complete enslavement. The response today from everywhere, not only in Germany, has been widespread and profound hostility toward America. There has been a great deal of puzzling over the origin of this. Resentment, envy, but also the errors made by the American government and its citizens, all play a role. It is especially startling to notice that everywhere where one finds anti-Americanism, antisemitism flourishes. The general malaise caused by cultural decline seeks a scapegoat, and for the aforementioned reasons, it finds the Americans, and, in America itself, once again the Jews who supposedly rule America.[21]

The anti-Americanism unveiled by Horkheimer is represented today by an alliance of strange bedfellows: Islamists – acting in the tradition of Sayyid Qutb – and some parts of the European Left. To be sure, also for Horkheimer, the home of the Western civilization is Europe of which America is an extension. True, this continent of the old world itself generated the crusades, colonialism, two world wars, genocidal Hitlerism, and last but not least, communist Stalinism. However, the genocide of the Holocaust which Horkheimer literally survived in fleeing to America, did not hinder him from stating that the West is today '*eine Insel der Freiheit in einem Ozean der Gewaltherrschaft*' ('an isle of freedom surrounded by an ocean of violent rule').[22]

The recommendation that Horkheimer makes to those who subscribe to 'critical theory' is to defend the idea of the West against any totalitarianism. He phrases it in the following way:

> One should judge on the free world by its notion (*Begriff*), and be committed to it in a critical manner, however, to stand up to its values. On these grounds, one has to defend the West against totalitarianism, be it the one of Hitler or Stalin, or of other varieties. It is the right and the obligation of everyone who follow critical theory to defend the West despite its shortcomings . . . because it is in our age an isle of freedom to which critical theory belongs that struggles to survive in an environment of an *Ozean der Gewaltherrschaft*/rule of terror.[23]

In his lifetime, Horkheimer knew only two varieties of the phenomenon that he mentions: Stalinism and Hitlerism. In my book *Europa ohne Identität* dedicated to the memory of Max Horkheimer I insert the quoted extract (see note 23) on the first page as a motto. I add there a reference to a new variety of totalitarianisms: Islamist religious fundamentalism.[24] The decision to add this chapter to the present book on the theme 'Islamism and the Left' occurs in a mindset of bridging, not one of confrontation.[25] My life as an immigrant in Europe includes an active membership of the European Left in the 1960s which continued until the early 1970s. In those years I was on the editorial board of the Left's theoretical journal *Das Argument* (West Berlin), and also published some major articles in *Sozialistische Politik*, as well as in other journals of the Left. My very first book *Die arabische Linke* (Frankfurt, 1969) was published in the book series *Dritte Welt* ('Third World') in Frankfurt which I had co-established.[26] By then, this book series was heavily influenced by the views of the Left. By then I managed to push the acceptance of the Middle East as the Arab part of the 'Third World'.

The earlier reference to the two intellectual sources of Western Third World-ism, namely Herbert Marcuse's *One-Dimensional Man* and Frantz Fanon's *Les Damnes de la terre*, is also based on a life on the European Left. The critique of what Marcuse named 'onedimensionality' was the identification of consumerism with the 'West', which led him to an admiration of the non-Western world, also in its upheaval against modernity and industrialization. I witnessed a public discussion in Frankfurt in which Adorno did not refrain from qualifying Marcuse's thought in public as an expression of a 'vulgar Marxism'.

Fanon added to this vulgar Marxism a pairing with the cited de-legitimation of Europe in a mystification of the Third World. Fanon promised a revolution that achieves freedom, but the Third World never delivered. Fanon asked brothers and sisters in the Third World to dismiss what he named in derogatory terms 'talkative Europe'; they should move on and act as people described as the 'wretched of the Earth'. The Third World was believed to be engaged in a cosmic revolution for the liberation of the world. And what comes afterwards?

What followed is this: in Africa there were and are dictators like Idi Amin and Robert Mugabe, in Asia Pol Pot and in the Middle East Saddam Hussein and Qadhafi's 'Green Revolution'. It is a shame that Mu'amar Qadhafi enjoyed being hosted by the president of the *Republic de la France*, Nicolas Sarkozy. True, Islamism opposes all of these authoritarian regimes, but is caught in their logic, however, in a religionized form. One segment of this ideology is Islamized anti-semitism. Do not be mistaken: totalitarianism is not the proper alternative to authoritarian rule.

Horkheimer, who was victimized by antisemitism, would not only be shocked today, but he would also feel supported in his reservations. If Horkheimer were alive and could learn that the genocidal ideology of antisemitism is spreading in the world of Islam in the name of Third World-ist authenticity he would be shattered. The agenda of de-Westernization is presented by the Islamists as a quest to establish *Hakimiyyat Allah* ('God's rule'). This rule and its ideology are the new totalitarianism to replace democracy. This so-called 'liberation theology' targets what is called 'Jews and crusaders as evil-doers'. The Left seems not to know that the agenda of authenticity is based on cultural purification by contemporary Islamists who want to purify Islam from 'the Enlightenment', dismissed by them as a 'Jewish idea'.[27] Is this the liberation theology? Is the Islamist reference to 'The Protocols of the Elders of Zion' an act of liberation in an uprising against the 'Jewish conspiracy' that is driven by the intention to 'Westernize' the world of Islam?[28]

The Islamist anti-globalization and upraising against Western imperialism is perceived as a revolt against 'world Jewry'. In this Islamist imagination the adopted antisemitism is espoused with anti-Americanism. Sayyid Qutb is the mastermind of this thinking.[29] Horkheimer did not live to witness Islamism, though he related anti-Americanism to the evil of antisemitism. Scholars like the Cornell professor Buck-Morss and others argue that Islamists are favourable to modernity. This is true. But what is the modernity that Islamists – like Anwar al-Jundi – are embracing? They are favourable only to the instruments, but not to the values of modernity. In their research, Roger Griffin and Jeffrey Herf have shown how, as fascism as an agenda of 'reactionary modernism'[30] did the same. This is not the *Philosophical Discourse of Modernity* outlined by Jürgen Habermas.[31]

Islamism perceives itself to be the expression of the new world revolution. This is more than an Islamist variety of the Third World-ist revolution. This thinking was first articulated by Sayyid Qutb, who in the following phrasing provides a reinterpretation of jihad as 'world revolution':

> The Islamic perspective is based on theocentrism/*rabbaniyya* . . . It prescribes jihad in the pursuit of a world revolution . . . to accomplish peace for humanity . . . This is the nature of Islamic peace which is not based on pacifism . . . Islam is therefore a permanent jihad to accomplish the rule of God on earth within the framework of proper order.[32]

In another book titled *Our Fight Against the Jews* Qutb identified one specific target of this revolution: The Jews.[33] What has happened to the Left such that today it supports political Islam that embraces a new racism against 'Jews, crusaders and unbelievers'? Please allow me this recourse: I as a young boy, who came in 1962 at the age of eighteen, from Damascus to Frankfurt, I embraced the ideals of the Left. As a European humanism that entails freedom, enlightenment and liberation. Today, I no longer see these elements in the thinking of the Left. Therefore, I wonder and then ask the question: what happened? An anti-Western irrationalism, for which the totalitarian and antisemitic Islamism is a case in point, is not the humanist and rational critique of the injustice of capitalism as presented by the Frankfurt School. So how could Susan Buck-Morss approve Islamism in the name of critical theory? Based on research that has lasted for three decades by a Muslim who is committed to the Hellenist tradition[34] in classical Islam, I shall in this study enlighten readers about the politicized Islam of Islamism and ask: isn't it better to maintain what Horkheimer has recommended? He requested from the community of 'critical theory' not only criticism of totalitarianism in general, known to him in the shape of Hitlerism and Stalinism, but also the defence of Western values. Horkheimer was aware of the prospect of unfolding further varieties of totalitarianism. If it holds that Islamism is also a totalitarian ideology, then the community of the Left and of liberals is challenged to reconsider its support for political Islam.

Why the project of intercivilizational bridging excludes the politicization of Islam into Islamism

The view of the Cornell professor Buck-Morss that Islamism is 'not a religious discourse' overlooks the combination of religion and politics in contemporary Islamist ideology. The result is a variety of religious fundamentalism that is clearly not a theology of liberation. Islamism is based on the religionization of politics and the politicization of religion. The radical geopolitical changes in the post-bipolar international environment have promoted the return of the sacred. The rise of Islamism as a new totalitarian movement predates these developments. Early Islamists did not talk about the 'Third World'. Their concern was with a remaking of the world in the pursuit of establishing a religious order that they named *Hakimiyyat Allah* ('Allah's rule'). This order is based on an invented shari'a elevated to the constitution of an Islamic state which is not the Islamic variety of democracy, but rather an indication of a new totalitarianism.[35]

The religionization of conflict by political Islam as represented by a transnational movement leads to polarization, not to bridging. Islamist movements are organized along the lines of a religionized ideology. The politicization of religion in point happens in the pursuit of re-making the world. The ideology puts forward political claims in divine language to make them non-negotiable. Therefore the inter-civilizational conflict becomes intractable when religionized. This leaves no room for a dialogue with the cultural other, and thus bridging in cooperation with those moderate Islamists is a mere illusion.

Within Islamist totalitarianism as based on the binary politicization of religion there are two directions. One of them legitimates a new pattern of warfare (jihadism), while the other forgoes the resort to violence and is represented by peaceful Islamists. These admit participation in institutions and are therefore named 'institutional Islamists'. Both varieties aim to replace the existing Westphalian order with a new world order based on Islamic tenets; they share the very same binary worldview and goals, if not the means.[36]

A prominent example for peaceful Islamists who participate in the demo-cratic game of balloting are the AKP-Islamists of Turkey. However, AKP-Islamists clearly engage in a 'creeping Islamization' even though they – for tactical reasons – refrain from an endorsement of the shari'a state as their divine order.[37] Despite all these differences, peaceful Islamism is a variety of religious fundamentalism and relates to the new conflict between the secular and the religious.[38]

Secular democracy is challenged by Islamism that wages a heated war of ideas against Western values.[39] This is not well understood in the ongoing distorting and blurring political debate on political Islam. This not only damages scholarship, but also the mindset of the Left, which is no exception. I state this as a liberal Muslim scholar committed to enlightenment in Islam and also to an intercultural bridging between the competing civilizations. I want to bring enlightenment about a radically changed world in a new international environment of politicized religion which represents a counter-enlightenment. In short, Islamism cannot be included in the project of intercivilizational bridging. On all levels, Islamism fuels the intercivilizational conflict and makes it intractable.

The Third World-ist Islamism is not what Marcuse and Fanon hoped for

The distinction between Islam and Islamism (see note 5) needs to be introduced and combined with an enlightenment about earlier and current expectations of Third World-ism supposed to lead to a liberation. At the outset I argued that Marcuse and Fanon laid the seeds. The revolution that the Left has been yearning for is in its substance different from the one Qutb proclaimed in his call for 'jihad as an Islamic world revolution'. Even though Sayyid Qutb's language reveals some borrowing from Marxism, jihadist Islamists are to be classified as the political Right. Certainly, Marcuse and Fanon had different concerns in their mind. The major Islamist thinkers, al-Banna, Qutb and Qaradawi have a different agenda.

At first, Islamists associate Islam with politics in their concept of *din-wa-dawla* ('unity of religion and state'). This is a recent addition, both in terms of language and in the substance of its meaning. The cited formula relates to the rise of a new movement addressed as Islamism and it is based on an invention of tradition; it did not exist in earlier times. The goal of Islamism is to establish a divine order named *Hakimiyyat Allah* ('the rule of Allah'). This formulation of political Islam, which was coined along with the foundation of The Society of the Muslim Brothers, established in Cairo in 1928, is also a new one. The founder of this movement is Hasan al-Banna. He is the grandfather of Tariq Ramadan, who is celebrated by the liberal Left (wrongly) as the voice of Islamic anti-globalization. Ramadan never dissociated himself unequivocally from his grandfather.

Today, the Islamist tradition of al-Banna and Qutb is continued by the 'Muslim Brother' Yusuf al-Qaradawi, known as the global Mufti of al-Jazeera TV. This Sheikh al-Qaradawi is associated with the claim of purification. He blames the 'imported solutions'(i.e. secularism, Marxism, liberal democracy etc.) for the present crisis in the world of Islam and argues that only 'Islam is the solution' (*al-Islam huwa al-hall*).[40] This ideology of cultural purification must be an alert for the Left, supposed to be committed to humanism.

I have no doubt that Marcuse and Fanon, whom I admired when I was young and a Marxist, have nothing in common with Islamism. They did not know of the development crisis that gives rise to a crisis of Islam expressed in a defensive cultural discourse and thus to the rise of political Islam. In a crisis of development and of legitimacy the politicization of religion takes place in a search for an alternative. Politicized Islam, namely, has been the answer in this search for more promising options for a better future. One is tempted to compare the current crisis situation in the world of Islam with the crisis of the Weimar Republic in Germany prior to the takeover by the Nazis in 1933. In both cases, responses to a crisis situation are not always democratic and not promising at all. Political Islam presents itself as a concept of political order on the grounds of divine precepts – *Hakimiyyat Allah*

('God's rule') – that resemble secular fascism. The overall and global phenomenon is the return of the sacred that creates a challenge to secular democracy and
above all to all values of cultural modernity. It is by no means a renaissance of religion.

In short, Islamism is the Islamic variety of religious fundamentalism and this is
not what Marcuse and Fanon had in their political dreams. Islamism is also a cultural
response, not a 'creative space' for any creative debate on modernity. On the side,
a jihadist actionism arises and it moves the defensive culture to the offensive in
fighting a new pattern of warfare. Along with this jihadist challenge based on the
jihadization of Islam one encounters a totalizing shari'a that Islamism presents.
In the course of this shari'atization which establishes divides within Islam, as well
as between Muslims and the rest of humanity, two concepts are espoused to one
another: global jihad and the shari'a-based order. To be sure, this is not a 'discourse
about modernity'. Some people who write about political Islam are advised to read
the literature of Islamism before theorizing. Most Marxists, as well as the Left-
wing community in general, have great difficulties in understanding the meaning
of religion and its place in society and politics. It is not a mere superstructure, as
a pure reflection of an economic basis, but is rather a cultural meaning in itself.
Add to this the necessary understanding of the general phenomenon of religious
fundamentalism. The great Marxist philosopher Ernst Bloch was among the
very few Marxist thinkers who were able to understand the meaning of religion.
Bloch was in a position to abandon pure reductionism in his work that helped to
understand the 'return of the sacred' in a political shape.[41]

Stated in a nutshell, the world revolution of global jihad in the twenty-first
century does not fulfil the hopes of Marcuse and Fanon. It neither provides a better
perspective for the Islamic civilization, nor liberates humanity from repression. If
Muslims were to join a universal democratic peace, then they would not only need
to dissociate their faith from religious fundamentalism, as a concept of divine order,
but also to engage themselves in 'rethinking Islam'. For smoothing the way for an
Islamic cultural acceptance of pluralism through reform, Muslims need to engage
in critical reasoning beyond apologetics. The foremost thing I learned as a Muslim
from the Frankfurt School is exactly this, with the inference that every matter
can be subjected to critical reasoning, including one's own religion and culture.
This is what Muslims lack due to the absence of a tradition of criticism. In the
romanticization of the Third World by the Western Left in the footsteps of Fanon
and Marcuse these issues are fully misconceived and blurred.

Islam, civil society and the critical reasoning of cultural modernity

Today, Muslims need democracy, not the rule named *Hakimiyyat Allah*. To engage
in a rethinking of Islam on the grounds of religious reform is a requirement for the
introduction of the concept of democratic pluralism. This venture could contribute
to putting Islamic thought in harmony with modernity. Islamism is not the liberal
'open Islam' Muslims need not only to cope with their predicament with cultural

modernity, but also as a legitimacy for the acceptance of a civil society. The ideology of Islamism places a neo-absolutist religious belief above any critical reasoning. 'Islamist modernity' transfers traditional Islamic absolutism into a new totalitarianism. This is the basic difference between both: democratic Islam and Islamism.

Democracy and civil society are not only the better options for Islamic civilization, but also – in contrast to the agenda of Islamism – are the core elements of cultural modernity needed for bridging. There are Western-educated Muslims like Serif Mardin, who believe 'civil society is a Western dream . . . part of history of Western Europe . . . civil society does not translate into Islamic terms'.[42] I not only contest this view and present a different one, but also dismiss Mardin's thinking as closing the door for a bridging. The implication of the arguments of Mardin is that a civil society-based democracy as a culture of the democratic state is not compatible with Islam. This is not acceptable. Why?

The answer is that Muslims who deny themselves critical reasoning end up imprisoned in a worldview determined by Islamic shari'a. It is difficult to imagine an Islamic shari'a state that endorses critical thought on democracy as a political culture of dissent. The concept of 'Islamic state' is based on a fundamentalist notion of order, which is totalitarian, not democratic, since it allows no pluralism and no dissent and disagreement. The shari'a-state is the agenda of Islamism, which is interpreted and conceptualized as a variety of the overall new phenomenon of 'religious fundamentalism'. I can hardly understand how some people of the Left who are expected to subscribe to 'critical reasoning' – in the tradition of Horkheimer – could approve Islamism! Islamism contradicts democracy on all counts. The reader is reminded of the insight articulated in the preceding section: the civilizational project of Islamism is not the liberation Marcuse and Fanon hoped for. In addition the Islamist venture is not an Islamic model of a cultural modernity, but exactly the negation of it.

Critical reasoning has to grapple today with the return of the sacred to society and to politics. I reiterate the reference to the findings of the *Fundamentalism Project* conducted at the American Academy of Arts and Sciences, which are unfortunately ignored. The findings of this project were published in five volumes by Chicago University Press, but were denied access to the scholarly debate. These findings also did not receive the attention they deserve from the Left. This project provided an academic concept of fundamentalism which has been referred to in this study. The study of religion in international politics is another area. Some recent studies made an inroad in this direction, but one is disturbed by the poor knowledge of Islam and Islamism. In short, Buck-Morss does not stand alone. Even some contemporary masterminds of critical theory, such as Jürgen Habermas, seem to have difficulties in understanding that the 'return of the sacred' (see note 35) does not herald a 'post-secular society',[43] but is rather an indication of the new phenomenon of religious fundamentalism.

Instead of the needed critical reasoning one encounters defamations such as the accusation of 'Islamophobia'. In this context, it should be possible to mention that the accusation of orientalism becomes a means of censorship instead of one of enlightenment about prejudice. This is neither a spirit of scholarship nor a contribution to countering Islamophobia, but rather defamation and censorship. For conceptualizing the politicization of religion into a concept of order in a crisis of modernity the Left needs to revive the critique of religion to grasp the religionized view of the world. Islamism is neither a liberation theology nor anti-globalization, it is a totalitarian neo-absolutism.

To be sure, it is not an orientalism to state that Islamism is no liberation and to argue that Muslims need instead critical reasoning, not an engagement in accusations and defamations. While I dismiss Saidism I leave no doubt that the critique of 'orientalism' by Edward Said had (in its time) a valid point.[44] However, there has been a development from one extreme to the other of an 'orientalism in reverse'. This has been detrimental. The latter term was coined by the Syrian Yale-educated philosopher Sadik Jalal al-Azm, who criticized the impact of Edward Said. The critique of this concept presented by enlightened Muslims, themselves warning of a conspiracy-driven approach, has been fully overlooked, not only in Western scholarship, but also by the Left obsessed with identifying the West with capitalism. The critique of Islamic fundamentalism has been subject to the censorship of political correctness for any critical thinking about Islam and its politicization.

The conclusion is that a rethinking of Islam committed to critical theory requires an Islamic acceptance of dissent, as well as an embrace of political and cultural pluralism as a major feature of civil society. Islamism does not fulfil this requirement. Instead Islamists prefer to engage in polemics against 'crusaders and Jews' to whom the 'guilt' of the misery of Islamic civilization is attributed in an approach of self-victimization. The salvation is for them the Islamic shari'a state that can be unveiled as the most recent variety of totalitarianism. In contrast to most liberal and leftist supporters of 'Islamist anti-globalization', I know Islamism from within; it is not the Islamic path to modernity and pluralism on which a democratization project for the Islamic civilization could rest. Without a shared acceptance of the idea of democratic peace there can be no bridging.

Bridging in an age of religionization of conflict

Islamism has been introduced and placed in the context of Third World-ism in a critical dialogue with the Left inspired by the legacy of Horkheimer. The reference to tradition by Islamism is an invention made in the name of authenticity, but it is imbued with a distorted modernity. Islamism closes the door to bridging, because it religionizes, that is essentializes, the intercivilizational conflict in a binary mindset.

The adoption of modernity by Islamism is restricted to the techno-scientific instruments and it precludes the values of humanism based in cultural modernity. As a totalitarianism that rests on the politicization of Islam and the religionization of politics in the context of globalization, political Islam adopts only a semi-modernity. This venture resembles the 'reactionary modernism' (Herf) of the Nazis (see note 30). All Islamists, including the jihadists among them, refer to the meaning of religion, acting in the belief of being 'true believers', but they barely engage in a reflection of the reality they act within in relation to the religious symbols they employ. The symbols get a new meaning and they are applied while using modern technology (e.g. e-jihad) for fighting the crusaders and Jews viewed as enemies of Islam.

The reference to religion takes place in a process of religionization of conflict by religious fundamentalism. Islamists claim to be an expression of *al-sahwa al-Islamiyya* ('Islamic awakening'). Again, this is not a theology of liberation, as some contend. The reference to Islam in this religious fundamentalism is not instrumental, but based on a perception and on an interpretation of Islam itself. Therefore, Islamism is Islamic in its nature in the understanding of religion as a *fait social* (Emile Durkheim). It is not about scripture, nor about an ideal Islam that exists nowhere in reality. The critical theory of the Frankfurt School helps understand the political realities of an Islamic fundamentalism based on a re-imagined *umma* that cannot be reduced to an economic basis. No, culture is not a mere reflection of economy, it is not an *Überbau* ('superstructure'). For example: the real *umma* of Islam is characterized by a tremendous religious and cultural ever-changing diversity. In contrast, the notion of a cultural–political *umma*, viewed by the Islamists as a monolithic entity drives their political action. This is culture, not economy. Nevertheless, the Islamists use Marxist terms when they replace the proletariat by the *umma* and see in it the subject of an 'Islamic world revolution' (S. Qutb) to be carried out by a permanent jihad. The vision of this revolution is totalitarian. It is not poised to establish a free society, but rather a totalitarian rule named *Hakimiyyat Allah* ('God's rule'). As repeatedly argued, this rule is based on an invented shari'a. Given this totalitarian agenda as the goal of Islamist revolution, the question comes up: what does Islamism share with the Left?

It is by no means an essentializing orientalism, but the Islamist view itself that contends the existence of an essential Islam all Muslims are supposed to share. This is pure imagination employed in the service of a politicization of Islam. Here one encounters Islamist essentialism at work, unfortunately approved by postmodernist cultural relativists, who believe themselves to be against all essentialisms.

What seems to make the Left susceptible to admiring Islamism, and even its jihadism is the fact that it is a revolt against the West expressed in identity politics. However, theorists of the Left overlook the politicization of Islam resulting in a variety of religious fundamentalisms. One needs to speak also in plural of Islamisms. Despite honouring the existing great diversity within the global phenomenon of religious fundamentalisms, Martin Marty insisted in our *Fundamentalism Project* on discerning a 'family resemblance' that allows basic generalizations in the analysis without overlooking the nuances. Therefore, it is admittable to study religious fundamentalism as a general phenomenon and therefore to employ a general concept. In this understanding, the study of the Islamic variety of Islamic fundamentalism

addressed as Islamism and of its particularity, namely jihadism, leads to enlightenment about a new totalitarianism. This is the peculiarity of the Islamist variant of
religious fundamentalism, which engages in viewing political, social and economic
conflicts in a religionized manner. The drive of Islamism to re-make the world in
a reactionary, backwards–oriented world revolution indicates the return of religion
to world politics. It is not an Islamophobia to relate this drive to the fact of an
internationalist Islamism. The claimed Islamist revival of the Islamist universalist
worldview of *dar al-Islam* ('abode of Islam') viewed as a global entity results in the
expectation of mapping the entire globe in the 'abode of Islam'. The related 'remaking' claims are based on the politicization. The 'political Islam' of Islamism
envisions an enduring cosmic jihad for an Islamic world order. The fight for an
'Islamic state' is the local and regional aspect of an 'Islamic order' on the road of
a global direction. In this field there exists a great confusion. Even some experts
with an international reputation such as John Piscatori confuse pan-Islamism
(which is limited to uniting the *umma* in an imagined territoriality of *dar al-Islam*)
with Islamist internationalism that covers the whole universe. To be sure, an
imagined territoriality of *dar al-Islam* and an Islamist universalism translated into a
political internationalism are two different issues in that the latter claims to provide
a model valid for the world at large. Hence, the recent interest in the study of
religion in world politics. Due to the lack of proper knowledge, these issues are
confused in the Western debate also by the Left that deplorably makes no exception.
The assessment of Islamism by Buck-Morss cited in the introductory remarks serves
only one illustration. Buck-Morss speaks for the Left and reclaims even the critical
theory to undergird her argumentation. In contrast, this chapter argues that
Islamism can never be legitimated by the critical theory, if solid knowledge of both
political Islam and the Frankfurt School is in place.

Islamism, contestation and the global protest of religious movements

Despite all criticism, I do not overlook an existing social aspect of Islamism. In fact,
this is exactly what creates its appeal, be it to the Left in the West or to disaffected
Muslims at home. As Buck-Morss rightly argues and was earlier cited, Islamism is
'protest against present inequalities'. However, the contestation is articulated in
a religionized politics. Political Islam essentializes the issue and divides humanity
into 'Muslims' and 'unbelievers'. The traditional Islamic worldview determines
the ideology of these religious fundamentalists, albeit in a new shape. The duality
is that the new phenomenon is political, but it is also – intrinsically – related to a
traditional religious faith. It follows that a meaning is involved based on faith.
If this is ignored, the consequence would be to fall into the trap of reductionism ending up in deriving fundamentalism from its overall structural context in
reducing it to a social phenomenon of contestation. Islamism is, however, much
more. In other words – any explanation of Islamism reduced to the social bedrock

of non-religious factors – is completely wrong. In so arguing I am neither ignoring the social environment of fundamentalism, nor overlooking the related factors. What is being emphasized is that ideology and worldview do matter equally. At issue is a contestation articulated in religious terms. Religion is viewed here as a cultural system that determines the worldview. The articulation of social discontent in religious terms is much more than a cover for a social concern in that it also includes a meaning. At issue is a religio–ideological background and the related worldview. Not only Susan Buck-Morss, but also Jürgen Habermas (see note 43) seem not to understand the phenomenon of contemporary religio–political movements, which are based on the politicization of general Islamic beliefs to advance the goal of *nizam Islami* ('Islamic order') on global grounds. In this context the religious doctrine of jihad and the concept of shari'a ('law') were given a new meaning in the course of the return of the sacred in a political garb. The traditional Islamic worldview[45] assumes a new shape. Islamism is not Islam, but it is nonetheless based on a view of Islamic faith and on an interpretation of it.

Today, the writings of the founder of the Muslim Brotherhood, Hasan al-Banna – the grandfather of Tariq Ramadan – and also of the following Sayyid Qutb are spreading around the world of Islam far beyond the country of their origin, Egypt, where the ideology of Sunni-Islamism took its basic shape. The distinction is: Qutb provided the Muslim Brothers with a firm foundation and solid ideological grounds in contrast to the founder al-Banna who was more of an activist man of propaganda than theorist, even though he left twenty highly influential essays. Coupled with the writings of Qutb these essays are to be viewed as the core Islamist legacy continued today by Yussuf al-Qaradawi. At this point, it suffices to dismiss the placement of the founder of a totalitarian Islamist Movement of the Muslim Brotherhood, al-Banna, on an equal footing with the Islamic revivalist of the nineteenth century, al-Afghani. This intolerable equation, which is done by Tariq Ramadan – the grandson of al-Banna – is most controversial and does not hold water. The Left sympathizes with Ramadan, while Paul Berman ironically asks: who is afraid of this person?

No doubt, Islamist movements are movements of contestation and protest. However, Islamism both in its Sunni and Shi'i varieties pursues two major goals. These are first, a de-secularization[46] and second, the politics of de-Westernization of society within the framework of a new 'revolt against the West' (see note 2) understood as a purification in pursuit of remaking politics. The pursuit of both goals cannot be justified in the name of the Frankfurt School. Totalitarian Islamism is poised to accomplish a cultural purification directed against all Western values, and – as the Islamist Anwar al-Jundi states – the Jews who 'stand behind them'. The Jewish philosopher Horkheimer prescribes in his will the call to defend European values and I follow him as a Muslim. Islamism does not only contest Western hegemony, but also the cultural idea of the West itself. Unlike decoloniza- tion, the new revolt relates the rejection of Western dominance to the dismissal of all cultural patterns associated with Europe as the core of the West. The cultural modernity and its European humanism should be dissociated from Western hegemony. This differentiation is discarded by the Islamists as a 'Jewish idea' and this view makes clear that antisemitism is an essential part of the Islamist agenda.

Conclusion: Islamism and critical theory

This chapter departs from a revival of the critical theory of the Frankfurt School established by Max Horkheimer to argue against the Third World-ist upgrading of Islamist neo-absolutism misperceived as an anti-globalization. Islamism is not primarily against capitalism of the West, but vehemently against its humanist tradition. It is also argued that this movement is the new totalitarianism.[47] Herewith I find myself at some critical distance to the thinking of Susan Buck-Morss who alleges a positive connection between 'Islamism and critical theory' to give legitimacy to Islamist movements. On the basis of a familiarity with the legacy of Horkheimer and on a solid knowledge about Islamism,[48] I defend the secular world order[49] and the idea of the West that should not to be confused with capitalism. Western humanism is worth defending against any variety of totalitarianism.

I also defend Islam against the totalitarian ideology of Islamism. Islam is a cultural system and above all a religious faith, not what political Islam preaches: a *Hakimiyyat Allah* ('God's rule'). Let it be stated candidly: the view expressed by Western pundits and some people of the Left, that Islamists fight against globalization, is not supported by a study of the major Arabic sources of political Islam. Those Third World-ist Westerners who look at Islamism positively as anti-globalization are flawed in their thinking. They not only ignore the intercivilizational conflict, but also close the door to bridging between the civilizations.

To date, the highest authority in Islamist thought is Sayyid Qutb. His book *Ma'alim fi al-tariq* ('Signposts Along the Road') provides road signs for an inter-civilizational polarization. Qutb made the two-step strategy clear: first, to establish *hakimiyyat Allah* for *dar al-Islam* (again: this is neither the caliphate nor 'Islamic democracy'). The first step is a precondition for the second one, namely the Islamic world revolution aimed at accomplishing a world peace in Islamic terms, that is, based on an invented shari'a for the remaking of the world. The overall goal is the rule of *siyadat al-Islam* ('supremacy of Islam') to be established over the entire globe. This strategy guides Islamist internationalism and it is provisioned by Qutb as an *farida* ('religious obligation'). This is the meaning of 'jihad' understood as a world revolution of Islam against Enlightenment and humanism. Horkheimer writes in his will that it is obligatory for supporters of his critical theory to defend the West against totalitarianism. This is exactly an agenda opposed to the one of Qutb. Horkheimer (by the way, also Habermas) and Qutb have never been in the know about the work of the other. Those who defend the Islamist discourse in the name of critical theory, as Buck-Morss does, establish a wrong connection. The real connect is the rival agendas for the future of the world, not compatible with one another.

In short, Islamism is not a Third World liberation theology, but rather the Islamic variety of the global phenomenon of religious fundamentalism. It is based on a totalitarian ideology. However, there is a uniqueness in Islamism, namely in its pertinence to world politics as it relates to the claim of an Islamic world order. This is the core idea of an Islamist internationalism that resembles Leninism in its aim at re-making of the world. The drive for an 'Islamic world revolution' (Qutb) challenges the Weberian assumption of a disenchantment of the worldviewed as a process of secularization. Islamism is a project of a global de-secularization.

It is sad to see that some American supporters of critical theory, who fail to understand the nature of Islamism, end up supporting Islamism with leftist arguments. The Islamist variety in this process of politicization of religion, as a fundamentalism, discards the tradition of cultural modernity to which critical theory subscribes. True, Islamic fundamentalists are also a minority within Islam. However, it is not only a vocal, but also a most powerful minority empowered by global networks supported by immense financial funds. It is the best-organized opposition throughout the countries of Islamic civilization. Islamism also exists in the European and US diaspora creating difficult choices for all.

One may assume that by itself the fact that Islamic fundamentalists view the West as an entity characterized as an alliance of 'crusaders and Jews' would suffice for critical distance. At issue is an agenda for a religious dictatorship named 'God's rule' that legitimizes divine politics. The alternative to Islamism is democratic peace. Under a prevailing perception of Islam under siege this civilization is torn between culture and politics and it is in a deep crisis on all levels. The problem is the lack of proper knowledge in the West about the issue. There are few who understand.

Among those who address this issue candidly was the Holocaust survivor, the late Ernest Gellner. He criticized Islamic fundamentalism in favour of a European enlightenment. His position is based on understanding fundamentalism properly. The same Gellner was defamed by Edward Said in the *Times Literary Supplement* (*TLS*), because he failed to share Third World-ist Saidism. In his latest book Gellner wrote: 'Religious fundamentalism . . . gives psychic satisfaction to many . . . It is at present quite specifically persuasive and influential within one particular tradition, namely Islam.'[50]

As shown in this chapter it seems that Islamism has similar effects on the Left!

In conclusion, I state that Islamism is a counter-enlightenment based on a neo-absolutism that is elevated to a new totalitarianism. The will of Horkheimer includes the recommendation to take the side of freedom against any totalitarianism. I cannot repeat often enough that the conflict is not between Islam and the West. In contrast to Huntington I argue, there is a better Islam of rational medieval philosophers such as Avicenna and Averroës. The Marxist-Jewish philosopher Ernst Bloch, who knew Islam well, defended 'Avicenna and the Aristotelian left' against the orthodoxy of Islamic Salafism.[51]

In the past, Muslim rationalists were in a position to enrich medieval Islamic thought in a heritage based on Hellenist rationalism. This venture was unfortunately not in a position to be a lasting tradition. The reader is reminded of Chapter 4 where it is argued that Islamic rationalism presents a variety of humanism. That tradition is worth being revived as the alternative to Islamism, I suggest to reserve the notion of Islamic Revival to this tradition. At present, as in the past, civil Islam and its humanism could promote democracy and human rights and be a civilizational bridge. The revival of the Islamic rationalism of Averroës and Avicenna would incorporate Muslims into humanity along pluralist lines. If Islamist fundamentalism were to prevail, then there can be no bridging, but rather a 'closing of the Muslim mind'[52] in line with an existing medieval tradition. The alternative is a 'civil Islam'.[53]

If Horkheimer and his critical theory and the will based on it were to be taken seriously, then Western democrats – including the Left and the liberals – are supposed to take a stand against Islamist totalitarianism in a defence of Western humanism that has parallels in Islamic civilization. Horkheimer appreciated the West as an 'Insel der Freiheit in einem Ozean der Gewalt' ('Island of freedom in an ocean of violence'). In contrast, the Islamists defame the West as a marketplace 'for Jews and crusaders'. No Left can keep self-respect and share this antisemitic defamation by Islamism carried out as a contestation. Antisemitism is no contestation.

The contemporary Left is mistaken, because it equates contemporary capitalism with humanism. Marx himself was a great humanist. The reminder of the historical fact, that there existed in the past an Islamic humanism, helps an understanding that there can be cross-cultural bridges between the civilizations of Islam and the West. This is the option for a peaceful resolution of the intercivilizational conflict that this book proposes. The Third World-ist romanticization of Islamism as anti-globalism does not contribute to this end.

7
FROM CONFLICT TO BRIDGINGS

Conclusions

The foregoing pages of the present book on intercivilizational conflict unite six research papers rewritten with the intention to develop them into chapters of a coherent book. I might not have been as successful as I wish to be in this endeavour, but nonetheless I believe that this work is based on mature research that is united by a thread throughout chapters that reflect my major accomplishments in an academic life that spans forty years (1970–2010). The years of my study of Islam as a civilization in world affairs focus on value-conflicts. The name of the field of study that I have created in this venture for which I claim to be the founder is 'Islamology'. This is a book of Islamology.

The reader of the foregoing six chapters is now familiar with the fact that I, unlike Samuel Huntington, not only distinguish between 'clash' and 'conflict', but also between Islam and Islamism.[1] I am against any essentializing along alleged fault-lines. The notion of conflict deals instead with real differences that lead to tensions and generate conflicts that one can resolve. The focus on bridging within the framework of conflict resolution is the concern of Islamology. While researching in the final stages of the present project I had the honour and equally great window of opportunity to be invited to Seoul a few months after my retirement in September 2009. I received the invitation from the Academy of Korean Studies to deliver along with keynote speakers, Richard Bernstein and Shirin Ibadi, the first presentation at the Global Forum on Peace and Civilizations. The event was held in Seoul 3–4 December 2009. The fact that the paper I presented there includes conclusions to the research pursued over many years compelled me to include it here however in a rewritten draft, to serve as a conclusion to this volume. So I add it as Chapter 7. Its major idea is that a liberal Islam supports 'democratic peace' placed in opposition to 'global jihad'.[2] The reader is reminded of the approach of my research in the study of Islam and conflict. I do not refer to Islam as a faith and a cultural system, but rather to the politicization of Islam that results in a religionized politics. This is the distinction between Islam as faith and Islam as *fait social* in the contemporary politics of the twenty-first century.

Dialogue among civilizations as means of peaceful conflict resolution

The assumption of a value-based intercivilizational conflict that assumes a political shape is combined in the present book with thinking about conflict resolution. Within this framework a bridging between the civilizations is directed by the hope for global peace. This hope is associated with an agenda for a global democratization. Earlier it was expected that global democracy would replace the hardships of the Cold War after the end of the East–West conflict. However, this hope has faltered on the bedrock of the post-bipolar newly emerging conflicts. These were not predicted or even overlooked before. Bipolarity was not replaced by a global democracy based on a common understanding of one new civilization shared by all on the grounds of international peace. In contrast to that dream, a reality of intercivilizational conflict prevails and shapes world politics. The pre-existing conflict-ridden heterogeneity of civilizations that has been unveiled by post-bipolarity leads to a new pattern of conflict. Against all odds the vision of a 'democratic peace' continues to be the only promising future prospect for humanity even under these unfavourable conditions. There can be no stable world peace without fulfilling the basic requirement for it, namely global democracy.

In the recent past there have been two competing schools of thought struggling with one another over the outlined issue. The debate was launched in 1993 and again in 1996 by the late Harvard Professor Samuel P. Huntington when he pronounced the unpromising scenario of a 'clash of civilizations'. The rival school of thought came into being as a contradiction articulated in 1999 in response to Huntington. The counter-agenda was outlined by the then-acting president of Germany, Roman Herzog, in opposition to Huntington.

The point of departure is a concern identified as an effort at 'preventing the clash of civilizations'.[3] This notion does not deny the existence of conflict. True, if one contends that something has to be 'prevented', then one concedes that 'this something' does exist. I have been arguing throughout this book that there are tensions, but what they generate is not a 'clash', but rather a conflict between the civilizations. Each civilization has its own values and at times these may not be compatible with one another. Thus, the emergence of value-conflicts. There are scholars who argue for a global village and support this view with a reference to the instruments of 'advanced scientific technology' that are expected to be shared. These scholars overlook the fact that the use of the same modern technology does not generate consensus over the values of peace of democracy. Therefore, under the circumstances of a simultaneity of globalization and fragmentation, there is a need for a dialogue between the civilizations to establish common values. The intercivilizational value-conflict can be peacefully solved with the help of such dialogue, but a 'clash' cannot, because it essentializes and polarizes.

To sum up the concern of the present book I state that the argument for bridging is presented without denying an existing intercivilizational conflict. Bridging happens on the grounds of a cross-cultural morality that advocates a combination of peace and democracy. This is a concern that reflects a mindset committed to peace among the civilizations. The breeding ground of hope for a new civilization of peace in a reality of multiple civilizations is the existing potential for a cross-cultural morality that is also a humanism. The values of peace and democracy could underpin a universal worldview to be shared in an intercivilizational dialogue. What is that? To give an answer, let me elaborate on the core argument that I present in this book, the same one that I presented in December 2009 in Seoul operating on the premiss of a cross-cultural community that shares the mindset of peace between the civilizations.

Intercivilizational dialogue and bridging

The major assumption on which this book rests is that there is one humanity characterized by diversity expressed in the fact of multiple civilizations. The cultural valuerelated differences among them generate tensions that could lead to conflict. In the tradition of Hedley Bull I think that references to the history of ideas in political philosophy could be helpful for the understanding of current issues. The fourteenth-century Muslim philosopher Ibn Khaldun (died 1406) claimed to be the founder of *Ilm al-Umram* ('science of civilizations'). He suggested a view of different groups of peoples in terms of their belonging to different civilizations. The latter are based in each case on an *asabiyya* (*esprit de corps*) that guarantees the coherence and stability of each civilization. Yet, in that age of Ibn Khaldun there existed no overwhelming globalization and thus no need to find ways for living together in peace between the different civilizations in one structure. Today, pluralism in the sense of acknowledging the cultural other, is essential for world peace. It is not only about the West. Asia, in its west, south and South East includes many civilizations, of which Islam ranks at the top. Great portions of the Islamic world community of the *umma* exist in Asia. For the east of Asia where Muslims are, in contrast to other parts, a tiny minority, Islam matters as well. The Muslim neighbourhood is embedded in an international environment that affects the aspiration of peace and democracy. In world politics the major conflict is, however, between Islam and the West, often addressed by political theorists – such as John Brenkman – as a 'geopolitics of Islam' that equally matters to Asia.[4] This book, written by a scholar concerned with international studies who is at the same time a secular Muslim, combines three issue areas and relates them to one another. These are: the heterogeneity of civilizations, international conflict and the concern for shared values in the pursuit of peaceful conflict resolution. Underpinning the inquiry into these areas is the dream of global peace and democracy believed to materialize in the course of bridging. It is argued that intercivilizational dialogue could serve as a means for this post-bipolar conflict resolution driven by the aspiration to accomplish and establish peace and democracy on global grounds. In this book

I distinguish between the structural globalization generated by global economic networking facilitated by the modern advanced technology and the cultural fragmentation generated by value-conflicts (see Chapter 2). To be sure, democracy is based on a value system and therefore I do not place democracy (values) and technology (instruments) on an equal footing in their effects. For instance, religious fundamentalists are modernists who embrace modern science and technology instrumentally, while they vehemently reject all of the value of cultural modernity.[5]

The notion of 'dialogue among civilizations'[6] viewed as a means for peaceful conflict resolution implies a dissociation from the controversial and highly disputed contribution by Samuel Huntington. His *Clash of Civilizations* rightly refers to a reality characterized by a 'heterogeneity of civilizations'. This is a theme that has moved to the fore, but fault-lines must not be the result. As early as the 1960s the great Sorbonne scholar, the late Raymond Aron, predicted that the East–West conflict could not last forever; he argued that this conflict was, at that time, veiled – what he named – the 'heterogeneity of civilizations'.[7] I add to this the insight that this heterogeneity generates an intercivilizational conflict. I repeat: a conflict is not a clash. Today, Aron's prediction is verified by a reality suppressed in politics and scholarship. As stated, there is no one civilization, but multiple ones and therefore world peace cannot be discussed properly without admitting the fact that people adhere to values and to worldviews that emanate from different civilizations. In this context, value-conflicts emerge. The light at the end of this tunnel could be the intercivilizational dialogue as a means for peaceful conflict resolution in the course of bridging.

Having stated Aron's insight about the heterogeneity of civilizations with the inference that there is no one world civilization, but instead sheer diversity, the next step would be to acknowledge that this diversity is not only a blessing. Diversity can be paired with mutual intercivilizational fertilization. This would be in place in a positive scenario. Otherwise diversity could become a menace when it is a source of conflict. At issue are values that are not always compatible with one another (e.g. shari'a vs legislative law). Thus, there is no common and shared understanding about the meaning of democracy and peace. How could this obstacle be overcome?

In the contemporary debate two extremes dominate: one of clash, the other of a 'convergence' of civilizations. In contrast to these extremes there are scholars who even deny the existence of civilizations altogether to speak instead of a very unspecific 'humanity' while ignoring diversity. Do not be mistaken: it is not only wrong but also consequential to identify humanity with one civilization. This is a dangerous approach, because there are Western scholars who speak of 'one civilization' and mean by this the West, as did W. McNeill.[8] There are others who deny the intercivilizational conflict, and place the relations between Europe and Islam in one 'Christian–Islamic civilization'. In real history there never existed such a thing. This book goes beyond this thinking to seek better avenues, one of which is conflict resolution in an intercivilizational dialogue that acknowledges a diversity of civilizations.

The reality of a diversity of civilizations is determined both by fertilization and by conflict. Based on two normative approaches, one of the potential of sharing values and the other of a meaningful dialogue, this book seeks to establish international relations as intercivilizational relations. If a sharing of universal values, such as individual human rights, secular democracy, pluralism, tolerance and civil society is feasible, then a cross-cultural morality and a shared discourse based on rational knowledge is within reach. I prefer to use these terms in the context of diversity instead of speaking in the singular about one civilization. In a process of global cross-cultural communication, peoples of different, even rival and competing civilizations (e.g. Islam and other civilizations in Asia and in the West) could talk to one another. They can establish a dialogue shaped by tolerance and aimed at peaceful conflict resolution, also in a democratic way. There are regional civilizations (e.g. China, India) and others that claim universality (Islam and the West). This claim is the problem in a world based on diversity. Therefore, a political culture of pluralism in which peace among civilizations could thrive promises an exit from the dilemma. Both civilizations, the West and Islam, are culturally different, but they can share among themselves and with others a cross-cultural international morality that combines the acknowledgment of difference with shared core values. This is what cultural pluralism is about. There can be no bridging without consent to this pluralism.

Islam as a civilization in the age of conflict among civilizations

The focus of the present book is the study of conflict combined with an inquiry into the potential for an intercultural dialogue viewed as a means of peaceful conflict resolution. The approach is general, however, with a focus on the history of Islam and Europe. All foregoing chapters acknowledge that there were positive records of mutual impact, but this acknowledgement does not ignore, however, the fact that both civilizations were also at odds. In the past and in the present this happened to the extent of becoming enemies waging war against one another, be it jihad or crusades in the past, and jihadism and 'war on terror' in the present. There exists an inimical image of Islam in the West maintained through continued stereotyping. Similarly, in the world of Islam the West does not enjoy a friendly image. Under the present conditions of post-bipolarity these intercivilizational issues touch on world politics. Today, there is a crisis of the 'order' of the world. Some observers suspect that the debate on civilization and world politics was launched by the West itself in a desperate search for a world political enemy supposed to substitute communism. It was suggested that Islam is the 'candidate' for this function. However, this view is utterly wrong. This issue is the reality of a 'heterogeneity of civilizations' and the conflicts that emerge in this context. It has already been acknowledged that this diversity could become a source of conflict in world politics. In the past, Islamic civilization resorted to jihad worldwide for the spread of Islam.[9] This expansionist mentality is revived today in an Islamist internationalism that becomes a source of conflict.

Islamist internationalism predates post-bipolarity. The increasing interest in Islam is not merely the outcome of the general effects of globalization. The issue is rather the pertinence of geopolitics of Islam in post-bipolar world politics. This matters most to the Mediterranean being the basin of the geopolitical European–Islamic border, but it also affects Asia in all of its parts. It is unfortunate that non-Muslims, be they Europeans or Asians, know so little about Islam. Images and cultural perceptions replace knowledge and have become the most important source of viewing Muslims. When it comes to conflict and bridging in intercivilizational relations it is unfortunate to see that ignorance about the cultural other is an impediment to peace. The simplistic talk about Islam as if it were a monolithic, holistic entity indicates this ignorance. Islam in Asia is not the same as Islam in Africa. The problem is that Western scholars of Islam who internationally dominate the field are usually trained either as anthropologists or as philologians concerned with classical languages. Social and historical phenomena on a global scale cannot be properly explained by philologians or anthropologists, as they are also neither informed about nor interested in the social and political developments in that part of the globe. Nonetheless, they have their firm views and are righteous and suppress other views about the modern Islamic societies in the process of peer-reviewing. This imposition is sad, but true.

The pertinent matter is that Islam in Asia and elsewhere is more than a religion; it also assumes the shape of a cultural system.[10] The politicization of this cultural system in a crisis-ridden context is happening in the international environment of a post-bipolar world and this process leads to giving religious fundamentalism a boost. In the present post-bipolar world time, this movement threatens peace and undermines the inclusion of the world of Islam into the envisioned process of global democratization. Hence, the need for a change in religion's pendulum between culture and politics in all world regions. This turn could be the acceptance of a cross-cultural international morality shared by all. Religion is to be restricted to a faith and to the related religious–cultural practices in order to keep it free from political abuse. No doubt, the ethics of Islam allows an international morality as political ethics that helps integrate Muslims in a peaceful world politics. But, there is an urgency to stop the politicization of religious worldviews, as these are related to claims that polarize and lead to a conflict. When this happens, then the dreadful 'Clash of Civilizations' becomes a self-fulfilling prophecy. Therefore this clash has to be averted in an intercivilizational dialogue.

Very often the question is asked, why the focus lies on Islam in this debate on global civilization and peace. The reason is that Hinduism, Buddhism or Confucianism, do not raise universal claims. In contrast, Islam – as much as Western Christianity does – claims to be a world religion for entire humanity. This religion represents a universal orientation with some political connotations. Even though I strictly distinguish between the faith of Islam and the contemporary political ideology of Islamism (see note 1), I admit that Islam is more prone to a politicization than any other religion. The political aspects involved explain the centuries-old rivalry between the two universal civilizations. Islamic civilization continues to be based on religion, but Europe has changed its identity. In the course of the Renaissance and Enlightenment Christianity underwent a secularization, replacing the orientation of Christian Jerusalem with the secular one of Greek humanism.[11] However, Western civilization kept its universal outlook, if in a secular shape. In this process, Christian Europe has become the secular West. The history of Islam and Christian or Western civilization is not only marked by the Islamic jihad and the Christian crusades in the past, and by colonialism and anti-colonial jihad in modern history, but also by positive encounters of cross-cultural fertilization.

Today, Europe[12] hosts about 23 million Muslims in its West and 12 million in its south east, but Islam is not as at home as it is, for instance, in Asia. From the point of view of peace, politicized Islam generates bloody conflicts between states (India and Pakistan) and within states such as in China (Xinjiang), Thailand, Malaysia, Philippines and even Indonesia. In Europe the lack of integration in society and polity makes young Muslims susceptible to al-Qaeda-jihadism.[13] Those tensions fuel the existing intercivilizational conflict.[14]

Religion and politics in Europe and Islam

Among the basic features of our present age is the return of religion to the public square. The classical work of Norbert Elias is generally accepted with the hypothesis that there are global standards of civilizational developments. These are today determined by the secular West, not by Christianity, or any other religion.[15] The transformation of 'Western Christendom' into Western civilization resulted from the secularization of Christianity in Europe. The major steps were the Renaissance, the Reformation and the Enlightenment as well as the French Revolution. Religious reforms accompanied the transition to modern society and the unfolding of cultural modernity. Since the age of the Enlightenment and the French Revolution we may no longer speak of a Christian religion-based civilization in Europe. Let it be reiterated for the sake of clarity, that the new Western civilization is predominantly secular. In comparison to the developments in Western Europe, the Islamic civilization continues to be overly determined and characterized by the religion of Islam and by its specific *Weltanschauung*. The return of religion is often viewed as 'Islamic revival'. People seem to overlook the fact that Islamic rationalism in medieval Islam was paired with secular humanism. This tradition was suppressed. If this had not been the case, a development could have taken a different course to contribute to an Islamic model of secularization. This was not the case. The lesson for today is that a cross-cultural morality linking all civilizations to one another in an ethics of peace and dialogue has to be secular. Why? The religious precepts of one religion cannot be accepted by the believers of other religions. On these grounds the book has argued in one of its chapters for a revival of the legacy of Islamic humanism.

The swinging pendulum of religion between culture and politics does not promote moderation and peace, but rather a politicization in an exposure to modernity. The revival of a religion-based political universalism compels us to ask whether this is an obstacle to the people of Islam joining a democratic global peace based on secular tenets.

The study of intercivilizational conflict pursued in this book is motivated and driven by the search for a peaceful solution. In the past there were the positive Western–Islamic encounters on the basis of reason and rationality. When religion becomes linked with politics violent conflict has generally been the result. For evidence one may look at the Islamic history of jihad conquests and – in contrast – at the Hellenization of Islam in the period between the ninth and twelfth centuries. Beyond such violence there were the Islamic influences on Europe on the eve of the Renaissance. These historical hints concern the past, but nevertheless continue to be topical. The increasing migration of Muslim peoples to Europe gives Islam a new significance for the old world. This means that a new reasoning on these issues is needed. Consequently, European–Islamic relations give rise to questions concerning the future of Europe with regard to the placing of religion and politics in society. The issue was addressed in a Cornell project as *Religion in an Expanding Europe*.[16] The ground for this reasoning needs to be secular to underpin a cross-cultural morality acceptable to all diverse religious communities now existing in Europe, the hub of Western civilization. In my view the twenty-first century compels Islam and the West to find ways for peaceful co-existence. By this I mean a secular peace between civilizations to be expanded to the rest of the world. A model for an intercivilizational dialogue could be established in this context with important consequences for bridging as a peace strategy, as this book has argued.

Understanding world politics and the heterogeneity of civilizations

The argument of heterogeneity of civilizations in terms of diversity put forward in this book implies that there are different understandings of state order, law, society, religion and knowledge as well as of the ethics of war and peace. This book squarely addresses these differences in civilizational terms by arguing that these are not new, but arise in a new shape to generate value-conflicts. Value-related differences between civilizations have existed throughout the history of humanity. There were also gaps of development in the 'civilizing process' (see note 15) that generate tensions. However, in their civilizational interaction with others people develop civilizational self-awareness. This can be negative and positive. The Mediterranean has always been a basin of these processes in the interaction between the Islamic and the Western civilization. As the historian Henri Pirenne has shown, the birth of Europe resulted from the Islamic challenge in the Mediterranean. Under conditions of globalization and modernity the conflict patterns change. No globalization can undo the heterogeneity of civilizations and it does not generate a new world culture, but rather cultural fragmentation and tensions, as argued in Chapter 2.

Today, no proper understanding of world politics is possible without accounting for the heterogeneity of civilizations. In an age of politicization of religion under conditions of post-bipolarity this reference to the civilizational approach to the study of world politics is nonetheless disputed. Some critics of this approach refer to globalization in the meaning of standardization and argue in favour of an emerging world civilization that bulldozes all cultural particularisms. This assumption is wrong. A reference to the flaws of the ideology of globalism brings to light the underlying fundamental errors. Globalists base their sweeping generalizations on wrong assumptions. Their claim that globalization eliminates all differences between cultures and civilizations through the effects of standardization is most questionable, for a 'McWorld' is nothing else than a fallacy on all counts. The spread of American popular culture is mistaken to be a wholesale standardization on global grounds. For instance, Asian Muslims, and others, may fully enjoy McDonald's hamburgers without sharing any of the American values held to be an indication of 'McCulture'! This book avoids these simplifications.

Another line of argument refers to the parabolic satellite dish claiming its unbeatable standardizing effects. In fact, this contention is baseless. For instance, Turkish migrants in Germany use these dishes to receive Turkish TV at home and continue to live in parallel societies. Our world does not become a 'McWorld' in terms of cultural standardization as some envisage. Well, colonialism, too, wanted to Westernize the world, but it failed to do so. In a joint project, my Indian colleague T.K. Oommen subtitled the book on identity that emerged from it in this manner: *From Colonialism to Globalism*.[17] This perception of such a historical continuity invokes collective memories that are not favourable to meeting the needs of cross-cultural morality in the search for conflict resolution in an environment imbued with intercivilizational tensions.

Dialoging with whom?

Civilizational unity and cultural diversity

In the terminology used in the present book cultures are viewed locally. They herald diversity within a given civilization. Therefore, culture and civilization are not the same and for this reason it is wrong to use the terms interchangeably. Nonetheless, these terms are often confused and negatively affect the debate about the pertinence of civilizations. As repeatedly shown, some also confuse the study of conflict in international politics and multicultural societies with the clash established by Huntington. This thinking distracts from the substance of the matter. To rectify this one needs to understand that culture and civilization are terms that have different meanings and are therefore not identical. In my study of International Relations I focus on culture and view it as a local system underpinned by a social production of meaning.[18] Seen from this angle, cultures are related in each case to a socially relevant set of values pertinent to a local framework. In my enquiry into civilizations I look at cultures that have a family resemblance and therefore tend to group together to form one civilization. Mostly, civilization is defined in terms of a shared view of the world. In short: cultures are local, civilizations are regional groupings of cultures which share a common worldview. For instance, Islam in India, or in South East Asia, is a different culture from the West African Islam of Senegal. Nonetheless, both belong to the very same Islamic civilization. In this meaning there exists one Islamic civilization, which consists of a great variety of local cultures, but humanity itself is not a civilization.

There are, of course, conflicts within the very same civilization. Ethnic conflicts within the Islamic civilization bring to an expression the politicization of differences among these local cultures (e.g. Turks and Kurds in Turkey). While these conflicts make world-political headlines, they are barely understood in the media. Above all, it is generally not well understood that ethnic conflicts are indications of developments within the Islamic civilization. In this sense, it is not correct to talk about an 'international conflict of cultures' or a 'battle of cultures' if this is meant to describe the intercivilizational dimension of conflict in world politics. Ethno-cultural and civilizational conflicts are different issues, and they ought not to be confused. The first are local and domestic, the latter refer to regional and international issues. These differentiations are pertinent for selecting a partner in an intercivilizational dialogue aimed at conflict resolution in the course of bridging.

In their rhetoric of universalism some civilizations claim universal validity for their views. It is detrimental to dialogue when a civilization claims for itself a world mission, as did the Islamic and the Western European civilizations in the past to their neighbours. In these cases there can be no real dialogue. It is not an indication of geocentric bias to focus on Islam and to state that other civilizations outside the Mediterranean were restricted to a regional status. In addition, Confucianism, for instance, lays no claims to universality, and is therefore more tolerant to others than Islam, or Christianity has ever been. It is necessary to mention both aspects, the positive and the negative, but for the sake of peace and a better future we need to focus on the positive heritage of intercivilizational fertilization without losing sight of the conflict.

In this book it has been established that value systems and normative positions between the civilizations are underlying the dissent. The West and Islam, for instance, have their own and therefore in each case different understandings of peace. For Muslims, world peace – as I understand it – can only be based on the expansion of the 'abode of Islam' to map the entire world. According to the Muslims' worldview, the world is divided into *dar al-Islam* ('abode of Islam') and *dar al-harb* ('house of war'). In the pursuit of peace this dichotomy needs to be overcome. This work to be done by Muslims themselves is still missing: the cited classical dichotomy has never been revised, even though no reality underlies it. I find it appalling that some representatives of the Muslim community in Great Britain define Europe in the age of Muslim migration as a part of *dar al-Islam*. This is not a mindset open to an honest dialogue.

In the past, Western politicians and scholars have seen the allegedly Westernized world along a similar dichotomy which was secular, but nevertheless self-centred. There are American scholars who define the clash between the two civilizations as 'Jihad vs McWorld'. This is simply wrong. In fact, we are dealing with a clash-mentality related to the politicization of two universal outlooks. On the surface one may think a 'new Cold War' between the secular and the divine is on the rise. It is obvious that 'McDonaldizing' the world could never amount to a contribution for abolishing the differences between Islam and the West, nor will it lay grounds for world peace. Peace is possible, but the grounds need to be different ones. Cultural and religious pluralism is a requirement for sustainable peace between the civilizations.

To date, the study of the civilizational dimension of conflict in world politics continues to be disputed and to be under pressure to find its way to the academe. To be sure I repeat that conflict and Huntington's 'fault-lines' are different issues. The academic study of the impediments to a real dialogue has to screen self-assertive identity politics. It is a fact that this identity politics is, by and large, based on a civilizational awareness of the self. Despite the existing networking, this awareness contributes to a divide in that it makes people separate themselves from others in asserting their belonging to a different civilization. As a Muslim scholar living between rival civilizations, I am deeply convinced that it is an illusion to believe that 'McWorld' will eliminate this phenomenon. In my book on *The Challenge of Fundamentalism* (see note 18), I further developed the formulation used earlier in Chapter 2 of this book 'simultaneity of globalization (in the field of politics, economics, communication and transport) and cultural fragmentation'. The latter relates to the lack of shared values.

Is an intercivilizational dialogue under conditions of a de-Westernization agenda feasible?

Historically, the process of globalization was generated by European expansion. In response, an emergence of civilizational self-awareness led to conflicts. The 'revolt against the West' is related to developments of value-conflicts that become global;[19] the universal validity of Western values in the context of a revolt against the hegemony of the West is contested. Anti-Westernism is more than a resentment, as it includes a demand for a de-Westernization of the world. This is the outcome that reflects the contemporary historical background for the emerging regional and international conflicts at the beginning of the twenty-first century. How feasible is bridging under these conditions?

For interpreting anti-Westernism as an effort at a de-Westernization leading to conflict in terms of value-conflicts, I simultaneously underline the fact that civilizations cannot serve as actors in world politics. This insight is well received. The exit strategy is dialogue on the level of cultures and civilizations. It concedes, to some extent, that there is a justification for the claim of de-Westernization, in particular when it indicates a resistance to cultural standardization. In principle, this resistance could lead to more plurality, but it is also perilous. For instance the demand for a de-Westernization raised by Islamists legitimized by the notion of authenticity ends up in a closed mindset and an agenda of cultural purification highly detrimental to the intercultural dialogue.[20]

Western cultural relativism fails to understand this self-assertive, mostly aggressive neo-absolutism.[21] Those Europeans who subscribe to cultural relativism also fail to understand that by relativizing their values they are, consequently, undermining them. However, such undermining of one's values and standards is not only self-defeating in such a situation but it is also a great obstacle to a cultural dialogue aimed at promoting peace. Some put the blame on others. There is a simultaneity in which the Islamists engage in a mindset of self-victimization, on the one hand, and on the other there are self-accusations by Westerners. Both are inappropriate for dialogue. One has to learn from the past that this kind of inflammatory dialogue leads nowhere. Let it be said in clarity, the cultural design of the dialogue should not conceal the nature of the new conflicts; they are political and economic, but have cultural undercurrents. Nonetheless, the importance of culture should not be overlooked or underestimated. In the dialogue cultural issues have moved to centre stage in domestic, regional and international communication. To understand the new post-bipolar environment, one has to acknowledge that culture matters.[22]

Between polarization and building bridges between the civilizations

Nearing the end, I reiterate, dialogue is a peaceful agenda to solve the civilizational conflict. Given the different options and scenarios, the preference for bridging through mediation and dialogue as an alternative to the 'clash' scenario makes it imperative to reach an intercivilizational consensus over commonalities. In my view, secular democracy and individual human rights are to be ranked as top priorities in this consensus. The reader is reminded of the notion of 'cross-cultural international morality' on which most views on bridging in the present book rest.

Prior to the resurgence of political Islam, Western observers held the view that democratization in the world of Islam would take place along the lines of a global/universal Westernization. In the last decade of the twentieth century there has been talk about worldwide democratization to be brought about by the end of bipolarity. Adverse changes and developments, however, have compelled me to rethink the issue as the end of the East–West conflict did not in itself create global democratic structures. Among the requirements for democratic transformation is a reconciliation of Islam with democracy. Referring to an authentic cultural underpinning for democratization in the Islamic world, I mean cultural and religious reforms. I am aware of the fact that the empowerment of Islamism is working against this process. Unlike the catastrophic security policies of the West I insist on a pursuit of a secular democratic response to Islamist terrorism.[23] Western flawed policies were repeated during the Arab Spring. Instead of a real democratization there has been an empowerment of Islamism.

The cultural effort at reconciling democracy and human rights with, at times, adversely oriented local cultures is a home-work (that is, the part of the job one has to do oneself) for the concerned peoples themselves. Eurocentric policies are by all means detrimental because they work like a missionary action. Euro-arrogance is as much damaging as the ignorance of Westerners about non-Western cultures; these are equally great obstacles. If we are to understand the nature of tensions and conflict between the civilizations, in the first place we need to acquire the necessary knowledge about the other civilizations. This is a basic precondition for a peaceful neighbourhood and also for the dialogue we need, based on mutual respect. Getting to know other civilizations means becoming acquainted with their ways of looking at the world in order to be in a position to co-exist with them. To be sure, the approach of understanding and tolerance does not preclude the possibility of saying: 'No, thank you!' This 'no' applies in the first place to Islamist efforts at hijacking democracy and human rights for giving legitimacy to their venture of re-making the world along their concept of divine order. Their contempt for secular concepts cannot be countered by one-way tolerance that would be a promotion of intolerance. One has also to quote Sir Karl Popper in his defence of the 'open society against its enemies', who stated that 'we should therefore claim, in the name of tolerance, the right not to tolerate the intolerance'. The non-negotiable premiss of intercivilizational dialogue is the acceptance of peace and democracy on the grounds of equality.

The findings

To sum up the conclusions of the present book on conflict and cultural dialogue among the civilizations the distinction between an intercivilizational dialogue and negotiation is essential. Dialogue is not business bargaining, nor is it a mere political negotiation as happens among governments. In an intercultural dialogue on the societal level the issue is intercivilizational peace in a drive to end all practices of mutual hostility. There is a need to share values about this peace in a dialogue that deals with conflicts not with shared politeness. I remind readers of the fact this book has emphasized, namely, that one should not forget that we can only talk to those who are capable of dialogue, i.e. are honestly ready to talk about an agreement to common values of peace and democracy. Islamists are Islamic fundamentalists who either refuse any dialogue with the 'crusading West' (the jihadists), or engage in the practice of doublespeak for tactical reasons, and pay lip-service to the rules (not the values) of democratic institutions next to all kinds of prevarications. Institutional Islamists willfully (*iham*) deceive in the pursuit of religio–political ends and cannot be democratic.[24] The dialogue with them is not a form of dialogue needed! In criticizing the Islamic side, I need to add that unfortunately also not all Europeans and Americans are capable of dialogue, either. Some Westerners lack honesty as well! For instance, the promotion of foreign trade – as is the case in Germany – is not a concern for intercivilizational dialogue, but an abuse of it. The same applies to the use of human rights in US foreign policy.[25]

   The necessity of bridging between the civilizations to be pursued as an intercultural dialogue has to be driven by a search for value-based commonalities between the civilizations. In this understanding of dialogue, as a pursuit for a global democratization,[26] and also as a means for peaceful conflict resolution between civilizations, the acknowledgement of conflict is imperative. Hereby one has to put the incommensurability of values and worldviews related to civilizations on the table. This is a challenge, but not a fault-line. Silence about this conceals conflict and then it can never be resolved. The statement of an intercivilizational conflict should not be defamed as an effort at finding a substitute for the previous East–West conflict. In our age, dialogue in world politics is an important method that brings people from different cultures and civilizations together to talk to one another in honesty and frankness about the promising avenues for a better future.

In short, dialogue between the civilizations should be a means for conflict resolution, not a forum for rhetorical pronouncements for the gallery. To be sure, a shared, cross-cultural morality is a basic requirement for this endeavour. I am aware of the potential that in this dialogue each party would be tempted to impose its own philosophy of life on others. As a result, value-conflict would also be inevitable in the dialogue itself. In this context, cultural relativism in the West, which denies the universality of values (e.g. those of human rights), is self-defeating and self-destructive. This relativist mindset ignores the fact that a form of neo-absolutism is developing in other civilizations, for example in political Islam, which I view as religious fundamentalism. In this case the limits for cultural pluralism become obvious.[27] The morality of pluralism is neither in line with fundamentalism nor with cultural relativism. In contrast, cultural pluralism shares the acknowledgement of diversity, but only within the framework of an acceptance of core values. There can be no peace between civilizations without sharing core values for a moral conduct of life accepted by all humanity.

Having determined dialogue among civilizations as a means of peaceful conflict resolution, I dissociate my thinking from the controversial and highly disputed contribution by Samuel Huntington on a 'clash of civilizations'. In a different reasoning I refer to the reality of 'the heterogeneity of civilizations' and this book moves this theme to the fore. At the end of the journey one is reminded of the Sorbonne scholar, the late Raymond Aron, who predicted that the East–West conflict could not last forever; he argued at the time that this conflict had veiled the heterogeneity of civilizations and generated an intercivilizational conflict. Today this prediction is verified by a reality suppressed in politics and scholarship. World peace cannot be discussed properly without admitting the fact that people belong by values and worldview to different civilizations. In this context there are value-conflicts and this book suggests an intercivilizational dialogue as a means for peaceful conflict resolution.

Given the heterogeneity of civilizations this book contests the idea of one world civilization and acknowledges diversity. This diversity is a blessing when intercivilizational mutual fertilization is in place, but it is the opposite when it becomes a source of conflict. This happens when values do not match with one another (e.g. shari'a vs legislative law). This book takes pains to go beyond the two approaches that dominate the related debate: one of 'clash', the other of a 'convergence' of civilizations. In contrast to these extremes it is peculiar when some scholars deny the existence of civilizations altogether to speak instead of a very unspecific humanity while ignoring diversity. Also the intercivilizational conflict is denied, for instance between Europe in Islam. Another peculiarity is those who contend a 'Christian–Islamic civilization'. In this book I have chosen to go beyond all of these highly questionable approaches to seek better avenues.

All of the preceding chapters leave ideological approaches behind and instead acknowledge the reality of a diversity of civilizations. This includes both fertilization and conflict. Based on two normative approaches, first, the potential of sharing values and second, dialogue, this book is an effort to look at intercivilizational relations. If a sharing of universal values such as those of individual human rights, secular democracy, pluralism, tolerance and civil society is feasible then a cross-cultural morality and a shared discourse based on rational knowledge are within reach at the end of the tunnel. In this global, cross-cultural communication, peoples of different, even rival and competing civilizations (e.g. Islam and the West) could talk to one another in a dialogue aimed not only at conflict resolution, but also at establishing cordiality. This 'Encountering the stranger' is the proper 'global communication' and is a promising path for a better future of humanity.[28] There are regional civilizations (e.g. China, India) and others that claim universality (Islam and the West). The focus of this book was on the latter because it is an international relations-based inquiry founded on assumptions of a world based on diversity and a political culture of pluralism in which peace among civilizations could thrive in a global context. The fact that the conclusions of the present book on the civilization of the West and Islam were presented at an academy in a country, Korea, that belongs to neither (see the reference in note 3), provides evidence for the global pertinence of the present subject in all points to humanity.

NOTES

1 Intercivilizational value-conflicts and bridging in the pursuit of post-bipolar peace

1 See B. Tibi, *Islam between Culture and Politics* (New York: Published in Association with Harvard University's WCFIA by Palgrave, 2001, 2nd enlarged edition, 2005) and also by the same: *Political Islam, World Politics and Europe: Democratic Peace and Euro-Islam versus Global Jihad* (Oxford and New York: Routledge, 2008).

2 B. Tibi, *Islamism and Islam* (New Haven: Yale University Press, 2012, forthcoming).

3 Thomas S. Kuhn, *The Structure of Scientific Revolutions* (Chicago/IL: University of Chicago Press, 2nd edition, 1970), Chapters 5–8.

4 Raymond Aron, *Paix et Guerre entre les Nations* (Paris: Colmann Levy, 1962), Chapter 8. It is unfortunate that in *Clash of Civilizations* Samuel P. Huntington, (New York: Simon & Schuster, 1996) ignores this book by Aron. Huntington's rhetoric is contradicted by the contributions included in Roman Herzog *et al.*, *Preventing the Clash of Civilizations* (New York: St. Martin's Press, 1999), herein essay by B. Tibi on cross-cultural morality, pp. 107–26, and also B. Tibi, 'Jihadism and Intercivilizational Conflict', in: Shahram Akbarzadeh and Fethi Mansouri, eds, *Islam and Political Violence* (London: Taures, 2007), pp. 39–64. See the references in note 1 and also Bruce Lincoln, *Holy Terrors. Thinking About Religion after September 11* (Chicago/IL: University of Chicago Press, 2005), Chapter 2.

5 In his book *The Foreigner's Gift. The Americans, the Arabs and the Iraqis in Iraq* (New York: Free Press, 2006), Fouad Ajami describes this liberation from Saddam's dictatorship which as a system has been identified by the Iraqi Samir al-Khalil (alias Kanan Makiyya) as: *Republic of Fear. The Politics of Modern Iraq* (Berkeley: University of California Press, 1989). Despite all critiques of Bush and his wrong policies one should never forget Saddam's atrocities; see also Said Aburish, *Saddam Hussein, The Politics of Revenge* (New York: Bloomsbury, 2000), and Middle East Watch, ed., *Human Rights in Iraq* (New Haven: Yale University Press, 1990).

6 See Helmut Anheier and Y. Raj Isar, eds, *Conflicts and Tensions*, vol. 1 of *The Culture and Globalization Series* (London: Sage 2007), and B. Tibi, *Islam's Predicament with*

Modernity. Religious Reform and Cultural Change (New York: Routledge, 2009), Chapter 5.

7   John Brenkman, *Cultural Contradictions of Democracy* (Princeton/NJ: Princeton University Press, 2007), p. 165.

8   See the report on Obama in: *New York Times*, 'America seeks bonds to Islam, Obama insists', 7 April 2009, frontpage.

9   Editorial of *International Herald Tribune*, 'Ending the clash of civilizations', 13 April 2009, p. 8. Obama visited in June 2009 a second major Islamic country, Egypt, and his message in his thoughtful speech in Cairo, 4 June 2009 was not only highly thrilling, but also resonated greatly.

10 On this perception see Graham Fuller and Ian Lesser, *A Sense of Siege. The Geopolitics of Islam and the West* (Boulder/CO: Westview, 1995). For a conceptual – however realism-oriented and therefore state-centred – approach on the place of perception see Robert Jervis, *Perception and Misperception in International Politics* (Princeton/NJ: Princeton University Press, 1976).

11 The classical study on this subject is by the late Turkish scholar Niyazi Berkes, *The Development of Secularism in Turkey* (New York: Routledge, new edition, 1998).

12 Fore more details see Zeyno Baran, Divided Turkey, in: *Journal of Democracy*, vol. 19, 1 (2008), pp. 55–69, and B. Tibi, 'Turkey's Islamist Danger. Islamists Approach Europe', in: *Middle East Quarterly*, vol. 16, 1 (2009), pp. 47–54.

13 See Chapter 6 on secularization and de-secularization in B. Tibi, *Islam's Predicament with Modernity* (note 6), pp. 178–208.

14 See the authoritative work by Fernand Braudel, *A History of Civilizations* (London: Penguin Press, 1994), and specifically on Islamic civilization see Marshall Hodgson, *The Venture of Islam*, 3 vols (Chicago/IL: University of Chicago Press, 1974).

15 William McNeill, *The Rise of the West. A History of the Human Community* (Chicago/IL: University of Chicago Press, 1963).

16 European expansion gave the world a new shape, see Philip D. Curtin, *The World and the West. The European Challenge* (New York: Cambridge University Press, 2000), but the related project of a Westernization of the globe failed; see Theodore von Laue, *The World Revolution of Westernization* (New York: Oxford University Press, 1987).

17 The authority of Bull is acknowledged by the Harvard professor Stanley Hoffmann who prides himself on being a disciple of Raymond Aron; he similarly praised Hedley Bull in his essay, 'Hedley Bull and his Contribution to International Relations', in his collected essays, *World Disorders* (Lanham/MD: Rowman & Littlefield, 1998), pp. 13–34.

18 Hedley Bull, *The Anarchical Society* (New York: Columbia University Press, 1977), p. 273. This lack of unity of outlook matters to global communication. For more details see B. Tibi, 'Global Communication and Cultural Particularisms', in: R. Fortner and M. Fackler, eds, *Handbook of Global Communication and Media Ethics*, vol. 1 (Oxford: Wiley-Blackwell, 2011), pp. 54–78.

19 On tension and conflict as related to cultures see the contributions, in: Y. Raj Isar and Helmut Anheier, eds, *Conflicts and Tensions*, referenced in note 6. This volume includes my chapter on Islam, pp. 221–31.

20 For detailed references and for a discussion of this issue related to Daniel Bell's notion of the 'return of the sacred', see Part V added to the new post-9/11 edition of B. Tibi, *Islam between Culture and Politics* (New York: Palgrave, 2001, 2nd edition, 2005), pp. 224–72.

21 The notion of 'post-secular society' coined by Habermas is ignorant about this basic feature of the return of religion to politics; on this issue see B. Tibi, 'Habermas and the Return of the Sacred', in: *Religion – Staat – Gesellschaft*, vol. 3 (2002), pp. 205–96.

22 Mark Juergensmeyer, *The New Cold War* (Berkeley: University of California Press, 1993).

23 Daniel Philpot, 'The Challenge of September 11 to Secularism in International Relations', in: *World Politics*, vol. 55, 1 (2002), pp. 66–95.

24 The book by Fawaz Gerges, *America and Political Islam. Clash of Cultures or Clash of Interests?* (New York: Cambridge University Press, 1999) is based on such misperceptions and is therefore a misleading contribution and not useful.

25 On the issues of meaning and moral order see the basic books by W.C. Smith, *The Meaning and the End of Religion* (New York: Harper & Row, 1978), Robert Wuthnow, *Meaning and Moral Order* (Berkeley: University of California Press, 1987).

26 Tariq Ramadan in his *Aux Sources de Renouveau Musulman. D'al-Afghani à Hasan al-Banna* (Paris: Bayard, 1998), upgrades his grandfather Hasan al-Banna. For a contrast see the disclosure by Caroline Fourest, *Brother Tariq. The Doublespeak of Tariq Ramadan* (New York: Encounter Books, 2008) and the critical book by Paul Berman, *The Flight of the Intellectuals* (New York: Melville House, 2nd edition 2011).

27 Hasan al-Banna, 'Risalat al-jihad' ('Essay on Jihad') included in: *Majmu'at Rasa'il al-Imam al-Shahid* ('Collected Essays of the Martyr Imam') (Cairo: Dar al-Da'wa, 1990), pp. 271–92.

28 In the contribution to the anniversary of the Dutch journal *Nexus* the table is turned on the Islamists by B. Tibi, 'De Grammatica van een islamitisch humanisme', in: *Nexus* (2008), issue 50, pp. 592–616, (special issue 'Europees humanisme'). In that essay Islamists are denied authenticity, while the discarded tradition of Islamic rationalism is revived and granted authenticity. Also in Chapter 4 of the present book Islamic humanism is upgraded against totalitarian Islamism. See also my article on 'Islamic Humanism' in *Theoria* (referenced in note 71).

29 Olivier Roy, *Globalized Islam. The Search for a New Ummah* (New York: Columbia University Press, 2005).

30 Marshall Hodgson, *The Venture of Islam*, 3 vols (Chicago/IL: University of Chicago Press, 1977), and Bernard Lewis, *Islam in History* (Chicago/IL: Open Court Publishers, 1993).

31 Fred Donner, *The Early Islamic Conquests* (Princeton/NJ: Princeton University Press, 1981).

32 This interpretation is included in B. Tibi, *Kreuzzug und Djihad. Der Islam und die christliche Welt* (Munich: Bertelsmann, 1999), reprinted hereafter as paperback several times.

33 On the debate on the 'return of history' vs the 'end of history' see Introduction and Chapter 5 in: B. Tibi, *Political Islam, World Politics and Europe* (see note 1).

34 See the contributions in: Frank Lechner and John Boli, eds, *The Globalization Reader* (Oxford: Blackwell, 3rd edition, 2008).

35 See B. Tibi, *Islam's Predicament with Modernity* (see note 6), Chapter 7 on pluralism.

36 Qutb, *Ma'alim fi al-Tariq* ('Signposts Along the Road') (Cairo: Dar al-Shuruq, legal edition), p. 5 and pp. 150–51.

37 Peter Katzenstein and Robert Keohane, eds, *Antiamericanism in World Politics* (Ithaca/NY: Cornell University Press, 2007).

38 Martin Kramer, *Arab Awakening and Islamic Revival* (New Brunswick/NY: Transaction Publishers, 1993).

39 John Kelsay, *Islam and War. A Study of Comparative Ethics* (Louisville/NY: John Knox Press, 1993).

40 Daryush Shayegan, *Cultural Schizophrenia. Islamic Societies Confronting the West* (London: Syracuse University Press, 1992), Part 3.

41 On this industrialization of modern warfare see Anthony Giddens, *Nation State and Violence* (Berkeley: University of California Press, 1987), Chapter 9. What underlies this development is described by Geoffrey Parker in: *The Military Revolution. Military Invention and the Rise of the West. 1500–1800* (Cambridge: Cambridge University Press, 1988).

42 David Ralston, *Importing the European Army. The Introduction of European Army Techniques into the Extra-European World 1600–1914* (Chicago/IL: University of Chicago Press, 1990).

43 Charles Tilly, *The Formation of National States in Western Europe* (Princeton/NJ: Princeton University Press, 1975), p. 45.

44 B. Tibi, 'Old Tribes and Imposed Nation States', in: Philipp Khoury and Joseph Kostiner, eds, *Tribes and State Formation in the Middle East* (Berkeley: University of California Press, 1990) and also B. Tibi, *Arab Nationalism. Between Islam and the Nation-State* (London: Macmillan, 3rd enlarged edition, 1997).

45 H.L.A. Hart, *The Concept of Law* (Oxford: Clarendon, 1970), p. 221.

46 Hedley Bull, *The Anarchical Society* (referenced in note 18), p. 273.

47 Eric Hobsbawm and Terence Ranger, eds, *The Invention of Tradition* (New York: Cambridge University Press, 1992), p. 4.

48 Gary Bund, *Islam in the Digital Age* (London: Plutos, 2003).

49 William M. Watt, *Muslim-Christian Encounters* (New York: Routledge, 1991).

50 Mary Kaldor, *Global Civil Society* (Cambridge/UK: Polity, 2003) and Larry Diamond, *The Spirit of Democracy. The Struggle to Build Free Societies Throughout the World* (New York: Times Books, 2008).

51 See the other extreme to the 'clash' rhetoric expressed by Emanuel Adler *et al.*, eds, *The Convergence of Civilizations* (Toronto: Toronto University Press, 2006).

52 B. Tibi, *Islamism and Islam* (New Haven/CT: Yale University Press, 2012).

53 Anthony Reid and Michael Gilseman, eds, *Islamic Legitimacy in Plural Asia* (New York: Routledge, 2007).

54 Shari'a Islamism is not a constitutionalism as wrongly argued by Noah Feldman, *The Fall and Rise of the Islamic State* (Princeton/NJ: Princeton University Press, 2008). On the 'Islamic state' as an Islamist notion see B. Tibi, *The Challenge of Fundamentalism. Political Islam and the New World Disorder* (Berkeley: University of California Press, 1998, updated 2002), Chapter 8.

55 For more details see B. Tibi, 'The Return of the Sacred to Politics. The Case of Sharia'tization of Politics in Islamic Civilization', in: *Theoria. A Journal of Political and Social Theory*, vol. 55 (April 2008), issue 15, pp. 91–119. This argument runs counter to Noah Feldman (note 54).

56 See the contributions in the volume by Leonard Weinberg, ed., *Democratic Responses to Terrorism* (New York: Routledge, 2008); the volume includes a chapter by B. Tibi on 'Islamism and Democracy'.

57 Brenkman (as quoted in note 7), here p. 165.

58 Martin Marty and Scott Appleby, eds, *The Fundamentalism Project*, 5 vols, (Chicago/IL: University of Chicago Press, 1991–95).

59 Robert Lee, *Overcoming Tradition and Modernity. The Search for Islamic Authenticity* (Boulder/CO: Westview, 1997), p. 21.

60 Hasan Hanafi, *al-Usuliyya al-Islamiyya* ('Islamic Fundamentalism') (Cairo: Madbuli, 1989).

61 See the chapter by Nancy Ammermann, in: Martin Marty and Scott Appleby, eds, *Fundamentalism Observed* (Chicago/IL: University of Chicago Press, 1991), pp. 1–65.

62 Introduction to *Understanding Fundamentalisms* which is volume 1 of the 5 volumes referenced in note 58, pp. ix–x.

63 Bruce Lawrence, *Defenders of God. The Fundamentalists Against the Modern World* (San Francisco/CA: Harper & Row, 1989).

64 Norbert Elias, *The Civilizing Process*, 2 vols (New York: Pantheon Books, vol. 1 1978 and vol. 2 1982).

65 See the interesting books by Bruce Lincoln, *Holy Terrors. Thinking About Religion After September 11* (see note 4) and Jean Bethke Elshtain, *Just War Against Terror* (New York: Basic Books, 2003).

66 Johannes J.G. Jansen, *The Dual Nature of Islamic Fundamentalism* (Ithaca/NY: Cornell University Press, 1997).

67 See note 43 above. This question is also posed by scholars who confuse universality of values with Eurocentrism such as Turan Kayaoglu, 'Westphalian Eurocentrism in IR-Theory', in: *International Studies Review* 12, 2 (June 2010), pp. 193–217.

68 Daniel Philpott, 'The Challenge of September 11 to Secularism in International Relations' (referenced in note 23), pp. 65–99. This dimension is not well understood by scholars (e.g. James Piscatori and Gilbert Achcar) who confuse pan-Islamism and Islamist Internationalism; see the references in the next note.

69 See for instance James Piscatori, 'Imagining Pan-Islam', in: Shahram Akbarzadeh and Fethi Mansouri, eds, *Islam and Political Violence* (referenced in note 4), and even worse with greater distortion the sections on pan-Islamism in Gilbert Achcar, *The Arabs and the Holocaust. The Arab-Israeli War on Narratives* (London: Saqi, 2010).

70 For more details see B. Tibi, *Political Islam, World Politics and Europe* (referenced in note 1), Chapters 1 and 3.

71 See Chapter 4 of the present book as well as the essay by B. Tibi, 'Bridging the Heterogenity of Civilizations: Reviving the Grammar of Islamic Humanism', in: *Theoria. A Journal of Political and Social Theory*, vol. 56 (2009), issue 120, pp. 65–80.

72 This is the subtitle of the book authored by Roman Herzog and others referenced in note 4 above on *Preventing the Clash of Civilizations*.

73 See the references in note 35 above.

2 Intercultural dialogue as a global communication in pursuit of bridging

1 The contributions included in the volume authored by Germany's former president Roman Herzog and others, *Preventing the Clash of Civilizations* (New York: St. Martin's Press, 1999) consider dialogue as the alternative to 'clash'. In the contribution by B. Tibi, 'International Morality and Cross-Cultural Bridging', pp. 107–26 (Chapter 10) the dimension of 'conflict resolution' is added to the intercultural dialogue.

2 The concept employed here draws on Jürgen Habermas, *The Philosophical Discourse of Modernity* (Cambridge/MA: M.I.T. Press, 1986).

3 See the *Handbook of International and Intercultural Communication*, edited by Malefi K. Asante and William B. Gudykunst (London: Sage, 1989) and the more recent *Handbook of Global Communication and Media Ethics*, edited by Robert Fortner and Mark Fackler, 2 volumes (Oxford: Wiley-Blackwell, 2011). This new handbook includes a contribution by this author, 'Global Communication and Cultural Particularisms', here vol. I, pp. 54–78. Although the present chapter heavily draws on that contribution, it is an original chapter exclusively completed and rewritten for the present book.

4 See the contrasts represented by Stephan Stetter, *World Society and the Middle East* (New York: Palgrave, 2008) and Scott Appleby, *The Ambivalence of the Sacred. Religion, Violence, and Reconciliation* (Lanham/MD: Rowman & Littlefield, 2000). Appleby was a co-chair and co-editor of the five volumes of *The Fundamentalism Project* (Chicago/IL: University of Chicago Press, 1991–95), who seems to have changed his views.

5 Benjamin Barber, *Jihad vs. McWorld* (New York: Ballentine Books, 1996).

6 Hedley Bull, *The Anarchical Society. A Study of Order in World Politics* (New York: Columbia University Press, 1977), p. 273.

7 On these tensions see the contributions in: Helmut K. Anheier and Y. Raj Isar, eds, *Conflicts and Tensions*, vol. 1 of *The Culture and Globalization Series* (London: Sage, 2007) in which is my chapter, 'Islam. Between Religious-Cultural Practice and Identity Politics', pp. 221–31.

8 On the conflict between Islam and the West as an intercivilizational conflict, see B. Tibi, 'Jihadism and Intercivilizational Conflict. Conflicting Images of the Self and the Other', in: Shahram Akbarzadeh and Fethi Mansouri, eds, *Islam and Political Violence* (London: Taures, 2007), Chapter 4.

9 For more information on identity politics see Michael Kenny, *The Politics of Identity* (Cambridge/UK: Polity, 2004), and also the reference made in note 7.

10 On the notion of defensive culture see B. Tibi, *The Crisis of Modern Islam* (Salt Lake City: Utah University Press, 1988), introduction.

11 The classical global travelling in Islamic history is the subject matter of Roxanne Euben, *Journeys to the Other Shore. Muslim and Western Travellers in Search for Knowledge* (Princeton/NJ: Princeton University Press, 2006).

12 Myron Weiner, *The Global Migration Crisis* (New York: Harper Collins, 1995).

13 See the contributions in Roland Hsu, ed., *Ethnic Europe* (Stanford/CA: Stanford University Press, 2010), and B. Tibi, 'Ethnicity of Fear? The Ethnicization of Islam in Europe', in: *Studies in Ethnicity and Nationalism/SENA*, vol. 10, 1 (2010), pp. 126–27.

14 The nonsensical term 'epistemological imperialism' was coined by the British Muslim Ziauddin Sardar, ed., *Islamic Futures. The Shape of Ideas to Come* (London: Mansell, 1985) in his pursuit of 'postcolonial studies' taught at UK universities.

15 Hedley Bull differentiates between international system (interaction) and international society (value-based community) in his book, *The Anarchical Society* (referenced in note 6), pp. 13–14.

16 See B. Tibi, 'Europeanizing Islam or the Islamization of Europe. Political Democracy vs. Cultural Difference', in: Peter Katzenstein and Timothy Byrnes, eds, *Religion in an Expanding Europe* (New York: Cambridge University Press, 2006), pp. 204–24.

17 The notion of 'Islam's geo-civil war' was coined by John Brenkman, *The Cultural Contradictions of Democracy. Political Thought Since September 11* (Princeton/NJ: Princeton University Press, 2007), pp. 165–69. Brenkman outlines a scenario that could be prevented, if liberal Muslims were to establish a culture of pluralism in Islam. In this regard the whole world is concerned, but Asia is an important case in point as shown in the contributions to Anthony Reid and Michael Gilseman, eds, *Islamic Legitimacy in a Plural Asia* (New York: Routledge, 2007), among which is the chapter by B. Tibi, 'Islam and Cultural Modernity', Chapter 3, pp. 28–52, see also note 36.

18 The origin of the debate is the essay by Daniel Bell, 'The Return of the Sacred?', included in his book *The Winding Passage. Essays 1960–1980* (New York: Basic Books, 1980), pp. 324–54. Bell questions the Weberian formula of a 'disenchantment of the world/ *Entzauberung der Welt*' understood as a secular rationalization (see note 30). This classical debate has been resumed in the light of the post-9/11 developments in the new

Chapter 11 added to the enlarged edition of B. Tibi, *Islam Between Culture and Politics* (New York: Palgrave, 2001, 2nd edition, 2005). See also Daniel Philpott, 'The Challenge of September 11 to Secularism in International Relations', *World Politics*, vol. 55, 1 (2002), pp. 66–95.

19 Manuel Castells, *The Power of Identity* (Oxford: Blackwell, 1997), p. 8.

20 On Islamic nativism see Mehrzad Boroujerdi, *Iranian Intellectuals and the West. The Tormented Triumph of Nativism* (Syracuse/NY: Syracuse University Press, 1996), and on cultural schizophrenia Daryush Shayegan, *Cultural Schizophrenia. Islamic Societies Confronting the West* (London: Saqi, 1992).

21 B. Tibi, 'The Interplay Between Social and Cultural Change', in: George Atiyeh and Ibrahim Oweis, eds, *Arab Civilization* (Albany/NY: SUNY, 1988), pp. 166–82. See also the work accomplished in The Culture Matters Research Project/CMRP, that was conducted at the Fletcher School/Tufts University 2003–06. The chair of the project, Lawrence Harrison, acted as the editor of the two volumes *Developing Cultures* (New York: Routledge, 2006).

22 Roland Inglehart, *Modernization and Postmodernization* (Princeton/NJ: Princeton University Press, 1997).

23 Ibid., p. 72.

24 Ibid., p. 106.

25 Stephan Stetter, *World Society and the Middle East* (New York: Palgrave, 2008), pp. 26–29. In contrast, Najib Armanazi, *al-Shar' al-Duwali fi al-Islam* ('International Law in Islam') (London: Riad E. Rayyes, 1990), demonstrates how much values do matter in Islamic reasoning.

26 See Chapter 2 on the Islamic worldview in: B. Tibi, *Islam between Culture and Politics* (see note 18). On its contemporary Islamist shape see B. Tibi, 'The Worldview of Sunni-Arab Fundamentalists', in: Martin Marty and Scott Appleby, eds., *Fundamentalisms and Society* (Chicago/IL: University of Chicago Press, 1993), pp. 73–102.

27 For an example of a self-assertive Islamist response see Mohammed Imara, *al-Sahwa al-Islamiyya wa al-tahaddi al-hadari* ('Islamic Awakening and the Civilizational Challenge') (Cairo: Dar al-Shuruq, 1991).

28 Jamal al-din al-Afghani, *al-A'mal al-Kamilah* ('Collected Works') (Cairo: Dar al-Katib al-Arabi, 1968), p. 328.

29 See Robert Kagan, *The Return of History and the End of Dreams* (New York: Alfred Knopf, 2008), in particular pp. 80–85. On the debate on the end of history, or in reverse, the return of history see B. Tibi, *Political Islam, World Politics and Europe: Democratic Peace and Euro-Islam versus Global Jihad* (Oxford and New York: Routledge, 2008), Introduction and Chapter 5.

30 See the references in note 18 and on the notion of disenchantment see Max Weber, *Soziologie, Weltgeschichtliche Analysen, Politik.* (Stuttgart: Kröner 1964), p. 317.

31 Franz Borkenau, *Der Übergang vom feudalen zum bürgerlichen Weltbild* (Darmstadt: Wissenschaftliche Buchgesellschaft, reprint 1980). Borkenau belonged to the scholarly community of the Frankfurt School established by Max Horkheimer who fled Nazi Germany 1933 to survive the Holocaust, but returned to Frankfurt after the war. I had the honour to study with Horkheimer in Frankfurt.

32 See the contributions by John Roth and Leonard Grobb, eds, *Encountering the Stranger* (Seattle/WA: University of Washington Press, 2012).

33 Hedley Bull, *The Anarchical Society* (see note 6), p. 10 and p. 11.

34 Ibid., p. 13.

35 Hedley Bull, 'The Revolt Against the West', in: Hedley Bull and Adam Watson, eds, *The Expansion of International Society* (London: Clarendon Press, 1984, reprint 1988), pp. 217–28, here pp. 222–23.

36 B. Tibi, *Islam's Predicament with Modernity. Religious Reform and Cultural Change* (New York: Routledge, 2009), in particular Chapter 2 on knowledge and Chapter 7 on pluralism. On the notion of 'post-secular society' coined in the aftermath of 9/11 by Jürgen Habermas, in his *Glauben und Wissen* (Frankfurt: Suhrkamp, 2001), see the critique by B. Tibi, 'Habermas and the Return of the Sacred', in: *Religion – Staat – Gesellschaft*, vol. 3 (2002), pp. 265–96.

37 Unforgettable in this regard is the work of Norbert Elias, *The Civilizing Process*, vol. 1: *The History of Manners* and vol. 2: *Power and Civility* (1982). The full reference is given in note 64 to Chapter 1.

38 The source of this school of thought is Edward Said, *Orientalism* (New York: Random House, 1979). A Yale-educated Muslim from Damascus, Sadiq J. al-Azm accused Said of engaging in 'an Orientalism in reverse'; see S. al-Azm, *Dhihniyyat al-Tahrim* ('The Mentality of Taboos') (London: Riad El-Rayyes, 1992). For an overview on this inflammatory debate B. Tibi, *Einladung in die islamische Geschichte* (Darmstadt: Primus, 2001), Chapter 4.

39 See *The Globalization Reader*, eds, Frank Lechner and John Boli (Oxford: Blackwell, 2008) that includes as Chapter 43 my contribution on religionized politics. The understanding of 'globalization' by Stetter, *World Society and the Middle East* (note 25) is flawed.

40 On Eurocentrism see Roy Preiswerk and Dominique Perrat, eds, *Ethnocentrism and History* (New York: NOK Publisher, 1978).

41 Ibn Khaldun's *al-Muqaddima* ('Prolegomena') exists in a numbers of editions in numerous translations and is therefore not referenced here specifically.

42 On this Islamic expansion between the seventh and the seventeenth centuries see B. Tibi, *Kreuzzug und Djihad. Der Islam und die christliche Welt* (Munich: Bertelsmann, 1999). The authoritative work on the history of Islamic civilization is Marshall Hodgson: *The Venture of Islam. Conscience and History in a World Civilization*, 3 vols (Chicago/IL: University of Chicago Press, 1977).

43 Elias, *The Civilizing Process* (note 37), vol. 1, p. 247.

44 Ibid., p. 256.

45 Ibid., p. 255. On the groundbreaking work of Norbert Elias, see the monograph by Stephen Mennell, *Norbert Elias: An Introduction* (Oxford: Blackwell, 1989).

46 The argument that a universalization of values does not match with globalization of structures is elaborated upon by B. Tibi, *Islam between Culture and Politics* (note 18).

47 William McNeill, *The Rise of the West. A History of the Human Community* (Chicago/IL: University of Chicago Press, 1963). Later on McNeill acknowledged in a self-critical way this criticism.

48 An example of this flawed thinking is the illusion of Weltethos based on a misconception of the realities on the ground. This wishful thinking is propagated by Hans Küng in his numerous books full of repetitions not worth being listed in detail.

49 Fernand Braudel, *A History of Civilizations* (London: Penguin, 1994).

50 See Paul Lubeck, 'The Challenge of Islamic Networks', in: Nezar AlSayyad and Manuel Castells, eds, *Muslim Europe or Euro-Islam* (Lanham/MD: Lexington Books, 2002), pp. 69–90, here p. 79. See also the chapter on: 'Islamic Radicalization in the European Union', by M. Laskier, in: Hillel Frisch and Efraim Inbar, eds, *Radical Islam and International Security* (New York: Routledge, 2008), pp. 93–120. See Frantz Fanon, *Les Damnés de la Terre* (Paris: Maspero, 1961) and Chapter 6 of the present book, as well

as my article, 'The Political Legacy of Max Horkheimer and Islamist Totalitarianism', in *Telos* (Fall 2009), issue 148, pp. 7–15. The article deals with the revival of a new Third World-ism based on the wrong assessment of Islamism, a theme also addressed in Chapter 6 of the present book.

51 Jürgen Habermas, *The Philosophical Discourse of Modernity* (see note 2).

52 B. Tibi, 'Culture and Knowledge: The Islamization of Knowledge as a Postmodern Project?', in *Theory, Culture and Society* vol. 12, 1 (1995), pp. 1–24, see also Chapter 2 on knowledge in my book *Islam's Predicament with Modernity*, pp. 65–94.

53 R. Bendix, 'Modernisierung in internationaler Perspektive', in W. Zapf, ed., *Theorien des sozialen Wandels*, 2nd edition (Cologne and Berlin: Kiepenheuer & Witsch, 1970), pp. 505ff., particularly p. 506.

54 Ibid., p. 507.

55 Ibid., p. 511. See also the chapter 'Tradition and Modernity Reconsidered', in R. Benedix, *Nation-building and Citizenship* (Berkeley: University of California Press, new edition 1977), pp. 361–434.

56 On Westernization see Theodore v. der Laue, *The World Revolution of Westernization* (New York: Oxford University Press, 1987).

57 On Hellenism and its adoption by Islamic rationalism see Chapter 8 in my book *Islam's Predicament with Modernity* (see note 36). There, the reader will find multiple references on this theme.

58 On this complexity see Chapter 11 on semi-modernity in *Islam's Predicament with Modernity* (see note 36).

59 On this problem of religious pluralism in Asia see the volume *Islamic Legitimacy in a Plural Asia* (see note 17).

60 One has to free this concept from the Huntingtonian charges inflicted on it.

61 See my contributions to vols 1 and 2 of *Developing Cultures* (see note 21): 'Cultural Change in Islamic Civilization', vol. 1, pp. 245–60 and 'Egypt as a Model of Development for the World of Islam', vol. 2, pp. 163–80.

62 *World Society and the Middle East* (referenced in note 25), p. 27.

63 Ibid., p. 28.

64 Ibid., p. 171 and p. 27.

65 *Conflicts and Tensions* (referenced in note 7).

66 See Anwar al-Jundi, *Ahdaf al-Taghrib fi al-alam al-Islami* ('The Goals of Westernization and the Islamic World') (Cairo: al-Azhar, no date, probably 1977); and also Ali M. Jarisha and Muhammed Sh. Zaibaq, *Asalib al-ghazu al-fikri li al-alam al-Islami* ('Methods of Intellectual Invasion of the Islamic World') (Cairo: Dar al-I'tisam, 1987), pp. 37ff., 92ff. These authors view secularization as a 'Jewish conspiracy directed against Islam'. See Chapter 3 on Islamist antisemitism in my forthcoming Yale University Press book *Islamism and Islam*.

67 Roman Herzog *et al.*, *Preventing the Clash of Civilizations* (see note 1).

68 On this issue there are two rhetorics opposed to one another, one is of a 'clash' by S.P. Huntington in *The Clash of Civilizations*, and the other is of convergence, see Emanuel Adler *et al.*, eds, *The Convergence of Civilizations* (Toronto: University of Toronto Press, 2006). In a proper global communication one is advised to write-off both.

69 See the reference to Stetter, *World Society* in note 25 and the wishful thinking by Richard Bulliet, *Islamo-Christian Civilization* (New York: Columbia University Press, 2004). In history there never existed such a thing.

70 Maxime Rodinson, *La Fascination de l'Islam* (Paris: Maspero, 1980), and Franz Rosenthal, *The Classical Heritage in Islam* (New York: Routledge, 1994).

3   The new intercivilizational Cold War of ideas and alternatives to it

1   On this perception spreading among Muslims see Graham Fuller, *Sense of Siege. The Geopolitics of Islam and the West* (Boulder/CO: Westview Press, 1995). Islamists upgrade these Muslim fears to an accusation of Islamophobia used instrumentally in a war of ideas to outlaw any criticism of Islamism. For more details see my chapter in Eric Patterson and John Gallagher eds, *Debating the War of Ideas* (New York: Palgrave, 2010), pp. 157–73.

2   The notion of the religionization of politics has been coined and illustrated in the case of the politicization of Islam in world politics by B. Tibi, *Islam's Predicament with Modernity. Religious Reform and Cultural Change* (New York: Routledge, 2009), see in particular Chapter 5. On political religion see the general work by Emilio Gentile, *Politics as Religion* (Princeton/NJ: Princeton University Press, 2006).

3   On this post-bipolar intercivilizational conflict that relates to 'religionized politics' (see the previous note and Chapter 1) that is not yet well recognized in international studies, see the special issue of the British journal *Totalitarian Movements and Political Religions* published in 2009 (vol. 10, 2 June 2009). Earlier, the Hannah Arendt Institute for the Research on Totalitarianism/HAIT, based at the University of Dresden/Germany, conducted a similar research project on 'political religions'. The results are included in: Gerhard Besier and Hermann Lübbe, eds, *Politische Religion und Religionspolitik* (Goettingen: Vandenhoek & Ruprecht, 2005). The HAIT-volume includes my case study on AKP in Turkey viewed as an example for institutional Islamism, which is also a political religion, on pp. 229–60. On the relation between political religion and civilizations see B. Tibi, 'Jihadism and Intercivilizational Conflict', in: Shahram Akbarzadeh and Fethi Mansouri, eds, *Islam and Political Violence. Muslim Diaspora and Radicalism in the West* (London: Taures, 2007), text on pp. 39–64, and the related notes are on pp. 201–6.

4   On Islamism as a politicized Islam see B. Tibi, *Political Islam, World Politics and Europe: Democratic Peace and Euro-Islam versus Global Jihad* (Oxford and New York: Routledge, 2008), and the follow-up monograph by the same author: *Islamism and Islam* (New Haven/CT: Yale University Press, 2012).

5   See Bruce Lawrence, *The Defenders of God* (San Francisco/CA: Harper & Row, 1989). Eric Hofer, *The True Believer* (New York: Perenial Library, 2002, reprint of 1951).

6   See Walid Phares, *The War of Ideas. Jihadism against Democracy* (New York: Palgrave, 2007), who has a different view, and the more pluralistic volume Eric Patterson and John Gallagher, eds, *Debating the War of Ideas* (New York: Palgrave Macmillan, 2010).

7   Sayyid Qutb, *Ma'alim fi al-tariq* ('Signposts along the Road') (Cairo: Dar al-Shuruq, 13th legal edition, 1989), pp. 201–02. On Qutb as the authority on political Islam see Roxanne Euben, *The Enemy in the Mirror. Islamic Fundamentalism* (Princeton/NJ: Princeton University Press, 1999), Chapter 3, and David Cook, *Understanding Jihad* (Berkeley: University of California Press, 2005), pp. 202–6.

8   Sayyid Qutb presented jihad in a modern understanding and in an invention of tradition as an Islamic world revolution in his book: *al-Salam al-alami wa al-Islam* ('World Peace and Islam') (Cairo: al-Shuruq, 10th legal edition 1992), pp. 172–73.

9   Sayyid Qutb, *al-Islam wa Mushkilat al-hadarah* ('Islam and the Problematique of Civilization') (Cairo: al-Shuruq, 9th legal reprint 1988).

10   Sayyid Qutb, *Ma'alim fi al-tariq* (note 7), pp. 5–9.

11   On this debate B. Tibi, *Political Islam* (note 4), Introduction and Chapter 5.

12   See Efraim Inbar and Hillel Frisch, eds, *Radical Islam and International Security* (New York: Routledge, 2008).

13   This is the antisemitic contention made by the Saudi professors Ali Mohammed Jarisha and Mohammed Zaibaq, *Asalib al-Ghazu al-fikri lil alam al-Islami* ('Methods of the Intellectual Invasion of the World of Islam') (Cairo: Dar al-I'tisam, 1987), almost on every page. For further information on Islamist antisemitism see Chapter 3 in my Yale University Press book: *Islamism and Islam*.

14   B. Tibi, 'Public Policy and the Combination of Anti-Americanism and Antisemitism in Contemporary Islamist Ideology', in: *The Current*, vol. 12 (Winter 2008), pp. 123–46.

15   John Kelsay, *Islam and War. A Study in Comparative Ethics* (Louisville/KY: John Knox Press, 1993), p. 117. For a discussion on this book see the article by B. Tibi, 'J. Kelsay and Sharia Reasoning in Just War in Islam', in: *Journal of Church and State*, vol. 53, 1 (2011), pp. 4–26.

16   John Kelsay, *Arguing the Just War in Islam* (Cambridge/MA: Harvard University Press, 2007).

17   See the reference in note 2 above.

18   Jarisha and Zaibaq, *Asalib* (referenced in note 13), p. 202.

19   Anwar al-Jundi, *Min al-taba'iyya ila al-asalah* ('From Dependency to Authenticity') (Cairo: Dar al-I'tisam, no date), pp. 183–8, see also the reference in note 14.

20   See note 4 above. Also in matters of security Islam and Islamism are different issues analysed by B. Tibi, 'Between Islam and Islamism', in: Tami A. Jacoby and Brent Sasley, eds, *Redefining Security in the Middle East* (New York: Palgrave, 2002), pp. 62–82.

21   'America seeks bonds to Islam, Obama insists', *New York Times*, 7 April 2009, frontpage; and: 'Obama invites Muslims to a new dialogue in Cairo', *International Herald Tribune*, 5 June 2009, frontpage.

22   See the contribution by the US Ambassador to Jakarta in 2002, in Ralph Boyce, 'US Foreign Policy. Our place in the community of nations', in: Karlina Helmantia and Irfan Abubakar, eds, *Dialogue in the World Disorder* (Jakarta: AIN-Hidayatullah Islamic State University, 2004), pp. 9–24; this volume also includes B. Tibi, 'Islamic Civilization and the Quest for Democratic Pluralism', pp. 159–202.

23   For a criticism see B. Tibi, 'Islamist Parties. Why they Can't be Trusted?', in: *Journal of Democracy*, vol. 19, 3 (2008), pp. 43–48, and the case study by B. Tibi, 'Turkey's Islamist Danger. Islamists Approach Europe', *Middle East Quarterly*, vol. 16, 1 (2009), pp. 47–54 (see also note 3 above).

24   See the wrong and highly misleading assessment by Robert Leiken and Steven Brooke, 'The Moderate Muslim Brotherhood', in: *Foreign Affairs*, vol. 86, 2 (March/April 2007), pp. 107–21.

25   Zeyno Baran, 'Turkey Divided', in: *Journal of Democracy*, vol. 17 (2008), pp. 55–69 and also her book *Torn Country: Turkey between Secularism and Islamism* (Stanford/CA: Hoover Institution Press, 2010).

26   The following books on Egypt provide reason to worry, because they are based on a misconception about the Movement of the Muslim Brothers (MB) and also muster US support for this Islamist movement and indirectly help it to come to power with a legitimation: Raymond Baker, *Islam without Fear. The New Islamists in Egypt* (Cambridge/MA: Harvard University Press, 2003), and most recently Bruce Rutherford, *Egypt after Mubarak* (Princeton/NJ: Princeton University Press, 2008). It is amazing to see how these people support one another. The endorsement for Rutherford on the book cover is written by Baker.

27   Caroline Fourest, *Brother Tariq. The Doublespeak of Tariq Ramadan* (New York: Encounter Books, 2008), and Melanie Phillips, *Londonistan* (New York: Encounter Books, 2006), pp. 174–75.

28 On this issue the book by the then president of Germany: Roman Herzog, *Preventing the Clash of Civilizations* (New York: St. Martin's Press, 1999), includes the contribution by B. Tibi, 'International Morality and Cross-Cultural Bridging', pp. 107–26.

29 For a major and still valid introduction into this subject see: Nazih Ayubi, *Political Islam* (New York: Routledge, 1991, reprinted 1994), see also the reference in note 34 below.

30 For more details see the two monographs on Islamism, published 1998 and ten years hereafter 2008 by B. Tibi: *The Challenge of Fundamentalism. Political Islam and the New World Disorder* (Berkeley: University of California Press, 1998, updated 2002); ten years later: *Political Islam, World Politics and Europe* (referenced in note 4). The third and conclusive monograph is *Islamism and Islam* to be published by Yale University Press in 2012.

31 For more details see the historical survey by David Fromkin, *A Peace to End all Peace. The Fall of the Ottoman Empire and the Creation of the Modern Middle East* (New York: Avon Books, 1989). After the fall of the last Islamic Empire Turkey was established as a secular order. This process is analysed in a book ranked as classic by Bernard Lewis, *The Emergence of Modern Turkey* (London: Oxford University Press, 1979).

32 Hedley Bull, 'The Revolt against the West', in: Hedley Bull and Adam Watson, eds, *The Expansion of International Society* (Oxford: Clarendon Press, 1984), pp. 217–28, quoted from p. 223

33 One of these pundits is Gilles Kepel, who for instance in his *Jihad. Le Fin de L'Islamisme* (Paris: Gallimard, 2000), engages in the self-delusion of an 'end of Islamism'. Kepel not only ignores all facts that contradict his wrong forecast, but seems also not to be knowledgeable about the distinction between Jihadist and institutionalist Islamism.

34 See the classic by Richard Mitchell, *The Society of the Muslim Brothers* (London: Oxford University Press, 1969). In a letter to the editor of *Washington Post* published under the heading 'Misjudging the Muslim Brotherhood', John Esposito and John Voll wrongly defend this movement against the accusation of being the source of all religious extremism in the Middle East. They are wrong as is Robert Leiken (see note 24). The fact is that almost all Islamist jihadist groups are offshoots of the Muslim Brotherhood. The founder of this movement, al-Banna, is the one who transferred classical jihad into terrorist jihadism, as shown in note 38 below.

35 On these repercussions see Adeed Dawisha, *Arab Nationalism in the 20th Century* (Princeton/NJ: Princeton University Press, 2003), Chapter 10 on '1967 and After', pp. 252–81, and B. Tibi, *Conflict and War in the Middle East* (New York: new expanded edition St. Martin's Press, 1998, first published 1993 in association with Harvard/CFIA), Chapters 3 and 4 on the 1967 war and its aftermath.

36 See the new chapters added to the third edition of 1997 of B. Tibi, *Arab Nationalism*.

37 This is a coinage by Yusuf al-Qaradawi, *al-Hulul al-Mustawrada wa kaif janat ala ummatuna* (The Imported Solutions and how they Damaged our Umma), vol. 1 of a 3-volume book trilogy, published in Cairo and Beirut in the 1970s under the title: *al-Hall al-Islami* (Beirut: Mu'assat al-Risalah, 1970–80), and reprinted many times. Qaradawi acts today as the heir of Sayyid Qutb.

38 On the ideas and the impact of Sayyid Qutb see Mohammed Dharif, *al-Islam al-Siyasi fi al-watan al-Arabi* ('Political Islam in the Arab World') (Casablanca: al-Ma'arif, 1992), pp. 102–10 and the references made in note 7. The work of Hasan al-Banna, *Risalat al-Jihad* ('Essay on Jihad'), reprinted in his selected writings *Majmu'at Ras'il al-Imam al-Shadid Hasan al-Banna* ('Collected Essays') (Cairo: Dar al-Da'wa, 1990), pp. 271–92 is also of great impact. For an English translation of some of al-Banna's writings see Charles Wendell, ed., *Five Tracts of Hasan al-Banna.* (Berkeley: University of California Press,

1978). For an analysis of the development from classical jihad to jihadism see my book, *Political Islam, World Politics and Europe* (note 4), Chapter 1.

39   On the totalitarian character of jihadist Islamism see B. Tibi, *Der neue Totalitarismus. Heiliger Krieg und westliche Sicherheit* (Darmstadt: Primus Verlag, 2004), and by the same author: 'The Totalitarianism of Jihadist Islamism', in: *Totalitarian Movements and Political Religions*, vol. 8 (2007), pp. 35–54.

40   On this history see B. Tibi, *Kreuzzug und Djihad. Der Islam und die christliche Welt* (Munich: Bertelsmann, 1999).

41   See the selected writings of al-Afghani, translated and edited by Nikki Keddie, ed., *An Islamic Response to Imperialism. Political and Religious Writings of al-Afghani* (Berkeley: University of California Press, 1968), and also the monograph by Rudolph Peters, *Islam and Colonialism. The Doctrine of Jihad and Modern History* (The Hague: Mouton, 1979).

42   See B. Tibi, 'Culture and Knowledge: The Politics of the Islamization of Knowledge. The Fundamentalist Claim to De-Westernization', in: *Theory, Culture, Society*, vol. 12, 1 (1995), pp. 1–24, and the chapter on knowledge in the book by the same author: *Islam's Predicament with Modernity* (referenced in note 2).

43   See Graham Fuller, *The Centre of the Universe. The Geopolitics of Iran* (Boulder/CO: Westview Press, 1991).

44   B. Tibi, 'Secularization and De-Secularization in Islam', in: *Religion – Staat – Gesellschaft*, vol. 1, 1 (2000), pp. 95–117, and also on this subject Chapter 6 in my book, referenced in note 2.

45   On this Wahhabi impact see Stephen Schwartz, *The Two Faces of Islam. The House of Sa'ud from Tradition to Terror* (New York: Doubleday, 2002), in particular Chapter 8 on the Wahhabi International. In contrast, N. DeLong, *Wahhabi Islam* (New York: Oxford University Press, 2004) dissociates Wahhabism from Bin Laden, which is not only wrong, but also a distortion. The apologetics of Saudi Wahhabi ideology is a disservice to understanding contemporary Islam.

46   Beverley Milton-Edwards, *Islamic Politics in Palestine* (London: Tauris, 1996).

47   On the PLO and the competition between the secular and religious movements in Palestine see Amal Jamal, *The Palestine National Movement. Politics of Contention* (Bloomington: Indiana University Press, 2005) and Loren Lybarger, *Identity and Religion in Palestine. The Struggle Between Islamism and Secularism in the Occupied Territories* (Princeton/NJ: Princeton University Press, 2007).

48   On this venture of Islamology see my book: *Islam's Predicament . . .* (note 2), pp. 7–11 and 21–24.

49   For a most disturbing example see: Dale Eikelman and James Piscatori, *Muslim Politics* (Princeton/NJ: Princeton University Press, 1996).

50   See the five volumes of *The Fundamentalism Project* conducted at the American Academy of Arts and Sciences and published by University of Chicago Press between 1990 and 1995, edited by Martin Marty and Scott Appleby.

51   See B. Tibi: 'Post-bipolar Order in Crisis: The Challenge of Political Islam', in: *Millennium: Religion and International Relations* (2000), pp. 843–59. In this context culture moves to the fore as discussed in the contributions to the *Culture Matters Research Project*, chaired by Lawrence Harrison and published by him as an editor in two volumes under the title *Developing Cultures* (New York: Routledge, 2006).

52   Hedley Bull, *The Anarchical Society. A Study of Order in World Politics* (New York: Columbia University Press, 1977), see pp. 13–14, italics mine.

53   On Islamic internationalism see B. Tibi, *Political Islam, World Politics and Europe* (referenced in note 4), Part 2.

54 See Jürgen Habermas, *The Philosophical Discourse of Modernity. Twelve Lectures* (Cambridge/MA: MIT Press, 1987), first essay pp. 1–22.

55 This debate is resumed in the new Chapter 11, completed after 9/11 for the second edition of B. Tibi, *Islam between Culture and Politics* (New York: Palgrave, in association with Harvard's WCFIA, 2001, new expanded edition 2005), and on the theme itself in general see Eric Hanson, *Religion and Politics in the International System Today* (New York: Cambridge University Press, 2006).

56 On Max Weber's *Disenchantment of the World* see his collected writings: *Soziologie – Weltgeschichtliche Analysen – Politik* (Stuttgart: Kröner 1964), pp. 317–20.

57 Jürgen Habermas, *The Philosophical Discourse* (see note 54), quoted from p. 1. Habermas changed his views after 9/11. For a criticism see B. Tibi, 'Habermas and the Return of the Sacred. Is it a Religious Renaissance or a new Totalitarianism', in: *Religion – Staat – Gesellschaft*, vol. 3, 2 (2002), pp. 265–96.

58 On this issue of knowledge see the references in note 42 above.

59 Qutb, *Ma'alim* . . . (see note 7), p. 169.

60 Qutb, *al-Salam* . . .(note 8).

61 Ibid., pp. 172–73.

62 Larry Diamond, *The Spirit of Democracy. The Struggle to Build Free Societies Throughout the World* (New York: New York Times Books, 2008).

63 On the venture of shari'a-Islamism wrongly viewed by some Westerners as constitutionalism see B. Tibi, 'The Return of the Sacred to Politics as a Constitutional Law: The Case of the Shari'atization of Politics in Islamic Civilization', in: *Theoria*, 115 (2008), pp. 91–118. The contested view is represented among others, representatively by Noah Feldman, *The Fall and the Rise of the Islamic State* (Princeton/NJ: Princeton University Press, 2008).

64 Karl Popper, *The Open Society and its Enemies*, 2 vols (London: Routledge and Kegan, 1945).

65 See Chapter 4 of the present book and on the tradition of Islamic rationalism see Herbert A. Davidson, *Alfarabi, Avicenna and Averroes on Intellect. Their Cosmologies, Theories of the Active Mind, and Theories of Human Intellect* (New York: Oxford University Press, 1992), Chapter 6 on Averroës.

66 Raymond Aron, *Paix et Guerre entre les Nations* (Paris: Calman-Lévy, 1962).

67 Robert Spencer, *Onward Muslim Soldiers: How Jihad Still Threatens America and the West* (Washington/DC: Regnery, 2003), p. XIII.

68 B. Tibi, *Islam's Predicament with Modernity* (referenced in note 2), in particular Chapters 1 and 5.

69 Among the few books that meet professional International Relations standards on this subject one finds: Rouhollah K. Ramazani, *Revolutionary Iran. Challenge and Response in the Middle East* (Baltimore/MD: Johns Hopkins University Press, 1987).

70 There are two varieties of Islamist internationalism. The one of Iranian-Shi'i Islamism is dealt with in Chapter 4 on Iran by B. Tibi, *Political Islam, World Politics and Europe* (note 4), and on Sunni internationalism of al-Qaida see Peter Berger, *Holy War Inc. Inside the Secret World of al-Qaeda* (New York: Free Press, 2001); on the competition with Shi'i internationalism see B. Tibi, *Political Islam, World Politics and Europe*, Chapter 3. On jihadist Islamism in Europe see Lorenzo Vidino, *al-Qaeda in Europe. the New Battleground of International Jihad* (Amherst/NY: Prometheus, 2006).

71 John Kelsay, *Islam and War* (note 15), p. 118.

72 These 'enclaves' connect immigration to security; on this see B. Tibi, *Islamische Zuwanderung. Die gescheiterte Integration* (Munich: Deutsche Verlags-Anstalt, 2002), and

also Chapter 6 in: Myron Weiner, *The Global Migration Crisis. Challenge to States and to Human Rights* (New York: Harper Collins, 1995). These themes are also addressed in Chapter 6 of my book, *Political Islam, World Politics and Europe* (referenced in note 4) and also in Chapter 5 of the present book as well as in my Chapter 7 in R. Hsu, ed., *Ethnic Europe* (Stanford/CA: Stanford University Press, 2010).

73 See B. Tibi, 'Bridging the Heterogenity of Civilizations. Reviving the Grammar of Islamic Humanism', in: *Theoria. A Journal for Political and Social Theory*, vol. 56, 120 (2009), pp. 65–80.

74 See the excellent translation of Farabi's *al-Madina al-Fadila* by Michael Walzer, ed., *Al-Farabi on the Perfect State. Abu Nasr al-Farabi: Mabadi ara' ahl al-madina al-fadila* (Oxford: Oxford University Press, 1985) and the Farabi chapter in B. Tibi, *Der wahre Imam* (Munich: Piper, 1996), Chapter 4.

75 Leslie Lipson, *The Ethical Crises of Civilizations. Moral Meltdown or Advance?* (London: Sage, 1993), pp. 62–63.

76 Ibid.

77 Mohammed Abed al-Jabri, *Arab Islamic Philosophy* (Austin: University of Texas Press, 1999), pp. 120–30.

78 Kelsay, *Islam and War* (see note 15), p. 117; see also Kelsay's new book *Arguing the Just War in Islam* (Cambridge/MA: Harvard University Press, 2007). On Kelsay's contribution see B. Tibi, *John Kelsay and Shari'a Reasoning in Just War in Islam*, in: *Journal of Church and State*, vol. 53, 1 (Winter 2011), pp. 4–26.

79 The classic on this subject matter continues to be the book by Niyazi Berkes, *The Development of Secularism in Turkey*, new edition (New York: Routledge, 1998). The secular republic of Turkey established by Kemal Atatürk is undermined at present by AKP Islamists ruling Turkey since 2002. See B. Tibi, 'Turkey's Islamist Danger. Islamists Approach Europe', in: *The Middle East Quarterly* (referenced in note 23).

80 Hasan al-Sharqawi, *al-Muslimun, Ulama wa Hukama* ('Muslims as Ulema and Wise Men') (Cairo: Mu'ssasat Mukhtar, 1987), p. 12.

81 Kelsay, *Islam and War* (see note 15), p. 25.

82 On the fundamentalist agenda of 'Remaking Politics' and 'Remaking the World', see the contributions included in: Martin Marty and Scott Appleby, eds, *Fundamentalisms and the State. Remaking Polities, Economies and Militance* (Chicago/IL: University of Chicago Press, 1993), in particular Parts 1 and 3.

83 See the contributions in Zeyno Baran, ed., *The Other Muslims. Moderate and Secular* (New York: Palgrave, 2010), in particular herein Chapter 9 by B. Tibi, 'Euro-Islam', pp. 157–74.

84 This political scientist is Marc Lynch, Veiled Truths, in *Foreign Affairs* (July/August 2010). This article is not only an unbalanced but also an outrageous review article about the book by Paul Berman, *The Flight of the Intellectuals* (New York: Melville House, 2010) in which Islamism is courageously criticized.

4 Which Islam for bridging?

1 The standard work by Fernand Braudel, *A History of Civilizations* (London: Penguin Press, 1994) lists Islam as a civilization. The foremost history of Islam as a civilization is Marshall Hodgson, *The Venture of Islam. Conscience and History in a World Civilization*, 3 vols (Chicago/IL: University of Chicago Press, 1974). This seminal work establishes also the scholarly legitimacy for addressing Islam as a civilization.

2   See the debate in Chapter 1 where the significant difference between the analytical notion of 'conflict' and Samuel P. Huntington's rethoric of 'clash' is elaborated on. For a critique see the volume by Roman Herzog *et al.*, *Preventing the Clash of Civilizations* (New York: St. Martin's Press, 1999), and my contribution to herein on pp. 139–68. This 'preventing' acknowledges the conflict and the fact of multiple civilizations. There is no Islamo–Christian civilization as well as no world civilization. It is therefore highly flawed to argue like Richard Bulliet, *The Case for Islamo-Christian Civilization* (New York: Columbia University Press, 2004). No such a thing ever existed in real history. See B. Tibi, *Kreuzzug und Djihad. Der Islam und die christliche Welt* (Munich: Bertelsmann, 1999).

3   The source of this formula is Raymond Aron, *Paix et Guerre entre les Nations* (Paris: Calmann Ley, 1962). The German translation was published in 1986 by S. Fischer in Frankfurt.

4   Therefore, Peter Katzenstein, ed., *Civilizations in World Politics. Plural and Pluralist Perspectives* (New York: Routledge, 2010) deserves praise despite the great flaws of the volume.

5   On this notion see Chapter 1 of the present book and B. Tibi, 'Jihadism and Intercivilizational Conflict', in: Shahram Akbarzadeh and Fethi Mansouri, eds, *Islam and Political Violence* (London: Tauris, 2007), pp. 39–64.

6   In this chapter I maintain that there existed an Islamic grammar of humanism which is defined in civilizational terms and add to this historical fact the insight that humanism is universal and can be shared on cross-cultural grounds. Due to their different meanings, the terms culture and civilization are not used interchangeably, as done by Huntington and many others. By culture I mean a social production of meaning, which is local; the reference to civilization relates to a grouping of local cultures characterized by family resemblance. In a civilizational set up cultures that are related to one another through the connect of shared values and worldviews create a civilization based on a shared *Weltanschauung*. See the references in note 1.

7   William McNeill, *The Rise of the West. A History of the Human Community* (Chicago/IL: University of Chicago Press, 1963).

8   On this issue see Helmut Anheier and Y. Raj Isar, eds, *Tensions and Conflicts*, vol. 1 of *The Cultures and Globalization Series* (London: Sage, 2007). See herein my chapter: 'Islam: Between Religious–Cultural Practice and Identity Politics', pp. 221–31.

9   Erasmus Foundation, ed., *The Limits of Pluralism. Neo-Absolutism and Relativism* (Amsterdam: Praemium Erasmus-Foundation, 1994). This volume includes a controversy between E. Gellner, pp. 163–66 and C. Geertz, pp. 167–73, amended by B. Tibi, pp. 29–36 on political Islam.

10   Jürgen Habermas, *The Philosophical Discourse of Modernity* (Cambridge/MA: MIT Press, 1986), p. 17.

11   Max Weber's notion, *Die Entzauberung der Welt*/the disenchantment of the world can be found in his *Collected Writings: Soziologie – Weltgeschichtliche Analysen – Politik* (Stuttgart: Kröner, 1964), p. 317.

12   Ernest Gellner, *Postmodernism, Reason and Religion* (London and New York: Routledge, 1992), p. 85, see also note 9 above.

13   Quoted from the article on 'International Relations Theory' by J. Vasques and M.T. Henehan, in: *Routledge Encyclopedia of Government*, 2 volumes (London: Routledge, 2004), here vol. 2, pp. 857–78, the quote p. 865.

14   Joel Kraemer, *Humanism in the Renaissance of Islam* (Leiden: Brill, 1986) p. VII and on the Hellenization of Islam: William Montgomery Watt, *Philosophy and Theology* (Edinburgh: Edinburgh University Press, 1962, many reprints), Parts 2 and 3.

15 Islamism is the ideology of political Islam that heralds as a religious fundamentalism in a new variety of absolutism (see note 9). For more details on political Islam see B. Tibi, *The Challenge of Fundamentalism. Political Islam and the New World Disorder* (Berkeley: University of California Press, 1998, updated edition 2002). On the related conflict see the reference in note 5.

16 John Brenkman, *The Contradictions of Democracy. Political Theory since 9/11* (Princeton/ NJ: Princeton University Press, 2007), p. 165.

17 For more details B. Tibi, *Die islamische Herausforderung* (Darmstadt: Primus, 2007), Chapters 5 and 6.

18 B. Tibi, 'Ethnicity of Fear? The Ethnicization of Islam in Europe', in: *Studies in Ethnicity and Nationalism/SENA*, vol. 10, 1 (2010), pp. 126–57.

19 Christian Meier, *Die Entstehung des Politischen bei den Griechen* (Frankfurt: Suhrkamp, 1983).

20 Jürgen Habermas, *The Philosophical Discourse of Modernity* (Cambridge/MA: MIT Press, 1987), p. 17.

21 See Jürgen Habermas, *Glauben und Wissen* (Frankfurt: Suhrkamp, 2001), and the critique by B. Tibi, 'Habermas and the Return of the Sacred', in: *Religion – Staat – Gesellschaft*, vol. 3, 1 (2002), pp. 265–96.

22 B. Tibi, *Europa ohne Identität? Die Krise der multikulturellen Gesellschaft* (Munich: Bertelsmann, 1998), Chapters 9 and 10. The Dutch edition was published under the title: *Europa zonder Identiteit* by Deltas, 2000.

23 This reading of Islamic rationalism is also inspired by Ernst Bloch. This great philosopher presented me, as a young student of twenty, with a dedication in his book: *Avicenna und die Aristotelische Linke* (Frankfurt: Suhrkamp, 1963), in which he sides with Islamic humanism against the Islamic orthodoxy, dubbed by him the '*Mufti Welt*' ('Mufti world') of the *fiqh*. On the conflict of rational philosophy and *fiqh* in Islam, see my book: *Der Wahre Imam* (Munich: Piper, 1999) Part 2 and also the reference in note 27.

24 For an example, see the volume edited by Emmanuel Adler and others, *Convergence of Civilizations* (Toronto: University of Toronto Press, 2006). These authors go to exactly the opposite extreme to replaces the 'clash' rhetorics (see note 2) with convergence rhetorics; both have in common ignorance of real history, hereby preferring to engage in a construction of a myth.

25 Christian Meier, *Die Entstehung des Politischen bei den Griechen* (see note 19), on the notion of '*Koennensbewusstsein*', in particular pp. 484–99.

26 On this subject see Will Duran, *The Renaissance*, vol. 5 of: *The Story of Civilization*, 11 vols (New York: Simon & Schuster, 1981), on Averroes (1126–1198), pp. 47, 538, 539. On Avicenna (980–1037), p. 537 in the Renaissance volume.

27 On the conflict between *fiqh* ('sacral jurisprudence') and *falsafa* ('rational philosophy') in Islam see the chapter by B. Tibi, 'Politisches Denken im klassischen und mittelalterlichen Islam', in: Iring Fetscher, ed., *Piper Handbuch der politischen Ideen*, 5 vols, here vol. 2, *Mittelalter* (Munich: Piper, 1993), Chapter 3, pp. 87–174.

28 Leslie Lipson, *The Ethical Crisis of Civilization. Moral Meltdown in Advance?* (Newbury Park/CA: Sage, 1993), p. 63. The German–Jewish scientist Edgar Zilsch, who fled Germany in 1938 acknowledges in his masterpiece: *Die sozialen Ursprünge der neuzeitlichen Wissenschaft* (reprint: Frankfurt: Suhrkamp, 1976), pp. 49–61, the Islamic–humanist contribution to the rise of a modern science in the West based on humanism. He traces the roots of modern science back to the combination of humanism and engineering.

29 Lipson, *The Ethical Crisis*, p. 62.

30 On Islamic migration to Europe see B. Tibi, *Political Islam, World Politics and Europe: Democratic Peace and Euro-Islam versus Global Jihad* (Oxford and New York: Routledge,

2008), Chapters 5 and 6. The concept of Euro-Islam to be presented in Chapter 5 of the present book is proposed both as a framework for integration and also for countering an Islamization. On this concept see also B. Tibi, *Euro-Islam. L' Integrazione mancata* (Rome: Marsilio, 2005); Chapter 5 includes further references.

31   On the tradition of shari'a reasoning see John Kelsay, *Arguing the Just War in Islam* (Cambridge/MA: Harvard University Press, 2007), Chapters 2 and 3, and B. Tibi, 'John Kelsay and Shari'a Reasoning in Just War in Islam', in: *Journal of Church and State*, vol. 53, 1 (2011), pp. 4–26; see also the references in notes 23 and 27 as well as the contributions included in *The Cambridge Compendium to Arab Philosophy*, eds, Peter Adamson and Richard Taylor (Cambridge: Cambridge University Press, 2005). On Islam and the European Renaissance see B. Tibi, *Kreuzzug und Djihad. Der Islam und die christliche Welt* (Munich: Bertelsmann, 1999), Chapter 5.

32   Ernst B. Haas, *When Knowledge is Power* (Berkeley: University of California Press, 1990), see also Chapter 2 on knowledge in B. Tibi, *Islam's Predicament with Modernity* (New York: Routledge, 2009).

33   Sayyid Qutb, *Ma'alim fi al-tariq* (Cairo: Dar al-Shuruq, 11th legal edition, 1989), preface, the quote is compiled from pp. 5–7.

34   The formulation *al-hulul al-mustawradah* ('The Imported Solution') is used as the title of volume one of the trilogy by the leading contemporary Islamist and his heir of Qutb Yusuf Qaradawi, *Hatimiyyat al-hall al-Islami* ('The Islamic Solution') (numerous prints and editions), in which he contests the Greek origins of democracy and dismisses it altogether in his Islamist project of a cultural purification.

35   Franz Rosenthal, *The Classical Heritage in Islam* (London: Routledge, 1992).

36   See Ziauddin Sardar, *Islamic Futures* (London: Mansell, 1985).

37   See the volume by the former President of Germany, Roman Herzog *et al.*, *Preventing the Clash of Civilizations* (cited in note 2), it includes as Chapter 10: B. Tibi, 'International Morality and Cross-Cultural Bridging', pp. 107–26.

38   Mohammed Abed al-Jabri, *Arab Islamic Philosophy* (Austin: University of Texas CMES, 1999). The quote is compiled from pp. 121, 124, 128.

39   See the article on the political philosophy of al-Farabi in the compendium referenced in note 31 and the Farabi-chapter in B. Tibi, *Der wahre Imam* (referenced in note 23), Chapter 4. Among the writings of al-Farabi is his seminal work *al-Madina al-fadila*. It was made available with an English translation by Richard Walzer as editor of: *Al-Farabi on the Perfect State* (Oxford: Oxford University Press, 1985).

40   On the high ranking of Aristotle in Islamic political philosophy see the contributions included in: Charles E. Butterworth, ed., *The Political Aspects of Islamic Philosophy. Essays in Honor of Mushin S. Mahdi* (Cambridge/MA: Harvard CMES, 1992).

41   Maxime Rodinson, *La fascination de l'Islam* (Paris: Maspero, 1980).

42   On this notion of intercivilizational conflict see my contribution referenced in note 5.

43   See note 30 and B. Tibi, 'A Migration Story. From Muslim Immigrants to European Citizens of the Heart?', in: *The Fletcher Forum for World Affairs*, vol. 31, 1 (Winter 2007), pp. 147–68. In my view, Muslim immigrants could only then become 'European citizens of the heart', if they were willing to embrace European humanism, which has a precedent in the grammar of their own tradition of humanism dismissed in Islamic civilization.

44   See the references in note 2 and 37. See also Robert Reilly, *The Closing of the Muslim Mind. How Intellectual Suicide Created the Modern Islamist Crisis* (Wilmington/DE: ISI Books, 2010).

45 For an example of this mindset see Ali M. Jarisha and Muhammad Sh. Zaibaq, *Asalib al-ghazu al-fikri li'l alam al-Islami* ('Methods of Intellectual Invasion of the Islamic World') (Cairo: Dar al-I'tisam, 1978). See the chapter on purity and Islamist purification in B. Tibi, *Islamism and Islam* (New Haven/CT: Yale University Press, 2012, forthcoming), pp. 177–200.

46 Within the framework of an intercivilizational dialogue that I have been pursuing in the past decades, I went also to Pakistan. My lectures held in Karachi/Pakistan in 1995 were covered by the Pakistani Press. See the report by S. Ahmed, 'Ways to avert clash between Islam and the West stressed', in: *DAWN* (Karachi), 27 October 1995, and also the article: 'Cross-cultural talks for peaceful coexistence urged', in: *DAWN*, 26 October 1995. The volume of the collected papers of the Karachi dialogue is published under the title: *Is there a Clash of Cultures?*, (Karachi, 1998), includes Tibi's chapter on pp. 9–23. See also the interview with B. Tibi, 'The clash of civilizations was not invented, but it was used, abused for other reasons', in: *NEWSLINE* (Karachi), November issue 1995, pp. 99–100.

47 On the meaning of the institutionalization of cultural innovations see Robert Wuthnow, *Meaning and Moral Order* (Berkeley: University of California Press, 1987), Chapter 8.

48 See Chapter 7 on the introduction of democracy into the world of Islam included in my new book *Political Islam, World Politics and Europe* referenced in note 30. See also the chapter: 'Education and Democratization', in: Alan Olson, ed., *Educating for Democracy* (Lanham/MD: Rowman & Littlefield, 2004), pp. 203–19.

49 See the classic on this subject by David Apter, *The Politics of Modernization* (Chicago/IL: University of Chicago Press, 1965).

50 Hedley Bull, *The Anarchical Society. A Study of Order in World Politics* (New York: Columbia University Press, 1977), p. 273.

51 See Clifford Geertz, *The Interpretation of Cultures* (New York: Basic Books, 1973), Chapter 4 and the book by B. Tibi, *Islam and the Cultural Accommodation of Social Change* (Boulder/CO: Westview Press, 1990), in which the approach of Geertz is employed in Chapter 1.

52 Helmuth Plessner, *Die verspätete Nation* (Frankfurt: Suhrkamp, 1974, new printing), pp. 33–34.

53 On semi-modernity see Chapter 1 in: B. Tibi, *Islam's Predicament with Modernity*, pp. 303–19 and also the chapter by B. Tibi, 'The Worldview of Sunni-Arab Funda-mentalists', in: Martin Marty and Scott Appleby, eds, *Fundamentalisms and Society* (Chicago/IL: University of Chicago Press, 1993), pp. 73–102.

54 See Aron referenced in note 3.

55 Hedley Bull, 'The Revolt Against the West', in: Hedley Bull and Adam Watson, *The Expansion of International Society* (Oxford: Clarendon Press, 1984), pp. 217–28.

56 For a debate on the argument of the return of history, that is not the end of it, see the debate Tibi vs Fukuyama in the book on *Political Islam* (note 30), in particular the Introduction and Chapter 5 there.

57 Theodore H. v. Laue, *The World Revolution of Westernization* (New York: Oxford University Press, 1987).

58 See the references in note 2 and B. Tibi, *Krieg der Zivilisationen* (Hamburg: Hoffmann und Campe, 1995). The expanded and revised second edition was published in Munich 1998 by Heyne Verlag in which I was compelled to add a new Chapter 7 for a critique on the critique of Huntington. To be sure, the notion 'war of civilizations' is not about the 'military', but about a war of ideas and worldviews. There I dissociate my work from Huntington. See the work of Walid Phares, *The War of Ideas. Jihadism against Democracy* (New York: Palgrave, 2007), and Eric Patterson and John Gallagher, eds, *Debating the War of Ideas* (New York: Palgrave, 2010).

59 See John Brenkman, *Contradictions of Democracy* (referenced in note 16), where he argues that a 'geo-civil dimension' emerges out of 'Islam's civil war', p. 165.

60 Here one has to acknowledge a value conflict. In my view an embrace of the values of democracy is the solution. In my book on *Political Islam. World Politics and Europe* (note 30), Chapter 7, I argue that democracy is a humanism-based political culture, and it is not limited to a simple procedure of voting, as US foreign policy of democratization suggests. For instance, there were in Iraq after the liberation from Saddam's 'republic of fear' elections, but certainly and by no means a process of democratization. The related culture of humanism is not yet in place, instead one encounters in Iraq a culture of ethnic and religious strife.

61 Bull, *The Anarchical Society* (note 50), p. 13.

62 Francis Deng and Abdullahi An-Na'im, eds, *Human Rights in Africa. Cross-Cultural Perspectives* (Washington/DC: Brookings, 1990). The volume includes Chapter 5 on Islam and human rights, pp. 104–32. See also Michèle Schmiegelow, ed., *Democracy in Asia* (New York: St. Martin's Press, 1997), which includes my chapter on Islam and democracy, pp. 127–46.

63 See the references in note 62. The Oslo papers were published in: Tore Lindholm and Kari Vogts, eds, *Islamic Law Reform and Human Rights* (Oslo and Copenhagen: Nordic Human Rights Publications, 1993). The volume includes among others M. Arkoun, pp. 11–14, B. Tibi, pp. 79–96. The Dutch-Amsterdam-Project on European humanism was published in the special issue no. 50/2008 of the journal *Nexus* under the title 'Europees Humanisme in Fragmenten': see the chapter in Dutch on Islamic humanism on pp. 592–616.

64 The book by Benjamin Barber, *Jihad vs. McWorld* (New York: Ballantine Books, 1996), expresses American naivité, not the substance of the conflict in point.

65 On Europeanizing Islam as an alternative to the Islamization of Europe (Political Democracy vs. Cultural Difference) see Chapter 5 of the present book and the references made there.

66 On the fight between rationalist humanism and the *fiqh*-orthodoxy in Islamic medieval thought see my chapter: 'Politisches Denken im klassischen und mittelalterlichen Islam', in: Iring Fetscher, ed., *Piper Handbuch der politischen Ideen*, 5 vols, here vol. 2, *Mittelalter* (Munich: Piper, 1993), Chapter 3, pp. 87–140.

5 Euro-Islam as a vision for bridging

1 See Zeyno Baran, *Torn Country. Turkey Between Secularism and Islamism* (Stanford/CA: Hoover Institution Press, 2010).

2 On the Islam diaspora in Europe see the two seminal volumes that emerged from a research project at the Dutch University of Leiden: W.A.R. Shadid and P.S. van Koningsveld, eds, *Political Participation and Identity of Muslims in Non-Muslim States*, vol. I, *Muslims in the Margin. Political Responses to the Presence of Islam in Western Europe*, vol. II (Kampen/Netherlands: Kok Pharas Publ., 1996). Volume I includes my chapter: 'Islam, Hinduism and the Limited Secularity in India. A Model for Muslim-European Relations in the Age of Migration?', pp. 130–44. The answer to the question asked is negative: India's dealing with its Islamic minority is not a model for Europe. On the Islamist (not Islamic) intrusion to Europe see: Russell Berman, *Freedom or Terror. Europe Faces Jihad* (Stanford/CA: Hoover Institution Press, 2010) and also the book by Lorenzo Vidino quoted in note 5 below.

3 See Jocelyne Cesari, *Where Islam and Democracy Meet* (New York: Palgrave, 2004). Cesari is among those scholars who overlook existing conflicts and prefer to report a success

story about a reality that does not exist. Other books characterized by this mindset are, among others: Jonathan Lawrence and Justin Vaisse, *Integrating Islam* (Washington/DC: Brookings, 2006), and Jytte Klausen, *The Islamic Challenge. Politics and Religion in Western Europe* (New York: Oxford University Press, 2005).

4 Francis Fukuyama, 'Identity, Immigration and Liberal Democracy', in: *Journal of Democracy*, vol. 17, 2 (April 2008), pp. 5–20.

5 Lorenzo Vidino, *The New Muslim Brotherhood in the West* (New York: Columbia University Press, 2010).

6 Fukuyama (see note 4), p. 6.

7 B. Tibi, 'Ethnicity of Fear? Islamic Migration and the Ethnicization of Islam in Europe', in: *Studies in Ethnicity and Nationalism/SENA* 10, 1 (2010), pp. 126–57. The politicization of the related conflict results in an effort for the 'Islamization of Europe'. See the related chapter in: J. Millard Burr and Robert Collins, *Alms for Jihad* (Cambridge: Cambridge University Press, 2006), pp. 237–62. Following a Saudi lawsuit this book was withdrawn from the market.

8 For a reference to the notion coined by Max Weber, *Entzauberung der welt* ('Disenchantment of the world'), see Max Weber, *Soziologie – Weltgeschichtliche Analysen – Politik*, Selected Writings (Stuttgart: Alfred Kröner, 1964), p. 317.

9 On the notion of 'return of the sacred' and its current topicality supplied with references see B. Tibi, *Islam Between Culture and Politics* (New York: Palgrave, 2nd enlarged edition 2005), Chapter 11. Next to the reference in note 50 below see the forthcoming papers of the project *The Return of Religion to the Public Square* conducted at the Central European University, Department of Law/Budapest, edited by Renata Uitz.

10 B. Tibi, *Islam's Predicament with Modernity. Religious Reform and Cultural Change* (New York: Routledge, 2009).

11 On this criticism see Paul Berman, *The Flight of the Intellectuals* (New York: Melville House, 2010), p. 150. For a contrast to Ramadan see B. Tibi, 'A Migration Story. From Muslim Immigrants to Citizens of the Heart', in: *The Fletcher Forum for World Affairs*, vol. 31, 1 (2007), pp. 147–68. In fact, Ramadan pursues an Islamist identity politics. This politics seems to fuel the intercivilizational conflict. On this issue see Chapter 16 by B. Tibi, in: Helmut Anheier and Y. Raj Isar, eds, *Conflicts and Tensions* (London: Sage, 2007), pp. 221–31. Jihadist movements recruit marginalized Muslims in Europe. See Lorenzo Vidino, *al-Qaeda in Europe. The New Battleground of International Jihad* (Amherst/NY: Prometheus Books, 2006).

12 Paul A. Silverstein, *Algeria in France* (Bloomington: Indiana University Press, 2004). B. Tibi, *Mit dem Kopftuch nach Europa. Die Türkei auf dem Weg in die EU* (Darmstadt: Primus, 2nd edition, 2007).

13 *Amsar* are the settlements built by Muslim invaders in the course of their *futuhat*-conquests that can be identified in modern terms as colonial settlements (see Efraim Karsh, *Islamic Imperialism*, New Haven/CT: Yale University Press, 2006). On these *amsar* see Khalid Yahya Blankinship, *The End of the Jihad State* (Albany/NY: SUNY, 1994), page reference 'amsar', index p. 371. On the related conquests see Fred M. Donner, *The Early Islamic Conquests* (Princeton/NJ: Princeton University Press, 1981).

14 See the section with the autobiographical asides 'Between Four Worlds' in the introduction to my book *Islam's Predicament* (referenced in note 10), pp. 15–19.

15 B. Tibi, 'A Migration Story' (referenced in note 11).

16 Jytte Klausen, *The Islamic Challenge* (referenced in note 3). For a contrast see B. Tibi, *Islamische Zuwanderung. Die gescheiterte Integration* (Munich: DVA, 2002).

17 B. Tibi, *Islamism and Islam* (New Haven/CT: Yale University Press, 2012).

18 B. Tibi, 'Europeanizing Islam or the Islamization of Europe', in: Peter Katzenstein and Tim Byrnes, eds, *Religion in an Expanding Europe* (New York: Cambridge University Press, 2006), pp. 204–24.

19 Ralph Ghadban, *Tariq Ramadan und die Islamisierung Europas* (Berlin: Verlag Hans Schiler, 2006). On political Islam in Europe see B. Tibi, *Political Islam, World Politics and Europe: Democratic Peace and Euro-Islam versus Global Jihad* (Oxford and New York: Routledge, 2008), Chapter 6.

20 Caroline Fourest, *Brother Tariq. The Doublespeak of Tariq Ramadan* (London: Encounter Books, 2008).

21 According to the printed programme of the Johnson Foundation this was the title of the presentation of Tariq Ramadan made at the Swedish Conference held in June 15–17, 2006 in the outskirts of Stockholm. I was among the speakers in the panel with Ramadan, but after exposure to the ordeal of listening to the 'doublespeak' I felt compelled to leave with great dismay in a protest to head directly to the airport while liberal Europeans, who are a hopeless case, continued to listen.

22 Emmanuel Adler *et al.*, eds, *The Convergence of Civilizations* (Toronto: Toronto University Press, 2006).

23 B. Tibi, 'Euro-Islamic Religious Pluralism for Europe. An Alternative to Ethnicity and to Multiculturalism of Fear', in: *The Current*, vol. 11, 1 (2007), pp. 89–103, and also my chapter in the book by Roland Hsu, ed., *Ethnic Europe* (Stanford/CA: Stanford University Press, 2010), pp. 127–56.

24 See Lawrence and Vaisse referenced in note 3.

25 B. Tibi, *Europa ohne Identität?* (Munich: Bertelsmann, 1998), hereafter printed in three editions.

26 See the book by Efraim Karsh, *Islamic Imperialism* (referenced in note 13 above).

27 These are the views of Ramadan as summarized by Abdullah Saeed, Muslims and non-Muslims Rule, in: Anthony Reid and Michael Gilsenan, eds, *Islamic Legitimacy in a Plural Asia* (New York: Routledge, 2007), p. 25. The volumes include a chapter with a radically different approach from the one of Ramadan by myself based on an Islamic embrace of cultural modernity, not on Ramadan's Islamization. The chapter is B. Tibi, 'Islam and Cultural Modernity', published in the same volume, pp. 28–52.

28 See B. Tibi, *Kreuzzug und Djihad* (Munich: Bertelsmann, 1999), and also the chapter on Islam in: Terry Nardin, ed., *The Ethics of War and Peace* (Princeton/NJ: Princeton University Press, 1996), pp. 128–45.

29 For more details see Fouad Ajami, *The Arab Predicament* (New York: Cambridge University Press, 1981), on pp. 28–29 where Ajami refers to my place in the Arab Left. This fact is also documented in my contribution to Edward Said, ed., *The Arabs of Today. Perspectives for Tomorrow* (Columbus/OH: Forum Associates, 1973), included as the chapter 'The Genesis of the Arab Left', pp. 31–42.

30 On this subject see Nazih Ayubi, *Political Islam* (London: Routledge, 1991), followed by the two monographs by B. Tibi, *The Challenge of Fundamentalism* (Berkeley: University of California Press, 1998, updated 2002) and *Political Islam, World Politics and Europe* (referenced in note 19). A third one is to be published by Yale University Press (see note 17).

31 See the chapter on customary Islam in West Africa in: B. Tibi, *Crisis of Modern Islam* (Salt Lake City: Utah University Press, 1988), pp. 68–80.

32 On Islam in France see Alec Hargreave, *Multiethnic France* (New York: Routledge, 2007).

33 See the coverage about that French project by B. Tibi, 'Euro-Islam oder Ghetto-Islam', in: *Frankfurter Allgemeine Zeitung*, 7 December 1992, p. 14. The paper in point, B. Tibi,

'Les conditions d'un Euro-Islam', and it was published hereafter in: Robert Bistolfi and Francois Zabbal, eds, *Islams d'Europe* (Paris: L'Aube, 1995), pp. 230–34. The related story is told in the chapter Euro-Islam to the second edition of my book: *Im Schatten Allahs* (Munich: Ullstein, 2003), pp. 491–529.

34 *TIME*, vol. 158, No. 26, 24 December 2001, p. 49.

35 Nezar AlSayyad, 'Muslim Europe or Euro-Islam. On the Discourse of Identity and Culture', in: AlSayyad and Manuel Castells, eds, *Muslim Europe or Euro-Islam* (Lanham/MD: Lexington Books, 2002), pp. 9–29, here p. 19.

36 W.M. Watt, *Muslim-Christian Encounters* (London: Routledge, 1991).

37 See the book by Robert Kagan, *The Return of History and the End of Dreams* (New York: Alfred Knopf, 2008) and the introduction to my book *Political Islam, World Politics and Europe* (referenced in note 19).

38 Lorenzo Vidino, *Al-Qaeda in Europe* (referenced in note 11).

39 B. Tibi, 'International Morality and Cross-Cultural Bridging', in: Roman Herzog *et al.*, *Preventing the Clash of Civilizations* (New York: St. Martin's Press, 1999), pp. 107–26.

40 B. Tibi, 'Jihadism and Intercivilizational Conflict', in: Shahram Akbarzadeh and Fethi Mansouri, eds, *Islam and Political Violence* (London: Taures, 2007), pp. 107–26.

41 Graham Fuller, *The Sense of Siege. The Geopolitics of Islam and the West* (Boulder/CO: Westview, 1995).

42 John Kelsay, *Islam and War* (Louisville/KY: John Knox Press, 1993), p. 118.

43 Akbarzadeh and Mansouri, eds, *Islam and Political Violence* (referenced in note 40).

44 These papers are published as articles in the Dutch journal *Nexus* in the volumes of 2005 (issue no. 41) and of 2008 (issue no. 50).

45 B. Tibi, *Islam's Predicament with Modernity* (referenced in note 10).

46 Hanif Kureishi, 'Karneval der Kulturen', in: *Neue Zürcher Zeitung*, 11 August 2005.

47 B. Tibi, 'The Totalitarianism of Jihadist Islamism', in: *Totalitarian Movements and Political Religions*, vol. 8, 1 (2007), pp. 35–54.

48 Henri Pirenne, *Mohamet et Charlemagne* (London: Allen & Unwin, 1939). See also the chapter on Pirenne in B. Tibi, *Kreuzzug und Djihad* (Munich: Bertelsmann, 1998), pp. 86–112.

49 On these civilizational Christian and Islamic traditions see Peter Brown, *The Rise of Western Christendom* (Cambridge/UK: Blackwell, 1996), and Marshall Hodgson, *The Venture of Islam* (Chicago/IL: University of Chicago Press, 1974).

50 See B. Tibi, 'The Return of the Sacred to Politics. The Case of Shari'atization of Politics in Islamic Civilization', in: *Theoria. A Journal for Political and Social Theory*, vol. 55 (2008), issue 115, pp. 91–119.

51 B. Tibi, 'Turkey's Islamist Danger. Islamists Approach Europe', in: *Middle East Quarterly*, vol. 16, 1 (2009), pp. 47–54.

52 See the reference in note 7 and the chapter included in Roland Hsu, ed., *Ethnic Europe* (referenced in note 23) by B. Tibi, 'The Return of Ethnicity to Europe via Islamic Migration', as Chapter 7, pp. 127–56.

53 Max Horkheimer, *Kritische Theorie*, 2 vols (Frankfurt: S. Fischer, 1966).

54 On this issue see B. Tibi, 'The Political Legacy of Max Horkheimer and Islamism', in: *Telos* (Fall 2009), issue 148, pp. 7–15.

55 Zeyno Baran, 'Turkey Divided', in: *Journal of Democracy,* vol. 19, 1 (2008), pp. 55–69.

56 For a full reference see note 35 above.

57 See the full reference in note 39.

58 See B. Tibi, 'The Quest of Islamic Migrants and of Turkey to Become European in a Secular Europe', in: *Turkish Policy Quarterly*, vol. 3, 1 (2004), pp. 13–28 and the chapter

'Euro-Islam' by the same author in: Zeyno Baran, ed., *The Other Muslims. Moderate and Secular* (New York: Palgrave Macmillan, 2010).

59 Peter Katzenstein, ed., *Civilizations and World Politics* (New York: Routledge 2010).

60 See the contributions in: Roland Hsu, ed., *Ethnic Europe. Mobility, Identity, and Conflict in a Globalized World* (Stanford/CA: Stanford University Press, 2010).

61 See for instance the German Islamophobic contribution by Hans-Peter Raddatz, 'Europe in the Conflict between Tolerance and Ideology', in: Andrew Bostom, ed., *Islamic Antisemitism* (Amherst/NY: Prometheus, 2008), pp. 643–49. Raddatz' contribution smacks of all negative aspects.

62 Thilo Sarrazin, *Deutschland schafft sich ab. Wie wir unser Land aufs Spiel setzen* (Munich: Deutsche Verlags-Anstalt, 2010, 17th edn). One commentator, John Vinocur, in the global edition of the *New York Times* argued that references to biological arguments, in particular if they come from a German, are today inadmissible.

63 B. Tibi, 'Bridging the Heterogenity of Civilizations: Reviving the Grammar of Islamic Humanism', in: *Theoria. A Journal of Political and Social Theory*, vol. 56 (2009), issue 120, pp. 65–80.

6 Intercivilizational conflict, bridging and critical theory

1 On the Third World and on its ideologization to a thirdworld-ism see the reference in note 13 below. For a comprehensive study on anti-colonial ideologies see the survey by B. Tibi, 'Politische Ideen in der Dritten Welt während der Dekolonisation', in: Iring Fetscher, ed., *Piper Handbuch für politische Ideen*, vol. 5 (Munich: Piper, 1987), pp. 361–402; for a case study and a comparison between a secular ideology that leans on European ideas (e.g. pan-Arab nationalism) and a religionized anti-Western ideology (e.g. Islamism) see B. Tibi, 'Arab Nationalism. Between Islam and the Nation State', 3rd expanded edition (New York: Macmillan, 1997), the chapter added to the 3rd edition.

2 Hedley Bull, 'Revolt against the West', in: Hedley Bull and Adam Watson, eds, *The Expansion of International Society* (Oxford: Clarendon Press, 1984), pp. 217–28.

3 The source of this invective in postcolonial studies shaped as cultural anti-Western studies is Professor Ziauddin Sardar, ed., *Islamic Futures. The Shape of Ideas to Come* (London: Mansell, 1985).

4 Anthony Giddens, *Beyond Left and Right. The Future of Radical Politics* (Cambridge: Polity Press, 1994).

5 For a comprehensive analysis of this distinction see the monograph by B. Tibi, *Islamism and Islam* (New Haven/CT: Yale University Press, 2012, forthcoming).

6 See the major book on the critical theory by Martin Jay, *The Dialectical Imagination. A History of the Frankfurt School* (Boston/MA: Little & Brown, 1973).

7 Susan Buck-Morss, *Thinking Post Terror. Islamism and Critical Theory on the Left* (London: Verso, 2003), Chapter 2 on 'Critical Theory and Islamism', pp. 41–56.

8 Ibid., p. 52.

9 Ibid., p. 43. For a criticism see B. Tibi, 'The Political Legacy of Max Horkheimer and Islamist Totalitarianism', in: *Telos* (Fall 2009), issue 148, pp. 7–15.

10 In their *The Globalization Reader*, the editors Frank Lechner and John Boli (Oxford: Blackwell, 2008) include a text by me with the interpretation of Islamism (political Islam) as a variety of religious fundamentalism; see the text included in that reader on pp. 358–63.

11 See Chapter 4 of the present book 'The grammar of European humanism' and the references made there. The theme humanism was the topic of the special issue of the

Dutch journal *Nexus*, no. 50, 2008. The issue was presented at an international congress on humanism, to celebrate the anniversary of the journal in a revival of European values. The event took place in Amsterdam in June 2008. In my presentation based on my contribution to the cited *Nexus*-issue 50/2008 on 'The Grammar of Islamic Humanism' (pp. 592–616) published in Dutch, I argued that an Islamic variety of humanism existed in medieval Islamic rationalism. The revival of that tradition could serve today as a cultural bridge, viewed as an alternative to the polarizing ideology of Islamism. The South African journal *Theoria* published in its issue 120 (Sept. 2009), pp. 65–80, a short English version of that Amsterdam paper which is referenced in note 25 below.

12 On Islamist antisemitism see Matthias Küntzel, *Jihad and Jew-Hatred. Islamism, Nazism and the Roots of 9/11* (New York: Telos, 2007), and B. Tibi, 'Public Policy and the Combination of Anti-Americanism and Antisemitism in Islamist Ideology', in: *The Current* (Cornell University), vol. 12 (Fall 2008), pp. 123–46.

13 On the cultural roots of Third World-ism see Peter Worsely, *The Third World* (Chicago/IL: University of Chicago Press, 1964, 2nd edition, 1970).

14 On Western civilization within the overall history of civilizations see Fernand Braudel, *A History of Civilizations* (London: The Penguin Press, 1994), and also David Gress, *From Plato to NATO. The Idea of the West and its Opponents* (New York: The Free Press, 1998).

15 Herbert Marcuse, *The One-Dimensional Man. Studies in the Ideology of Advanced Industrial Society* (London: Routledge & Kegan, 1964), p. 47.

16 Frantz Fanon, *The Wretched of the Earth* (London: Penguin Books, 1967), pp. 251–52. See the criticism of Fanon by a Jewish philosopher of the French Left, Alain Finkielkraut, *La Défait de La Pensée* (Paris: Editions Gallimard, 1987).

17 As a person who suffered this rule I continue to use and to subscribe to this notion of 'Oriental despotism' coined by Karl Wittfogel, not fearful of being condemned and bashed by the accusation of self-orientalization.

18 The result was three monographs completed in a time span of two decades on Islamism. These are: (1) B. Tibi, *The Challenge of Fundamentalism. Political Islam and the New World Disorder* (Berkeley: University of California Press, 1998, updated 2002); (2) B. Tibi, *Political Islam, World Politics and Europe: Democratic Peace and Euro-Islam versus Global Jihad* (Oxford and New York: Routledge, 2008) and (3) the forthcoming book *Islamism and Islam* (referenced in note 5).

19 Lorenzo Vidino, *al-Qaeda in Europe. The New Battleground of International Jihad* (Amherst/NY: Prometheus, 2006).

20 Max Horkheimer, *Kritische Theorie*, 2 volumes (Frankfurt: S. Fischer, 1968), here vol. 1, preface, p. XIII.

21 This statement by Max Horkheimer is included in: *Horkheimers Gesammelte Schriften*, and it is quoted here in accordance with the excellent translation by Andrei Markovietz, *Uncouth Nation. Why Europe Dislikes America* (Princeton/NJ: Princeton University Press, 2007), p. 199.

22 See Horkheimer, referenced in note 20, p. XIII.

23 Ibid.

24 See the dedication to Max Horkheimer in: B. Tibi, *Europa ohne Identitaet* (Munich: Bertelsmann,1998), in which it is stated that Islamism is the new totalitarianism. Almost one decade later this contention was supported with more details in this monograph B. Tibi, *Der neue Totalitarismus* (Darmstadt: Primus, 2004).

25 B. Tibi, 'Bridging the Heterogeneity of Civilizations. Reviving the Grammar of Islamic Humanism', in: *Theoria* 56 (Sept. 2009), issue 120, pp. 65–80.

26 B. Tibi, *Die arabische Linke* (Frankfurt am Main: EVA, 1969) reviewed in: *The Middle East Journal*, vol. 24, 3 (1970), pp. 391–92 by Hisham Sharabi. On the grounds of this review by the late Hisham Sharabi, his friend Edward Said invited me to make a major presentation at the Arab-American Association of University Graduates/AAUG in Boston (1972). That was my very first visit to the US. The paper 'The Genesis of the Arab Left. A Critical Viewpoint' delivered there was published in Edward Said, ed., *The Arabs of Today. Perspectives for Tomorrow* (Columbus/OH: Forum Associates, 1973), pp. 31–42 as my first US publication.

27 This antisemitic invective is included in the work of the Islamist Anwar al-Jundi; in his view, 'Enlightenment is a Jewish Idea'. This al-Jundi calls for a purification of Islam from the 'Jewish virus' in his books. See for example his *al-Mu'asara fi itar al-Asalah* ('Modernity in the Framework of Authenticity') (Cairo: Dar al-Sahwa, 1987), for instance p. 79 and p. 83.

28 Anwar al-Jundi, *Ahdaf al-Taghrib* ('The Targets of Westernization') (Cairo: al-Azhar, 1987). See the discussion of this work in Chapter 8 on authenticity in B. Tibi, *Islam's Predicament with Modernity*, pp. 237–64.

29 See note 12 and also the book, *America min al-dakhil bi minzar Sayyid Qutb* ('America from Inside Viewed Through the Lenses of S. Qutb'), written by S.A. al-Khalidi (al-Mansura/Egypt: Dar al-wafa'a, 1987). The reference denotes the source of Islamist antisemitism.

30 Roger Griffin, *Modernism and Fascism* (London: Palgrave, 2007) and Jeffrey Herf, *Reactionary Modernism. Technology, Culture and Politics in Weimar and the Third Reich* (New York: Cambridge University Press, 1984).

31 Jürgen Habermas, *The Philosophical Discourse of Modernity* (Cambridge/MA: MIT Press, 1987).

32 Sayyid Qutb, *al-Salam al-Alami wa al-Islam* ('World Peace and Islam') (Cairo: Dar al-Shuruq, reprinted 1992), pp. 170–72 on the idea of an Islamic World Revolution.

33 Sayyid Qutb, *Ma'rakatuna ma'a al-Yahud* ('Our Fight Against the Jews') (Cairo: al-Shuruq, 10th legal edition, 1989). This book by Qutb is analysed in a full section in the Cornell article by B. Tibi referenced in note 12.

34 See the three monographs on political Islam referenced in note 18.

35 For more details see B. Tibi, 'The Return of the Sacred to Politics. The Case of Shari'atization of Politics in Islamic Civilization', in: *Theoria. Journal of Social and Political Theory*, vol. 55, 1 (April 2008), issue 115, pp. 91–119. On Islamist jihadism see B. Tibi, 'The Totalitarianism of Jihadist Islamism and its Challenge to Islam and to Europe', in: *Totalitarian Movements and Political Religion*, vol. 1, 8 (2007), pp. 35–54.

36 See my two articles on these two varieties of Islamism (institutional and jihadist) in the special issue (vol. 10, 2, 2009) of the British journal *Totalitarian Movements and Political Religion*. Both varieties share the challenge to world order. On this see Daniel Philpott, 'The Challenge of September 11 to Secularism in International Relations', in: *World Politics*, vol. 55, 1 (2002), pp. 66–95.

37 Zeyno Baran, 'Divided Turkey', in: *Journal of Democracy*, vol. 19, 1 (2008), pp. 55–69. See also eight presentations on Islamism and democracy published in the *Journal of Democracy*, vol. 19, 3 (July 2008).

38 Mark Juergensmeyer, *The New Cold War? Religious Nationalism Confronts the Secular State* (Berkeley: University of California Press, 1993) suggests, as his book title denotes, that there is a competition between the religions and the sacred that underpins a new Cold War.

39　For more details see my chapter in: Eric Patterson and John Galleger, eds, *Debating the War of Ideas* (New York: Palgrave: 2010).

40　Yusuf al-Qaradawi, *Hatmiyyat al-Hall al-Islami* ('The Determined Islamic Solution'), 3 vols. Vol. 1, *al-Hulul al-Mustawrada* ('The Imported Solutions') (Beirut: al-Risalah, reprint 1980).

41　Daniel Bell coined the term 'The Return of the Sacred' in 1977 in a LSE Lecture that is included in Bell's collection of essays *The Winding Passage* (New York: Basic Books, 1980), pp. 324–54. For a resumption of this debate in the aftermath of 9/11 see the new Chapter 11 added to the second enlarged edition of B. Tibi, *Islam between Culture and Politics* (New York: Palgrave, published in association with Harvard's WCFIA, 2005, first 2001), pp. 234–72. For an appropriate understanding of religion see Ernst Bloch, *Thomas Münzer als Theologe der Revolution* (Frankfurt: Suhrkamp, reprint 1972), a major book that continues to be inspiring.

42　See Serif Mardin, 'Civil Society and Islam', in: John Hall, ed., *Civil Society* (Cambridge/ UK: Polity, 1995), pp. 278–300. In contrast to Mardin I believe that Islam could embrace civil society, see my contribution to: Leonard Weinberg, *Democratic Responses to Terrorism* (New York: Routledge, 2008), pp. 41–62.

43　Jürgen Habermas, *Glauben und Wissen* (Frankfurt: Suhrkamp, 2001) and in the context of September 11 the critique by B. Tibi, 'Habermas and the Return of the Sacred', in: *Religion – Staat – Gesellschaft*, vol. 3, 2 (2002), pp. 265–96.

44　The source of postmodern Saidism is: Edward Said, *Orientalism* (New York: Vintage Books, 1979). For critique on Edward Said's thinking qualified as an 'orientalism in reverse' see Sadik J. al-Azm, *Dhihniyyat al-Tahrim* ('The mentality of Taboos') (London: El Rayyes Books, 1992), pp. 17–86. This criticism was suppressed and therefore it deplorably was denied debate in Western scholarship. On this debate on orientalism see the survey in Chapter 4 in: B. Tibi, *Einladung in die islamische Geschichte* (Darmstadt: Primus Verlag, 2001), pp. 136–90.

45　On the Islamic worldview see Chapter 2 of the book by B. Tibi, *Islam between Culture and Politics* (referenced in note 41), pp. 53–68.

46　B. Tibi, 'Secularization and De-Secularization in Islam', in: *Religion – Staat – Gesellschaft*, vol. 1, 1 (2000), pp. 95–117.

47　See my book *Der neue Totalitarismus* referenced in note 24 above.

48　See my article in *Telos* referenced in note 9 above.

49　See Turan Kayaoglu, 'Westphalian Eurocentrism in International Relations Theory', in: *International Studies Review* 12, 2 (2010), pp. 193–217. Therefore, I disagree with Kayaoglu on Westphalian Eurocentrism.

50　Ernest Gellner, *Postmodernism, Reason and Religion* (London: Routledge, 1992), p. 84.

51　See Ernst Bloch, *Avicenna und die Aristotelische Linke* (Frankfurt: Suhrkamp, 1963), and on Islamic rationalism see Herbert A. Davidson, *Alfarabi, Avicenna and Averroes on Intellect* (New York: Oxford University Press, 1992). For the place of Islamic rationalism in a history of ideas in Islam see B. Tibi, *Der wahre Imam. Der Islam vom Mohammed bis zur Gegenwart* (Munich: Piper, 1996), Part 3. Worth reading is also Franz Rosenthal, *The Classical Heritage in Islam* (New York: Routledge, 1994).

52　Robert Reilly, *The Closing of the Muslim Mind. How Intellectual Suicide Created the Modern Islamist Crisis* (Wilmington/DE: ISI Books, 2010).

53　Robert Hefner, *Civil Islam. Muslims and Decmocratization in Indonesia* (Princeton/NJ: Princeton University Press, 2000).

7   From conflict to bridgings

1 See B. Tibi, *Islamism and Islam* (New Haven/CT: Yale University Press, 2012, forthcoming).

2 See the contributions included in Michael Brown *et al.*, eds, *Debating Democratic Peace* (Cambridge/MA: M.I.T. Press, 1996) and the implementation of this thinking to the subject in point by B. Tibi, *Political Islam, World Politics and Europe: Democratic Peace and Euro-Islam versus Global Jihad* (Oxford and New York: Routledge, 2008).

3 See Roman Herzog *et al.*, *Preventing the Clash of Civilizations* (New York: St. Martin's Press, 1999) with contributions that contradict Samuel P. Huntington, *The Clash of Civilizations and the Remaking of the World Order* (New York: Simon & Schuster, 1996). The volume by Herzog *et al.* includes B. Tibi, 'International Morality and Cross-Cultural Bridging' as Chapter 10, on pp. 107–26. The proceedings of the dialogue event of the Academy of Korean Studies mentioned in the preliminary remarks to this chapter were published by Academy as: *2009 Civilization and Peace* (Seoul/Korea and Edison/NJ: Jimoondang, 2010). This volume includes B. Tibi, 'Dialogue Among the Civilizations as Means of Peaceful Conflict Resolution', pp. 33–50.

4 John Brenkman, *The Cultural Contradictions of Democracy. Political Thought since September 11* (Princeton/NJ: Princeton University Press, 2007), pp. 165–69.

5 On this splitting of modernity by Islamists into values and instruments see the survey completed by B. Tibi, 'The Worldview of Sunni-Arab Fundamentalists: Attitudes Toward Modern Science and Technology', in: Martin Marty and Scott Appleby, eds, *The Fundamentalism Project*, 5 vols, here vol. 2: *Fundamentalisms and Society* (Chicago/IL: University of Chicago Press, 1993), pp. 73–102. This interpretation is developed further in Chapter 11 on semi-modernity by B. Tibi, *Islam's Predicament with Modernity* (New York: Routledge, 2009), pp. 303–19.

6 See Fred Dallmayr, *Dialogue Among Civilizations* (New York: Palgrave, 2002).

7 Raymond Aron, *Paix et Guerre entre les Nations* (Paris: Calmann-Lévy, 1962), Chapter 13.

8 In the book by William McNeill, *The Rise of the West. A History of Human Community* (Chicago/IL: University of Chicago Press, 1963) the West is elevated to the 'civilization of humanity'. This mindset is criticized by Eric Wolf, *Europe and People without History* (Berkeley: University of California Press, new edition 1997).

9 The violent intrusion of Islam in Asia is authoritatively documented on the example of the Indian sub-continent by Fernand Braudel, *A History of Civilizations* (London: The Penguin Press, 1994), pp. 232–36. See also, however, the controversial interpretation by Efraim Karsh, *Islamic Imperialism* (New Haven/CT: Yale University Press, 2006). On the current Islamist revival of this expansive internationalism with a claim of 'return of history' see B. Tibi, *Political Islam, World Politics and Europe* (note 2), Part 2.

10 See B. Tibi, *Islam between Culture and Politics* (New York: Palgrave, 2nd expanded edition after 9/11, 2005), Chapter 2 on culture and cultural system, Chapter 4 on globalization/fragmentation, Chapter 10 on intercultural dialogue and the new Chapter 11 on 9/11.

11 See Leslie Lipson, *The Ethical Crisis of Civilization* (London: Sage, 1993), pp. 62–66.

12 On Islam in Europe see B. Tibi, *Political Islam, World Politics and Europe* (note 2), in particular Chapters 5 and 6.

13 On Islamism in Europe see Lorenzo Vidino, *Al-Qaeda in Europe. The New Battleground of International Jihad* (Amherst/NY: Prometheus Books, 2006).

14 See the contributions in the research-based volume edited by Helmut Anheier and Y. Raj Isar, *Conflicts and Tensions*, vol. 1 of *The Cultures and Globalization Series* (London:

Sage, 2006). This volume includes as Chapter 18 a chapter by B. Tibi on Islamic cultural identity politics as a source of conflict, pp. 221–31.

15 Norbert Elias, *The Civilizing Process*, 2 vols (New York: Pantheon Books, 1978/1982).

16 See Peter Katzenstein and Timothy Byrnes, eds, *Religion in an Expanding Europe* (Cambridge: Cambridge University Press, 2006). The volume includes Chapter 8 on Islam in Europe, pp. 204–24, by B. Tibi.

17 T.K. Oomen, ed., *Citizenship and National Identity. From Colonialism to Globalism* (London and New Delhi: Sage, 1997). The volume includes Chapter 7 by B. Tibi on religious fundamentalism and ethnicity, pp. 199–225.

18 See B. Tibi, *The Challenge of Fundamentalism. Political Islam and the New World Order*, updated edition (Berkeley: University of California Press, 2002), Chapter 5; see also the reference in note 10.

19 Hedley Bull, 'The Revolt Against the West', in: Hedley Bull and Adam Watson, eds, *The Expansion of International Society* (Oxford: Clarendon Press, 1984), pp. 217–28.

20 See Chapter 8 on authenticity in my book, *Islam's Predicament with Modernity* (referenced in note 5), pp. 237–64.

21 See the strong critique of cultural relativism by the late Ernest Gellner, *Postmodernism, Reason and Religion* (London: Routledge, 1992), in particular p. 85.

22 See the results of *The Culture Matters Research Project/CMRP*, published by Lawrence Harrison, ed., *Developing Cultures*, 2 vols (New York: Routledge, 2006). This author was a member of the CMRP team and is a contributor to both volumes.

23 See the contributions included in: Leonard Weinberg, ed., *Democratic Responses to Terrorism* (New York: Routledge, 2008), herein Chapter 4 by B. Tibi, on 'Islam, Islamism and Democracy', pp. 41–62.

24 B. Tibi, 'Islamist Parties. Why They Can't be Democratic', in: *Journal of Democracy* 19, 3 (July 2008), pp. 43–48.

25 See the materials in *Harvard's Human Rights Journal* vol. 5 (Spring 1992) on 'Human Rights Issues in US Foreign Policy', pp. 137–205.

26 Larry Diamond, *The Spirit of Democracy. The Struggle to Build Free Societies Throughout the World* (New York: New York Times Book, 2008).

27 See the proceedings of the dialogue over this issue held in Amsterdam and published by the Erasmus Foundation, ed., *The Limits of Pluralism. Neo-Absolutisms and Relativism* (Amsterdam: Praemium Erasmianum Foundation, 1994), and Chapter 7 on pluralism in my book *Islam's Predicament with Modernity* (referenced in note 5), pp. 209–36. Furthermore see the dialogue proceedings of the Academy of Korean Studies/Seoul referenced in note 3 above.

28 See my contributions to these themes in: Robert Fortner, ed., *The Handbook of Global Communication and Media Ethics* (Oxford: Wiley-Blackwell, 2011); and in: Leonard Grob and John Roth, eds, *Encountering the Stranger: A Jewish–Christian–Muslim Trialogue* (Seattle/WA: University of Washington Press, 2012, forthcoming).

BIBLIOGRAPHY

Aburish, Said, *Saddam Hussein. The Politics of Revenge* (New York: Bloomsbury, 2000).

Adamson, Peter and Richard Taylor, eds, *The Cambridge Compendium to Arab Philosophy* (Cambridge: Cambridge University Press, 2005).

Adler, Emanuel *et al.*, eds, *The Convergence of Civilizations* (Toronto: Toronto University Press, 2006).

Afghani, Jamal al-din al-, *al-A'mal al-Kamilah* ('Collected Works') (Cairo: Dar al-Katib al-Arabi, 1968).

Ajami, Fouad, *The Arab Predicament* (New York: Cambridge University Press, 1981).

—— *The Foreigner's Gift. The Americans, the Arabs and the Iraqis in Iraq* (New York: Free Press, 2006).

Akbarzadeh, Shahram and Fethi Mansouri, eds, *Islam and Political Violence. Muslim Diaspora and Radicalism in the West* (London: Taures, 2007).

AlSayyad, Nezar and Manuel Castells, eds, *Muslim Europe or Euro-Islam* (Lanham/MD: Lexington Books, 2002).

AlSayyad, Nezar, 'Muslim Europe or Euro-Islam. On the Discourse of Identity and Culture', in: Nezar AlSayyad and Manuel Castells, eds, *Muslim Europe or Euro-Islam* (Lanham/MD: Lexington Books, 2002), pp. 9–29.

Anheier, Helmut and Y. Raj Isar, eds, *Conflicts and Tensions*, vol. 1 of *The Culture and Globalization* Series (London: Sage, 2007).

Appleby, Scott, *The Ambivalence of the Sacred. Religion, Violence, and Reconciliation* (Lanham/MD: Rowman & Littlefield, 2000).

Apter, David, *The Politics of Modernization* (Chicago/IL: University of Chicago Press, 1965).

Armanazi, Najib, *al-Shar' al-Duwali fi al-Islam* ('International Law in Islam') (London: Riad E. Rayyes, 1990).

Aron, Raymond, *Paix et Guerre entre les Nations* (Paris: Colmann Levy, 1962).

Asante, Malefi K. and William B. Gudykunst, eds, *Handbook of International and Intercultural Communication* (London: Sage, 1989).

Atiyeh, George and Ibrahim Oweiss, eds, *Arab Civilization: Challenges and Responses* (Albany/NY: SUNY, 1988).

Ayubi, Nazih, *Political Islam* (New York: Routledge, 1991, reprinted 1994).

Azm, Sadik J. al-, *Dhihniyyat al-Tahrim* ('The Mentality of Taboos') (London: El Rayyes Books, 1992).

Baker, Raymond, *Islam without Fear. The New Islamists in Egypt* (Cambridge/MA: Harvard University Press, 2003).

Banna, Hasan al-, 'Risalat al-jihad' ('Essay on Jihad'), in: *Majmu'at Rasa'il al-Imam al-Shahid* ('Collected Essays of the Martyr Imam') (Cairo: Dar al-Da'wa, 1990), pp. 271–92.

Baran, Zeyno, 'Divided Turkey', in: *Journal of Democracy*, vol. 19, 1 (2008), pp. 55–69.

—— ed., *The Other Muslims. Moderate and Secular* (New York: Palgrave, 2010).

—— *Torn Country. Turkey Between Secularism and Islamism* (Stanford/CA: Hoover Institution Press, 2010).

Barber, Benjamin, *Jihad vs. McWorld* (New York: Ballentine Books, 1996).

Bell, Daniel, *The Winding Passage. Essays 1960–1980* (New York: Basic Books, 1980).

Berger, Peter, *Holy War Inc. Inside the Secret World of al-Qaeda* (New York: Free Press, 2001).

Berkes, Niyazi, *The Development of Secularism in Turkey* (New York: Routledge, new edition, 1998).

Berman, Paul, 'Who is Afraid of Tariq Ramadan?', in: *The New Republic* (June 2007), issue 4, pp. 37–63.

—— *The Flight of the Intellectuals* (New York: Melville House, 2010).

Berman, Russell, *Freedom or Terror. Europe Faces Jihad* (Stanford/CA: Hoover Institution Press, 2010).

Besier, Gerhard and Hermann Lübbe, eds, *Politische Religion und Religionspolitik. Zwischen Totalitarismus und Bürgerfreiheit* (Goettingen: Vandenhoek & Ruprecht, 2005).

Bistolfi, Robert and Francois Zabbal, eds, *Islams d'Europe* (Paris: L'Aube, 1995).

Blankenship, Kalid Yahya, *The End of the Jihad State* (Albany/NY: SUNY, 1994).

Bloch, Ernst, *Avicenna und die Aristotelische Linke* (Frankfurt: Suhrkamp, 1963).

—— *Thomas Münzer als Theologe der Revolution* (Frankfurt: Suhrkamp, reprint 1972).

Boroujerdi, Mehrzad, *Iranian Intellectuals and the West. The Tormented Triumph of Nativism* (Syracuse/NY: Syracuse University Press, 1996).

Bostom, Andrew, ed., *Islamic Antisemitism* (Amherst/NY: Prometheus, 2008).

Boyce, Ralph, 'US Foreign Policy. Our Place in the Community of Nations', in: Karlina Helmantia and Irfan Abubakar, eds, *Dialogue in the World Disorder* (Jakarta: AIN-Hidayatollah Islamic State University, 2004), pp. 9–24.

Braudel, Fernand, *A History of Civilizations* (London: Penguin Press, 1994).

Brenkman, John, *The Cultural Contradictions of Democracy. Political Thought Since September 11* (Princeton/NJ: Princeton University Press, 2007).

Brown, Michael *et al.*, eds, *Debating Democratic Peace* (Cambridge/MA: M.I.T. Press, 1996).

Brown, Peter, *The Rise of Western Christendom* (Cambridge/UK: Blackwell, 1996).

Buck-Morss, Susan, *Thinking Post Terror. Islamism and Critical Theory on the Left* (London: Verso, 2003).

Bull, Hedley, *The Anarchical Society* (New York: Columbia University Press, 1977).

—— 'The Revolt Against the West', in: Hedley Bull and Adam Watson, eds, *The Expansion of International Society* (Oxford: Clarendon Press, 1984).

—— and Adam Watson, eds, *The Expansion of International Society* (Oxford: Clarendon Press, 1984).

Bulliet, Richard, *The Case for Islamo–Christian Civilization* (New York: Columbia University Press, 2004).

Bund, Gary, *Islam in the Digital Age* (London: Plutos, 2003).

Burr, J. Millard and Robert Collins, *Alms for Jihad* (Cambridge: Cambridge University Press, 2006).

Butterworth, Charles E., ed., *The Political Aspects of Islamic Philosophy. Essays in Honor of Mushin S. Mahdi* (Cambridge/MA: Harvard CMES, 1992).

Castells, Manuel, *The Power of Identity* (Oxford: Blackwell, 1997).

Cesari, Jocelyne, *Where Islam and Democracy Meet* (New York: Palgrave, 2004).

Cliteur, Paul, *The Secular Outlook: In Defense of Moral and Political Secularism* (Oxford: Wiley-Blackwell, 2010).

Cook, David, *Understanding Jihad* (Berkeley: University of California Press, 2005).

Curtin, Philip D., *The World and the West. The European Challenge* (New York: Cambridge University Press, 2000).

Dallmayr, Fred, *Dialogue Among Civilizations* (New York: Palgrave, 2002).

Dawisha, Adeed, *Arab Nationalism in the 20th Century* (Princeton/NJ: Princeton University Press, 2003).

DeLong, N., *Wahhabi Islam* (New York: Oxford University Press, 2004).

Deng, Francis and Abdullahi An-Na'im, eds, *Human Rights in Africa. Cross-Cultural Perspectives* (Washington/DC: Brookings, 1990).

Dharif, Mohammed, *al-Islam al-Siyasi fi al-watan al-Arabi* ('Political Islam in the Arab World') (Casablanca: al-Ma'arif, 1992).

Diamond, Larry, *The Spirit of Democracy. The Struggle to Build Free Societies Throughout the World* (New York: Times Books, 2008).

Donner, Fred M., *The Early Islamic Conquests* (Princeton/NJ: Princeton University Press, 1981).

Davidson, Herbert A., *Alfarabi, Avicenna and Averroes on Intellect. Their Cosmologies, Theories of the Active Mind, and Theories of Human Intellect* (New York: Oxford University Press, 1992).

Duran, Will, *The Renaissance*, vol. 5 of: *The Story of Civilization*, 11 vols (New York: Simon & Schuster, 1981).

Eikelman, Dale and James Piscatori, *Muslim Politics* (Princeton/NJ: Princeton University Press: 1996).

Elias, Norbert, *The Civilizing Process*, 2 vols (New York: Pantheon Books, vol. 1 1978 and vol. 2 1982).

Elshtain, Jean Bethke, *Just War Against Terror* (New York: Basic Books, 2003).

Erasmus Foundation, ed., *The Limits of Pluralism. Neo-Absolutism and Relativism* (Amsterdam: Praemium Erasmus-Foundation, 1994).

Euben, Roxanne, *The Enemy in the Mirror. Islamic Fundamentalism* (Princeton/NJ: Princeton University Press, 1999).

—— *Journeys to the Other Shore. Muslim and Western Travellers in Search for Knowledge* (Princeton/NJ: Princeton University Press, 2006).

Fanon, Frantz, *The Wretched of the Earth* (London: Penguin Books, 1967).

Feldman, Noah, *The Fall and Rise of the Islamic State* (Princeton/NJ: Princeton University Press, 2008).

Fetscher, Iring, ed., *Piper Handbuch der politischen Ideen*, 5 vols (Munich: Piper, 1987–93).

Finkielkraut, Alain, *La Défait de La Pensée* (Paris: Editions Gallimard, 1987).

Fortner, Robert and Mark Fackler, eds, *Handbook of Global Communication and Media Ethics* (Oxford: Wiley-Blackwell, 2011).

Fourest, Caroline, *Brother Tariq. The Doublespeak of Tariq Ramadan* (New York: Encounter Books, 2008).

Fromkin, David, *A Peace to End all Peace. The Fall of the Ottoman Empire and the Creation of the Modern Middle East* (New York: Avon Books, 1989).

Fukuyama, Francis, 'Identity, Immigration and Liberal Democracy', in: *Journal of Democracy* vol. 17, 2 (April 2008), pp. 5–20.

Fuller, Graham, *The Centre of the Universe. The Geopolitics of Iran* (Boulder/CO: Westview Press, 1991).

—— and Ian Lesser, *A Sense of Siege. The Geopolitics of Islam and the West* (Boulder/CO: Westview, 1995).

Geertz, Clifford, *The Interpretation of Cultures* (New York: Basic Books, 1973).

Gellner, Ernest, *Postmodernism, Reason and Religion* (London and New York: Routledge, 1992).

Gentile, Emilio, *Politics as Religion* (Princeton/NJ: Princeton University Press, 2006).

Gerges, Fawaz, *America and Political Islam. Clash of Cultures or Clash of Interests?* (New York: Cambridge University Press, 1999).

Ghadban, Ralph, *Tariq Ramadan und die Islamisierung Europas* (Berlin: Verlag Hans Schiler, 2006).

Giddens, Anthony, *Nation State and Violence* (Berkeley: University of California Press, 1987).

—— *Beyond Left and Right. The Future of Radical Politics* (Cambridge: Polity Press, 1994).

Gress, David, *From Plato to NATO. The Idea of the West and its Opponents* (New York: The Free Press, 1998).

Griffin, Roger, *Modernism and Fascism* (London: Palgrave, 2007).

Haas, Ernst B., *When Knowledge is Power* (Berkeley: University of California Press, 1990).

Habermas, Jürgen, *The Philosophical Discourse of Modernity* (Cambridge/MA: M.I.T. Press, 1986).

—— *Glauben und Wissen* (Frankfurt: Suhrkamp, 2001).

Hall, John, ed., *Civil Society* (Cambridge/UK: Polity, 1995).

Hanafi, Hasan, *al-Usuliyya al-Islamiyya* ('Islamic Fundamentalism') (Cairo: Madbuli, 1989).

Hanson, Eric, *Religion and Politics in the International System Today* (New York: Cambridge University Press, 2006).

Hargreave, Alec, *Multiethnic France* (New York: Routledge, 2007).

Harrison, Lawrence, ed., *Developing Cultures* 2 vols (New York: Routledge, 2006).

Hart, H.L.A., *The Concept of Law* (Oxford: Clarendon, 1970).

Harvard's *Human Rights Journal* vol. 5 (Spring 1992), 'Human Rights Issues in US Foreign Policy', pp. 137–205.

Hawkesworth, Mary and Maurice Kogan, eds, *Encyclopedia of Government*, 2 vols (London: Routledge, 2004).

Hefner, Robert, *Civil Islam. Muslims and Democratization in Indonesia* (Princeton/NJ: Princeton University Press, 2000).

Helmantia, Karlina and Irfan Abubakar, eds, *Dialogue in the World Disorder* (Jakarta: AIN-Hidayatollah Islamic State University, 2004).

Herf, Jeffrey, *Reactionary Modernism. Technology, Culture and Politics in Weimar and the Third Reich* (New York: Cambridge University Press, 1984).

Herzog, Roman et al., eds, *Preventing the Clash of Civilizations* (New York: St. Martin's Press, 1999).

Hobsbawm, Eric and Terence Ranger, eds, *The Invention of Tradition* (New York: Cambridge University Press, 1992).

Hodgson, Marshall, *The Venture of Islam. Conscience and History in a World Civilization*, 3 vols (Chicago/IL: University of Chicago Press, 1974).

Hofer, Eric, *The True Believer* (New York: Perenial Library 2002, reprint of 1951).

Hoffmann, Stanley, *World Disorders* (Lanham/MD: Rowman & Littlefield, 1998).

Horkheimer, Max, *Kritische Theorie*, 2 vols (Frankfurt: S. Fischer, 1966).

Hsu, Roland, ed., *Ethnic Europe. Mobility, Identity, and Conflict in a Globalized World* (Stanford/CA: Stanford University Press, 2010).

Huntington, Samuel P., *Clash of Civilizations* (New York: Simon & Schuster, 1996).

Imara, Mohammed, *al-Sahwa al-Islamiyya wa al-tahaddi al-hadari* ('Islamic Awakening and the Civilizational Challenge') (Cairo: Dar al-Shuruq, 1991).

Inbar, Efraim and Hillel Frisch, eds, *Radical Islam and International Security* (New York: Routledge, 2008).

Inglehart, Roland, *Modernization and Postmodernization* (Princeton/NY: Princeton University Press, 1997).

Jabri, Mohammed Abed al-, *Arab Islamic Philosophy* (Austin: University of Texas Press, 1999).

Jacoby, Tami A. and Brent Sasley, eds, *Redefining Security in the Middle East* (New York: Palgrave, 2002).

Jamal, Amal, *The Palestine National Movement. Politics of Contention* (Bloomington: Indiana University Press, 2005).

Jansen, Johannes J.G., *The Dual Nature of Islamic Fundamentalism* (Ithaca/NY: Cornell University Press, 1997).

Jarisha, Ali M. and Muhammed Sh. Zaibaq, *Asalib al-ghazu al-fikri li al-alam al-Islami* ('Methods of Intellectual Invasion of the Islamic World') (Cairo: Dar al-I'tisam 1978).

Jay, Martin, *The Dialectical Imagination. A History of the Frankfurt School* (Boston/MA: Little & Brown, 1973).

Jervis, Robert, *Perception and Misperception in International Politics* (Princeton/NJ: Princeton University Press, 1976).

Juergensmeyer, Mark, *The New Cold War. Religious Nationalism Confronts the Secular State* (Berkeley: University of California Press, 1993).

Jundi, Anwar al-, *Ahdaf al-Taghrib fi al-alam al-Islami* ('The Goals of Westernization and the Islamic World') (Cairo: al-Azhar, no date, probably 1977).

—— *Min al-taba'iyya ila al-asalah* ('From Dependency to Authenticity') (Cairo: Dar al-I'tisam, no date).

—— *Ahdaf al-Taghrib* ('The Targets of Westernization') (Cairo: al-Azhar, 1987).

—— *al-Mu'asar fi itar al-Asalah* ('Modernity in the Framework of Authenticity') (Cairo: Dar al-Sahwa, 1987).

Kagan, Robert, *The Return of History and the End of Dreams* (New York: Alfred Knopf, 2008).

Kaldor, Mary, *Global Civil Society* (Cambridge/UK: Polity, 2003).

Karsh, Efraim, *Islamic Imperialism* (New Haven/CT: Yale University Press, 2006).

Katzenstein, Peter, ed., *Civilizations in World Politics. Plural and Pluralist Perspectives* (New York: Routledge, 2010).

—— and Timothy Byrnes, eds, *Religion in an Expanding Europe* (New York: Cambridge University Press, 2006).

—— and Robert Keohane, eds, *Antiamericanism in World Politics* (Ithaca/NY: Cornell University Press, 2007).

Kayaoglu, Turan, 'Westphalian Eurocentrism in International Relations Theory', in: *International Studies Review* 12, 2 (2010), pp. 193–217.

Keddie, Nikki, ed., *An Islamic Response to Imperialism. Political and Religious Writings of al-Afghani* (Berkeley: University of California Press, 1968).

Kelsay, John, *Islam and War. A Study of Comparative Ethics* (Louisville/NY: John Knox Press, 1993).

—— *Arguing the Just War in Islam* (Cambridge/MA: Harvard University Press, 2007).

Kenny, Michael, *The Politics of Identity* (Cambridge/UK: Polity, 2004).

Kepel, Gilles, *Jihad. Le Fin de L'Islamisme* (Paris: Gallimard, 2000).

Khalidi, S.A. al-, *America min al-dakhil bi minzar Sayyid Qutb* ('America from Inside Viewed Through the Lenses of S. Qutb') (al-Mansura/Egypt/Dar al-wafa'a, 1987).

Khalil, Samir al-, *Republic of Fear. The Politics of Modern Iraq* (Berkeley: University of California Press, 1989).

Khoury, Philipp and Joseph Kostiner, eds, *Tribes and State Formation in the Middle East* (Berkeley: University of California Press, 1990).

Klausen, Jytte, *The Islamic Challenge. Politics and Religion in Western Europe* (New York: Oxford University Press, 2005).

Kraemer, Joel, *Humanism in the Renaissance of Islam* (Leiden: Brill, 1986).

Kramer, Martin, *Arab Awakening and Islamic Revival* (New Brunswick/NY: Transaction Publishers, 1993).

Kuhn, Thomas S., *The Structure of Scientific Revolutions* (Chicago/IL: University of Chicago Press, 2nd edition, 1970).

Küntzel, Matthias, *Jihad and Jew-Hatred. Islamism, Nazism and the Roots of 9/11* (New York: Telos, 2007).

Laue, Theodore von, *The World Revolution of Westernization* (New York: Oxford University Press, 1987).

Lawrence, Bruce, *Defenders of God. The Fundamentalists Against the Modern World* (San Francisco/CA: Harper & Row, 1989).

Lawrence, Jonathan and Justin Vaisse, *Integrating Islam* (Washington/DC: Brookings, 2006).

Lechner, Frank and John Boli, eds, *The Globalization Reader* (Oxford: Blackwell, new 3rd edition, 2008).

Lee, Robert, *Overcoming Tradition and Modernity. The Search for Islamic Authenticity* (Boulder/CO: Westview, 1997).

Leiken, Robert and Steven Brooke, 'The Moderate Muslim Brotherhood', in: *Foreign Affairs*, vol. 86, 2 (March/April 2007), pp. 107–21.

Lewis, Bernard, *The Emergence of Modern Turkey* (London: Oxford University Press, 1979).

—— *Islam in History* (Chicago/IL: Open Court Publishers, 1993).

Lincoln, Bruce, *Holy Terrors. Thinking About Religion after September 11* (Chicago/IL: University of Chicago Press, 2005).

Lindholm, Tore and Kari Vogts, eds, *Islamic Law Reform and Human Rights* (Oslo and Copenhagen: Nordic Human Rights Publications, 1993).

Lipson, Leslie, *The Ethical Crises of Civilizations. Moral Meltdown or Advance?* (London: Sage, 1993).

Lybarger, Loren, *Identity and Religion in Palestine. The Struggle Between Islamism and Secularism in the Occupied Territories* (Princeton/NJ: Princeton University Press, 2007).

Lynch, Marc, 'Veiled Truths: The Rise of Political Islam in the West', in: *Foreign Affairs* (July/August 2010).

Marcuse, Herbert, *The One-Dimensional Man. Studies in the Ideology of Advanced Industrial Society* (London: Routledge & Kegan, 1964).

Mardin, Serif, 'Civil Society and Islam', in: John Hall, ed., *Civil Society* (Cambridge/UK: Polity, 1995), pp. 278–300.

Markovietz, Andrei, *Uncouth Nation. Why Europe Dislikes America* (Princeton/NJ: Princeton University Press, 2007).

Marty, Martin and Scott Appleby, eds, *The Fundamentalism Project*, 5 vols, (Chicago/IL: University of Chicago Press, 1991–95).

McNeill, William, *The Rise of the West. A History of the Human Community* (Chicago/IL: Chicago University Press, 1963).

Meier, Christian, *Die Entstehung des Politischen bei den Griechen* (Frankfurt: Suhrkamp, 1983).

Middle East Watch, ed., *Human Rights in Iraq* (New Haven/CT: Yale University Press, 1990).

Milton-Edwards, Beverley, *Islamic Politics in Palestine* (London: Tauris, 1996).

Mitchell, Richard, *The Society of the Muslim Brothers* (London: Oxford University Press, 1969).

Nardin, Terry, ed., *The Ethics of War and Peace* (Princeton/NJ: Princeton University Press, 1996).

Oommen, T.K., ed., *Citizenship and National Identity. From Colonialism to Globalism* (London and New Delhi: Sage, 1997).

Parker, Geoffrey, *The Military Revolution. Military Invention and the Rise of the West. 1500–1800* (Cambridge: Cambridge University Press, 1988).

Patterson, Eric and John Gallagher, eds, *Debating the War of Ideas* (New York: Palgrave Macmillan, 2010).

Peters, Rudolph, *Islam and Colonialism. The Doctrine of Jihad and Modern History* (The Hague: Mouton, 1979).

Phares, Walid, *The War of Ideas. Jihadism against Democracy* (New York: Palgrave Macmillan, 2007).

Phillips, Melanie, *Londonistan* (New York: Encounter Books, 2006).

Philpott, Daniel, 'The Challenge of September 11 to Secularism in International Relations', in: *World Politics*, vol. 55, 1 (2002), pp. 66–95.

Pirenne, Henri, *Mohamet et Charlemagne* (London: Allen & Unwin, 1939).

Plessner, Helmuth, *Die verspätete Nation* (Frankfurt: Suhrkamp, 1974, new printing).

Popper, Karl, *The Open Society and its Enemies*, 2 vols (London: Routledge & Kegan Paul, 1945).

Qaradawi, Yusuf al-, *al-Hall al-Islami* ('The Islamic Solution') 3 vols (Beirut: Mu'assat al-Risalah, 1970–80).

Qutb, Sayyid, *al-Islam wa Mushkilat al-hadarah* ('Islam and the Problematique of Civilization') (Cairo: al-Shuruq, 9th legal reprint, 1988).

—— *Ma'alim fi al-Tariq* ('Signposts Along the Road') (Cairo: Dar al-Shuruq, 13th legal edition, 1989).

—— *Ma'rakatuna ma'a al-Yahud* ('Our Fight Against the Jews') (Cairo: al-Shuruq, 10th legal edition, 1989).

—— *al-Salam al-alami wa al-Islam* ('World Peace and Islam') (Cairo: al-Shuruq, 10th legal edition, 1992).

Raddatz, Hans-Peter, 'Europe in the Conflict between Tolerance and Ideology', in: Andrew Bostom, ed., *Islamic Antisemitism* (Amherst/NY: Prometheus, 2008), pp. 643–49.

Ralston, David, *Importing the European Army. The Introduction of European Army Techniques into the Extra-European World 1600–1914* (Chicago/IL: University of Chicago Press, 1990).

Ramadan, Tariq, *Aux Sources de Renouveau Musulman. D'al-Afghani à Hasan al-Banna* (Paris: Bayard, 1998).

Ramazani, Rouhollah K., *Revolutionary Iran. Challenge and Response in the Middle East* (Baltimore/MD: Johns Hopkins University Press, 1987).

Reid, Anthony and Michael Gilsenan, eds, *Islamic Legitimacy in Plural Asia* (New York: Routledge, 2007).

Reilly, Robert, *The Closing of the Muslim Mind. How Intellectual Suicide Created the Modern Islamist Crisis* (Wilmington/DE: ISI Books, 2010).

Rodinson, Maxime, *La Fascination de l'Islam* (Paris: Maspero, 1980).

Rosenthal, Franz, *The Classical Heritage in Islam* (New York: Routledge, 1994).

Roy, Olivier, *Globalized Islam. The Search for a New Ummah* (New York: Columbia University Press, 2005).

Rutherford, Bruce, *Egypt after Mubarak* (Princeton/NJ: Princeton University Press, 2008).

Saeed, Abdullah, 'Muslims and non-Muslims Rule', in: Anthony Reid and Michael Gilsenan, eds, *Islamic Legitimacy in a Plural Asia* (New York: Routledge, 2007), pp. 14–27.

Said, Edward, ed., *The Arabs of Today. Perspectives for Tomorrow* (Columbus/OH: Forum Associates, 1973).

—— *Orientalism* (New York: Vintage Books, 1979).

Sardar, Ziauddin, ed., *Islamic Futures. The Shape of Ideas to Come* (London: Mansell, 1985).

Sarrazin, Thilo, *Deutschland schafft sich ab. Wie wir unser Land aufs Spiel setzen* (Munich: Deutsche Verlags-Anstalt, 2010, 17th printing).

Schmiegelow, Michèle, ed., *Democracy in Asia* (New York: St. Martin's Press, 1997).

Schwartz, Stephen, *The Two Faces of Islam. The House of Sa'ud from Tradition to Terror* (New York: Doubleday, 2002).

Shadid, W.A.R. and P.S. van Koningsveld, eds, *Political Participation and Identity of Muslims in Non-Muslim States*, vol. 1; *Muslims in the Margin. Political Responses to the Presence of Islam in Western Europe*, vol. 2, (Kampen/Netherlands: Kok Pharas Publ., 1996).

Sharqawi, Hasan al-, al-Muslimun, *Ulama wa Hukama* ('Muslims as Ulema and Wise Men') (Cairo: Mu'ssasat Mukhtar, 1987).

Shayegan, Daryush, *Cultural Schizophrenia. Islamic Societies Confronting the West* (London: Saqi, 1992).

Silverstein, Paul A., *Algeria in France* (Bloomington: Indiana University Press, 2004).

Smith, W.C., *The Meaning and the End of Religion* (New York: Harper & Row, 1978).

Spencer, Robert, *Onward Muslim Soldiers: How Jihad Still Threatens America and the West* (Washington/DC: Regnery, 2003).

Stetter, Stephan, *World Society and the Middle East* (New York: Palgrave, 2008).

Tibi, Bassam, *Die arabische Linke* (Frankfurt: EVA, 1969).

—— 'The Genesis of the Arab Left', in: Edward Said, ed., *The Arabs of Today. Perspectives for Tomorrow* (Columbus/OH: Forum Associates, 1973), pp. 31–42.

—— 'Politische Ideen in der Dritten Welt während der Dekolonisation', in: Iring Fetscher, ed., *Piper Handbuch für politische Ideen*, 5 volumes, here vol. 5 (Munich: Piper, 1987), pp. 361–402.

—— *The Crisis of Modern Islam* (Salt Lake City: Utah University Press, 1988).

—— 'The Interplay Between Social and Cultural Change', in: George Atiyeh and Ibrahim Oweiss, eds, *Arab Civilization* (Albany/NY: SUNY, 1988), pp. 166–82.

—— *Islam and the Cultural Accommodation of Social Change* (Boulder/CO: Westview Press, 1990).

—— 'Old Tribes and Imposed Nation States', in: Philipp Khoury and Joseph Kostiner, eds, *Tribes and State Formation in the Middle East* (Berkeley: University of California Press, 1990), pp. 127–52.

—— *Conflict and War in the Middle East* (New York: new expanded edition St. Martin's Press, 1998, first published 1993 in association with Harvard/CFIA).

—— 'Politisches Denken im klassischen und mittelalterlichen Islam', in: Iring Fetscher, ed., *Piper Handbuch der politischen Ideen*, vol. 2, Mittelalter (Munich: Piper, 1993), Chapter 3, pp. 87–140.

—— 'The Worldview of Sunni-Arab Fundamentalists', in: Martin Marty and Scott Appleby, eds, *Fundamentalisms and Society* (Chicago/IL: University of Chicago Press, 1993), pp. 73–102.

—— 'Culture and Knowledge: The Politics of the Islamization of Knowledge. The Fundamentalist Claim to De-Westernization', in: *Theory, Culture, Society*, vol. 12, 1 (1995), pp. 1–24.

—— *Krieg der Zivilisationen* (Hamburg: Hoffmann und Campe, 1995).

—— 'Les conditions d'un Euro-Islam', in: Robert Bistolfi and Francois Zabbal, eds, *Islams d'Europe* (Paris: L'Aube, 1995), pp. 230–34.

—— *Der wahre Imam* (Munich: Piper, 1996, new paperback edition 2001).

—— 'Islam, Hinduism and the Limited Secularity in India. A Model for Muslim-European Relations in the Age of Migration?', in: W.A.R. Shadid and P.S. van Koningsveld, eds, *Political Participation and Identity of Muslims in Non-Muslim States*, vol. 1 (Kampen/Netherlands: Kok Pharas Publ., 1996), pp. 130–44.

—— 'War and Peace in Islam', in: Terry Nardin, ed., *The Ethics of War and Peace* (Princeton/NJ: Princeton University Press, 1996), pp. 128–45.

—— *Arab Nationalism. Between Islam and the Nation-State* (London: Macmillan, 3rd enlarged edition, 1997).

—— 'Islam and Democracy', in: Michèle Schmiegelow, ed., *Democracy in Asia* (New York: St. Martin's Press, 1997), pp. 127–46.

—— 'Religious Fundamentalism, Ethnicity and the Nation-State in the Middle East', in: T.K. Oommen, ed., *Citizenship and National Identity. From Colonialism to Globalism* (London and New Delhi: Sage, 1997), pp. 199–225.

—— *Europa ohne Identität? Die Krise der multikulturellen Gesellschaft* (Munich: Bertelsmann, 1998).

—— *The Challenge of Fundamentalism. Political Islam and the New World Disorder* (Berkeley: University of California Press, 1998 updated 2002).

—— 'International Morality and Cross-Cultural Bridging', in: Roman Herzog *et al.*, eds, *Preventing the Clash of Civilizations* (New York: St. Martin's Press, 1999), pp. 107–26.

—— *Kreuzzug und Djihad. Der Islam und die christliche Welt* (Munich: Bertelsmann, 1999).

—— *Europa zonder Identiteit* (Deltas, 2000).

—— 'Post-bipolar Order in Crisis: The Challenge of Political Islam', in: *Millennium: Religion and International Relations* (2000), pp. 843–59.

—— 'Secularization and De-Secularization in Islam', in: *Religion – Staat – Gesellschaft*, vol. 1, 1 (2000), pp. 95–117.

—— *Einladung in die islamische Geschichte* (Darmstadt: Primus Verlag 2001).

—— *Islam between Culture and Politics* (New York: Palgrave, 2001, 2nd enlarged edition, 2005).

—— 'Between Islam and Islamism', in: Tami A. Jacoby and Brent Sasley, eds, *Redefining Security in the Middle East* (New York: Palgrave, 2002), pp. 62–82.

—— *Islamische Zuwanderung. Die gescheiterte Integration* (Munich: Deutsche Verlags-Anstalt, 2002).

—— 'Habermas and the Return of the Sacred. Is it a Religious Renaissance or a new Totalitarianism', in: *Religion – Staat – Gesellschaft*, vol. 3, 2 (2002), pp. 205–96.

—— *Der neue Totalitarismus. Heiliger Krieg und westliche Sicherheit* (Darmstadt: Primus Verlag, 2004).

—— 'Islamic Civilization and the Quest for Democratic Pluralism', in: Karlina Helmanita and Irfan Abubakar, eds, *Dialogue in the World Disorder* (Jakarta: UIN-Hidayatullah Islamic State University, 2004), pp. 159–202.

—— 'The Quest of Islamic Migrants and of Turkey to Become European in a Secular Europe', in: *Turkish Policy Quarterly*, vol. 3, 1 (2004), pp. 13–28.

—— *Euro-Islam. L'Integrazione mancata* (Rome: Marsilio, 2005).

—— 'Politischer Konservatismus der AKP als Tarnung für den politischen Islam? Die Türkei zwischen Europa und dem Islamismus', in: Gerhard Besier and Hermann Lübbe, eds, *Politische Religion und Religionspolitik. Zwischen Totalitarismus und Bürgerfreiheit* (Göttingen: Vandenhoek & Ruprecht, 2005), pp. 229–60.

—— 'Egypt as a Model of Development for the World of Islam', in: Lawrence Harrison and Peter L. Berger, eds, *Developing Cultures. Case Studies*, vol. 2 (New York: Routledge, 2006), pp. 163–80.

—— 'Europeanizing Islam or the Islamization of Europe. Political Democracy vs. Cultural Difference', in: Peter Katzenstein and Timothy Byrnes, eds, *Religion in an Expanding Europe* (New York: Cambridge University Press, 2006), pp. 204–24.

—— 'A Migration Story. From Muslim Immigrants to European Citizens of the Heart?', in: *The Fletcher Forum for World Affairs*, vol. 31, 1 (Winter 2007), pp. 147–68.

—— *Die islamische Herausforderung* (Darmstadt: Primus, 2007).

—— 'Euro-Islamic Religious Pluralism for Europe. An Alternative to Ethnicity and to Multiculturalism of Fear', in: *The Current*, vol. 11, 1 (2007), pp. 89–103.

—— 'Islam and Cultural Modernity', in: Anthony Reid and Michael Gilsenan, eds, *Islamic Legitimacy in a Plural Asia* (New York: Routledge, 2007), pp. 28–52.

—— 'Islam between Religious-Cultural Practice and Identity Politics', in: Helmut Anheier and Y. Raj Isar, eds, *Conflicts and Tensions* (Los Angeles/CA: Sage, 2007), pp. 221–31.

—— 'Jihadism and Intercivilizational Conflict', in: Shahram Akbarzadeh and Fethi Mansouri, eds, *Islam and Political Violence. Muslim Diaspora and Radicalism in the West* (London: Taures, 2007), pp. 39–64.

—— *Mit dem Kopftuch nach Europa. Die Türkei auf dem Weg in die EU* (Darmstadt: Primus, 2nd edition, 2007).

—— 'The Totalitarianism of Jihadist Islamism and its Challenge to Islam and to Europe', in: *Totalitarian Movements and Political Religions*, vol. 8 (2007), pp. 35–54.

—— 'De Grammatica van een islamitisch humanisme', in: *Nexus* (2008), issue 50, pp. 592–616.

—— 'Islam, Islamism and Democracy: The Case of the Arab World', in: Leonard Weinberg, ed., *Democratic Responses to Terrorism* (New York: Routledge, 2008), pp. 41–62.

—— 'Islamist Parties. Why They Can't be Democratic', in: *Journal of Democracy*, vol. 19, 3 (2008), pp. 43–48.

—— *Political Islam, World Politics and Europe. Euro-Islam and Democratic Peace vs. Global Jihad* (New York: Routledge, 2008).

—— 'Public Policy and the Combination of Anti-Americanism and Antisemitism in Contemporary Islamist Ideology', in: *The Current*, vol. 12 (Winter 2008), pp. 123–46.

—— 'The Return of the Sacred to Politics. The Case of Sharia'tization of Politics in Islamic Civilization', in: *Theoria. A Journal of Political and Social Theory*, vol. 55 (April 2008), issue 115, pp. 91–119.

—— 'Bridging the Heterogeneity of Civilizations: Reviving the Grammar of Islamic Humanism', in: *Theoria. A Journal of Political and Social Theory*, vol. 56 (2009), issue 120, pp. 65–80.

—— *Islam's Predicament with Modernity. Religious Reform and Cultural Change* (New York: Routledge, 2009).

—— 'The Political Legacy of Max Horkheimer and Islamist Totalitarianism', in: *Telos* (Fall 2009), issue 148, pp. 7–15.

—— 'Turkey's Islamist Danger. Islamists Approach Europe', in: *Middle East Quarterly*, vol. 16, 1 (2009), pp. 47–54.

—— 'Ethnicity of Fear? Islamic Migration and the Ethnicization of Islam in Europe', in: *Studies in Ethnicity and Nationalism/SENA* 10, 1 (2010), pp. 126–57.

—— 'Euro-Islam: An Alternative to Islamization and Ethnicity of Fear', in: Zeyno Baran, ed., *The Other Muslims: Moderate and Secular* (New York: Palgrave Macmillan, 2010), pp. 157–74.

—— 'Reform, Change and Democratization in the Middle East in Post-Bipolarity', in: *International Studies Review*, vol. 12, 2 (June 2010), pp. 309–15.

—— 'The Return of Ethnicity to Europe via Islamic Migration', in: Roland Hsu, ed., *Ethnic Europe* (Stanford/CA: Stanford University Press, 2010), pp. 127–56.

—— 'Global Communication and Cultural Particularisms: The Place of Values in the Simultaneity of Structural Globalization and Cultural Fragmentation', in: Robert Fortner and Mark Fackler, eds, *The Handbook of Global Communication and Media Ethics*, 2 volumes, here vol. I (Oxford: Wiley-Blackwell, 2011), pp. 54–78.

—— 'John Kelsay and "Sharia Reasoning" in Just War in Islam', in: *Journal of Church and State*, vol. 53, 1 (2011), pp. 4–26.

—— *Islamism and Islam* (New Haven/CT: Yale University Press, 2012, forthcoming).

Tilly, Charles, *The Formation of National States in Western Europe* (Princeton/NJ: Princeton University Press, 1975).

Totalitarian Movements and Political Religion, vol. 10, 2 (June 2009).

Vasques, J. and M.T. Henehan, 'International Relations Theory', in: Mary Hawkesworth and Maurice Kogan, eds, *Encyclopedia of Government*, 2 vols (London: Routledge, 2004), here vol. 2, pp. 857–78.

Vidino, Lorenzo, *al-Qaeda in Europe. The New Battleground of International Jihad* (Amherst/NY: Prometheus, 2006).

—— *The New Muslim Brotherhood in the West* (New York: Columbia University Press, 2010).

Walzer, Richard, ed., *Abu Nasr al-Farabi: Mabadi ara' ahl al-madina al-fadila* ('Al-Farabi on the Perfect State') (Oxford: Oxford University Press, 1985).

Watt, William Montgomery, *Philosophy and Theology* (Edinburgh: Edinburgh University Press, 1962, many reprints).

—— *Muslim–Christian Encounters* (New York: Routledge, 1991).

Weber, Max, *Soziologie – Weltgeschichtliche Analysen – Politik* (Stuttgart: Kröner, 1964).

Weinberg, Leonard, ed., *Democratic Responses to Terrorism* (New York: Routledge, 2008).

Weiner, Myron, *The Global Migration Crisis. Challenge to States and to Human Rights* (New York: Harper Collins, 1995).

Wendell, Charles, ed., *Five Tracts of Hasan al-Banna* (Berkeley: University of California Press, 1978).

Wolf, Eric, *Europe and People without History* (Berkeley: University of California Press, new edition 1997).

Worsely, Peter, *The Third World* (Chicago/IL: University of Chicago Press, 1964, 2nd edition 1970).

Wuthnow, Robert, *Meaning and Moral Order* (Berkeley: University of California Press, 1987).

Zilsch, Edgar, *Die sozialen Ursprünge der neuzeitlichen Wissenschaft* (reprint: Frankfurt: Suhrkamp, 1976).

INDEX

References to notes are denoted by the letter 'n'. The prefix 'al' is ignored in the sorting order for personal names.